animal signs, authentically illustrated by Douglas Allen. Also included is a tree guide with photos of the bark, leaves, seeds and profiles of major American species.

The how-to sections on hunting, fishing, camping, cooking, horse packing and photography include hundreds of practical ideas. These tips, techniques and projects will show you how to use your head and hands in the woods, to adapt to your surroundings and derive from them the necessities of life, and how to use the simplest man-made products in meeting wilderness challenges. All of these projects derive directly from the author's field experiences, his acquaintance with Indians, Eskimos, guides, trappers, prospectors and others who have learned how to live apart from civilization.

Complete Book of Outdoor Lore and Woodcraft is illustrated with 450 photos and explanatory drawings. It deserves a place in every outdoorsman's pack.

The Author

Clyde Ormond lives in Rigby, Idaho, on the same land his father once homesteaded. Formerly a school teacher and principal, and for the past thirty-five years a prolific outdoor writer, he has hunted, fished and camped in most of North America's wilderness. Mr. Ormond has distilled his vast knowledge and rich experiences into ten books and hundreds of articles for outdoor magazines.

Complete
Book
of
Outdoor
Lore
and
Woodcraft

Clyde Ormond

Complete Book of Outdoor Lore and Woodcraft

Drawings by
Ernest Kurt Barth
Douglas Allen
Nicholas Amorosi

OUTDOOR LIFE BOOKS
New York

HARPER & ROW PUBLISHERS
New York

Copyright © 1964, 1970, 1981 by Clyde Ormond

PUBLISHED BY
Outdoor Life Books
Times Mirror Magazines, Inc.
380 Madison Avenue
New York, NY 10017

DISTRIBUTED TO THE TRADE BY
Harper & Row Publishers, Inc.
10 East 53rd Street
New York, NY 10022

Library of Congress Catalog Card Number: 81-47715
ISBN: 0-06-014962-0

Manufactured in the United States of America

To Lucille Anderson Ormond

Contents

20. **Fishing How-To**

Foreword

by Don DeHart, big-game guide and outfitter

Clyde Ormond has traveled the trails and rivers up and down the North American continent for over thirty years, hunting, fishing, and absorbing the lore of the unspoiled wilderness of our vast and beautiful land. He is a natural woodsman and the keenest, most observing person I have ever traveled with.

I have known Clyde for a good many years. We have spent weeks at a time in the mountains. From Alaska's arctic wastes to the mountains of the North and Southwest, we have tramped and ridden the trails together. He has tremendous ability in observing and recording what he sees, either by camera or notebook, and what he files away in his memory is fantastic. When he starts to write, he is able to call upon a veritable filing cabinet of valuable information. And he is always very sure that what he writes is absolute fact. So, I can truthfully say, I know of no man better equipped to write a book on outdoor lore and woodcraft.

Clyde is no armchair writer. On our treks in the far back country, I've seen him spot the tracks of a wolf or wolverine on a sand bar, or sight a moose or a grizzly bear from a distant mountain. He is able to see game at a distance long before the average man can. Some of my professional guides, on seeing him for the first time, have remarked, " 'Spose we better take it easy with this dude writer.'' Much to their surprise and chagrin, at the end of a long day's hunt this "dude" writer came into camp in the lead.

I believe this book to be one of the best ever written on the subject. In my judgment, it will fill the need for a basic guide to the outdoors. It is not only interesting reading, but may serve as a serious textbook, and will stimulate those who read it to heed the "call of the wilderness" that has long been an inspiration for many of us.

Don DeHart
Slana, Alaska

Introduction

To most people the outdoors means that part of our country which has not yet been exploited by buildings, industry, or agriculture. To the more imaginative the outdoors also means an escape from the prosaic cares of the day, where the human spirit may find complete physical change and freedom. We go into the outdoors for a physical and spiritual uplift, and it is with this aspect that this book is concerned.

The North American outdoors may be broadly divided into mountains, forests, seacoasts, deserts, swamps and bayous.

The appeals of rugged mountains are many and varied—the blue spires reaching to the heavens; the cool clean air of high altitudes; the vastness and tenacity of mountainous upheavals. To each the appeal is different, but I have yet to find a person who didn't, in some personal way, love the mountains.

I have stood on thin shelving ledges in Idaho's Sawtooth Mountains where the slip of a boot meant a plunge to eternity. The sight of a Rocky Mountain goat, staring at me from above like some venerable patriarch, made the climb worthwhile. In the remote, foggy Aleutians, we were rewarded for the day's hard climb to a mountaintop by nothing more than the feel of whipping rain and wind, mixing in vortex between two oceans. In the primitive Wind River Mountains, we were repaid for the difficult trek over glacial wash above timberline by the sudden sight of ink-blue lakes in the innumerable pockets of rock below.

The surprises of mountain country are myriad and diverse: Wild flowers splashing in color at the base of melting glaciers. The thump of a deer, startled and flashing gray among the timber. Pug marks of the wary cougar in the dust of a trail up a switchback. Red-frosted acres of ripe blueberry bushes on an Alaskan slope. Grizzly spoor in a wild raspberry patch. Peaks of eternal white in the Canadian Rockies. The laughing trickle of an ice-cold creek, quenching to the thirst and soothing to the ear. A bright outcropping of mineral on the bare face of a cliff. The sheer inspiration of unscalable peaks.

These are the things the observing person sees in mountain country; and America is blessed with mountains.

The rugged Rockies stretch from southern New Mexico to northeast Alaska. Many of the peaks reach fourteen thousand feet in elevation, with Mount McKinley thrusting over twenty thousand feet upward into the sky. This great curving range generally parallels the western seacoast. With such secondary ranges as the Coastal Range, the Wasatch Mountains in Utah, and the Bitterroots bounding Idaho and Montana, the pleasures of mountains are within convenient access to anyone in the western portions of the continent.

Similarly, the Appalachian system of mountains parallels the eastern seacoast, extending all the way from the St. Lawrence River southward to Alabama and Georgia. With such smaller ranges as the Green, White, Black, Adirondacks, Blue Ridge, Alleghenies, and Smoky mountains, the Appalachian system offers the joys of mountains to those living in the East.

Mountains and forests go together like trout and a fly rod. There are no smells quite like green pine needles or the campfire smoke of dry aspen. Few sights are more inspiring than the carpets of tall conifers on the mountain slopes. There is no simpler lesson in courage and tenacity than a strong oak. What music can compare with the low moaning of wind in pine tops or the hush of a breezeless forest at dusk?

The sights, sounds, and smells of the forest are innumerable and coupled with surprises: The burst of a grouse from almost beneath one's feet. The chatter of a tree squirrel which has detected the invader's presence. The sudden sight of a lake below the trail, with the dark shadow of a moose nosing beneath the surface for food. A chipmunk's nearly inaudible patter as he races away on fallen maple leaves. The V of a mallard brood swimming a river.

As with mountains, America has a priceless heritage of forests. To the city or plains dweller, it is hard to realize that approximately one-third of our total land area is composed of forests. In the United States, excluding Alaska, there are 625 million acres of forest land. These forests are sufficiently spread throughout the country so as to offer enjoyment for all. As one example, there are now national forests set aside in forty-one states.

Canada, too, has an amazing acreage in forests, with one million square miles of forested lands. Alaska has coniferous forests over the majority of its land area, and Mexico has areas of forests along its "spine" and in its tropical lowlands.

All these vast orchards of the Almighty offer pleasures and deep joys to those who will but take time to explore them.

The seacoasts, those almost limitless, tenuous lines where land is wedded to water, also offer varied forms of enjoyment to the outdoorsman.

My first real acquaintance with an ocean came some years back. I had previously flown over two oceans, fished offshore for big-game species, and had watched the fearless divers at Acapulco dare the sea by diving from the high cliffs above. I had swum in the ocean's languid, salty brine off a protected beach. I had skirted the open leads of the Arctic by dog team.

But the ocean first revealed part of its true character to me late one night off a rocky shore. The weather was wild and boats had been kept offshore for two days. All that night, the roar of the breakers could be heard for miles. They rolled in to smash upon the rocks below us, their rebellion and torture dying in rhythmic undefeat, in sprays of falling water.

This is the appeal and fascination of the seacoasts for many—the magnetism of awesome and often brutal power.

Others enjoy the seacoasts for the offshore fishing, the skin diving, boating, and swimming in sheltered bays and inlets. Still others love the seacoasts during hot summers for the feel of warm wet sand on bare feet, the sun's warmth on near-nude bodies. Many camp in trailer communities on shore, where they can hear the continuing pound of the surf.

Seacoasts bound the entire continent, ranging in latitude from the warm beaches, caves, and harbors of Florida, California, and Acapulco, Mexico, through the rocky shores of New England, to the ice-bound coast of the Arctic, where anchor ice prohibits any use of the coastline for most of the year.

Another considerable part of our outdoors is the desert. To many people a "desert" is a hot, dry, inhospitable place, devoid of all life. A true desert is, of course, so devoid of water that plant and animal life are either scant or nonexistent. But North American has only one true desert—the Mojave Desert of California.

The modified deserts and arid regions are an integral part of the continent's playground. These broad areas of limited rainfall reach from central New Mexico to north-central Canada, with east-west boundaries highly irregular, and often overlapping forest and mountain areas.

During the intense heat of midsummer, the arid regions lie dormant. With spring rain, the desert comes vividly to life. There is no more beautiful sight than the Southwestern desert in full bloom. Few colors are more lovely than the yellow blossoms of the prickly pear, or the rainbow hues of Arizona's Vermillion Cliffs.

Few plants are more awe-inspiring than the giant saguaro cactus reaching its spiny arms towards heaven. And with the cool of evening, the desert's own forms of animal life become active.

Just last month I traveled a section of desert near the Mexican border. At first glance, the rolling, scrubby acres appeared lifeless. But by timing the trek for four o'clock in the afternoon and later, we moved about in the waist-high prickly pear and saw javelina, quail, whitetail deer, and one large rattlesnake before darkness had set in. The desert's "people" had come to life after the day's siesta.

To those outdoors-loving people who have learned that the deserts are not dead, our arid lands provide a wealth of enjoyment, offering such pleasures as rock-hunting, exploring, prospecting, and color photography.

The swamps and bayous are the mysterious lands of the continent. In no area can a person lose himself more completely than in the heavy foliage along winding waterways. Few sounds are more eerie than the call of birds and wild animals in such hushed, unfamiliar settings. Nothing torments the imagination faster than the solitude of swamps and bayous where vision is limited and legend takes on reality.

Swampland is, of course, terrain which is inundated by water until its soil becomes spongy. Marshlands are low, level lands where drainage has been hindered by heavy vegetation, hard subsoil, or large areas of adjacent level lands. In flooded lands of this type, rivers won't maintain a single channel, but cut away into numerous offshoots which drain into a lacelike network of waterways called bayous.

The principal swamp-bayou areas are found in the delta regions of the Mississippi; in Florida and Louisiana; in the Great Lakes region between the U.S. and Canada; the Dismal Swamp country of North Carolina and Virginia; and oddly enough, in the Far North. Opposite factors of climate and weather produce both the swamps of the South and the muskeg of the North.

Warm weather, rain, and river runoff produce the swamps. In Alaska and Canada, permafrost and hard pan soil act as a shelf under the summer runoff of melting snows headed for the Arctic and Pacific. With the lush growth of insulating moss between, water has no place to go, forming the boglike muskeg which is comparable to the swamplands of the South.

I have an old trapper friend in British Columbia who, before the advent of the Alaska Highway, made six separate annual trips for supplies with pack horses from Fort Nelson to Fort St. John. These laborious overland treks were in bush and muskeg country, over two hundred and fifty miles each way. Naturally, he came to learn the route of least muskeg and bog. Later, the military flew this man over the same horse route while he dropped flags indicating his course. The pilot road for the Alcan, now called the Alaska Highway, followed that old horse trail.

Swamplands attract the waterfowl hunter, he who thrills to the cry of a dog pack on the trail of a varmint, whose heart leaps to the gobble of a wild turkey. For others, the interest may lie in exploring, poling a thin boat along an old trapping route, in photographing the wild grace of jumping mallards, or in capturing on canvas the desolation of mangrove trees in a sepulchral setting.

As with any worthwhile pursuit, the full enjoyment of the outdoors entails certain fundamental hazards. In forests deep enough to impart the full flavor of the wilderness, there is the mild hazard of becoming lost. In mountainous regions, this danger may be accompanied by the possibility of falling, of sudden avalanches, or of encountering a dangerous animal. The desert's dangers are thirst, sunstroke, and poisonous insects or snakes. In the seacoast swamp areas, there is always the hazard of traveling on water, and, along the ocean, the danger of storms.

Such dangers are relative. The tendency has always been to accent the hazards of being in the outdoors, rather than to stress the deep pleasures and benefits which are the real reasons for going. This is understandable, largely because hazards are tangible. The inspirations, pleasures, and deep benefits are intangible and harder to explain; but they are satisfying beyond description.

It is true that the hazards of any area or endeavor should be understood, so that they may be avoided. We learn to handle automobiles so that we may have the benefits of transportation. We use hammers, axes, and knives for their utility in keeping with the purposes for which they were developed. This should be our fundamental attitude in the enjoyment of the outdoors. The inspiration, benefits, deep joys, and real communion with the Almighty far, far outweigh the hazards.

Many have discovered that two weeks retreat into the outdoors from the business world, in the company of majestic mountains and chattering creeks, breathing the redolence of pine needles and wild huckleberries, is sufficient to rejuvenate them for the remaining fifty weeks indoors. For millions the tug of a trout on a flyline, the unexpected flash of wild game, the enduring honesty of great trees and rivers, and a sense of nature's unrelenting life cycle, feed both body and soul. They realize that the farther man travels down that long, complex road out of the wilderness and into the air-conditioned cells of comfort he calls office and home, the greater his periodic need to return.

CLYDE ORMOND
Rigby, Idaho

1

Hiking into the Outdoors

Hiking across the uneven terrain of the outdoors, unlike everyday walking on the concrete sidewalks of cities, is something of an art. It was an art practiced with perfection by the American Indian as he stalked game along wilderness trails before the white man came. From the Indians the early mountain men learned the lore of wilderness travel, and it has been passed on through generations of outdoorsmen.

The art of hiking is basically a matter of learning to conserve your energy, of discovering the easiest way of navigating across rough terrain, often while wearing a heavy pack, without tiring yourself unduly. The pace at which you travel, the routes you select along the way, and the case with which you traverse difficult or dangerous obstacles—these are the signs of how expert a hiker you are.

First of all, if you intend to hike a considerable distance, set a comfortable pace. If you are hiking with a friend, the slower should never try to match the pace of the faster. Trying to keep up with a fast walker is the surest way to tire yourself and spoil your excursion. It is better to set your own comfortable pace, lagging behind if necessary, and catch up while the faster one rests.

It is a cardinal rule in outdoor walking that the steeper the elevation, the shorter your steps should be. The same applies to rough terrain. The more rocky or obstructed the going, and the more slippery the surfaces, the shorter should be your steps. Nothing will tire you quicker than taking long, fast steps uphill; and taking long, fast steps downhill over slippery logs, grass, or rocks is inviting a fall.

Another vital rule in hiking is to step over and around obstructions. It takes the same energy to lift your body a foot off the ground as it takes to walk approximately 13 feet on the level. When confronted by blowdowns, large rocks, or other obstructions on the trail, the experienced hiker steps over them and conserves his energy. The same applies to small objects on the trail, which are apt to roll and unbalance the hiker. It is always better to plant the feet between the innumerable rocks, twigs, and mounds—even though it entails breaking stride—rather than chance a fall.

Another rule of hiking in any kind of terrain is to follow the route of least resistance. It is wise to take advantage of the routes selected by those who have previously traveled the same course. In regions of true wilderness, where few if any humans have been, the best routes are generally marked in some fashion by wild game. There are no better engineers for finding the easiest way through wild country than such animals as deer, sheep, elk, and caribou.

Often the trails left by these road builders will be faint, but the observant outdoorsman will spot them. Sometimes a trail through heavy forests will be pockmarked by deer in their seasonal or daily movements. In areas of the Far North, trails will be worn a foot deep, like separate "buggy-tracks," by brown bear; or cut deeply into the high ridges by caribou. Often the routes of the wild animals will show only as openings through bush, worn grass at a creek crossing, or faint dung along a ridge. The experienced hiker looks for such signs, and gives thanks to the game for reducing his effort.

In the mountains the least obstructed routes generally follow the ridges. Before leaving one crest, the experienced hiker carefully scans the valley or canyon bottom, locates the longest, lowest ridge across to the opposite mountain, and marks it as his route. It is wise when hiking in the mountains to keep as much as possible of the elevation one has gained. Often the easiest opposing ridge won't be straight across but along a longer route following a mild course around an entire canyon apex. Just as it is always less laborious to step around a small pocket in the terrain, so it is with valleys and canyons. Hiking *around* their apexes—depending upon the ultimate objective, of course—often is less tiring in the long run than "lopping down, and puffing up again." One reason for traveling along ridges in mountain country is that less blowdown timber occurs on ridges than on either side of the mountain.

The seasoned outdoorsman soon learns to glance at any mountain and tell, from its steepness, whether it is negotiable or not. Some mountains are simply not worth the effort to climb, unless you are hunting goats or sheep or are equipped with mountain-climbing gear. A good guide for any hiker is the "angle of repose"—the degree of inclination at which it is too steep for foliage to grow, and slides and bare earth appear. Generally speaking, one shouldn't try to climb these areas, but find a more gradual, though round-about, route.

On any mountainside that can't be climbed along a man-made or game trail, the best procedure is to zig-zag upward rather than take a straight course. That is, one should climb in an angling route for a few rods; then, where the thinness of foliage or absence of rocks suggests, turn sharply and climb a few rods in the opposite direction before reversing. This technique utilizes the muscles of the right and left side of the body evenly, and gives the sides of the feet, which must dig in on the uphill side with each step, a chance to rest.

Treacherous Terrain

One of the best tools to help in crossing treacherous ter-rain is a staff about 4 to 6 feet long and 1½ inches in diam-eter. Light, dry wood, such as a small jack pine cut to suit-able length makes an adequate one. A staff becomes a third leg in uncertain footing and often prevents a nasty fall. With such a staff, you can poke firmly into a stream bottom and, by moving either one leg or the staff at a time (never both together), always have two "legs" to give you balance. You can probe for holes, big rocks, or soft spots in the bottom of muddy streams. If you are with a partner, you can hold the staff between you and support each other.

In crossing the glacial creeks of the Far North, a staff of driftwood or scraggly timber found on the spot often repre-sents the difference between crossing or staying on the same side. Such creeks, even in midsummer, have their source only a few miles away in the high glacial fields above. When you ford them in early morning, the creeks are low and clear, the flow reduced by the cold of the night. After a warm day, they are roaring, muddy demons, three times as deep, and vicious enough to roll rocks of glacial wash the size of buckets down in a seething boil that can often be heard for miles.

A good rule for crossing creeks and streams is to ford them either at the slow end of a deep pool or just before a long stretch of placid water breaks into a riffle. At these two places the water will be shallower and the current slower. Usually this is the widest part of the stream.

A hiking staff is also useful in desert areas. In some desert country, like portions of Arizona, there is a saying of the oldtimers that "everything that grows either sticks or bites you." This isn't literally true, but poisonous snakes and insects, and the various forms of cacti, keep the hiker constantly on his guard. He must continuously wind in and out among the sharp-tined cacti plants, some of which would penetrate the tough hide of a horse's leg, and be on the watch for harmful reptiles. A staff is useful for breaking an occasional spine out of the way or for defending yourself against desert rattlers.

A staff also is valuable when crossing swampland, muskeg, or other spongy ground. With it you can probe ahead in treacherous places for uncertain footing. You can use it as a pole for literally vaulting potholes you could not otherwise jump.

In crossing such watery areas, a fact to remember is that most swampland, if negotiable at all, has some solid high ground. Generally this ground borders the actual water level and permits travel between areas of inundation. Often small lakes, channels, and boggy areas are joined by necks of relatively solid footing. These must often be crossed in a series of jumps between hummocks of vegetation. The point to remember is that the ground is most solid in those parts where vegetation roots appear. For instance, in boggy areas having such vegetation as moss, grass, and sparse willows, the most solid footing occurs at the roots of the heaviest foliage—in this case, the willows. I have crossed Canadian muskeg, either on foot or horseback, where small spruce trees would wiggle as far as 20 to 30 feet ahead of me. Yet by sticking to the footing afforded by these spruce and the smaller arctic birch, crossing was fairly safe. However, had I stepped where only caribou moss grew among the water puddles, I would have sunk in. In those areas, incidentally, the hardpan creating the boggy situation was approximately 4 feet below the surface.

Finally, when a mishap does occur in boggy country, and you fall through into muck or water, a staff long enough to catch solid footing on at least one side can be a lifesaver. If you do fall in boggy terrain, try to land "spread-eagle"—that is, with arms and legs outspread. This distributes the body's weight over a greater surface. I have an Eskimo friend who has twice saved his own life in this fashion when falling through thin ice in the Arctic. He landed with arms outstretched, holding his short *oonok*, or hunting pole, in his mittened hands. The pole, anchoring on ice at either side, held his weight sufficiently so that he could inch his way back to safety by squirming along the ice on his belly.

This trick of landing spread-eagle often saves a life in steep, mountainous country. If you slip on a steep slope, trying to keep your feet may tumble you over a cliff or down the slope. If you land spread-eagle, friction and a low center of gravity help to halt your slide.

How Far Each Day

How far a hiker should walk in a day depends on such factors as the season of the year, the difficulty of the terrain, his age and physical condition, the purpose of the hike, and the amount of weight he needs to carry.

Some adults, unused to walking, cannot hike a half-mile without being tired. Others, hardened by outdoor living and mountain climbing, can walk all day and still be in fair shape. According to the standard set by President Theodore Roosevelt, a U.S. Marine should be able to walk a total of fifty miles in twenty hours. This is no reason for the beginner to attempt anything of that nature. Actually, pack horses average only two and a half to three miles per hour on mountain trails. That pace is too fast for a man. And there is little need for any outdoorsman, ever, to walk fifty miles in one around-the-clock period. Actually, one hikes for pleasure. When this is diminished by too strenuous an effort, the purpose is largely defeated.

On any trip, plan the hike so you reach your objective early in the day. If the hike is to be four miles round trip, you should be at the end of two miles well in advance of the half-day mark. You should rest, then turn back while there is still more than a half-day left, or before you are excessively tired. The hike back, on a single day's trek, invariably takes longer and is more tiring. Where the entire day is spent hiking towards a given objective, the last half, similarly, takes more time and energy than the first. This should be remembered so that a margin of strength may be left, and the full hike made more enjoyable.

This is especially true of hiking through deserts, swamps, or muskeg areas. In the desert the midday sun saps energy fast, and the afternoon portion of the day is hottest. Similarly, in boggy or muskeg areas the soft underfooting unexpectedly takes the hiker's energy before he is aware of how tired he is.

A good way for any beginning hiker to approach the matter of how far to hike in a day is not to set too definite an objective on his first hike—that is, not decide to hike to Clear Creek and back but see how far he can pleasurably hike toward Clear Creek before getting very tired, or in less than half of his available time. If he makes it to the creek, pleasurably, fine. If not, he should head back, then try for longer distance the next time.

Generally speaking, any person in good physical shape and health should be able to hike from three to five miles a day in easy country. Seasoned outdoorsmen can hike ten to twenty in rolling forest country, if necessary, with no pack or just a light load.

Footwear for Hikers

Shoes or boots are the most important single item of clothing for hiking, since the feet take the most punishment. Generally speaking, hiking shoes should be 6 to 8 inches high, light in weight, and have a "cord" type of sole. Heavy boots, cowboy boots, oxford-type shoes, canvas sneakers, calked boots, or boots having no heels (wedge type), are not good for prolonged hikes.

Recently, jogging has become a widely adopted form of exercise and activity, and shoes especially for the purpose have been developed. Basically, these shoes are low-cut, have heels continuous with their soles, and are padded in the areas of greatest stress. They are usually well-built and adapted especially for the purpose of jogging or running on flat surfaces.

Joggers may feel that these shoes would do as well for hiking over various types of terrain. On soil surfaces, or when on easy rolling trails such as in mildly undulating forest country, jogging shoes do fairly well. But they have several drawbacks for rough or mountain travel. They tend to pull off at the heels when you are climbing a steep in-

A light, rugged boot suitable for hiking.

cline. They lack the hard square-cut heel necessary to keep from "rolling" and stumbling when going downhill or over small rocks. Again, the mildly upturned toes of jogging shoes won't "bite in" at the toes on hills, and there is no protection for the ankles in rocky country.

Hiking shoes should be light, as the weight of heavy boots, multiplied by the thousands of times the feet must lift them, requires an excessive expenditure of energy. Cord soles were for many years the best soles developed for holding firmly to most surfaces—rocks, wood, and grass. In more recent years, another type of sole has been developed which is comparable, and for extremely rough or rocky going, even somewhat better. That is the Vibram® sole. This sole is protected by registered trademark. It is made of a hard-rubber compound, and features, on its surface, a series of deep channels and square-cut ridges—something like a winter snow tire for an automobile.

The design is patterned so as to present resistance in all directions, to prevent slipping. In rough travel the sole will "bite in" on rocks, logs, and other odd-shaped surfaces better than most soles, and the material seems to wear forever. It is a somewhat bulky sole, and the main thing to watch for when choosing footwear with Vibram soles is to get a boot as light in weight as is consistent with good quality.

Leather soles are not good for mountain hiking as they tend to slip on rocks and smooth surfaces. The same is true of wedge-type soles—they become miniature skis in mountain country. Where terrain is consistently swampy or filled with muskeg, a good choice is the rubber-bottom, leather-top pac. These, too, should be light, about 8-inches high, and have heels.

Many Canadians use moccasins for hiking. Once the feet

Moccasins are good for hiking in wet or muskeg terrain, but the feet must be toughened to their use.

are hardened to their use, these are fine in country that is rolling, wet, or has a moss or muskeg surface. Work moccasins that tie on and come high over the ankles are the most useful. For use in snow these are often supplemented by a rubber "slipper" with cleat soles. Good moose-hide moccasins will dry out at night without being stiff in the morning—and that's a decided advantage.

For serious hiking only good-quality shoes should be worn. The intermittent wetting, constant twisting and banding, and uneven wearing to which shoes used in outdoor hiking are subjected will not only ruin poor-quality footgear quickly, but will cripple the wearer. Seams will part; heels will loosen; tacks will work their way into the

11

feet after several wettings; inner soles will become lumpy. Too often the front ends of such shoes, after being dried a few times, will lose their shape and resemble the curled front ends of skis. Some dry out hard as rocks. The results can even be disastrous when such a boot goes to pieces while the hiker is afield.

Hiking shoes should be purchased a half-size and a width larger than a person's dress shoes. Under the hiker's constant weight, feet spread out laterally to a considerable degree. After long hours of walking, the feet also swell slightly. All this takes up the extra half-size. Also, a thicker sock should be worn in a hiking shoe than in a dress shoe. In fact, when fitting a hiking shoe, it is a good policy to take along an extra-heavy sock and try on the new shoe over it.

Once the new shoe is taken home, it should be broken in by stepping into a tub of water, with the shoes fully laced, for three to five seconds. Then the shoe should be worn until it dries thoroughly on the foot. This shapes a new hiking shoe to the foot, and loosens and flexes leather and stitching to the point where it is wearable. After this initial wetting and drying, a good shoe grease or dressing should be applied, unless the shoe has been pretreated with a silicone preparation which makes it fairly waterproof. Broken in in this manner, the shoe should be worn for several days in advance of a long hike—even a few hours each evening around the house will help.

Good hiking shoes, conditioned in this manner, will take repeated wetting and drying in the outdoors without too much damage. After a wetting, shoes should be dried slowly at night near a camp stove or campfire. Treated with another coat of shoe dressing, they will be ready for wear the next day.

Too many people spoil good shoes by trying to dry them too fast. Often they set them in back of the camp stove or too near the fire and go about something else. When the odor of burning leather greets their nostrils, it is too late, and the shoes are practically ruined. Instead, shoes should be dried slowly. They should be set considerably away from intense heat and off the ground where they would draw additional moisture. Good ways to dry shoes are to hang them from a tree limb in the sun or from the ridgepole of a tent, or set them against the sunny side of a flat rock. Hanging shoes upside down allows them to drain as well as dry.

Foot Care for Hikers

An outdoorsman can patch up a minor burn or cut, or a blister from swinging an ax, and still enjoy himself. A small wound on his foot will cripple him. Proper foot care is essential to the enjoyment of any hike.

The difficulty with getting your feet wet on a hike is that sand and gravel often get into your shoes along with the water. Such gritty particles lodge between the toes and between folds of the skin, particularly at the underside of the first toe-joints. They also stick to the socks and work into the weave of the knitting. They grate against the foot's tender skin like sandpaper. Also, wet socks—particularly cotton ones—wrinkle, lose their shape, and gradually work down inside the shoes, where they quickly blister the feet.

The best way of caring for the feet after getting them wet is to thoroughly wash shoes, socks, and feet. Next, shake the shoes till they are as free of water as possible. Wring the socks dry and shake out further moisture. Wipe the feet dry with a handkerchief. Lacking a handkerchief, use the wrung-out socks to dry the feet, then wring the socks out again. Put socks and shoes on and continue hiking. There will be ten times less damage and discomfort to the feet if these precautions are taken.

In desert hiking, where the feet are not apt to get wet but do heat up, to prevent galling it is wise to stop occasionally, remove shoes and socks, and for several minutes fan your feet with your hat to cool the skin. When putting on the socks again, put the left sock on the right foot, and vice versa. This helps eliminate creases and makes the socks wear more evenly, thus prolonging their resistance against holes. Similarly, in forest hiking, when you come to a creek after an hour or so of hot hiking, it is refreshing to take off shoes and socks and dunk the feet into the cool water.

A final suggestion: Make certain never to wear socks with holes in them on lengthy hikes. The material around the edge of a hole in a sock, once dampened by perspiration, tends to roll, forming a hard ring which is sure to cause blisters.

The Hiker's Clothes

The season of the year and the expected weather determine the hiker's clothing. Usually, the majority of hikes are made in summer and fall in the colder climates, and in comparable weather in the warmer climates.

For mile-weather hiking, cotton undergarments, shirt, and pants are best. A hiker sweats while walking, and the evaporation tends to chill him when he stops. Therefore, garments should be relatively light, and loose enough to allow for freedom of movement and easy evaporation.

This is especially true when hiking under intense sun or in desert areas. Under such conditions, wear light-colored clothing, as dark coloration draws more heat. Good colors for intense heat and sunlight are the suntans and mild tints of green and blue. Also, to avoid sunstroke or heat exhaustion, travel in desert areas during the evening and morning hours, if possible, reserving midday for resting. A white handkerchief placed under the hat rim and draped over the nape of the neck helps to keep the sweltering sun off that area.

On a hike in more temperate regions, carry a light jacket or woolen shirt to wear when pausing to rest, as the evaporation of heavy perspiration causes one to cool off quickly. If light showers are expected, a nylon jacket is fine. Otherwise a light poplin jacket will generally suffice to turn any wind and keep you warm. One of the best jackets for the purpose is the top part of a suit of Dacron-insulated underwear. This garment has unbelievable warmth for its few ounces of weight, launders easily, and is inexpensive. Woolen sweaters are not suitable for hikes through country where brush or foliage occur—they snag too easily.

For mile-weather hiking, socks are the one item that should be made of wool. Light wool socks are more comfortable for most people than cotton socks. This is especially true once they are wet. Wool-nylon socks are also good.

During the late fall months, when cold nights are the rule and storms are to be expected, the best material for clothing is wool: medium-weight, tightly-woven wool pants and lightweight woolen shirts.

For extremely cold, snowy weather, light woolen underwear and heavy "mackinaw" woolen pants, together with lightweight woolen shirts and light down jackets, are a good combination. Heavier socks of wool, too, are needed if you are wearing pacs. Pacs are the best footgear for snowshoes, though some woodsmen prefer 10-inch felt gaiters worn inside four-buckle rubber arctics.

Regardless of season, pants used for long hikes should not have cuffs such as are standard for dress pants. Outside cuffs catch snow, rain, twigs, sand, and gravel, and become a hard rope around the ankles. Cuffs also hook on sticks and tend to trip the hiker. Hiking pants, like riding jeans, should have terminal leg seams turned only toward the inside. Pants should not be worn inside the boots, they funnel leaves, dirt, and sticks between socks and leather.

For mild weather both the shirt and pants should be of hard, tightly knit but porous material. This prevents the garments from being snagged and torn, and in insect country cuts down on the bites of mosquitoes, black flies, and gnats. Denim shirts and the Levi type of pants are useful in this respect, and make the pest problem a bit more endurable. For insect-pest regions, shirts should be long-sleeved and pants full-length regardless of warm temperatures.

There is one material that insects can't bore through—buckskin. Shirts, pants, and jackets of buckskin are the toughest of garments. Their utility is limited, however, for extended hiking in a variety of weather. Buckskin garments won't "breathe," and this makes evaporation and cooling almost impossible. Once the wearer stops to rest, his skin becomes clammy and cold.

One of the best kinds of headgear for most hiking is a medium-brim felt hat, light in color and western in style. A quality felt hat of this kind offers protection against light rain and snow, falling limbs and swishing branches, and shades the eyes from the direct rays of the sun. During a heavy downpour, the hat will shed most of the rain if the crown is left undented. During extremely cold weather, this kind of hat is still useful if worn with a pair of knitted earlaps. For desert hiking, a wide-brimmed cloth or straw hat is cooler but wilts easily in any appreciable storm.

For cool weather, and for camp chores, snug-fitting buckskin gloves are good. For colder weather, knit jersey gloves are warm, and leather, rabbit-lined gloves will suffice for all but extreme arctic weather, where down mitts are needed.

A neckerchief such as the Boy Scouts wear is helpful for protecting the back of the neck from insects and sunburn. A large bandanna handkerchief will do just as well, and will often double for other purposes, such as bundling up small items and covering the ears in cold weather.

The Laundry Problem

Laundering clothes in the outdoors presents quite a problem in certain regions and under certain conditions. Some hardy outdoorsmen simply wear what they have on for a trip's duration. The average person, however, becomes an outdoorsman each year for a period of only a few days to a month. Accustomed to changing clothes at home, he usually prefers to continue the habit in the outdoors.

Field trips of more than a day or so each should always be made with at least a partial change of clothing at hand. No "spares" are usually needed for such items as a heavy stag coat, raincoat, boots, or pacs. Changes of underwear, shirt, socks, and pants should always be taken along on the longer treks.

Generally the best time to do your washing outdoors is not on Mondays, but when it is most convenient to bathe or swim. If your pack contains a change of underwear, rinse out the worn garment after the swim, wring it out, and drape it over a rock or bush to dry while you bask in the sun. If the opportunity to bathe and wash doesn't occur when you can pause to dry things out, the washed articles can be bundled in a neckerchief, carried on the outside of the rucksack, and dried after the night's camp is made.

During colder weather, in regions where tents and overnight huts are necessary, laundering can be done inside. Although facilities for washing clothes may be limited, a bucket or washpan, soap, and water are all that are really necessary to do a good job of laundering.

Soak the soiled garment in warm water, not hot, after it has been soaped. Soaking for an hour or even less will loosen the dirt. Then rub the garment between the hands or up and down in the soapy water until it is reasonably clean. Rinse it in clear water and hang it up to dry.

When drying wet clothes, wring out all possible water and hang or drape them so the greatest surface will be exposed to heat, sunlight, or movement of the air. During the warm weather, air and sunlight are all that is needed. During a storm, some form of artificial heat must usually be employed.

During wet weather, the best place to dry clothes is a line just under the tent's ridgepole or a temporary frame set back from the camp stove. Make sure the clothes are not too close to either stove or gas lantern, where they may catch fire and burn up an entire outfit. Wet clothes can be hung outside during freezing weather. After they have frozen stiff, the moisture can be shaken out in the form of frost particles.

2

The Hiker's Pack

The size of the pack you carry into the outdoors will be determined by your build and physical condition, the intended duration of the hike, the type of terrain, and whether you go alone or with a partner.

Perhaps no two hikers will carry identical packs with the same expenditure of energy. It is difficult to pick a hiker at random and determine just what he can or should pack. There are, however, basic rules and standards to help each individual choose the best pack for himself.

Just as no one who has not practiced on one-day or overnight hikes should attempt a hike of several days' duration, so no one unused to a pack-load should attempt to carry a heavy pack on his first hikes. As the distance and difficulty of your hikes are gradually increased, so can the weight of the pack you carry.

As a guide to determining the size and weight of your pack, consider these facts: A husky fifteen- or sixteen-year old boy, in good physical shape, can carry a 25-pound pack, in rolling hill country, with no difficulty. Some fellows can carry a heavier pack, for more miles, than grown men. A healthy man of average build can carry a 30- to 35-pound pack, in reasonable terrain. Toughened by backpacking experience, he can handle up to 50 pounds.

Knapsacks

For simply hiking into the outdoors for a day's fun, you need to pack little more than a camera, lunch, personal incidentals, and a small, light emergency kit which will be described in detail in a later chapter. This gear may easily be carried in a small knapsack, such as the official Boy Scout model, or in a small rucksack capable of handling more bulk and weight. Most knapsacks or rucksacks will average from 14 to 15 inches wide, 5 inches thick, and from 15½ to 17 inches high. A larger rucksack is more useful for hikers who may wish to carry back more weight than they take; that is, for such purposes as prospecting, rock-hunting, or gathering small pieces of driftwood along the seashore.

Recently, an ultra-light knapsack has been developed, especially made for bicycling, skiing, and similar go-light trips. This triangular knapsack measures 5½ by 6½ by 13 inches, and goes laterally around the body just over the hips. It is called, inelegantly, the "fanny-pack," and also may be used to carry the very lightest of loads when hiking. It is useful especially when the hands must be entirely free.

Pack Basket—Tumpline

The woven pack basket is often used for portages on canoe trips, as it handles a variety of irregular-shaped bundles easily; and if the portage is short, the weight can be increased. Guides and seasoned outdoorsmen usually employ a tumpline for carrying bulky gear and heavy objects such as outboard motors, tents, and bed rolls. The tumpline consists of a leather band which goes around the forehead, and two leather straps which are tied to heavy bundles that ride on the user's back. Loads of 100 pounds or more can be lugged with a tumpline—an implement, incidentally, which would kink the neck of a person not used to it.

Packboards

The packboard is perhaps the best device for carrying a variety of loads under different circumstances. Packboards have been developed in several basic types. One consists of a vertical framework having the tops of the two side standards closer together than the bottom ends. Another type is the exact reverse, with the tops of the standards spread apart. Still another form of packboard is an integral board-and-sack. Another, of aluminum tubing, has a small horizontal shelf across the bottom to support the load. Each type of packboard has been developed for a special type of load and terrain. It has also been designed for the type of activity of the user. All have been designed with a view toward keeping the center of gravity as constant as possible and preventing horizontal leverage.

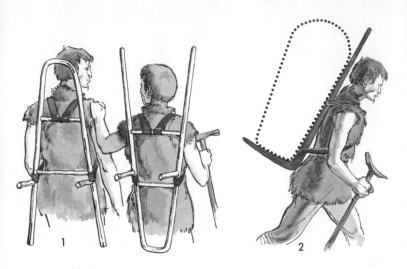

Modern backpacking equipment owes much to the ancient devices used by the primitive load-bearers of the East. The "A" frame and inverted "A" frame carriers (1), and the "L" frame carrier (2), were forerunners of the modern pack frame.

As examples of how these factors must be correlated, the carrier of a heavy burden over level terrain needs a packboard which will allow his load to be carried high on the back, about even with the shoulders, where it will in no way interfere with his leg movement, and in such a position that he may walk almost upright. Conversely, the person who must climb steep mountains, using his hands to help pull himself up over rocks and broken terrain, needs a packboard which will permit the load to be carried lower, at the small of his back. Otherwise he would be unbalanced, with a constant tendency to fall on his face. Again, the person who needs free arm and leg movement while wearing a pack, should have a board which distributes the load more evenly from his shoulders to the small of his back. In all cases, the heaviest portions of the load should always be

The principle of the basket carrier (3) has been adapted in the tumpline used by North Woods' packers today; and the fulcrum or pole carrier (4) taught us the principles of leverage and weight distribution.

set as closely against the wearer's body as possible. This adds to the mechanical advantage.

For general outdoor use in all kinds of terrain, a compromise packboard can be made. This type of packboard consists of two elements: (1) a wooden frame resembling a small ladder with three crossbars mortised into two side rails; (2) a canvas wrap which encircles this frame and is laced tightly together at the back. Web straps, fastened to the upper crossbar, pass through an opening in the face of the canvas wrap, over the user's shoulders, then down to his hips where they fasten, usually with buckles, to the lower ends of the frame's siderails.

This simple, all-around packboard has many virtues. It allows a heavy load to be placed well up on the shoulders and back where man's heavy burdens belong under average circumstances. It allows the same load to be reversed and tied upside down on the board, for steep climbing where the hands must be used. This packboard also prevents the load from rubbing against the wearer's back; the taut canvas

Homemade wooden packboard consists of a frame of two sidebars joined by crosspieces, and a canvas wrap which rests against the wearer's back. It carries gear of different shapes and sizes.

wrap creates an air space of approximately 1½ inches between load and wearer. This not only provides for ventilation, but evenly distributes the total weight over the greatest possible area. The large loops of the two shoulder straps allow the packboard to be easily put on and taken off, and are quickly slipped off in case of a fall. Finally, the packboard is light in relation to the load.

Years ago, I invented a smaller version of this packboard, which can be carried in the coat pocket on hunting trips and assembled in camp for lugging home the game. The canvas wrap is replaced with one of lighter drill, and the straps are smaller. At camp, the entire frame is either built from the ends of orange crates or shaped from small, dry pine slabs. Mortises are cut into the siderails with an ax, and the crossbars are nailed on. The wrap is then fixed rigidly along the ends by shoving two alder sticks through the seams, and laced with a shoelace tightly around the frame. The shoulder strap is attached with a loop knot to the middle of the top crossbar, run through the wrap opening and tied to the ends of the frame with nylon cord.

The makings of this miniature packboard folded into something little larger than six nails and a bandanna handkerchief; and for years we used it to carry the lunch, rope, camera, and elk bugle on the way out, and 15 pounds of heart and liver coming back to camp. A sack the same size as the board was later added for carrying small articles.

These all-purpose packboards still have to be made by the individual, though some commercial models are beginning to appear. Modified versions are available in the Trapper Nelson packboard; a rugged military model which consists of an integral pressed-wood frame-and-wrap, moulded to fit the wearer's back; and pack frames made of light aluminum tubing.

Aluminum pack frames have several advantages: They are very light for their strength and the load they can carry. Most joints, which are the weakest points in a wooden frame, are eliminated by bending and shaping the metal tubing. Also, they are equipped with a small shelf at the bottom, which prevents the load from sagging or slipping downward. One model of the aluminum pack frame is designed so that a small child can be carried along the trail papoose fashion.

When carrying a pack frame the hiker should lean slightly forward so as to bring the center of gravity over the legs and feet. The lower strap, which rests against the back just above the hips, acts as a fulcrum upon which the load rests, with lift being supplied by the wearer's hips and legs. With the frame evenly loaded, the total weight may be shifted slightly from shoulders to back, and vice versa, by a slight shifting of the walking posture.

Go-Light Gear

Let's consider an actual example of what might go into a one-man pack, assuming that it is for summer or mild-weather traveling. Further, let's assume that the hiker is experienced on shorter hikes, wants to stay a week, and is conditioned to carry 40 pounds easily.

In this case, the necessary items of gear and food will break down into just over half the weight for gear, and less than half for food.

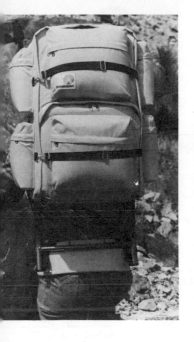

Two types of framed packs. At left, aluminum pack frame with detachable pack. The frame is molded to fit the wearer's back, has a padded belt that encircles the hips. Packbag contains two large internal compartments and four external pockets. Backpack below has an internal frame that molds to the contours of the back, features eight leather tabs to lash on extra equipment, tunnels behind the side pockets for carrying ski poles or fishing rods. *Courtesy Himalayan Industries, Inc.*

Placement of weight in a pack is determined by the wearer's activity. A hiker packing a heavy load on level terrain (left) should carry the heaviest part of his gear at about shoulder level (dark portion). Arrows show lift and pull from shoulders and upthrust from hips and legs. A rock climber (right) should pack the heaviest part of his load at the small of his back, bringing the center of gravity as close to his body as possible so the weight does not tip him forward. Courtesy Himalayan Pak Co.

The basic items will be:

Packboard	3 pounds or less
Ax	2½ pounds
Sleeping bag	4 pounds
Cooking and eating utensils	2 pounds
Down vest	½ pound
Raincoat	½ pound
Underwear, shirt, socks	2 pounds
Camera and film	2½ pounds

Tarp	2 pounds
Emergency kit	½ pound
Whetstone, matches, tooth-	½ pound
brush, first-aid kit, etc.	½ pound
Miscellaneous	2 pounds
Total	22 pounds

In addition, the hiker may want to carry a fishing rod, rifle, handgun, or binoculars.

The ax should have a single-bit, 1½-pound head, and a leather sheath. It won't exceed 2½ pounds.

Sleeping Bags

There are several types of sleeping bags which will stay within this weight limit and still be comfortable for mild to cool weather. One is the inside portion of the down mummy bag used by the Air Force in World War II. Another is a mummy bag lined with an olive-drab army blanket. Several of the light down robes, used a generation ago, will not exceed this weight, and are very useful.

One of the most interesting lightweight sleeping bags I've ever seen was given to me by an old lion hunter in Arizona. It is made of paper with a thin layer of fiber insulation. The bag itself is lined with a cotton flannel sheet. This bag, too, is warm for its light weight, and very useful in semidesert country where moisture isn't a problem but nights are cool.

Cooking Utensils

The cooking kit and eating utensils may be assembled in a variety of ways and still stay under the weight limit. Only a few pots and dishes are necessary. Two light, nested, aluminum pots will take care of all cooking except frying. One is usually used to heat water, the other to cook stew, vegetables, etc. With the water heated, the other pot may be used to cook dried fruit, since beverages will be of the instant kind and mixed in the cup.

Since every ounce of weight is vital on a hiking trip, and since no food can be wasted, most hikers carefully cook only as much as they can eat, and eat the main course right from the pot.

The weight of the cooking pots can be cut down by taking three nested tin cans of suitable size. Remove their tops, hammer down their edges so they won't cut, and use short pieces of thin wire for bails. Bails are left off until the pots are used.

A frying pan is heavy, has an awkward handle, and is useful only if the backpacker obtains fish or small game. Bacon can be cooked in the bottom of a pot. The frying-pan problem can be solved in one of two ways. One is to buy a small frying pan, cut a length off the handle, and rivet a small aluminum loop around the remaining portion. In use, a length of stick is whittled to correct size and shoved tightly into this loop, providing the pan with a long, cool handle.

Others solve the problem by cutting a gallon fruit can at a 2-inch height, leaving a 2-inch strip of metal all the way up one side to the top. All edges are bent over and hammered into a smooth rim, and the upright strip is bent into a handle. This frying pan will fit under two or three other pots in the pack.

The eating utensils may be reduced to an aluminum plate, aluminum cup, spoon, and fork. A belt knife or even a pocketknife does all the necessary cutting and spreading.

The weight of the spoon and fork can be further reduced by using the small plastic forks and spoons available for picnics. A usable spoon, or even a fork, can be whittled out of a piece of flat wood.

Clothing

Raincoats have been vastly improved within the last few years with the invention of polyethylene. The old-style, heavy, rubber-fabric raincoat can now be left at home, and a plastic one weighing only a few ounces substituted, if you will be reasonably careful of snags. Perhaps the most usable type is the parka-raincoat, which has a hood to cover the head and neck.

One of the nicest garments for cool evenings and mornings is the down vest. It weighs only a few ounces, is a marvelous windbreaker, and is very warm for its weight. The top part of insulated Dacron underwear, as mentioned before, is also a warm, light garment. Such items fill the bill better than the heavy woolen jackets or shirts once used for the purpose.

For a week's jaunt, an extra denim shirt is necessary, and also may be used as a jacket for warmth. Two pair of spare socks will suffice. The change of underwear should be of the same kind as the ones worn.

Camera

Most outdoorsmen now carry cameras. A big share of any trip's enjoyment is the "braggin" pictures one returns with and reviews many times. Unless one is a professional photographer, a 35-mm camera and a spare roll of 36-exposure film will do the picture-taking job.

Tarps

Except for an ax, a tarp is the most important part of the gear. The old standard in tarps for backpacking was an 8-foot square of waterproof 8-ounce canvas, sometimes with triangular-shaped ends (for forming the sides of a lean-to), and grommets along all sides. This served the purpose well, and is indeed today one of the best-known tarp materials where automobile, boat, plane, or horse transportation is available. Such a tarp is tough, snagproof, waterproof, and long-wearing. Its single fault is that it is too heavy for backpacking.

Realizing this, many hikers made their own tarps of muslin or drill. These were waterproofed, and often were made up at home into small one-man tents. These light, cotton materials weren't as snagproof or waterproof as the heavier canvas, but they made up for it in lightness.

Recently a material has been invented for tents and tarpaulins which is half the weight of canvas. This is a nylon base, coated on both sides with vinyl plastic. It is tough, completely waterproof, and stands hard wear very well. Tarps of this material are available in a variety of sizes from mail-order houses.

The best overall size for a hiker's tarp is 8 feet square. Most tarps of this new material are rectangular in shape. For occasional use, a size approximating 8-feet square will do. For the serious hiker who takes to the woods often, it's better to buy a large size, cut it down to 8 feet square, and re-hem it.

Regardless of material, one should have the local canvas shop put additional eyelets, or grommets, along all sides 18 inches apart. These prove most useful for tying down lean-tos and flys during wind, and for tightly wrapping bundles and gear.

Many old outdoorsmen and veteran hikers will say that even this load is too heavy. Many hikers, could do well in the woods without as much gear. But the purpose in being outdoors is not to see how much one can endure. The purpose is enjoyment, communion with nature, and rebuilding the body and spirit for the remainder of the year.

Cold-Weather Gear

For traveling in snow and below-freezing temperatures, heavier gear is needed. The sleeping bag should be of down. The tarp should either be made into a small, floored tent, or used as a Baker tent or lean-to, with an all-night fire burning in front so that reflected heat will keep the sleeper warm. Deep snow requires snowshoes; level country and dry, frosty snow, skis. Increasing a pack-load to a full limit of 50 pounds, and then using it on webs which sink in at every step, is a job for only the hardy.

The problem of carrying sufficient gear in snowy climes can be solved, however, by using a light toboggan. In steep country, thick underbrush, or varied snow conditions, a man in good physical shape can still drag 75 pounds for many miles with no difficulty. Under easier conditions, such as along snow-covered stream beds, over frozen lakes, or rolling, open country, 100 pounds is a mild load for a strong man.

The principle of the toboggan is that it distributes the load over a broad surface of snow, and its hard, polished undersurface reduces friction to a minimum. The center of gravity remains very low, preventing tip-overs in sloping country. For the winter traveler wishing to stay in the wilds for several days, the toboggan is an excellent way to transport his gear.

Food for the Trail

The old Hudson Bay standard for food in the wilderness was 3 pounds per man per day. The traditional staples were the three B's—beans, bacon, and bannock. Tea was the favorite trail drink, as it was light, easily made, and provided more heat than coffee. Bannock was made on the spot from flour. Salt was included, of course. Together with what meat he could find, this simple diet kept the woodsman well fed. All trail food was chosen not only for its nutritional value but for its relative lack of water content and resistance to spoilage.

These should be the factors considered in selecting today's trail foods. Thanks to dehydration, we now can have a far greater variety of palatable foods.

The four basic foods are:

1. Milk and milk products
2. Bread and the cereal group
3. Fruit and vegetables
4. Meat and meat products

Keeping these requirements in mind, here is a suggested list of food for the 40-pound pack-load, for one man for a full week's stay:

Bacon (in slab)	1 pound
Powdered eggs	½ pound
Cereals (rolled oats, wheat hearts, prepared cereal, etc.)	1½ pounds
Instant tea or coffee (Substitute chocolate or bouillon cubes)	½ pound
Sugar	1 pound
Prepared pancake mix	1 pound
Salt, pepper, seasoning	½ pound
Cured ham	1½ pounds
Dried fruit (peaches, apples, prunes, etc.)	1½ pounds
Cooking foil	
Chocolate bars	½ pound
Dry beans	1 pound
Powdered milk	1 pound
Raisins	½ pound
Dehydrated vegetables	1 pound
Dried soups (in envelopes)	½ pound
Rice	½ pound
Pilot biscuit, hardtack, or crackers	1 pound
Chipped beef	½ pound
Macaroni	½ pound
Cheese	½ pound
Total	16½ pounds

Such a list includes the four basic food groups, and when cooked properly will provide more than the average man can eat. And fish or game can be added for variety. In areas of mountain creeks, a bunch of fresh watercress, picked from cold water, adds tang to a meal. This list may, of course, be altered here and there according to the tastes of the individual.

In arranging meals, perishables should be consumed first. The ham, for example, might be used the first two days, with any remaining portion used in a pot of beans and ham for supper the third night. Combinations can also be made, such as a few raisins cooked with rice and sugared. Sugar, browned in a pan and mixed with boiling water, makes a fine hotcake syrup. Even a pocketful of threshed wheat, which has not been treated with chemicals, or pinole (described later), to chew on while walking is nourishing and pleasant.

With any grub list the hiker may make up, it's a good idea to try out at least a few of the dishes at home. Most people can stir hot water in soup-mix, soak beans overnight, or brew up a potful of dried fruit and water. But for any dishes you are uncertain about, such as pancakes in a tiny skillet, practice at least once at home where failure won't mean going hungry.

Foodstuffs for trail use should be packaged against both moisture and spillage. One of the best arrangements for such items as sugar, salt, beans, rice, and cereals is a double bag. The inner bag is a plastic container known as a refrigerator bag. The 1-quart size will hold a pint, or about half a pound of kernel goods, and still leave room to fasten the top with a doubled elastic band. This inner bag then goes inside a muslin bag sewed to size on the home sewing machine.

If you have the time, sew a loop seam and drawstring in the top of the muslin bag for tight closure. A simpler way is to use ordinary mailing tags. These have a tough string which you can tie around the top of the bag and label the contents on the tag.

Packing the Load

To assemble the pack, all foodstuffs, clothing, and gear are arranged on one corner of a folded tarp in a grouping approximately the size of the outside dimensions of the packboard. The entire bundle, except for the ax, is then wrapped in the tarp just as a Christmas package is wrapped—ends of tarp folded in and remainder wrapped around and around.

The wrapped pack is then laid on the back of the pack-board and lashed firmly. Usually the bedroll rides on top, and relatively high. If the lower end of the pack can be made a trifle smaller than the middle, this prevents the entire load from sagging when it's lashed down. The ax is shoved head upward through the lashings so there is no pos-sibility of losing it.

To shoulder such a pack alone, grasp the right strap in both hands (if you are right-handed) near its junction with the board. In a single hoisting movement, swing the load upward and to the right. At the end of this movement, and under the upward momentum, swing the right arm under the strap as far as possible toward the shoulder. The strap and weight usually come down with the strap over the up-per arm. In another upward hoisting motion with the body, and with the strap loosening under momentum again, place the strap fully over the right shoulder with the left hand. Next, lean forward and bend to the left, letting the pack not only rest on the back, but gently roll to a position where the left strap may easily be placed over the shoulder with the left hand. It's largely a matter of hoisting up quickly and placing the straps while momentum creates a mild slackness in the straps. Care should be used not to twist the body too much, to guard against a slipped disc or other spinal injury.

When resting, experienced hikers pick out any sort of elevation, such as a blowdown, large rock, or tree limb, on which to set the packboard. Loading again becomes just a matter of bending forward and slipping the arms through the straps.

3

Water Travel

The first craft that primitive man ever rode down a stream was probably a log. One may assume that, finding a particular log wasn't big enough to support his weight on water, he joined together two logs with roots or vines, thus constructing the first raft. Indeed, some of the earliest rafts of history were fashioned in this way. One consisted of three logs, the central log being longest, held apart with crossbars lashed to the logs. The Fiji Islanders built their war canoes on this catamaran principle derived from early rafts. Another step in the development of the raft came naturally when early man, in his need for lumber, tied trees together and floated them downstream. And when he learned to use dowels and sharp-edged tools, raft-making became far simpler.

Simple log rafts are still very useful in timbered country for crossing streams, moving around the shoreline of lakes, or even crossing them when occasion demands. They are useful in moving one's equipment down a river when traveling along the bank in wilderness country presents too many obstacles, or when there is too much weight for backpacking.

A log raft is easily made where conifer timber grows adjacent to a stream or lake. The only materials needed are dry timber, an ax, and some type of fastening such as spikes, baling wire, or rope.

Water Displacement

Before cutting into a stand of dry timber, however, the raft-maker should know something about the principle of water displacement. It will save him the annoyance of a day spent cutting timber, only to find that his finished raft sinks when he steps on it.

Briefly, water supports any type of craft if the volume of water displaced by that craft is equivalent in weight to the craft itself. To build a raft, then, it is necessary to have sufficient logs to displace enough water to support the weight of the raft and anyone riding on it.

Since the raft will be made of logs of varied shapes and sizes that taper from butt to tip, it would appear next to impossible for a man lacking a slide rule and a knowledge of engineering to estimate the amount of logs he'll need. Such is not the case. Anyone, by remembering a simple formula and by keeping all figures approximate, can estimate the proper weight to within a few pounds.

Let's take a practical example: Suppose that you come upon a high mountain lake, in lodgepole-pine country, where trout are jumping near the shoreline. You decide to make a simple raft in order to pole offshore and cast to them.

Just off to one side, we'll say, there is a stand of dry pines, some of which average 8 inches thick. The raft, let's suppose, will be 12 feet long, since timber of that length is handy and only one man will be using it. A 12-foot log, averaging 8 inches in diameter, is about all one person can drag to the water's edge.

If the log averages 8 inches thick midway of its length, it will have a radius of 4 inches. The formula for obtaining the volume, or cubic feet, of any cylinder, is to multiply the radius by itself, times *pi* (3.1416, or roughly 3-1/7), times the length. All figures, for our purpose, should be expressed in feet.

The 4-inch radius, or 1/3 of a foot, times itself, times 3-1/7, times 12, will equal 4.2 cubic feet, to the nearest tenth. The log, then, will displace 4.2 cubic feet of water. One cubic foot of water weighs 62.4 pounds. Multiplying 4.2 times 62.4, we get 262.08 pounds—the weight of water the log will displace.

This 8-inch pine log will weigh, if perfectly dry, 25 pounds per cubic foot, or 105 pounds. Subtracted from the weight of water displaced (262 pounds), leaves 157 pounds—the weight that the log will support in the water.

At this point some adjustments will have to be made. You will not want the raft to sink to the very top of the logs, as this would wet any load carried on it. Further, allowing the logs to ride well out of the water would not result in a direct proportion in log-height to total weight-lift, since the weight of the logs would remain constant, and have to be subtracted, regardless of the lessened weight. Again, if the timber happened to be partly wet, or after it had become water-logged from use, its own weight would increase well beyond 25 pounds per cubic foot. Also, if the upper sections of the 8-inch trees were to be used, as well they might, this would cut down on the total buoyancy. Maybe some would average only 6 inches. Lastly, since it would take you the better part of a day to build, you decide that you will make it a semipermanent conveyance; and that next month you will bring a partner or two along to enjoy the fishing. The total weight then would be 400 pounds or over on the completed raft.

For a complete safety and utility margin, then, the 157 pounds of buoyancy per log might well be cut way down to, say, 60 pounds. Assuming this figure, it would take about seven logs to support the total weight and allow the raft to ride well out of the water, as well as giving it enough width to prevent tipping.

Building the Raft

To make the logs into a raft, roll or drag them to the water's edge. The logs should be alternated—that is, every other one turned end for end—so that both ends of the finished raft are about the same size.

Join the logs together by spiking a crossbar of 4-inch pine near either end. Added rigidity can be achieved if all the underlogs are slightly notched on top, where the crossbars will be set. You will get added length from short spikes if the top part of each crossbar is slightly notched where

Two methods of constructing a raft: If only baling wire or rope is available, crossbars are lashed to logs, and diagonal brace is lashed to crossbars to keep raft rigid. If spikes are handy, logs can be notched for crossbars, which are themselves notched to allow for deeper penetration of the spike (left).

the spike will be driven. Avoid notching the crossbars too deeply, as this weakens the timbers. Notching the logs eliminates the need for a diagonal brace. All logs should be set as closely together as possible, to prevent a foot getting wedged—something that can be disastrous in fast water— and to prevent water from splashing on the duffel. Limbs

A sail can be rigged on a raft to take advantage of prevailing winds. Uprights are spiked to the crossbar and guyed with ropes on either side. Top crosspiece, lashed to uprights, prevents them from spreading. A tarp makes a suitable sail, and it can be spiked or tied through grommets at the four corners.

should be cut off close to the log, and the logs rotated to get the closest fit.

Eight-inch spikes, set one to each junction, will hold a raft together for average use. For use in wild water, or for heavier loads, each junction may be lashed with baling wire, and the ends bent down so as not to catch gear or person. Where weight is at a premium, sufficient baling wire to do the entire job will weigh less than the necessary spikes. When backpacking into an area where you expect to raft across streams, a coil of such wire sufficient to do the job may be carried on the packboard. Figure two loops at each junction, or 6 feet of wire—85 feet of wire for the entire raft. If the crossbars are lashed with baling wire, a diagonal brace should be added to hold the raft perfectly rigid.

If considerable duffel is to be moved, a small platform may be built in the raft's center. The load should first be enclosed in a waterproof tarp and wrapped so that splashed water will drain off, not into, the gear. Then the load should be lashed solidly to the raft in case you run into fast water or a sudden storm.

Propelling a Raft

Rafts of this type are ordinarily poled rather than rowed or paddled. A light pole of dry timber, long enough to reach the lake or stream bottom at its deepest point, is all that's needed. Stand toward the rear of the raft, poke the thick end of the pole into the bottom, then push downward and back. As the raft is forced away from you, continue pushing by alternating your hands upward along the pole's length. If you are traveling with a partner, one can pole on either side of the raft.

If a pole of sufficient length isn't available, a paddle may be made from a dry log, and spiked to a short pole handle. Cut the log in half and then split a slab of wood off the flat side of one half. Often it is easier to cut away the sides, leaving a plank at the middle. This is accomplished by scoring both sides with the ax at 3-inch intervals, then slicing off the side chips until a plank remains. In either case, the plank is roughly shaped, and spiked or wired to the handle. By alternately paddling a few strokes on each side, you can propel a raft in a slow, zig-zag fashion.

A breeze blowing in the right direction will move a raft slowly, and will move it faster if a sail is used. A simple sail can be erected on two upright poles fastened to the forward crossbar, guyed with ropes, and held rigidly apart by a cross member attached at either end. The sail may be a tarp tied at each of its four corners.

When floating gear on a raft down streams or large rivers, learn in advance whether there are any sizeable waterfalls, narrow chutes, or stretches of wild water. Such water can upset a raft. Lives and cargoes have been lost in such places. Where treacherous water is known to be ahead, rafts can be poled to the bank well in advance, cargoes portaged around, and the raft guided through with ropes and retrieved below.

Rubber Life Rafts

The rubber life rafts developed by the military during World War II, though intended for ocean survival, have been used by civilians for boating and fishing on small inland waters. These rafts carry prodigious weights for their own size. The original military rafts are now largely exhausted, but commerical versions are available. Where such craft can be transported to small inland waters, they are still very useful for sporting purposes.

When using a rubber life raft of any type, certain safety precautions must be observed to prevent mishap. First, because of its shallow draft, wide bottom, and odd shape, a rubber raft is almost uncontrollable in wind. It should not be used far out on lakes where sudden wind is a possibility. Again, for the same reasons, people must remain low in it to maintain any stability. When you stand up in a rubber raft, the entire craft is apt to kick out from under you like a thin wooden chip. Also, the short oars with which it is equipped are too flimsy to get a real hold in the water when fast turning or quick control is needed. Lastly, deterioration of the rubber fabric, due to age, weathering, and poor care, often makes these older rafts virtual death traps on a hot lake. If the raft is pumped too full, and the warmth of the day expands the air in the tubes, a blowout is apt to occur. I watched this happen at Water-Dog Lake in Wyoming. One of the fishermen was using a one-man rubber boat far out on the lake. The big tube of his raft gave way, and the smaller tubes wouldn't support his weight. He happened to be a good swimmer, and that saved his life.

In general, a rubber raft should have several separate air compartments. It should not be overloaded or overinflated and should be used reasonably close to shore.

Boats for Wilderness Travel

The most basic forms of the boat are still useful to the outdoorsman. One of these is the scow, which is little more than a rectangular box constructed of planking. It is moved either by poling or rowing, and is often used as a ferry. An improvement over the scow is the punt. This is generally a boat of 14 to 16 feet in length, with square ends, and either straight or sloping sides. Sometimes a skeg is placed at the stern to aid in steering.

Specialized boats for use in marsh country are often long and slim, with pointed bow and square transom, and are often poled. On one type, called a rail boat, a flat, elevated platform is built just ahead of the transom. The poler stands on this and shoves the craft along with a long pole.

One type of waterfowl boat has pointed ends, a high coaming, and is decked over except for a small space in the craft's center. The decking serves to protect the user from splashed water, and may be covered with foliage, grasses, or rushes for camouflage.

A more generally useful craft in inland country is a flat-bottomed skiff. This boat has a pointed bow, square stern, and comes in lengths of 14 feet or larger. It is propelled either with pole or oars.

An all-purpose craft has been developed for use on inland waterways which combines the features of many other small boats. Such a boat usually has a pointed, upturned bow, a flat, or semirounded bottom, and a square transom. There is an appreciable flare to the sides, and the front of the bow is partially decked over. The boat is propelled by oars or a small outboard motor. It is made either of planking, plywood, aluminum, or bonded fiberglass. Boats of this kind are generally 14 to 16 feet in length. Smaller ones are available which can be carried on the top of a car and used for fishing small inland waters.

Almost every outdoorsman today knows how to handle a small outboard motor and appreciates its great advantages. However, in much of the remaining back country, boats must be rowed or poled. Poling a boat is similar to poling a raft: Sit or stand toward the rear of the boat, poke the pole into the bottom, and push. By alternating sides, you can keep the craft moving in a fairly straight line.

For rowing, oars, usually made of ash, are used, varying in length from 6 to over 7 feet, depending on the width of the boat's beam. Six-foot oars have 2-foot blades, and when set in the locks leave a space of approximately 6 inches between the handles when they are brought together. Longer oars still have this approximate distance between the handles, but have proportionately longer blades.

The safest oarlocks are those that have a small-diameter pin which goes through the oar and locks it in place. The lock itself fits into a metal base firmly attached with screws to the boat's railing. The lock also has a small hole drilled in the lower end of the post. This allows a cotter key or nail to be inserted and bent over, thus fastening the lock to the boat.

This arrangement is safe on lakes and prevents losing an oar. However, on streams or during wind, or when the boat must be used near rocky shores, it's better not to lock the oar into the lower element. Often an oar has to be suddenly removed and used as a pole to prevent crashing against rocks or shore.

When traveling down rivers, especially those having areas of rough water, the bow should be pointed upstream. The rower gains several advantages by pointing the bow upstream. First, in fast water, he can row upstream, against the current, and slow his downstream pace. In white water, the rower sees exactly where he is going, and with a stroke of the oars can keep the craft riding parallel to the downstream waves. Also, by slowing the pace with judicious upstream rowing, he can cause the boat to ride gently with the troughs and crests of waves, preventing the shipping of water over the ends of his craft. The technique of keeping a small boat riding with heavy water, not against it, must be practiced to be learned.

Heavy water and high waves are sometimes unexpectedly encountered on small lakes, especially in mountainous country. An abrupt "blow" may come from a sudden change in temperature or pressure of the atmosphere, sending a virtual gale of wind tearing down a canyon. When caught on a lake in such a blow, head immediately for shore. If shore can't be reached in time, turn the boat's bow into the oncoming waves, allowing the wind to blow the boat to shore. The bow tends to split and ride up over the waves rather than receive their full force, as would the broader surface of the sides.

A rowboat should be equipped with a can or pail of at least 2-quart size for bailing out water caused by waves or leakage.

In case of an upset, the safest procedure is to *stay with the boat*. Winds will eventually blow the craft to shore. River currents will also carry the helpless craft to milder water, and eventually to the bank. In analyzing many boating mishaps, it has been found that those who drowned felt certain they could swim to shore. The lone survivor was usually the person who elected to stay with the boat—often the timid one of the group.

Development of the Canoe

One of the most romantic forms of inland water transportation is the canoe, and like the raft and the boat, canoes have had an interesting development. The birth of the canoe probably came when primitive man, riding his log downstream, conceived the idea that he might be able to ride inside the log instead of on it. The dugout canoe had its beginnings in that historic moment.

The dugout canoe, or pirogue, had to be patiently carved out of a single suitable tree trunk. There were various ways to do this, but the bulk of the wood was removed by burning the log (always stopping the fire before the shell became too thin), and chopping out a cavity with a primitive adze.

The shape of the dugout had certain advantages over the log raft, notably the pointed ends and the upturned bow and stern. Simple keels, to aid in steering, were often incorporated in early dugouts. The early dugouts also had their disadvantages. Trees available in some areas were often too small, and dugouts made from them were too narrow and unstable. Often their gunwales were too low.

To improve the dugout canoe, certain modifications were attempted which in part paralleled the development of the log raft. The gunwales of the dugout were raised by the addition of hewn planking along each side—comparable to the addition of logs along each edge of the raft. Finished dugouts were often split down the middle, to give added beam width and stability, and the halves joined together at the bottom with a hewn plank. This, of course, necessitated similar shaped and curved center planking at the upturned bow and stern. The overall result was comparable to the stage of the raft where a flat, solid, reasonably watertight floor was achieved.

The next breakthrough in the development of the canoe came when man conceived the notion that stretching tough pliable skin over a wooden framework could be substituted for solid planking. It is entirely possible that this came about during the patching of solid dugouts. For centuries, animal skins had been used for clothing, tents, and water bottles. In the process of wedging skins into cracks, or over holes in wood, man may have gotten the idea of a skin and framework canoe.

The skin canoes and skin boats themselves have had an interesting development. As late as the white's settlement of America, bullboats were extensively used. These were small crafts made by stretching buffalo hides over willow framework. Some bullboats were cup-shaped and had about as much stability in water as a chip in a swill bucket, but they did serve to ferry or float occupants.

The Eskimo kayak is another form of the skin-over-framework design. The kayak is a long, narrow craft, pointed at either end, which is propelled by a double-ended paddle. The skin covering of the early models included not only the bottom, but all the deck area with the exception of a small round aperture, or cockpit, at the craft's center. The paddler sat in this opening and buttoned a skin apron, worn around his waist, over the aperture, making the entire craft watertight. With such an arrangement, he could capsize, roll over and come upright without shipping water. Indeed, during heavy waves, the user of a kayak often purposely capsized, then came up beyond an oncoming wave, to avoid strain on his light craft.

In the Arctic today, there are two remaining forms of the skin canoe which serve useful purposes. One is the tiny skin boat used mainly to retrieve hair seals shot in open water. This puny craft—about 7 feet long—is pointed at both ends, and is made from the hide of a single *oogruk*, or bearded seal. The framework is made of hand-shaped driftwood or whalebone. The sealskin is placed over the bottom of the canoe's skeleton, then laced with leather thong completely around the gunwales. The entire craft weighs only a few pounds and is hauled on a dog sled by the seal hunter. It is propelled for short distances with a single paddle, or with a paddle tied at each gunwale with thong and used as oars.

The other type of skin canoe, merely a larger version, may measure 28 feet in length. It, too, has a skeleton built of driftwood and whalebone. Six or seven sealskins sewed together into a shell are then laced around the gunwales. The skeleton of this type of craft will last for many years, and is placed upside-down on a whalebone rack during the winter. The covering is stored inside until the spring whaling season. I was told by the Eskimos that, with normal use, the skin of this seaworthy craft will last for three years. In such a craft, a crew of eight Eskimos will go to sea, kill bowhead whales weighing up to 60 tons, and bring the oil, blubber, and bone back to their villages. Not all in one load, of course.

The romantic birchbark canoe was an American Indian invention and was one of the most successful of the handcrafted canoes. A craft of light weight and high utility, it was made in great numbers in North America until the stands of suitable paper birch were depleted.

From early times, canoes have had certain advantages over boats for many types of water. They are light and therefore portable. They will handle large loads of duffel and cargo in rapid water. When rough water is encountered, an average-sized canoe can be portaged by one man. Canoes travel fast, with a minimum of effort and water disturbance. They may be taken into wilderness areas where larger, heavier types of watercraft could not be hauled.

Modern Canoes

The American canoe evolved from the birchbark stage to the canvas and wood canoe popular in grandfather's time. Today, the best canoe for the outdoorsman is the aluminum or fiberglass type. It is rugged and durable. The best size for the average person is a 17-footer. A canoe of this length, with a 36-inch beam and semiflat bottom, is very stable and will support two men and their gear easily in most water. It will have a depth amidships of just over 13 inches, and will weigh from 60 to 80 pounds, depending on the gauge of the aluminum or weight of the fiberglass used. Such a craft will haul 600 to 800 pounds safely. If greater stability is desired, wider-than-average models are available and, for additional safety, they can also have air chambers fastened along the gunwales.

Their relatively light weight puts both types of canoes in the same class as the early birchbark canoe, in that one man can portage it without undue difficulty. More, these canoes, unlike the wood and canvas models, will not become water-logged after being used, and the material never needs refinishing. They will also stand more abuse than the canvas models. And, because of mass production, the price is reasonable. Best of all, they will turn upright after being capsized. For use with an outboard motor, square-sterned models are available. They are used, usually, for fishing and traveling on sheltered lakes.

Any heavy gear hauled in a canoe should be placed as near amidships as possible. This makes it easier to handle the craft in fast water or wind, where it must respond immediately to the paddle. All loads should be lashed down in case of an upset. This applies especially to the ax, grub, and supplies most needed for survival. Small packages needed during the day, such as a lunch, may be stored outside the main cargo. It's a good notion, too, to place a light covering of spruce boughs on the canoe's bottom under the cargo. If any water is shipped, it will drain from under the load and can be bailed out. The boughs serve the same purpose as the elevated platform on the raft. The weight distribution should be such that when completely loaded and in the water, the canoe rides with the stern just a trifle lower in the water than the bow.

How to Paddle a Canoe

Paddles for a canoe, unlike oars for a boat, should be related in size to the man, not the craft. A paddle should be just a bit shorter than the person using it. However, for best results the man in the stern should use a paddle just 5 inches shorter than his height. Several types of hardwood are used for paddles, but ash is perhaps the best choice.

Unlike the rower of a boat who must use oars from a fixed position, the canoe paddler has an unfixed paddle and can work from several positions in the craft. For this reason, he has a greater variety of strokes available to him.

The basic stroke used in moving the craft forward is easier understood and practiced when two paddlers move the craft. Primarily, this stroke is made on the mechanical principle of a wheel and axis—the blade in the water represents the wheel's outside, and the canoeist is the axis. Any force at the paddle's end therefore tends to rotate the craft away from the direction of the stroke. With a paddler in the bow and stern paddling on either side, each offsets the lateral movement caused by the other's stroke.

For this type of stroke, the paddle blade is dipped deeply into the water and pulled back alongside the craft, the inside of the blade being turned slightly outward toward the end of each stroke. The movement of the arms is similar to the opposing motion of the pistons on a steam locomotive. The hand on the top of the paddle pushes forward as the lower hand goes back and, towards the end of the stroke, up. The stroke should not be made with the knob hand used as a pivot and all movement made with the lower hand; neither should the lower paddle hand remain stationary and all the movement made with the knob hand. Rather, the stroke should be made by a combination of pulling with the lower hand and pushing with the upper.

When only one man paddles a canoe, the finish of this basic stroke has to be altered so as to compensate for the lateral movement of the canoe. This may be done with two basic strokes:

One stroke begins with the blade of the paddle at right angles to the canoe. Once the stroke is begun, however, the blade is turned at a gradually increasing angle, like the feathering of an airplane propeller, with the inside of the blade toward the stern. The stroke is completed with the blade traveling closely against the side of the canoe. The different pitch at the end of the stroke tends to move the stern in an opposite direction, compensating for the opposite lateral movement caused by the first part of the stroke.

The second stroke is similar, but at the end of the stroke, and with the change in pitch not so pronounced, the paddle is moved outward against the water. The pattern of this stroke is similar to a fish hook, with the finish of the stroke being the shank. This outward motion offsets the initial tendency for the craft to move in the opposite direction. Both strokes are basic for the lone canoeist, and if done in a gradual rhythmic flow of movement, will keep the canoe on a straight course.

A single canoeist paddling from the bow executes the basic forward stroke by dipping the paddle into the water against the bow and pulling backward just beyond the body, finishing the stroke with the inside edge of the blade behind the outside edge.

To cause a canoe to back up, the first basic forward stroke mentioned is used in reverse.

To make a canoe move toward the paddle, the blade is reached outward from the craft, dipped in, and drawn toward the paddler.

If the canoeist wants the craft to turn in the direction opposite to his paddle, he dips the paddle in, either at bow or stern, and pushes outward in a generally sweeping motion.

Two paddlers, executing either of these two strokes, can turn the craft either right or left rapidly by making such strokes on opposing sides of the craft. Modifications of these strokes are made by either drawing or pushing the paddles in a diagonal direction, either toward or away from the canoe.

Sailing a Canoe

A temporary sail can be erected in a canoe to catch a favorable wind on a lake. This may be made by attaching a tarp or cloth to two 6-foot staves set upright nearly the canoe's width apart. The bottoms of the staves are braced at the bottom of the canoe by either the feet or packages of duffel, and the uprights are held in the hands, like the two rolls of a scroll.

A mild breeze will scoot the canoe along. If it turns into a stiff wind, the entire arrangement may be quickly lowered to prevent an upset. Attaching such a sail permanently is a mistake, as it may easily cause the canoe to capsize.

Packing and Portaging

Portaging involves heavy work, but in bad water is the lesser of two evils. While initially packaging and arranging duffel for canoe travel, some thought should be given to the problem of portaging. Gear should be divided according to weight and bulk, so that at the portage it won't have to be rearranged into portable packages. All large packages of gear should be within the weight tolerance of the packboard, pack basket, or tumpline.

Some of the best containers for carrying gear on canoe trips are the watertight portable ice packs used by the military in the tropics during World War II. These come in three sizes: Perhaps the most usable one is 19 inches high, 12 inches wide, and 9 inches thick. These containers are made of rugged fabric and rubber. On both larger sizes there are web shoulder straps and adjusting buckles, with ends molded integral with the container and positioned similarly to those on a packboard. It is thus possible to pick up the loaded container and carry it on one's back. The smaller container doesn't have shoulder straps, but has a web strap that makes it possible to carry the loaded package like a haversack slung over one shoulder.

To carry a canoe, place the two paddles across the center thwarts. Lash their knobs wide apart against the gunwales on one thwart and lash the blades to the other thwart so they slightly overlap each other. During portaging, the blades ride on the carrier's shoulders while he supports the forward portion of the canoe with his hands.

If the portage is long, it may be necessary to pad the shoulders with a rolled-up shirt or jacket. Some canoeists use a wooden yoke which fits over the shoulders and partially around the neck, similar to the old yokes used by western homesteaders for carrying two pails of water. Such yokes support the canoe's weight better, but represent an additional item to take along and portage.

For two men, shouldering a canoe is a simple chore. It is more difficult for one man, but there is a knack to it. Turn the canoe away from you onto its side and stand midway of its length. Bend over the craft and lift it onto one knee. Then, reach over and grasp the far end of the thwart and boost it upward in a rolling motion, helped by a lift from the knee, onto your back. Adjust it so that the paddle blades, or the yoke, is in position on your shoulders, and balance the craft with your hands at the gunwales.

To place the canoe into water without damaging it, set the stern into the water first. Then lift the bow until it is clear of any rocks, and gradually feed the canoe into the water. Two men do this easier than one. Each grasps an

Army surplus ice packs are excellent waterproof containers for carrying gear on canoe trips. Shoulder straps permit carrying the container like a pack during portages.

opposite side of the thwart or gunwale, lifting the canoe clear of the shore. One man must handle it by the bow.

Rough-Water Tactics

In streams too shallow or too rough to risk possible injury to the craft's bottom, a canoe often must be "lined" through the shallows by attaching a length of rope to each end and manipulating the craft from shore while it is in mid-stream. A coil of 100 feet of 3/8-inch hemp rope is just right for a 50-foot length at both bow and stern. Nylon rope is better, as it is far stronger for its diameter.

In going upstream, the man with the bow line, which should be longer than the stern line, walks a bit ahead of the canoe. This angles the craft into the current, where it may be pulled forward and controlled by the lines.

When lining a canoe downstream, the bow line is kept shorter. This tends to keep the stern headed out. The canoe may be moved outward against the pull of the lines, or allowed to drift in closer depending upon the need.

There are no set rules for running fast water in stretches where it must be ridden out instead of lining or portaging. Fast water is fast because of the pull of gravity. Normally, where fast water occurs the bottom of the stream is rocky. This is a hazard for both the canoeist and the boatman when running wild water; hence, the deepest channel should be chosen through rapids. Here the current is the fastest, but it is safest since it is deep. Only experience in observing the riffles, eddies, swirls, backwashes, and oily chutes of fast water will enable a person to detect the submerged rocks which create them, and estimate the depth of the water.

The canoeist's best procedure is to stay parallel with the main current. Enough forward speed should be maintained to prevent back currents catching the craft and turning it sidewise. The responsibility for sighting dangerous rocks and currents rests with the bow paddler. The stern paddler anticipates the bow man's change of direction, and supports the action.

Kneeling is the safest position for paddling a canoe, as it keeps the center of gravity low. Do not sit and paddle in any kind of water representing even a mild danger.

Repairing the Craft

Everyone who travels on the water should know how to repair minor damage to his craft. The farther you are away from tools and materials for making repairs, the more you need to know. With the older wood and canvas canoes, minor repairs of the fabric covering are made as follows:

1. The canoe is dried out.

2. The edges of the break are carefully lifted away around the immediate puncture.

3. A piece of canvas somewhat larger than the puncture is dipped in marine glue or waterproof cement and pressed into place under the outer shell, and the outer canvas covering is firmly pressed down against it.

A bag of powdered resin and a catalyst are better for the purpose, but necessitate leaving the craft out of the water overnight while the material hardens. This type of resin is very useful for welding broken wood in a canoe.

In cases where the wood has been too badly damaged, it sometimes has to be replaced on the spot with dry timber from the shoreline. Bending wooden parts, after steaming them in a container of hot water, represents a challenge, but it can be done with patience.

Aluminum canoes are repaired in a somewhat different way. If the break is too severe, the only cure is to have the craft welded by a professional. Fortunately, with aluminum canoes little or no metal is wasted or completely ruined when minor damage occurs. The edges of a break or puncture can be hammered into shape again, using a stone and a piece of wood in the same way that car fenders are repaired. The leak can then be filled with resin and left to set. If no resin is available, use chewing gum, old-fashioned pine gum, or a strip of adhesive tape. If spruce or pine gum is used, it works better when warmed with a bit of bacon fat.

Wooden boats often spring leaks en route and have to be repaired. Many times leaks at junctions can be repaired by removing fasteners and replacing the screws with longer ones. Leaks between seams may be plugged with caulking compound, or by pounding lamp wicking, or even cotton cloth which has been soaked in liquid cement, into the openings. A screwdriver or pocketknife is often the only tool needed. If the leak is bad, it is wise to dock the boat, let it dry thoroughly, and fill the crack with a mixture of the powdered resin and catalyst.

A new material called "apoxy resin" will weld almost anything. It is particularly useful for repairing fiberglass craft. A repair kit containing all the necessary items for repairing fiberglass craft, including sheets of plastic cloth, costs only a few dollars and is obtainable at most sporting goods stores and marinas. If the puncture is small, a gob of the resin mixture is applied directly over the hole. After thoroughly drying, it is sanded down and the repair is complete. For repairing larger holes, the craft must be completely dried out, and the damaged area sanded. A piece of the fiberglass cloth larger than the puncture is welded on with the resin, allowed to dry overnight, and sanded down. Fiberglass cloth has great tensile strength, and such a repair is usually quite permanent.

4

Finding Your Way

One of the hazards most feared by those going into the outdoors is getting lost. As is usual with any hazard, those who know least about it, its preventatives and its solutions, are the ones who fear it most. Actually, the risk of getting permanently lost in the outdoors and undergoing severe hardships and possible tragedy is a minor one. There are far more risks involved in our daily use of electricity, pressure-cookers, automobiles, power saws, or construction scaffolding than in hiking into the wilderness. Yet we accept these other calculated risks every day, since the proportion of benefit far outweighs the likelihood of misfortune. We should have the same attitude toward our journeys into nature.

One of the first things to do before setting off on a hike

into wilderness country is to leave word with the family or a neighbor just where you expect to go, and approximately how long you expect to remain. This is rescue insurance, in advance. Should you not return when expected, or within a reasonable time thereafter, others can begin looking for you. Many lost persons have been found while conserving their energies and waiting for a searching party. But you should expect this kind of favor only if you have an abiding willingness to help rescue others, *any* time the need arises.

Maps

The next precaution to take is to learn everything possible about the area. For this purpose, maps are your best source of information, unless the area is close to human habitation, in which case local information also helps. Any large-scale map of the state or province in which the area is located is good to begin with. Even the detailed highway maps in a road atlas are adequate. A map of this size will indicate mountains, peaks, rivers, large creeks, lakes, airports, roads, and the nearest towns or villages. Once the area you intend to explore has been located on this map, a more detailed map of the particular area should be obtained. This map should be of sufficiently large scale to show changes of elevation, all current or abandoned settlements or landmarks, all topographical features, townships (areas 6 miles square), degrees and minutes of latitude and longitude, and meridian lines. These meridian lines are survey lines and run in a true north-south direction.

Virtually every inch of North America has now been mapped, either by land or aerial survey. For the purposes of the average outdoorsman, detailed maps scaling four to six miles per inch will be sufficiently large. Maps of this scale are available from several sources, including the Department of Interior's Geological Survey, the Forest Service (maps of the National Forests in forty-one states), private map-makers catering to specialized interests such as mining and political surveys, and airports.

I have three detailed maps before me. One is the map of an entire state, obtained from a company making maps for prospectors. This one measures 29 by 36 inches, and shows all roads, creeks, and rivers, all sizeable lakes, county lines, township boundaries, National Forests, and all recorded mineral claims and locations. The marked boundaries of mineral locations, incidentally, are often helpful in getting one's bearings.

The second map is a detailed map of the Bridger Wilderness Area in Wyoming. This map is scaled to approximately six miles to the inch, and was obtained through a regional Forest Service office. It shows meridians, townships, all peaks and higher mountains, all creeks, lakes (numbering nearly 1000), roads and jumping-off spots around the Area's periphery, and the single horse trail traversing the region.

The third map is a detailed map of the Port Moller area in Alaska's Aleutian Islands, issued by the Geological Survey Division of the U.S. Department of the Interior. This map is scaled to 1:250,000, or four miles to the inch. It shows latitude to the quarter-degree, all water including two coast lines, settlements of any size, lakes, and islands. Of perhaps greatest value, this map shows all elevations from sea level with contour lines at intervals of 200, 250, 500, and 1000 feet.

For the serious outdoor traveler headed for remote wilderness country, the best maps are those issued by the U.S. Geological Survey, Federal Center, Colorado, or Washington 25, D.C. These cover all parts of continental United States and Alaska. Comparable topographic maps are available for Canada, and may be obtained from The Surveys and Engineering Branch, Department of Mines and Resources, Ottawa, Canada.

The Compass and How to Use It

Anyone going into strange country needs a compass. To many people, a compass is a little watchlike gadget which points north and shows them how to get out of the woods without getting lost. But a compass is only a precise instrument which indicates its own relationship to a given direction, as the earth relates in space to celestial bodies.

Here is an analogy that will give you a fair notion of how a compass acts: Imagine a railroad track which extends across the continent, headed in the general direction of a line between the sun at noon and the North Star. Assume that one end stops somewhere in northern Canada, and the other extends into the Pacific Ocean. Imagine further that there are similar parallel but slightly curving lines adjacent to this track, on both sides, which end in the same places. Lastly, imagine that you place a yardstick between the tracks of the railroad, paralleling them.

The tracks are comparable to the magnetic lines of force running through the earth, and ending in a "pole" in northern Canada; and an opposite pole out in the Pacific Ocean. The yardstick is the compass needle.   From this homely comparison, it will be readily seen that a compass needle doesn't point north, or, in fact, at anything. It is merely a magnetized needle which, in the earth's magnetic field, will run parallel to the lines of magnetic force. If the compass, then, were taken to a spot in northern Canada just over the northern pole of this great magnet, the needle would point straight down. And if taken out into the Pacific Ocean over the opposite pole, the compass needle would point upward. Place a compass needle west of the earth's magnetic lines of force, and the needle will point east as well as north. Similarly, if the compass were taken to the east coast, east of the magnetic lines in the earth, the needle would point west as well as north, or some degree of northwest.

Carrying this to an extreme, if a compass were taken east of the north magnetic pole it would point west. West of the magnetic pole, the needle would point eastward. Only over a varying magnetic line running through the United States from central Lake Superior-Kentucky-North Carolina and off the eastern coast of Florida will a compass needle point true north.

This deviation or declination in compass direction may easily be found for a given area at camp on the first clear night. Before dark, lay the detailed map on a chair, camp table, or box, and mark the north-south meridian line closest to that area so it can be read easily. This may be done by scribing along some kind of straightedge, such as the edge of a box, with a pencil. Draw the line across the entire length of the map.

After dark, take the map outside and lay it flat upon a table, alforjas box, or chair. It may even be placed upon the ground in an open area from which the stars can be seen. Then, with the aid of a flashlight, lay a straight stick about

2 feet long, or a section of fishing rod, over the marked meridian line, and entirely parallel to it. Next, place the eye somewhat above the stick or rod, and look continuously from its length towards the North Star (which you've located earlier, and as described later). This estimating movement is comparable to that of a golfer who glances several times down his intended swing toward a distant flag. Rotate the map without moving the stick until the stick points toward a distant point directly and vertically beneath the North Star. With two or three "tries," this can be done. The stick acts as a sighting radius.

Lastly, remove the stick without disturbing the map. Then place the compass directly over the marked meridian on the map, so that the north and south markings on the compass dial are precisely parallel to the marked meridian of the map. In such a position, the compass needle will be found to "deviate" somewhat from North Star north. Read this deviation in degrees, and write it down. Repeat the above procedure two or three times. If you find the deviation to be 12 degrees on the first try, 14 the second, and 10 the third, take the average. Your compass deviation, or declination, for the area is an approximate 12 degrees in a given direction—say,—12 degrees east of north.

If the entire procedure is repeated several times, and averages taken, it will be accurate enough for all practical purposes.

With these tools—map, compass, and degrees of deviation—it is a simple matter during the daytime, in strange country and in any kind of weather, to find "practical north." Simply reverse the process above. Lay the map on a flat surface. Place the compass over it so that the compass needle lies precisely over and parallel to the marked meridian on the map. With the compass held solidly upon the map, rotate the map itself until the needle points to the degree of variation for that area. Now both the map and the markings on the compass dial will be oriented.

Finding the North Star

Another and more accurate way to determine true north at a wilderness camp at night is to find the Big Dipper and the North Star of the Ursa Major constellation. When the seventh star, at the dipper's handle, is either vertically above or below the North Star, the star itself is in a true north position.

This direction may be marked at camp by lining up one straight side of a tree at a marked height with the top of a stake driven into the ground and lined up with the star. In daylight, a fishing line or cord may be tied tightly between the two points, if desired, making a simple woods' compass. The map, laid precisely under the taut string, will show surrounding land features in their true direction.

Shadow Stick

A unique method for determining directions in the woods was discovered by Bob Owendoff of Falls Church, Virginia. The method is so simple and reliable that the Army expects to adopt it.

All you need is a straight stick about 3 or 4 feet long. Set the stick in the ground in an open area where sun will strike it and cast a shadow. Mark the tip of the shadow with

Method of determining true north at night when North Star and Big Dipper are in alignment. Map placed beneath the string will orient the hiker to his surroundings.

a stone. After a few minutes, when the shadow has moved over the ground, place another stone at the tip of the shadow. Draw a straight line through both stones.

This line runs east and west. The first stone is at the west end of the line. Now, if you draw the shortest line from the base of the stick to the east-west line, you will have found north (in the Northern Hemisphere).

You can also tell time with the shadow stick. Just draw a line parallel to the east-west line through the base of the stick. Then add a semicircle between the two parallels and centered on the stick. The shadow is a moving hour hand. Noon is the north line, 6 P.M. the east end of the semicircle.

Route Sketching

An excellent method for finding one's way in the strange country is to sketch a map of the route of travel. This map should be begun at the point of departure into strange country. It should be drawn on some kind of tough paper which will withstand repeated folding, and should be enclosed in a waterproof envelope. Once the jumping-off place has been left, all vital information should be recorded. The best technique for doing this is to sketch the route as it unfolds, according to a reasonable scale of reduction, and place each bit of important data and all of the larger natural landmarks in proper position as you progress.

In practice it works like this: At the point of departure from familiar country, the initial thing to do is to draw a known boundary and note its true compass direction. This boundary may be an old road, a nearby river or creek, a deep canyon, or a row of mountains.

This landmark should be drawn to a scale that will permit the map to be completed on the available paper. For example, a map of average outdoor country covering a five-mile area can be sketched on a sheet 10 inches square, with a scale of half a mile to the inch. For rough or hazardous country, this scale can be increased to a quarter-mile per inch or larger.

One need not be an artist to sketch a simple map. Heavy lines may represent rivers, geographical boundaries, or roads. Continuing chain-links may represent mountains. High peaks may be indicated with an inverted letter V, and lakes may be drawn with a series of concentric circles. A vertical line topped with an inverted V makes a good "tree." If necessary, all may be more clearly identified with small lettering. Or, if space is limited, a legend may be made in the margin, such as: T = tree; L = lake; M = mountain; X = camp; B = bog, etc.

The next step consists of placing on the map all the more prominent landmarks within the limits of vision, recording their position on the compass from the point of departure and their estimated distance. Choose such landmarks as a large tree at the top of a distant hill, a distant peak, the end of a lake within sight, or the sharp bend of a river.

Up till now, the map will read something like this: Old logging road, with general course running north-north-east. The point of departure at the road's end. A peak, 36 degrees from this point, estimated as 4 miles away. Lake end, 287 degrees, 2 miles. Limestone promontory with tall fir tree, 2 degrees, 10 miles. Long wooded ridge, paralleling logging road, 260 degrees, ½ mile.

Incidentally, it is far more exact to record all compass directions in terms of degrees, not directions. Beginners learn to "box" a compass to the extent of sixteen directions. This isn't enough for the outdoorsman on extended trips into strange country. The variation of but a degree or

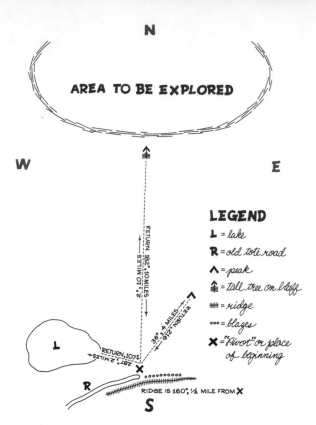

N

AREA TO BE EXPLORED

W   E

RETURN, 182°, 10 MILES
2, 10 MILES

36°, 4 MILES
RETURN, 216°

RETURN, 107½°
287°, 2 MILES

R

RIDGE IS 160°, ½ MILE FROM X

S

LEGEND

L = lake

R = old tote road

Λ = peak

= tall tree on bluff

= ridge

ᵒᵒᵒ = blazes

X = "Pivot" or place of beginning

Example of a field-drawn map that will help a hiker find his way out of strange country. From point of departure, X, he has recorded compass readings on three prominent landmarks, a tree atop a distant hill, a lake, and a peak. To return from area to be explored, he will overcompensate on his course from the tree so he comes out on road R. If he undercompensates, he will hit blazed row of trees.

two, when multiplied by an appreciable distance, can result in a sizeable error.

The map so far, simple as it is, can be extremely valuable to the hiker. For example, the peak recorded on the map can be used to find the way back by taking a compass reading exactly opposite from the recorded 36 degrees, or 216 degrees. This will point the way back to the end of the logging road. Similarly, a compass reading from the tall fir tree, at 182 degrees, will also point toward the end of the logging road.

Unfortunately, you cannot always head for a distant objective and reach it by hiking a straight line. Often you must detour a bit to avoid a swamp, a mountain cliff, areas of bad muskeg, or a lake.

When a zig-zag route is followed to an objective, in order to return a compensation must be made. If, for example, you veer off 10 degrees going, you must compensate 10 degrees in the opposite direction in order to return to your starting point. This is a matter not only of direction but of time. If you walk off course, say, for an hour, then you must compensate in returning for that distance. To do this, you must keep your wits about you and remember for how long, or for approximately how many miles, you have veered off course in order to offset this error on the return trip.

This cannot be done with accuracy. Often you will be tired when returning and mistakenly think you have traveled far enough in one direction to offset your shift in course. Also, the very nature of outdoor terrain makes it necessary to alter your course constantly. It is a good notion, for this reason, to locate the camp or point of departure along a creek, lake, old road, drain canal, ridge of hills, or similar boundary. Thus, if you miss your target, you can find it by going up or down the river or ridge.

The best way of doing this is to overcompensate on the return route. For example, suppose the camp is located near the eastern end of an old logging road, and that the direction of return is straight southward. Setting a course slightly west of south would bring you out on the road a bit west of camp. Knowing that you have overcompensated to the west, you can then proceed confidently east on the road until you find your camp.

Unless you are aware of your bearings, the tendency on a long hike is to go in a circle. It has been demonstrated that, while blindfolded, a person will travel in some degree of a circle. The tendency is more pronounced the farther he goes.

This can be quickly proven at home. In a field, select an object, say, 200 yards away. Then, with the eyes closed, walk toward it as far as is feasible without bumping into anything. On opening your eyes, you will find that you have traveled in a circle, or an arc of a circle, despite all effort to avoid it. Why this happens is debatable. Some claim that it is because the normal stride of one leg is longer than that of the other leg. Whatever the reason, the result is the same.

One way to avoid circling, on clear days, is to walk keeping the sun at your back, or at any consistent angle. Naturally, the position of the sun will gradually change, but for short periods of time this won't cause too great an error, if you make periodic checks with the compass for the true reading.

The best way to stay on course is to pick out two landmarks in a line at different distances in front of you. Behind you, at the starting point, pick another landmark. Walk directly on a line toward the two forward landmarks, keeping all three in a straight line. When you reach the first landmark in front of you, the farthest landmark then becomes the first, and you select another distant landmark up ahead for the second. As you pass each landmark, it in turn becomes the rear one. By keeping all three landmarks in

By lining up three landmarks, A, B, and C, a hiker can stay
on course without constantly consulting his compass. When
he passes rock B, it becomes rear landmark and he spots a
third beyond C.

a straight line, you can maintain a fairly straight course for
a considerable distance. This avoids constantly checking
with the compass every few rods, and keeps your attention
directed toward your objective.

In order to help you return to your camp or starting
point, it is a good idea to mark the general camp area in

some way so that it may bc located at an appreciable distance. If camp happens to be in conifer country, or near any tall tree, a good way of marking the location plainly is to shinny up a tree and tie a white dish cloth or spare shirt to the top. Such a flag can be seen for great distances, especially when using binoculars.

Blazing a Trail

A trail can be blazed from camp either on trees or brush. In some areas the defacing of living timber is prohibited so you must blaze the brush. (Blazing means to cut a strip of bark from a tree every so often along the route of travel to mark the trail for your return.) A blaze 6 inches long is sufficient, and if the strip of bark is left hanging it helps later to denote the age of the blaze.

When blazing brush, the tips are cut and bent over in the direction of the route. Brush should be blazed as near to your height as possible for easy visibility. It should also be done on twigs large enough not to be mistaken for the work of browsing moose.

Hardwood trees, or trees growing in arid climates, will retain blazes longer than trees growing in humid country. Also, larger trees will show blazes longer than small trees. Small, fast-growing trees will grow around the blazes, sealing them partially over. The foliage in Canadian and Alaskan bush country, because of the rank, humid growth, won't retain blazes too long. I have traveled along Canadian trails blazed by Tahltan Indians where only faint scars remained here and there on the scrub aspen or silver poplar. On the other hand, I have ridden over the trails made by

Sheep Eater Indians in Idaho's rugged interior where their blazes on the big ponderosa pines were as plainly visible as the drawings they left in surrounding caves. These were made before the white man's settlement.

Too much blazing defeats the purpose and becomes confusing. This is especially true if two travelers happen to be in the same area and both blaze. In any case, blazes should be uniform in size and similar in characteristic. Then the maker can identify them as his own.

Using Nature's Signs

A seldom-used method of getting one's bearings is to learn the direction of the prevailing winds in the particular area. This may be done in clear weather by paying attention to breezes. When they appear, dry dust is sifted downward and will follow their direction. When the first clouds appear, their general direction will indicate the wind's direction. Heavy storm will normally come with the direction of prevailing winds.

One should not be misled by thermal breezes, the daily movement of air in mountains. Normally, warming air will rise, cooling air descend. This means that faint breezes will follow ridges upward in the morning and follow them downward at night. The changing weather will alter the course of winds, but if you observe the general pattern for several days, you can usually decide from what compass direction the prevailing winds come. This knowledge can be useful in foggy, stormy weather when neither the sun is visible during the day nor the stars at night.

For example, deciduous trees will shed their leaves in greatest bulk in the direction opposite from that of the prevailing winds—the winds blow them there. Again, if snow is on the ground, the pattern of its drifting will indicate the wind's course. On the windward side of large trees, the snow will tend to pack into a shelf. On the opposite side, because of eddying backcurrents, it will build up into a ridge. The trees themselves will often indicate the direction of the prevailing winds; branches, and even the trunk, may be bent in the opposite direction.

Trees may be used in other ways as compasses. On solitary trees, moss is apt to be thickest on the bark on the north side. This is not a dependable guide, however, when trees are growing in clumps and there is ample shade. Again, the bark of large trees will be thicker on the north side, as will the individual growth rings. Both may be measured by chopping into opposite sides of the tree and making a comparison.

Wild plants and flowers, too, may often be used as compasses. Where blossoms and stems form on a plant in an open area, they normally turn in the direction of the sunlight, just as plants in home windows, and garden flowers such as dahlias, will seek sunlight. This means that the preponderance of the flowers and stems will usually occur on the south and east sides of the plant. Where flowers have fallen, the remaining stems of many plants will still hold a readable message for the observing person.

Getting Lost

While it is true that very few people become permanently lost and meet with disaster because of it, there are few outdoorsmen who have *never* become confused in the woods. The person who maintains that he's never been confused in the woods has never spent much time there, or else he is kidding you. This temporary confusion is not serious in itself, but it is all too often the point at which many people allow the situation to become critical.

The biggest danger in getting lost is the normal tendency to panic. The cure can be as certain. The person who has the self-control to defeat his own panic won't stay lost very long.

The first thing to do on becoming lost is to accept the fact calmly and stop traveling. Regard the situation as but a temporary nuisance, like fixing a flat tire. Next, try to locate an identifiable landmark. If you have followed the rules and have a compass and maps, both detailed and field-made, this is simple. The compass will show directions. The field-made map will indicate approximately how far you are from camp. The detailed map will show other identifiable landmarks within striking distance.

In looking for landmarks, one should climb to the highest elevation possible within the immediate area. Lakes, streams, distant mountains, open areas, and valleys or canyons all show up well when seen from high above. If storm or sudden fog has blotted out the surroundings so this cannot be accomplished, the wise thing to do is to stop, conserve your strength, and wait until the weather clears and landmarks become visible again. Often this requires staying out overnight or, in some cases, an extra day or so. This will be uncomfortable, but not necessarily harmful or fatal. The human body has enormous stores of energy and sustenance, some that are rarely tapped. Men have survived after a complete fast of thirty days or more. So the scarcity of food need not prove fatal, as long as water is available.

The secrets of survival are to conserve and ration your

strength; make yourself as comfortable as possible; augment the body's energies with any form of food carried along; add to the supply of food, if possible, with edible wild plants, wild fruit, fish, or any small game; and lastly, build a fire and keep it going both day and night, piling on green boughs to make it smoke and smolder during the daylight hours. This will keep you warm and provide a signal day and night. There are few remaining places where a big smoldering fire cannot be spotted by someone. State Fish and Game Departments have regular patrol flights over the more remote fishing and hunting areas in their territory. In National Forests, a continuously smoking fire is certain to be detected by the Forest Service rangers, either from a lookout station or plane.

Civilian rescue groups, such as sheriff's posses, now operate in most of the more rugged areas. They use jeeps, saddle horses, snow tractors, and snowmobiles, aircraft, and boats. In addition, state and provincial air rescue groups now operate widely over the continent.

The best way to signal an airplane is to form the letters SOS on the ground. In open areas of snow, dark-colored saplings or poles can be laid on the white snow in the shape of these letters. On sandy beaches, especially if the sand is white, the letters may be spelled out with rows of rocks. Charred wood from a fire also makes a good contrast against light surfaces. In clear air, domestic chickens can be seen from a plane at 2000 feet. Contrasting letters 6 to 10 feet in size can be seen by most low-flying planes.

There has been developed in recent years a system of signaling known as the Ground-Air Emergency Code. The code consists mainly of large symbols stamped out in the snow or formed on the ground. The code symbols and their meaning are shown in the accompanying table.

CODE LETTER	MEANS
L	Require fuel and oil.
LL	All is well.
△	Safe to land here.
⌐L⌐	Aircraft badly damaged.
K	Indicate direction to proceed.
▷	Will attempt to take off.
→	Am proceeding in this direction.
N	No, or negative.
Y	Yes, or affirmative.
⊥L	Not understood.
W	Require engineer.
□	Require compass and map.
¦	Require signal lamp.
I	Serious injuries. Require doctor.
II	Require medical supplies.
X	Unable to proceed.
F	Require food and water.
≫	Require firearms and ammunition.

A flare has been developed recently for use by lost persons signaling for help. It is called the Penguin Aerial Flare and consists of a small tubelike device which is held in the hand and shoots flare cartridges. A flare is threaded into the device and set off. It leaves the tube with a report comparable to that of a .22 blank cartridge and rises to a height of over 100 feet. As it rises, it leaves a bright red trail, and at the height of the rise bursts into a bright red ball of flame and gives off a loud report. It will burn for from three to five seconds.

5

Forecasting the Weather

Outdoor trips can be delayed or completely ruined by adverse weather. Because of this, a basic knowledge of weather, and some ability in forecasting it, is vital to the outdoorsman. Though man is constantly learning more about the secrets of weather, much is still unknown. A standing joke is the wide disparity between the weather man's daily predictions, and the weather we actually get. This is largely due to the unstable nature of the many factors influencing the weather.

The Atmosphere

A knowledge of fundamental weather forecasting begins with an understanding of the earth's atmosphere and its relationship to the earth's surface. Briefly, the earth is completely surrounded by a band, or layer, of air into which a constantly varying amount of water is being evaporated. This evaporation of water into the air comes from the ocean areas—the greater part of the earth's surface—and inland waterways, as well as from the moist earth itself. This water vapor, seemingly in defiance of the law of gravity, accumulates in the air; condenses when the right combination of temperature, elevation, and saturation occurs; then drops as rain or snow. This is nature's way of irrigating the land areas of the earth.

The actual pattern by which this occurs begins to become evident when we understand that the layer of atmosphere is not constant as to pressure. The "normal" pressure of the atmosphere is equivalent to the weight of approximately 30 inches of mercury at sea level. At higher elevations, where there is less remaining air above, it is less. Indeed, a mercury column, showing to what height the air pressure would push mercury in a vacuum, was the earliest barometer, an instrument for measuring atmospheric pressures. Smaller barometers, based on the action of atmospheric pressures on a flat metal box which has been partially vaccumized, are available to the serious outdoorsman to whom weather changes are most vital.

Due to changes in temperature and elevation, and largely because of the earth's rotation on its axis, the pressures throughout the atmospheric band vary. Areas of low pressures are known as "lows" and areas of higher pressures are called "highs." The vapor in the air, being in the aggregate heavier than air, moves toward areas of low pressure, and fills in what are known as the "troughs." When sufficient moisture has accumulated, it forms clouds, condenses, and becomes rain or snow.

Winds are caused by unequal atmospheric pressure, and as a large area of moisture fills in a low-pressure area, winds form and become an integral part of the "low." It might be said then that "highs" indicate fair weather until the high pressures of the area are dispelled and that "lows" indicate building storms and wind, until the low-pressure area is moved, by masses of air movement, out of that region. "Low" areas may cover several states, or parts of states. The winds accompanying a low, in the Western Hemisphere, habitually blow around the low cell in a counter-clockwise pattern.

As these clouds and winds form, they vary in intensity and place, because of differences in temperature and humidity, where they "bump into" areas of different pressures, and so forth. For one thing, clouds are generally higher by day than by night. They are higher in the tropics than at the earth's poles. And where the average height of clouds may range in summer from 10,000 to 12,000 feet, their average height in winter may be only one-third that height. All clouds are charged to some extent with electricity, which is most pronounced during thunderstorms. In a basic way, high clouds don't shed their moisture; low cloud formations do. Light-colored clouds are not apt to shed moisture; dark, dirty-colored clouds are.

Cloud Formations

For the outdoorsman, simple weather forecasting may well begin by observing forming clouds and interpreting the winds that accompany them. Correlated with changes in temperature and matched to the season of the year and area, this information is enough to predict weather for the immediate future—at least far enough ahead to plan sensibly for outdoor activity.

Clouds are of four basic types: cirrus, cumulus, stratus, and nimbus. Broadly speaking, cirrus clouds are those feathery puffs of clouds high in the atmosphere, with slender fingers running out in all directions. A halo around the sun is simply light filtering through cirrus clouds. Cumulus clouds are big, white, rounded masses of individual clouds with a soft and fluffy appearance, and which often appear in fair weather in a blue sky. Stratus clouds are generally long horizontal banks or bands of clouds

Cirrus clouds are thin, white, feathery puffs which usually indicate fair weather. In abundance, however, they mean rain in twenty-four hours.

which form near the earth's surface, massing together so as to nearly cover the sky. Nimbus clouds are low masses having no definite contour, and from which rain or snow is usually falling.

These primary formations often overlap and modify as they descend, and become combination patterns. Such formations are known as cirro-cumulus, strato-cumulus, cumulo-nimbus, etc.

With only this meager knowledge, it is possible to predict simple weather probabilities and changes:

Suppose it has been clear and calm, but a breeze gradually comes up, which settles into a steady and increasing wind. If the wind holds steady from the normal direction of storm for that area and season, it means a "low" is forming somewhere in that direction; that the actual storm is to the right of the person facing the wind, and that it might be smart to get the tent set up and the gear inside before dark.

Suppose a fresh breeze springs up during a prolonged rain. The rain has been from the southwest (normal for that area and time of year), but the new breeze is from the north and continues to come. This probably means that the low-pressure area may have bumped into an adjacent high-pressure area moving in from the north. The "high" is pushing the "low" out. It is likely to clear, and the weather turn cooler.

Perhaps it has been hot and sultry all day. By afternoon, banks of low, dirty-colored clouds form on the horizon and build fast. This may mean a localized "low," rapidly building because of the heat. If the cloud banks continue forming, a stiff wind may suddenly blow up ahead of them, and there may be a thunderstorm. If distant rumbling can be heard, or if distant lightning flashes can be seen before the wind arrives, the storm is liable to break any moment.

Cumulus clouds, fluffy horizontal masses in a blue sky, generally mean fair weather. They normally increase during the day but disappear at night.

Cumulus clouds building vertically in large banks are warning signs of possible brief showers, usually in the afternoon or evening.

Weather Signs

It is useful to learn to recognize and interpret outdoor "signs" of weather changes. These signs are all about. Many are universal; others are localized in significance. Such signs occur in the atmosphere and heavenly bodies, in the foliage, and in the behavior patterns of birds, insects, and the different species of wildlife.

As examples of atmospheric signs which may be used to predict weather changes, the following have been observed by enough outdoorsmen to make them fairly reliable:

A pronounced halo around the sun or moon in summer means probable rain within a day or so. A bright silvery moon in late summer or fall indicates frost.

In winter, when "sun dogs" (rainbow-colored arcs on either side of a halo) appear around the sun, either in early morning or late evening, it is a sign of much colder weather in the near future.

The old rhyme, "Rainbow in morning, sailor take warning; rainbow at night, sailor's delight," has much basis in fact.

A heavy dew on grass and weeds in early morning is an indication of clear weather for the remainder of the day. If the grass is dry in early morning, and the air has a hot, hushed and dry feeling, a storm is probably on the way.

The colors of the sky give some indication as to forthcoming weather changes. A bright blue color, changing from pale blue at the horizon to a deep indigo-blue at the zenith means clear weather. A hazier, grayer blue means dust in the air from winds, and possibly approaching storm. A "mackerel sky"—bits of high clouds speckled somewhat like the markings of a mackerel, and the total formation lying in a long elliptical shape—means winds aloft and approaching storm.

Stratus clouds are long grayish bands near the earth's surface. Their increase means rain is in the offing.

Nimbostratus, a form of nimbus clouds, are dark-gray masses close to the earth's surface from which rain or snow is falling or will fall. All photos courtesy of U.S. Department of Commerce, Weather Bureau.

When smoke coming from a campfire hugs the ground as it rolls away, it means a storm is coming. Smoke that rises straight aloft from a fire means continuing clear weather.

For campers or hikers along the coastal areas, the incidence of tides has a bearing on the weather. A falling tide lowers the atmospheric pressure; and with humid air, rain is more likely at low tide than at high tide.

High visibility over ocean water indicates coming rain since a normal haze over salt water is moved out by shifting air movements.

In many areas, better television reception is obtained when a thick cloud cover is overhead—the waves "bounce" downward from it. Similarly, a lowering cloud ceiling will cause sound waves to resonate. When distant sounds are loud and hollow-sounding, a rainstorm is on the way.

Odors afield become stronger under the influence of a low-pressure area. A high-pressure area pins them down—hence, when odors are strong storm is on the way or to be expected.

Foliage grows according to the prevailing winds, with its leaves lying in a natural position. Overturned leaves mean a shift in wind direction.

A sultry hot night, during a normally cool season of year, means approaching storm.

Low, blue-black storm clouds which rapidly build on the horizon in the direction from which prevailing rainstorms come, mean excessive rain and possible thundershowers. Preceded by sultry heat, and sudden gusts of cool air moving ahead, they mean hail.

Wildlife Behavior

The behavior of wildlife, if interpreted correctly, will provide clues to weather changes; indeed, wildlife are among our best weather prophets.

If elk, deer, or similar species behave peculiarly despite no contact with the sights, smells, or sounds associated with man, it usually means coming storm. With a big storm only hours away, elk will often bolt or stampede for no detectable reason.

During late fall, if elk suddenly begin migrating out of the high country, and apparently lose some of their fear of the presence of man, it means that heavy snowstorms are on the way—snows that would lock them in the high ranges. Elk will often move twenty-four hours ahead of such violent snowstorms.

Wild geese, similarly, move ahead of frigid weather southward to warmer climates as the bitter temperatures proceed. A temperature of 28 degrees will normally move geese from the lakes of the North country, which would freeze them in. If long wedges of migrating geese or whistling swans appear headed southward, you can bet that frigid weather is not far behind.

Grouse that stay all winter in timber country will bury themselves completely under the snow surface, their only air provided by a small hole. However, when their triangular tracks begin appearing on the snow, you may be sure the weather is about to clear of storm.

Waterfowl fly higher during clear weather, lower during stormy weather. When birds begin appearing, or start singing or flitting about after prolonged storm, it means that clear weather is not far away.

Prior to a summer thunderstorm, Chinese pheasants will usually crow repeatedly in areas just ahead of the coming storm.

In wooded country during the fall season, owls will often hoot intermittently throughout the night. This, in my own experience, has always meant storm of some sort within a period of three days.

The black bear is something of a long-range weather forecaster. If he hibernates deep, and gathers a considerable amount of twigs for his bed, it usually means a cold winter with shallow snow. If a bear hibernates close to the surface, it normally means heavy winter snow.

If, in the spring, a black bear emerges from hibernation, then goes back to his den, it usually means that rain or a spell of hot weather has interrupted his sleep, but more cold weather is yet to come.

All of these weather signs will be affected to some degree by seasonal weather patterns and the particular region in which you live. However, when region, season, and weather history are taken into consideration, these signs will prove to be valuable indicators for short-term weather predictions.

Dangerous Weather

It is one thing to be able to predict bad weather to a reasonable degree, and yet another to be able to meet bad weather as it occurs in the outdoors. This means, in short, that the outdoorsman must be able to ride out bad weather with patience and philosophy and keep his equipment and himself dry during storm. He must also know how to meet dangerous weather.

Dangerous weather, for the outdoorsman, consists largely of thunderstorms, excessive windstorms such as cyclones and tornadoes, and to a lesser degree, unseasonal or violent snowstorms.

Thunderstorms are bred by heat, and reach a high degree

of savagery on high mountain-tops, which are known as "weather breeders." They often come on the heels of hot, sultry weather when there is a hushed calm to the air. An experienced outdoorsman can almost "feel" a thunderstorm coming.

The natural reaction to being caught in a thunderstorm, is to get under something for protection. In wooded country, there may be no cover except trees, and the result is often fatal. High trees draw lightning. A single tall tree in an open area is worst of all, and most apt to be hit. Certain species of trees are more vulnerable to lightning than others; for example, it is said that oaks are hit more often than beeches.

The best place to be during lightning storms is close to the ground. One should not move; a moving animal or person is more apt to be struck than a stationary one. If caught in a thick wooded area, one can often do no better than to get under the protection of the shortest, thickest trees, and huddle till the electrical violence passes.

If you are caught in an open meadow, the safest procedure is to lie flat on your stomach. Rain usually accompanies lightning storms, but it is better to get soaked on the back than to be struck by lightning. If you can reach a brushy area before the storm gets too near, a good place to huddle is under the lowest, thickest foliage. A thick stand of any kind of foliage is far less apt to attract lightning than a single tree or bush.

During a lightning storm, you should not hold any implement containing steel. An ax, for example, with a metal bit and wet handle soaked with the salt from human perspiration, makes a fine invitation for electricity.

Violent wind can often be dangerous. It can blow you against trees or rocks, or topple rocks, dry trees, or limbs onto you. As in thunderstorms, safe places are close to the ground, in ditches or similar depressions in the earth, in a cave if available, under a rocky ledge (not one having loose rocks) or beneath an overhanging dirt bank. Regardless of the terrain, there will be *some* place accessible that is low and protected.

Cyclones and tornadoes are among the most violent of wind storms. Cyclones are tropic-bred. They are large storms, covering great areas. The inward-whirling movement of air characteristic of cyclones is thought to be induced in part by the cold air of polar regions meeting the rising hot, humid air. Cyclones are always accompanied by torrential rains and winds of high velocity.

Some warning of the approach of a cyclone is given by the sky. The sunrises and sunsets are bloody red. The air is sultry and oppressive. Cirrus clouds change to cirro-stratus, the barometer drops fast, the sky rapidly becomes overcast, and nimbus clouds occur. Soon, wind, water, and clouds are lashed to a fury, and the cyclone is on.

The only safe place in a cyclone is a storm cellar with the lid on. If you cannot get out of the storm area, stay close to the ground, behind solid embankments or rocky bluffs, or cling to something completely stationary.

A tornado is a small, localized whirling of air, like the cyclone in that both rotate counterclockwise in the Northern Hemisphere. Tornadoes are found only in the United States. They cross the land surface at from twenty to forty miles per hour, generally from west-south-west to east-north-east. The wind velocity, at the same time, may reach up to 400 miles per hour. Tornadoes are characterized by a dipping, twisting funnel, dropping down from low cumulo-nimbus squall clouds.

Like thunderstorms, tornadoes are bred from sultry

weather conditions. The worst months for tornadoes are May through July, with the mid-winter months the least susceptible to these violent, funneling winds.

As with cyclones, the best place to be, if you are in the path of a tornado, is in a cellar with the lid on. However, due to the slow land speed, and their general direction being known, you can usually avoid an approaching tornado by traveling rapidly at right angles to its path.

A heavy fall of snow, especially if unexpected or if accompanied by wind, can be mildly dangerous to the outdoorsman. Generally speaking, such a storm can be predicted far enough in advance for a person to reach camp or adequate shelter before it gets too bad. In any case, a heavy snowstorm should be accepted with patience. If you stay in one place, keep a fire going, and conserve your strength, you'll be safe. With clearing weather, you can find your way to camp, or out of the country, without becoming lost.

6

A Shelter for the Night

Unless one is fortunate enough to stay in a wilderness cabin, or unless he uses a camper, trailer, or motor home, the best outdoor shelter is a good tent, properly set up. The experience of generations has gone into tent making, and models are now available to suit every purpose. Whenever possible, the person going into the outdoors should take full advantage of the variety and high quality of modern tents.

Where the question of weight rules out packing a tent, the next best shelter is a tarp. The 8-by-8 foot tarp mentioned earlier for use with a packboard can be fashioned into various types of shelters. Often this can be done with nothing except simple framing material found on the spot.

If you are caught in a rainstorm while hiking with a packboard, you can in less than a minute shed the packboard, unroll the tarp, and slip under it with your duffel until the shower passes.

A tarp is one of the most versatile of shelters. Pitched over a ridgepole lashed to a tree, and the sides pegged down, an 8-foot tarp will keep a sleeper dry in heavy storm.

Tarp Shelters

For a more permanent shelter, you can utilize material at hand as a temporary framework over which the tarp can be spread. For instance, in timber country you can lay the end of a long sapling or pole on a fallen log, the other end on the ground. Then spread the tarp over this sampling in the shape of a letter A, leaving a space of about 1½ feet between the log and the upper end of the tarp. The sides of the tarp, of course, are pulled down tight and staked with cords from the grommets to wooden stakes or any available brush. The high end should be uphill. There is room under this shelter for you, your gear, and sleeping bag. If may be cramped, depending on the height of the log, but you will sleep dry.

A more roomy and comfortable A-tent arrangement can be made by fastening one end of the sapling to a blowdown or handy tree, and supporting the other end with two short shear poles. A shelter of this type can be 3 feet high and over 5 feet wide inside—room enough for sleeping and for storing gear. If a raincoat is in the duffel, you can hang it over the end, in case the wind direction changes.

In erecting any kind of shelter, attention should be given to the lay of the land with respect to drainage. It should be placed on high ground, in an area where considerable rain won't drain under it, and in a position so your head is as high or higher than your feet. If at all possible, it should be placed with its side toward the direction of the rain. Where this is impossible, the raincoat covers the open end.

You can quickly make another effective shelter by tying the end of a sapling to a tree trunk at about a 6-foot height. The other end of the sapling rests on the ground. Place the tarp over this ridgepole and tie one corner to its upper end near the tree, the opposite corner to the lower end. If the length of the pole, from tree to ground, is just over 11 feet, the tarp will just reach. If you want a space between the tree and the edge of the shelter for getting inside conveniently, then the ridgepole may be longer, and the upper end of the tarp tied farther back. The loose corners of the tarp are spread apart, and the edges of the tarp are tied down to stakes. The steepness of this shelter will allow rain to run off. Since a tree builds up the earth higher around its base, your head should be nearest the tree. Also, you have more room in that position for your head and shoulders, and you won't have to sleep with canvas in your face.

If two shear poles are substituted for the tree, even more room is afforded at the front of the shelter, and you can keep a fire burning at the entrance. When using these shear poles as a support for the front end of the ridgepole, the tops of both poles should be slanted toward the rear of the

Ridgepole can be supported by two shear poles and the tarp pitched in this manner. Back of tarp should face toward the wind.

shelter—otherwise the shelter will tip over forward. In this arrangement, it is best to have the back end face into the wind. A fire placed in front of such a shelter will reflect heat on a sleeper and can be used for cooking. If the fire is kept small, it may be built close enough to the shelter's front for you to sit on the end of your sleeping bag and cook, loaf about, or simply wait out a storm.

An even better form of tarp shelter may be made in the form of a lean-to. If two trees can be found close enough together, a ridgepole can be tied between them. If only one tree is available, shear poles can be set under one end of the ridgepole and the other end tied to the tree. In an area without any standing timber, shear poles can be used to support both ends of the ridgepole. To keep the finished shelter from toppling over sidewise, tie a guy rope

With ridgepole lashed to two trees, tarp can be pitched as a lean-to. In chilly weather, heat from a fire built in front will be reflected onto bed at rear.

to each shear pole where it joins the ridgepole and stake it at each side.

Once the ridgepole is set up solidly, lay several poles just over 8 feet long so they extend from the ridgepole to the ground. If the bottom ends are sharpened with an ax and stuck into the earth, the tops won't need too much anchoring, except for the two outside poles, which must be tied firmly to the ridgepole. The tarp is then spread over this framework and tied to the bottom of the outside poles.

Those outdoorsmen who often use lean-tos of this type usually sew a tapered flap to opposite sides of the tarp. These flaps become the sides of the lean-to, forming a three-sided shelter, or half of an A-tent.

With this type of shelter, the sleeping bag is laid lengthwise along the rear. A fire in front of the lean-to, if kept burning all night, warms the sleeper by heat reflected downward from the tarp slope, similar in principle to the reflector oven. The shallowest part of the lean-to, nearest the sleeper, is the warmest.

In swamp or muskeg country where the only available framework for a shelter may be underbrush, low bushes, or willows; or in desert country where the only "timber" is sagebrush, the tarp shelter is equally effective.

A clump of low willows can be used to support a tarp. Clear away all stalks and other brush from the side away from the wind. Then spread one side of the tarp over the clump, tie the eyelet cords to individual stalks, and lay the opposite side on the ground, stretched taut, and peg it down with willow stakes cut from the brush. The result isn't shapely, but it's a shelter.

Similarly, in sagebrush country, one side of the tarp may be spread over several closely-set sages, tied, and the opposite edge staked to the earth. The rear end can be made windproof by stuffing it with sagebrush tips built into a brushy "wall."

In low, swampy areas which are traversed mainly by boat, and where suitable framework is not available, you can use a boat or canoe to make a tarp lean-to. Turn the boat or canoe on its side and anchor it. Lay one edge of the tarp on the upper edge of the boat, and hold it down with heavy objects—oars, anchor, or anything handy. Stake the opposite edge of the tarp to the ground, and you have a waterproof shelter.

In the Arctic, the Eskimos who hunt during the winter always carry a short crosscut saw and square-bladed shovel on their dog sleds and, more recently, their snowmobiles. When staying out overnight, they cut blocks of packed snow with the saw, and build a small rectangular-shaped enclosure. They cover the top of the enclosure with a tarp, using snow and ice to hold the edges down. A small oil or kerosene stove provides some heat. The temperature outside may be 30 below zero. I spent one night in such a shelter near Cape Lisbourne in the Arctic Circle, together with two Eskimo guides. It was cramped and cold, but it was far better than no shelter.

Snow Trench or Cave

The same principle can be adapted to other winter travel in deep snow country and cold temperatures, such as cross-country skiing, snowshoe treks, and snowmobiling. If one is caught in a survival situation, it is possible in many instances to build a snow trench or snow cave, which will afford some protection if only to preserve body heat.

The snow trench can be built in flat open country where there is sparse brush or timber with which to build a shelter. It is made by scooping out a small trench, slightly larger than the person's body, and to a depth of about a foot. The snow may be scooped out with nothing more than a snowshoe, the rear end of a ski, or a tiny collapsible spade, such as the military used in World War II to dig foxholes. This tool can be carried in the saddlebags of the snowmobile for just such a possible emergency. If the snow is soft, much of it can be scooped out with a boot and the hands. As the snow is removed, it is used to build up the sides of the trench.

When the hollowed space is made (keeping the snow packed and built up as straight as possible for sides) it is covered over the top, with the exception of an open end, with anything available, such as branches, brush, a space-blanket, or the light rubberized nylon tarp often used to wrap packs on the pack-board. The tarp also might be carried in the snowmobile saddlebags.

At night, the user works his way inside from the open end, and the protection of his winter clothing, plus the body heat conserved inside the small trench, will make the difference between survival and freezing.

A snow cave is made in much the same way. It is dug into the windward side of any big available snowdrift. The removed snow is used in much the same manner to enlarge and build up the "cave," or hollow, on the outside.

Both types of sheleter should have the bottom covered with any available brush, boughs, and so forth, for insulation. With the warm clothing normally worn by winter travelers, especially the modern insulated suits made for snowmobilers, both emergency shelters will help conserve enough body heat to permit overnight survival.

The Husky sled-dogs of the Far North have utilized this principle for generations. With frigid weather, night, or impending storm, they simply curl up, furry nose-to-tail, and let any snow completely cover them. In the morning, or periodically during the night if the covering gets too deep, they burst forth, often from under several inches of the white stuff, shake, and apparently are as good as new.

In jack-pine country, one can even use a tarp to make a wigwam type of shelter. Tie three poles near their tops and spread them to form a tripod. Then lay a number of poles in the V at the top of the tripod to form a cone-like frame. Stretch the tarp over the framework, covering sufficient surface to make a weatherproof area on the ground beneath.

Lean-Tos and Other Frame Shelters

Many of the shelters previously described can be built without using a tarp, if none is available. It will take longer, require more material, and the shelter won't be quite as waterproof, but it will be usable.

The lean-to is perhaps the best. The sloping poles are laid along the ridgepole in the same manner, except that more are necessary to prevent the final covering from falling through. A thick covering of boughs then is laid over the sloping roof members. The best kind are green balsam, spruce, fir, or pine. These are not placed haphazardly in a pile, but laid individually in the manner that a house is shingled, beginning at the bottom, with the butts pointing upward. The next row is laid similarly, with the tips overlapping a portion of the first row. Successive rows of boughs are laid in this manner up to the ridgepole. It is wise to lay several additional poles across the roof, to hold down the boughs firmly in case of wind. The sides of the lean-to may be built of saplings angled against the roof, their butts sharpened and driven into the ground. More boughs are then woven in and out between these sloping uprights until a suitable side wall is built. This type of lean-to will act as a windbreak, especially if dirt is piled along its outside edges, and it will shed an appreciable amount of rain. Built in winter and covered with 3 to 5 inches of snow, it will make a very snug shelter.

Place sloping poles close together along a ridgepole to make a bough lean-to. Starting at bottom, lay boughs with butts upward, overlapping them like shingles.

In birch or aspen country, where plenty of large trees are available, sections of bark will make a fine covering for the roof of the lean-to. To remove the bark from a tree, girdle the trunk at 3-foot heights. Then vertically split the section of bark between on opposite sides. By pushing the toe of an ax blade between bark and tree, the bark may be pried away in a semicyclindrical shape.

Rows of this cupped bark are laid, convex side up, along the length of the lean-to. Smaller sections of bark are then placed over the joints of the first row—much as curved tile is laid on a roof. Two or three rows of bark placed this way will make a waterproof roof.

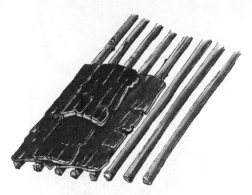

Sections of bark can be used instead of evergreen boughs as covering for a lean-to. Bark is laid convex side up in overlapping rows.

Evergreen boughs can be used to build other types of shelters. One is an A-shelter, made with a ridgepole lashed between two trees, or lashed to one tree and supported by shear poles at the other end. Long green boughs placed butts down, with their tops leaning against the ridgepole, form the sides. In areas where long boughs are not available, short saplings may be used for the sides and shorter boughs woven through them.

Another bough shelter consists of a frame of three poles—a ridgepole set with one end on the ground, and the other end lashed to two shear poles which are sharpened at their butts and driven into the ground. The shears should lean slightly toward the ridgepole. The sides are then formed of boughs.

One of the simplest shelters to make in cedar or juniper country is a tree shelter. Choose a thick cedar or juniper tree and cut off all the boughs on the side opposite the wind. Next, stand several saplings against the tree's over-

Evergreen boughs form the sides of this A-shelter. The butts are sharpened and driven into the ground.

hanging branches, leaning them toward the trunk. The boughs cut away are then woven into the side walls so that the result resembles the entrance to a wigwam.

Desert and Seacoast Shelters

Along seacoasts or in swampy areas where not too much timber is available, but where there is an abundance of grass or brush, a brush blind can be built using thin saplings as rafters and side studs. Others of smaller diameter are woven

This bough shelter consists of a frame of a ridgepole lashed to shear poles. Boughs are placed similarly to those in A-shelter.

back and forth between these, forming a rough mesh. Through this mesh, long grass may be woven to make a good windbreak or shelter for temporary storm. A raincoat over the top helps to waterproof it.

In desert areas containing tumbleweed, heavy winds will blow stretches of the dry weeds across the plains, until they are caught by an obstruction such as a fenceline or a patch of sagebrush. Under the wind's pressure, tumbleweeds will matt together, and often a great heap of these weeds can be hollowed out and fashioned into a windbreak or shelter.

Another desert shelter can be made only of sagebrush. In order for sagebrush to hold together, the walls of any shelter must be thick. The best shape is that of a large letter U, with the walls gradually shaped inward until the whole affair is canopied over, quite like the entrance of an Eskimo igloo. The result looks like an overgrown outdoor adobe

Saplings leaned against tree branch in shape of a wigwam can be woven with evergreen boughs to form a simple shelter.

baking oven similar to the ones New Mexico Indians still use.

Along many large rivers, seacoasts, or desert arroyos, where clay or sandy soil is predominant, and water has cut channels over the centuries, abrupt and sizeable cutbanks are often left. Often these vertical banks have depressions cut into their sides which may be enlarged into a space big enough to permit a sleeper to lie down. With a night fire out front, they make snug shelters. However, flash floods in desert arroyos often pour down an unbelievable amount of mud and water. One must stay above the ocean tides along any seashore, of course, and there is always the possibility of a sudden rise in the water level of a river. When you bed-down in a cutbank, be sure you choose a safe spot; otherwise you may be washed away during the night.

Rock Shelters

Rock shelters are often useful along rocky seacoasts and above timberline in mountainous country. The rock cairns built by waterfowl hunters are perhaps the best type. Like weed shelters, they are built in the form of a big letter U. The curved end of the shelter helps keep the built-up rock walls from tumbling. A fire at the opposite end helps keep you warm inside. With driftwood used as rafters, and a raincoat as roofing, a rock shelter becomes a snug, waterproof home.

Timberline in the conifer regions of most of the continent occurs at around the 10,000-foot elevation. Elevations above this are usually rocky in nature owing to soils having been weathered away and washed down. If you are hiking above timberline, it is wise whenever possible to descend into fringing timber before night overtakes you. But if you must spend the night up in the rocks, the first thing to do is to find the side of a bluff opposite to the prevailing wind. The leeward side of a bluff will have eddying currents of wind, but these are far more endurable than the blasts on the windward side. Look for shelving rock with a near-vertical or overhanging face. The back of such a place forms one wall and perhaps a partial roof. The ends of the shelter may be built up of flat rocks from talus slides. Heat from a fire in front will be reflected by the vertical wall or overhanging rock onto the sleeper. Smoke will be a problem, owing to the eddying wind currents, and the kindling perhaps only grass and bits of wood collected from the scrubby growth where the timberline tapers off.

Cave Shelters

When you can find them, caves provide good readymade shelters. Look for them when traveling in mountainous country. In many desert areas containing lava flow, caves are formed by the molten lava cooling around air pockets. Some caves formed this way are enormous; one even became a National Monument—The Craters Of The Moon. There are small ones spread throughout much of the lava desert of the West.

Some caution must be exercised in exploring caves. Caves are dark, so be sure to carry a good flashlight or lantern. Many caves are moist and drip water, making footing slick and hazardous. As one can easily get lost in the larger caves, never explore beyond the point where exit is certain. A 100-yard spool of fishing line tied near the entrance and uncoiled as you investigate will permit you to find your way back.

Small caves may be inhabited by bats, mice, packrats, or bobcats. Their presence may be indicated by smell, dung, or tracks in the dust of the cave floor. In using a cave for a shelter, stay near the mouth, just far enough inside beyond the overhang to prevent rain from coming in. Most caves smell better there. A fire at the cave's mouth will prevent any varmint from entering, or rodents from getting too close. I know of two men who used a rocky cave for a shelter, and during the night the big gray rats which also called it home nearly grazed up their sleeping bags.

Selecting a Campsite

In wooded country several factors influence the choice of a campsite: a suitable water supply; an area of ground level enough to pitch a tent or build a shelter and free from rain or snow drainage; the availability of wood for making a fire and shelter; and the incidence of mosquitoes or other insects.

A point of land that juts out into a lake or stream is a good place to pitch camp. Such a point is generally level enough for a tent or shelter. It allows a view in at least two directions. Water is handy. An open point of land catches available breezes and helps keep insects away. The danger of fire, caused by gusts of wind coming up, is minimized. And drainage is away from the campsite in three directions.

In desert travel, one usually carries his own water supply in a canteen. The main things to look for are some source of fuel for a fire, material for making a windbreak, and a spot for the sleeping bag free of desert cacti and other spined vegetation. Often this will be on the sheltered side of some low knoll, in a patch of high sagebrush. If you have brought along a tarp, and there is little danger of storm, lay it on the ground under the sleeping bag and fold half the tarp over the bed. Desert nights are cool, and dew will usually form towards morning. The tarp prevents any moisture from coming up from below, and keeps the dew off on top.

After the spring runoffs, good camping areas can be found on high gravel bars along riverways. The spring floods often carry huge piles of driftwood downstream, where they lodge in shallow water. After the heat of summer, the wood dries out and makes suitable firewood. If the shelter can be made against such a large pile, it not only furnishes fuel but acts as a windbreak. A little remodeling of the pile is often all that is necessary to have a suitable backdrop; and with a fire out front, such a spot can be very comfortable. Care should be taken to see that the spot is high enough above the prevailing waterline to be entirely safe from any sudden rise in water.

Old gravel bars, laid down centuries ago when a river was cutting its channel, are also good campsites. These overlook the river and normally have sufficient quicksand mixed with the gravel on the surface to be smoothed into a place for the bed. Pieces of old driftwood are usually found in such areas.

In high mountain country, the best place for a campsite is a small open space of level ground near a thick copse of timber and, if possible, near water. A lush growth of conifers or other foliage is usually a sign of the beginnings of a mountain spring.

When camping in snow, a thick copse of timber, as near a running creek as possible, provides a good windbreak and wood for fuel. If the creek is frozen or drifted over, it often can be found by digging. Often a spring in such an area will be warm enough at its origin so it does not freeze, and can be found by going a distance upstream. A boggy area, not covered with snow, sometimes indicates a spring. If no running water is present, snow can be melted, although snow water lacks the minerals to make it palatable, and tastes flat. One of the reasons why tea became such a popular trail drink, especially during the winter, is that snow water had to be used; and tea not only warmed the person but made the water taste better.

Choosing a campsite in swampland presents difficulties. Usually the highest possible elevation—a small ridge or a neck of land between bodies of water—will be the driest place for a camp. Dampness in the sleeping area often has to be offset by piling boughs, leaves, or grass into a heap and placing the bed on top.

Where sufficient time and fuel are available, the sleeping area can sometimes be dried out a bit by building a fire over it and letting it burn for an hour or so. This burns down any roots and brush stumps, and heats the ground beneath. Scrape the fire and coals away, sprinkle a layer of fresh earth over the blackened ashes, lay fresh boughs or grass over this, and place the bed on top. If you are without a bed or any sort, this arrangement will often keep you warm all night solely by the heat left in the ground from the fire. But make sure the fire has been extinguished or covered with earth before bedding-down, especially if dry fuel has been used. A fire blazing up beneath you in the middle of the night is not conducive to good sleep.

7

Firemaking

Fire, man's greatest discovery, has been a great civilizing influence; but, conversely, a warm campfire in the evening can also become the connecting link between modern man and his primal ancestry. However, no one has a moral right to use fire in the outdoors who will not assume responsibility for its hazards. A full understanding of the dangers of fire is necessary both to your safety and to your full enjoyment of the outdoors.

Hazards of Fire

The principal hazard of fire is that it will get out of control. There are many ways a campfire can do this. Sparks will fly from too large a fire or from wood which still holds moisture in its cells. A small fire often catches branches or brush which are too close for safety to the fire itself. As fire burns, it heats the surroundings and dries them out—often to the degree that otherwise green or wet material will burn. Ordinarily this occurs most unexpectedly. When the fire dies down, someone piles on a new supply of fuel—perhaps too much—and when the fresh fuel flames up, surrounding materials are ignited.

This is especially true near conifer trees. A fire under a green pine, for instance, will heat the boughs to the point where they easily catch fire. The green needles burn quickly; a flame shoots up the side of a tree, and the makings of a forest fire are there in seconds, for the fire will then jump from treetop to treetop where it can't be reached.

Wind is another cause of fires getting out of control. Often a fire will be safe until a sudden gust of wind, or a change in the wind's direction, either blows sparks into dry tinder or blows the flame itself into adjacent inflammable material. Many people don't realize that fire makes its own wind, and the larger the fire, the greater the draft in the immediate area. Wind is nothing more than air moved by a change in atmospheric pressure. There is a difference between relatively cool air, and the abrupt, red-hot air heated by a fire. This difference in pressures causes a sudden draft, or wind, causing a large fire built on a calm day to break into a roar.

Another, more insidious hazard of fire is its ability to creep along ground apparently barren of fuel. This is noticeably true in conifer woods where, as a result of blowdowns having accumulated over the ages, the top layer of ground is largely punk. Sometimes, after a fire has been thoroughly doused with water, live embers at the outer periphery will eat beneath the surface for some distance, come to the top, and catch onto dry needles.

Fire that gets out of control—often hours after apparently having been extinguished—does unbelievable damage. A burned conifer forest will take a hundred years to grow back again. I recently rode through a western forest that was almost completely consumed by fire forty years ago. One or two of the old charred stumps had a diameter of 18 inches. The new growth of pines averaged only 6 to 8 inches in diameter. Even when a fire consumes only part of the timber, the remaining trees are slowed down in growth from one-third to one-half. Scarred trees allow wood rot and insects to penetrate, further destroying their utility.

If you are aware of the dangers implicit in the use of fire in the outdoors, you can take the necessary precautions to prevent your campfire from ever getting out of control.

First of all, plan the camp so the fire will be on rocks, gravel, sand, or bare earth whenever possible. If only a grass or sod floor is available, clear off all grass down to damp earth in a 10-foot area and place the fire in the center of this circle. If you are in an area where doing this will leave an eyesore on the landscape, the turf may be shoveled away in blocks, piled up, and later replaced. To do this, simply cut down through the grass to a depth of 3 inches in a grid pattern to produce blocks of turf a foot square. After the first one is started, these are easily sliced off beneath the grass.

It is never safe to build a fire beneath a tree or against it. Neither is it safe to build a fire in a pile of dry driftwood along a stream bed—the wood needed should be removed from the pile. In desert country or rangeland, it is never safe to build a fire in a grassy area or in a high wind.

Fireplaces

Once a spot for the fire has been chosen and cleared, it increases the safety factor, and also the convenience when cooking, to make some kind of fireplace.

One of the simplest is three rocks placed in the form of a triangle. The fire is built in the center. Place the rocks with their flat surfaces up, then work them down into the ground so that the three top surfaces are even. This can be accurately determined by setting a pan of water on the rocks and noting on which side it spills.

A fireplace of rocks in the form of a stubby letter U has several advantages. The open end can be placed toward the wind, providing a draft for the fire. Fuel can be shoved in through this open end. Large cooking pots will rest on the sides, supported by hot coals built up nearly even with the top. Smaller pots may be hung over the fireplace on a dingle stick, rack, or tripod.

A dingle stick is a length of green sapling sharpened at the butt. It is shoved into the earth and angled over a rock support or a forked stick so that its tip hovers over the fire. A pot is hung on this end by the bail. The height is regulated by varying the distance of the supporting rock from the fire or by setting the forked-stick support higher or lower. Often Canadian guides merely bend a green alder or willow sapling toward the ground and tie the pot's bail to it with a wire fishing leader. The weight of the filled pot keeps the sapling bent, and a small fire can then be built under the pot.

A rack may be erected over the fireplace by shoving two forked sticks into the ground, one at either side, and laying a length of sapling into these forks. The ends of this horizontal bar may be tied to the forks for added support. Green saplings should be used, especially for the bar, otherwise it is apt to burn in two. A wire coat hanger, bent into a long loop with a hook at the bottom end makes a good potholder. So does a forked branch notched at the bottom end. The fork hangs on the bar; the notched end holds the pot.

A tripod of green saplings can be used to support pots over a rock fireplace as well as over other types of cooking fires. Three green saplings approximately 4 feet long form the tripod. Their butt ends are sharpened and shoved into the ground, straddling the fire. The tops are brought together and lashed in place. Wire is best, but cord or rope may be used if the fire is kept low.

With a bit more effort, a cooking crane can be made which will support heavy kettles and allow you to regulate the distance of the pot from the fire. The crane is begun by driving a 4- or 5-foot post into the ground by the side of the fireplace. Next, an arm is tied to this post with wire or rope so that it will be secure but still loose enough to swing when pushed. The outer end of the arm is tied to the top of the post with a rope. A pot, hooked to the end of the arm, can be swung over the fire or off to the side to regulate cooking heat.

Another type of fireplace, which is handy for a more permanent camp, is built of two rows of rocks set a foot or more apart with the fire between. Fewer rocks are necessary if a shallow pit is dug where the fire is made. Allow the fire to burn down to coals and rest the larger frying pans either across the rocks or directly on the coals. Dutch ovens are set on the coals, which are heaped upon the flanged lids. The heat can easily be regulated by shifting the coals along the space between the rocks. The Sheep Eater Indians often used this type of fireplace, and a few of the old rock rows are still visible in the West.

Where transportation permits, any of these cooking arrangements is improved by the addition of some kind of grid or length of flat metal. A piece of sheet iron placed across the sides of a rock fireplace provides a flat cooking surface that not only prevents spilling things but helps distribute the heat. A metal grid with legs is handy when it can be transported. It is set up directly over a bed of coals, with the four legs shoved into the ground, or else laid, with the legs folded under, across the top of a rock fireplace. A fine light grid may be made by bending light metal rods into a loop around each corner of the grate from an old electric oven, and cutting them at approximately 18-inch lengths. These legs will fold flat during transit.

One of the simplest fireplaces consists of two green logs 6 to 8 inches in diameter and about 3 feet long. These are laid on either side of the fire after it has burned down almost to coals. The green logs won't burn, and they permit the necessary draft to enter from either end. The cooking pots are simply set on the logs. Flatten the tops of the logs slightly with an ax, to prevent the pots from slipping. The size of the bed of cooking coals can be easily regulated by distributing them in the opening between the logs. Or the main fire can be kept going at one end, and the cooking coals raked toward the opposite end. The heat can be further regulated by moving the pots along the logs.

Often the outdoorsman must build a fire on wet ground, especially when camping in muskeg country in the North or in swampy areas in the South. The best method is to elevate the fire on a platform of poles and branches. Such a platform will soon dry out sufficiently to allow the fire to burn well. A fire built on wet ground is usually smoky and hard to keep going. The fire heats the ground, which in turn gives off steam that tends to put out the fire.

Building a Cooking Fire

Seasonal outdoorsmen all say to use hardwood for a cooking fire. This is fine in hardwood country. In other areas, one must use softwoods, pine splits, aspen branches, willows, mahogany clumps, damp driftwood, and even sagebrush. Many an early-day camper cooked up a fine mess of coffee and bacon over a fire burning nothing more aristocratic than buffalo chips.

Fuel for a cooking fire should be obtained, if possible, from standing timber. Even during the driest weather when the earth is parched, wood lying on the ground will have soaked up dampness. A fire made of such fuel will be smoky slow-going, and hard to regulate.

It is important to remember that fire catches most easily onto wood that has been shaped so that it has the greatest amount of surface area in proportion to its bulk. For example, fire from a match won't ignite a pine split 2 inches in diameter. But if the stick is split into six slats, and one of these is shaved into paper-thin shavings, a match would quickly set fire to the shavings, and the burning shavings would ignite the slats. The point to remember is that the initial fuel should be *thin*, with considerable air available to every surface.

One good way of starting a fire, using pine splits, is to split several lengths into sticks an inch in diameter. These are shaved into "fuzz sticks." It is not easy to be able to whittle a series of shavings along the length of a stick without breaking any of them off, but with a little practice it can be done. Three or four of these fuzz sticks are laid on the ground, each crossing over the top of the other. More of the inch-thick sticks are then stood around this pile like the poles of a wigwam. This arrangement allows air to circulate freely all around the shavings and wood. A match touched to the lower fuzz stick, on the windy side, will start the fire quickly and easily. All fires, incidentally, should be lit from the windy side.

Another method is to poke the fuzz sticks into the ground, leaning them together like the bundles of a wheat shock, and place larger sticks around them. A fine arrangement is to crosshatch several shaved sticks, like a small log pigpen, and lay larger wood on top. Any of these arrangements will allow free circulation of enough air to supply oxygen to the thin starting-fuel.

Waxed paper is a very useful fire-starter. Some purists would frown on it, but generally while they are shaving up a batch of "whittlin's," the other fellow's fire is under way. In damp weather, the waxed paper from a sandwich lunch will start a fire and keep it going until the heat dries larger twigs.

Another good fire-starter is a small wax candle. The tiny ones used to decorate birthday cakes will burn long enough to ignite even damp shavings. Carry a few in your coat pocket. Larger candles will serve the same purpose, will start even wetter wood, and can be used also for temporary camp lights.

A fine fire-starter can easily be made at home by rolling a foot-long section of newspaper into a solid stick and tying it with thread. Dip the roll of newspaper into a pan of melted paraffin wax until the hot wax saturates the entire roll. When the roll is dry, cut off half-inch lengths with a sharp knive. These can be carried in your pocket, and will quickly ignite a fire.

The woods themselves provide many suitable fire-starters. Regardless of the severity or duration of a storm, heart-wood from dead, standing timber will remain dry. A little chopping will yield chips and small pieces sufficient to get a blaze going. When the fire becomes large enough, damp wood can be dried over it.

Often a storm will hit standing timber only on one side. Chopping into the sheltered side of a wet tree will produce dry wood just under the bark. Or after a light storm, the cambium layer at the inner surface of tree bark will still be dry, and this also makes a fine fire-starter. The shredded bark of dry cedar, unless actually hit by rain, will make a good fire-starter, even in a heavy rainstorm.

Another good starter found in conifer country is pitch. This is found in old, dry conifer stumps and exposed roots of timber long dead. Such pitch in a resin-impregnated stump or root is yellowish in color, and shows yellow and gummy when shaved with a knife.

A few shavings of pitch will start a fire as though coal-oil had been poured over the kindlings. Experienced outdoors-men who have set up a permanent camp, look for such pitch roots as fire-starters. Even when plenty of dry wood is available, a few shavings of pitch wood will start a fire on a cool morning when otherwise one would be shivering and waiting for slower kindling to burn.

Generally speaking, a cooking fire should be small. Allow the fire to burn down to a bed of coals, if the available wood permits, and cook over it in its receding stage.

The fire for comfort should also be kept small. This minimizes danger and conserves both fuel and energy. Usually the fire used for cooking is later fed with available splits, tips of branches, or whatever is handy. This keeps one warm until bedtime. It should be a standing rule never to go to bed while a roaring fire is going.

Sometimes you will want your fire to last all night. The best way to do this is to lay two round logs 2 inches apart over the coals. By morning, the logs will have burned partly through; or if small, completely through, but the ashes will have fallen over the remaining coals, sealing them from air. Or the burned log ends will have charred over, with live fire underneath. By blowing hard next morning, either into the ashes or against the log ends, the smoldering fire can be coaxed into flames. A few shavings or tinder placed on the coals will help. It also helps to build the initial fire in a shallow pit. Its sides help seal off any air from the coals.

Keep Your Matches Dry

The most important necessity for firemaking in any area is dry matches. The best type for outdoor use are long wooden matches. The paper matches put up in book form, like those used by cigarette smokers, are next to useless in the woods. Even when dry, they have been properly dubbed "go-fur" matches—you light one, it goes out, and you go for another. After being wet, paper matches can't be lit.

The short wooden matches about 1½ inches long, called "safety" matches, are better but not ideal. They must be struck on the abrasive surface of their boxes, and this prevents their being carried loose in a pocket or match safe.

Standard wooden matches, 2½ inches long, can be lit by scratching them with a fingernail, by raking them across the pants, or by rubbing them on a hard, dry surface. These are the kind to carry on camping trips.

For extended trips especially, matches should be carried in some kind of waterproof match container. Several are available. One is simply a plastic tube, long enough to accommodate a dozen wooden matches, which closes with a screw-on cap over a waterproof washer. Another is similar, but has a small compass in the top, making a useful combination.

A good match container can be made of two fired shotgun shells—a 12 gauge and a 20 gauge. The smaller shell is filled with matches, shoved into the larger shell, and sealed tight at the junction with melted paraffin or a couple of turns of scotch tape.

An even simpler container, but slightly more bulky, is a small, round bottle having a screw-on metal cap. A glass bottle is susceptible to breakage, but a small one carried in a coat pocket rarely breaks.

Of course, one is apt to leave even a match container at home. For this reason, it is a good policy to carry at least three paraffined matches in some article of gear. A hunter can remove the buttplate of his rifle, bore a 5/16-inch hole 2½ inches deep into the wood of the stock; poke in three matches which have been dipped in melted paraffin; and replace the buttplate.

Another trick is to bore a small hole into the top standard of the wooden packboard frame. The matches are inserted, and the aperture closed tightly, either by a small cork, rubber stopper, or wooden dowel. This plug is then cut off flush with the standard, and the matches become a part of the packboard. When you need them, the plug is removed with a knife tip.

Fishermen, who get wet more often than others, can carry three treated matches wrapped in a tiny plastic refrigerator bag or strip of vinyl sealed with scotch tape. The puny package is then slipped into the envelope carrying the fishing license. Most license envelopes are somewhat waterproof themselves, and this doubles the protection. Matches so treated and wrapped will survive a complete inundation in a river or creek and come out dry.

Other places to carry a few extra matches are in a money belt or in the pocket of a knife-sharpening kit. During hunting season, three matches may be placed inside an empty cartridge of .30 caliber or larger shell, and sealed with a small wooden plug.

Fire Without Matches

In cases of emergency, when you might be caught in the woods without matches, there are four primitive methods of starting a fire.

Fire Drill

The first is fire by friction. The practical application of this principle is the fire drill. The idea is to make a bow that will revolve a spindle in a shallow notch in a board fast enough to create a spark.

The bow can be made from a curved branch of a length to permit at least a 30-inch of thong to be tied between its ends. It should be hefty enough to prevent undue springiness. A curved alder, aspen, or willow approximately an inch in diameter is suitable.

The bow string can be made from the leather laces of one's boots, a braided fishline, or nylon cord. A leather string a half-inch wide can be cut from a circular piece of leather by cutting from the edge in ever smaller circles until the center has been reached.

For the spindle and fire board, certain woods are better than others. Dry quaking aspen, dry willow, and dry cottonwood are among the best. The board is cut from a chunk of wood, reduced to about half-inch thick, 5 to 6 inches wide, and any length over a foot. One edge is squared like a board—flat on both sides, square on the edge. A half inch inside this edge, several cone-shaped holes are gouged halfway through the board. A V-notch is then cut from the board's edge to each hole. The apex·of the V should extend nearly to the hole's center.

The spindle may be fashioned from a slab of the same wood, or a length of dry willow or aspen a foot long may be used. The spindle is not left round, but shaved into a six-sided stick, or hexagon. The hexagon shape prevents the string from slipping. One end is tapered, and the tip is sharpened somewhat like a pencil, though blunter. The other end is rounded off.

A 3-by-4 inch chunk of wood an inch thick over which the hand will fit is used for a knob to hold the spindle. On one side a small round hole is made, which will fit over the spindle.

A pile of dry tinder such as cedar bark, broken up, shredded, and rolled in the hands until it is a dry dust, is placed under one of the notches in the fire board. The bow is assembled by tying the thong to one end, wrapping it twice around the spindle, pulling it taut, and wrapping it around the other end of the bow. It's best to wrap this end rather than tie it. The wrapping is held in the palm, and the thumb is placed between thong and bow. This way, the tension on the thong may be increased by pressing the thumb toward the palm.

The round end of the spindle is placed under the knob, the tapered end into a notched hole in the board. By sawing back and forth on the bow like an inspired cellist, the spindle can be revolved. The idea is to start lightly, then increase the pressure. Long strokes are best, and with the increased pressure, these strokes should be speeded up.

If all goes well, smoke will appear at the notch. When it boils up, drop the bow, tap the smoking dust in the notch onto the tinder, and blow long and gently against it. The tiny spark created may thus be fanned into flame.

Flint and Steel

Another primitive method of starting a fire is to strike flint sharply against steel. The steel must be an old file, the back of a pocketknife, or another object having a sharp corner or edge. The punk must be some material like the cotton wicking found in an old kerosene lamp. Finally, dry tinder such as mulched cedar bark is needed. All this assumes that you have a piece of flint.

With the dry tinder handy, the wicking is held in the hand on top of the flint. The steel is struck obliquely against the flint, so that any spark produced will land on the wicking. When that occurs, the wicking is placed quickly into the punk, held in the cupped hands, and blown against gently until the live spark catches onto the tinder.

Magnifying Glass

You can utilize the sun's rays to start a fire, if you have a magnifying glass. I have a reading glass 3 inches in diameter with a focal length of 7 inches with which I can start a fire every time. The only other necessities are a handful of punk and some shavings. The best punk is the dry, rotten

In an emergency, a fire can be started with some type of magnifying glass—the lens from a telescope or binoculars, a convex watch crystal, or even a flashlight lens. Here the author uses a large magnifying glass to focus the sun's rays on dry tinder. Shavings will be laid on once fire is started.

wood of a fallen and aged pine tree. Shredded cedar bark is also good. A handful, rolled into a ball and "bunched" on the ground, is ideal. The dry shavings are laid on this, once the blaze is started.

To make the fire, hold the magnifying glass at right angles to the sun, and move it back and forth until the rays are brought to a tiny pin-point of light on the tinder. Smoke will rise within seconds. The light should be kept steady on the point until the punk bursts into flame. Blowing lightly on the punk encourages this. When the live spark has burst into flame, the dry tinder and shavings are carefully laid on top.

Firearm and Cartridge

Another method of starting a fire is with a firearm and a live cartridge. Remove the bullet from the cartridge by tapping it judiciously all around with a rock or the back edge of a knife while holding it firmly on another rock. Tapping loosens the crimp and expands the brass at the seating area until the bullet may be twisted out with the fingers.

With the bullet removed, the powder is fired into such inflammable material as cotton wadding or charred cloth. The resultant spark is then fanned into flame by blowing on it. It helps to put part of the live powder from the cartridge case with the punk. A small wad of cloth can be placed in the cartridge mouth and fired through the bore.

In some rather extensive field experimentation, both with revolvers and rifles, I have found that this method of starting a fire is most difficult to accomplish. Modern, progressive-burning powders, lacking the resistance of a heavy bullet to build pressures and facilitate combustion, tend to "blow" out of the bore as unburned kernels of powder, instead of igniting either the forward portion of the charge or the tinder.

Extinguishing the Fire

It is just as important to know how to put out a fire as to know how to build one.

In general, it is always best to allow the fire to die down before attempting to put it out. It is easier if the fuel has been largely consumed; and the fire is more apt to be completely extinguished.

Next, the remaining wood may be slightly scattered, but *not* beyond the cleared area. This helps remaining fuel to burn up more quickly, and makes the bed of fire more shallow for soaking with water.

The final step is to drown the fire completely with water. Water should be poured onto a wood fire until it quits steaming. Careful attention should be given to the edges of the fire area. Occasionally the water is all dumped on the major part of the fire, with this thin border neglected. Afterward, fire creeps into adjacent dry grass or foliage.

In areas where sufficient water isn't available, such as in desert camps, the fire may be extinguished by allowing it to die completely, then burying it deeply with earth in which there is no foliage. If the earth is dug up in a circle just outside the fire area, the ditch formed acts as a safeguard against the possibility of fire creeping beyond.

8

The Water Problem

Next to air, the most important immediate need of the human body is water. The body is composed of 67 per cent water, with the moisture level being continuously depleted and replenished. Normally, the body will lose moisture by perspiration, and as waste through the kidneys. The latter will run on an average of 2½ to 3 pints per day, though slightly less during periods of excessive perspiration. It takes a minimum of at least 1½ pints of water per day to keep the human organism functioning. Dehydration usually takes place, if all water intake is stopped, after approximately three days, four days at the very maximum. These are facts every outdoorsman should remember in planning his trips into the outdoors. Man can survive on little food for long periods of time if he doesn't exert himself, and if he has water. Lacking water, his chances of survival greatly diminish.

In wooded mountainous country, the water problem tends to solve itself. High mountains act as watersheds for melting snow and rain, forming springs, streams, and lakes. Born fresh from the earth, these sources of water are normally pure; thus the higher you go into wilderness country, the less likelihood of your finding the water contaminated.

This is especially true of mountain springs, creek beginnings, and alpine lakes. Contamination normally comes with the increasing incidence of people and industrial and human wastes. Most outdoor travelers in the mountainous West, as an example, have no hesitancy in taking a drink from any mountain spring or creek they come across, but they would be reluctant to drink from the river created by these same springs and creeks farther down.

This is no assurance that a mountain creek or even a spring is not contaminated. There is no visible way in which contamination can be determined. The only sure way is to have a chemical analysis made of the water.

The old notion that a creek, traveling through gravel, will purify itself, may or may not be true. Water traveling through rocks and gravel, however, does tend to dissipate any contamination originating higher up by sheer volume or increased dilution.

In many of the more widely traveled areas of the outdoors, such as the National Forests, contaminated water is usually marked. Signs stating "Good Drinking Water," or "Unfit For Drinking," should be heeded. In remote areas, one's nose becomes a partial guide. Water that has a peculiar odor should not be drunk until tested.

As an example of this, there is an area in British Columbia where the creeks and lakes smell peculiarly sulfurous. In the early days of the Alaska Highway, the small cafes in the region used to serve pop with meals because the water in that region comes from springs containing Epsom salts, and to drink it results in violent diarrhea.

Purifying Water

There are several ways to purify questionable water. The oldest method is to boil it vigorously for at least five minutes. This kills any germs, but gives the water a flat taste, which can be offset somewhat by pouring the water back and forth between two containers.

An easier way to purify water is to treat it with chlorine or iodine. Chlorine tablets for this purpose are available at any drug store, with the required number of pills per gallon designated on the bottle. Household laundry products containing chlorine, such as Purex and Chlorox, will accomplish the same purpose. A small bottle of such a bleach taken along to treat questionable water isn't too much bother, considering the risks involved with impure water. The correct dosage for household bleach is eight drops per gallon of water. If the water is colored or turbid, use twelve drops per gallon. Tincture of iodine will also purify water. The ratio for iodine is sixteen drops per gallon.

When using any of these chemicals, the treated water should be allowed to stand for at least half an hour before drinking it. For this you may use any kind of container—even a birchbark kettle, described in Chapter 13. Water can even be boiled in such a bark kettle by heating rocks in a fire and dropping them into the water. If metal foil is available, a light "pot" may be made of the material, in which small amounts of water can be boiled by holding the pot directly above the fire. To make such a pot, find a green forked branch whose ends can be bent and tied in a knot or fastened with a string. A single branch-tip can sometimes be bent and tied into the shape of a small landing net or tennis racquet. Into this push a doubled sheet of aluminum foil, forming a pot at the bottom, and allowing an inch of foil to extend over the top all around which is folded down over the wooden loop. You can then pour water into this pot and hold it over the fire to boil.

Melted snow must sometimes be used for cooking water during the winter or in alpine areas above timberline. When using snow, dig down beneath the surface and get the whitest snow available. This occurs during the heaviest part of a storm, when the air is purest; and the whiter the snow the freer it is of dirt, conifer needles, etc. To purify snow water, either boil it for several minutes or treat it with one of the above chemicals. Many campers defeat the flat taste of snow water by making tea of it. Boiling the water for making tea purifies it in the same operation.

Ice and snow are both used for water by Eskimo hunters in the Arctic. They haul along several blocks of freshwater ice on the dog sled when hunting on the frozen ocean during winter. They melt the ice over a small oil or gasoline stove, prepare tea, and drink it scalding hot. Before tea was available to these hardy hunters, they used snow or ice water to cook meat, then drank the broth of the boiled meat.

Locating Water in the Mountains

In unfamiliar mountain country, water can be located by several methods. One of the best is to use topographical and aerial maps. With maps of this type, it's just a matter of ascertaining your current location, getting a compass bearing on a stream, and going to it.

If no map is available, the overall contour and elevation of the terrain will indicate where to look for water. Water seeks lower elevations, of course, and this means that canyons, low valleys, and gorge bottoms are the most likely spots to find water in mountainous country. Climb to the highest immediate elevation and scout the lower areas. Binoculars help in pin-pointing areas, but creeks, small lakes, and any sizeable streams can often be seen by the eye alone. As water is a fine reflector, a curve in a watercourse is apt to catch the sunlight and reveal itself.

Foliage is another sign of water. Green, lush vegetation, or a more luxuriant growth than normal, suggests moisture and possibly a watercourse. A row of high willows or large bushes in any canyon bottom often indicates water.

Mountainsides are also good places to scout for water, and especially any areas of pale-green foliage occurring in a tiny pocket along a mountainside. Springs and bogs on a sidehill are normally accompanied by a lighter tint in foliage coloration.

Water also can be found at high altitudes just below remaining glacial snow. Pockets in the earth's surface in the general drainage area below the snow, are apt to be water-filled.

Dry creek beds in mountainous country which show evidence of early-spring runoff will almost certainly have outcroppings of water farther down their courses.

In heavily timbered country, the thriftiest stands of trees will normally follow the areas of good surface moisture.

Game trails will help an observing person to locate water. In their natural pattern of woods movement, such species as deer, elk, and moose will normally intercept at least sufficient water to satisfy their thirst within the day's travel. Moose are especially helpful. They may be found high up on wooded plateaus during the heat of midday; but their tracks will show that they head for water both early in the day and toward dusk. In fact, the very presence of a moose normally indicates that water—often considerable quantities of it—is within walking distance. Upland birds such as the ruffed grouse also stay in the vicinity of water. The spoor of this bird usually means that a spring or creek is fairly close.

If you find a spring, scoop out the earth and rocks into a pocket, where the water bubbles up. By using the material scooped out to build a circular bank at the lower side, the pocket may be made large enough to dip up a full pail without muddying the water or getting any dirt into the bucket. Tiny springs will replenish themselves between dippings.

If the spring comes out of rocks, or trickles away downhill, you can make a small trough and "pipe" the water into a more accessible flow, under which you can set the pail.

A suitable trough of sufficient length can easily by made from a section of a straight pole, split lengthwise with an ax into halves. Gouge a V-notch along the center of one half with the toe of the ax, used as a chisel.

If a board is available, such as the slat from an orange crate, this can be made into a similar trough by splitting it in two lengthwise, then nailing the two pieces together at right angles to make a V-trough.

A strip of aspen bark cut wide enough to form a small crescent can be placed concave side upward to do the same job.

If a flat slab of rock can be found, it, too, can be made to create a small waterfall for the bucket.

A trough to pipe water from a mountain spring can be made of the split half of a straight pole with a V-notch gouged along its center. Rocks support the trough, which angles slightly downhill.

When making a trough, pile earth and rocks underneath to form a solid trestle to where the water falls from the end.

Water in the Desert

The water problem is always most severe in arid country where sources of a new supply are often far away. When the water supply is short, there are many things you can do to stretch the available amount. You can ration the amount of water on hand. You can prolong your body supply of moisture greatly by refraining from hard exertion. Every effort should be made to keep from perspiring, as nothing will deplete the body's store of moisture faster than perspiring heavily on a hot day. When moving about, keep a constant lookout for any wild fruit or berries which may be eaten to relieve thirst. Most wild berries are edible, and are high in water content. On the other hand, do not eat anything containing much salt, as this increases thirst.

In desert areas, certain cacti contain small quantities of water in their barrels. The barrel cactus is one of the best. Often the wild desert sheep in cactus country will butt these plants, break the stubby barrel, and eat the moisture-filled pulp inside. Similarly, if you chop into a barrel cactus and eat the pulp, you can get enough moisture to keep you going.

The lowly cactus known as the prickly pear also has in the pulp under the spines a considerable amount of moisture. This can be chewed, the moisture sucked out, and the dry pulp spit out. In many desert areas, jackrabbits derive most of their water supply from prickly pears.

When the water supply is very low, you can get some relief for a dry mouth by holding a small, smooth pebble at the side of your tongue. This does not, of course, add any moisture to the body, but does stimulate the salivary glands to produce more moisture in the mouth.

The bloom of most wild flowers, including desert flowers, is edible. If eaten at daylight, small amounts of dew may be present, and this helps if the emergency is extended.

To get an idea of the very minimum amount of moisture the human body can survive on, consider the Australian aborigine who survives in the salty, uninhabitable outback. He eats rodents, bugs, ants, and insects—their bodies contain moisture. He follows any rain cloud in the sky, even for miles, until it gives up its moisture, then licks it up from the earth. He digs in land depressions where previous rains have gathered until his fingers get down to wet earth; then sucks the moisture from it and spits out the sand. He eats the roots of shrubs for the meager moisture they contain.

Or consider the Arctic explorer at the other end of the earth who was caught on an ice floe, and survived for days with no fresh water except the condensation of his breath on his hair, mustache, and parka collar.

If, after a partial degree of dehydration, you find a water supply, you should exert all your will power not to drink too fast and too much. Drinking too much water after dehydration is comparable to drinking too fast after overheating from strenuous exertion; you are certain to get nauseated and sick. A good way to take water after intense thirst is to soak any available piece of cloth, such as a strip cut from a shirttail, place it in the mouth and suck it, gradually increasing the amount.

With sensible planning, you need never get into any emergency this extreme. It is good insurance to know, however, that if you do, *anything* containing water or moisture will prolong the time before dehydration takes place. This includes any birds that can be killed, birds' eggs, rodents, roots, flowers, insects, or even earth down at the moisture-level that may be dug into and sucked dry.

If the thought of eating crickets, mice, and grasshoppers repulses you, remember that under circumstances of starvation or extreme thirst, things look differently. A man starved for three days will eat almost anything. A man suffering extreme thirst will drink anything. Wasn't it John the Baptist who not only survived in the wilderness on nothing except wild honey and locusts, but actually flourished on the diet?

9

Meat for the Pot

Fresh meat is hard to carry on wilderness treks, and next to impossible to keep during the summer and fall months during which the majority of outdoor trips are taken. For this reason, the grub supply may have to be supplemented by wild game once you are on the trail. Usually this consists of such small game as rabbits, squirrels, and those species of upland gamebirds native to the area. Today's back-country explorer finds such game as useful as did his forebearers, and for extended jaunts has come to depend on it to a considerable extent for his meat supply.

In advance of any trek into an area where game is expected to be taken, learn the current regulations to make sure that such game may be legally in season during the time of the intended trip. Also, find out if the species likely to be found may be legally taken with rifled firearms. In some areas, for example, grouse may be taken only with shotguns.

144

Firearms

The best weapon for taking small game is a firearm. Through the decades, many types of firearms have been especially developed for meat hunting. One of the earliest was Marble's Game-Getter, a lightweight combination shotgun and .22 rifle with a skeleton stock. A selector made it possible to shoot either barrel. The gun was useful on small game at close ranges.

Another was Harrington & Richardson's Handy Gun, a .410 shotgun with a short barrel and no stock, just a pistol grip. Later, this gun was designated as a sawed-off shotgun by the Federal Government and was discontinued. Anyone owning this gun today must register it.

Other similar shotgun-rifle combinations have been manufactured. The Savage Arms Company, as an example, currently markets an over-under gun with .22 long rifle and .410 shotgun barrels. Recently, several types of survival guns have appeared which are designed for military personnel who are stranded in wilderness areas. Among the most successful of these is the Armalite AR-7 Explorer, an eight-shot automatic rifle chambered for the .22 long-rifle cartridge, which weighs under 3 pounds and can be broken down so the barrel and action fit inside the molded fiberglass stock. The rifle will then float. Skillfully used, it is one of the best weapons for bringing in meat for the camp. For extended wilderness stays, even where all gear must be backpacked, it would be wise to leave other duffel at home in order to include it. Up to a range of 50 to 75 yards, the rifle will shoot accurately enough to bag small game.

A less expensive but slightly bulkier gun for meat hunting is a bolt-action single-shot .22 rifle which may be handily taken down. An old one I have used for years measures just 26 inches when taken down into two pieces, and weighs under 3 pounds. Strapped to the back of a loaded packboard, it is easily carried.

An even lighter weapon for bagging grouse, rabbits, and squirrels (where permitted) is a lightweight .22 pistol. My old H & R 922, bought in the 1930 depression days for a few dollars, weighs only 23 ounces, and has bagged innumerable grouse and cottontails. Smith & Wesson's Airweight Kit Gun weighs only 14¼ ounces. It, too, handles the inexpensive .22 rimfire cartridges, which are greaseless and may be carried in bulk in a pocket.

These light, wilderness-adapted weapons are all older standbys. Today, many comparable models are available and are advertised by the big gun companies.

The best way to shoot small game with a pistol is to approach as closely as possible; then sit down slowly and hold the gun in both hands. Shooting should be deliberate, as at a paper target.

An accessory that helps to steady the handgun is a leather thong used as a neck lanyard. The ends of the thong are tied so as to get approximately a 27-inch loop. In the end opposite the knot, a loop large enough to slip over the grip is made by tying a single overhand knot. The lanyard is placed around the neck, the loop slipped over the grip, the gun held in both hands, and the lanyard drawn taut. When used in the sitting position, the lanyard steadies the aim to an unbelievable extent. Used in this manner, a handgun will account for small game up to 25 yards. For this range, the .22 long-rifle cartridge is usually sufficient. Only hollow-point shells should ever be used on small game. The newer .22 WMR cartridge is better for the purpose, but requires a heavier handgun, and is far more noisy.

Small game such as cottontails, snowshoe rabbits, and the fool-hen species of grouse such as the Franklin and pine hen, may all be stalked to within this range. I have repeatedly photographed snowshoe rabbits and grouse as close as 8 feet. It's better to spend time slowly stalking the game for one good shot, than to fire at random and scare it away.

Franklin grouse and pine hens are especially easy to bowl over with a rock. Ruffled grouse, except in wilderness country, are far more wary. So are adult sage grouse, squirrels, and cottontail rabbits, though an occasional young one of all these may be hit with a rock.

A Wyoming outfitter once told me that he had often caught fool hens, which are the most stupid species of grouse, with a length of fishing line tied to a long, slim willow or jack pine. He tied the line to the pole's end, then formed a loop at the line's other end. By moving slowly and carefully he could often approach a fool hen, lower the loop over its head, and with one quick jerk have grouse for supper

Hunting with a Sling

The ancient sling, such as Biblical David used against Goliath, is an effective emergency weapon. Used with stones about the size of a hen's egg, it has ample power for knocking down small game and grouse at several rods. It takes a little practice to learn to use a sling properly and develop the accuracy necessary for hitting small game.

A sling is made of two leather thongs and a "pocket." The tough leather laces used for heavy boots are fine for

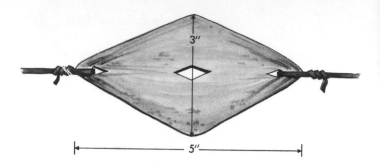

Pocket for hunting sling is made from triangular piece of leather with small, diamond-shaped hole cut in the center. Thongs are tied to each corner through slits.

the purpose, and may be used in an emergency. The leather pocket is made from soft leather such as buckskin, or, when vitally needed, from the tongue of a shoe or boot. This pocket is cut in a diamond shape, approximately 5 inches long by 3 wide. It helps to cut a tiny diamond-shaped hole in the exact center of the pocket, to permit the stone to nestle more firmly into the leather. At each corner of the longer dimension a slit is cut far enough inside the pocket's edge so that the remaining leather won't tear out under a strain. A leather thong is then tied into each of these cuts, using a slip knot or three half-hitches. A 2-foot sling is a good size for the beginner. Both thongs are cut 26 inches long, and a loop formed at the end of one with a bowline knot, for use around a finger.

To use a sling, place a round, smooth stone into the pocket and hold it with the left hand (for a right-handed thrower). Thread the looped thong over the middle finger of the right hand and hold it there by crooking the finger. Then grasp the other thong between the thumb and index finger at a point so that the two thongs are the same length between hand and pocket. Next, lower the pocket gently

Hunting sling is whirled around the head to get momentum, then thong-end held between thumb and index finger is released as rock comes forward in a right sweep. The stone is whipped forward and away with great force—but it takes practice to develop accuracy.

so that the stone holds the thongs taut, with the stone resting alongside the leg. In a sweeping motion, whirl the sling rapidly around the head at arm's length. Centrifugal force holds the stone in the pocket. At about the fourth whirl, as the rock comes from behind in a right sweep, let go of the loose thong-end, whipping the stone forward with considerable force. Like pistol shooting, becoming proficient with a sling requires ammunition of consistent size and lots of practice.

The Slingshot

A far more accurate though less powerful emergency weapon is the old-fashioned slingshot. In grandfather's day, any farm boy worth his salt not only owned a slingshot, but was quite deadly with it.

The rubber bands were strips 5/8″ wide cut from an old bicycle or auto tube. After they were tied to the arms of a crotch stick, they measured 8 to 9 inches long. The pocket was cut from the tongue of an old shoe.

Finding a suitable crotch was painstaking work. A good crotch had to fork evenly in the middle, and the forks themselves had to be at least 4 inches long. The butt, or handle, had to be 4 inches long and up to ¾-inch in diameter. The branches of plum or apple trees yielded the best crotches.

To assemble the slingshot, one end of each rubber band was fastened to a slit cut in the pocket. Usually one boy threaded the rubber band through the slit, bending it back over itself, while another boy wound string around the join, finishing with a square knot. The other end of each rubber band was folded lengthwise, laid against a circular notch cut around each of the crotch's forks a quarter inch from the tips, and similarly wound and tied with string. The notch held the rubber band from slipping off the end of the fork.

Ammunition for a slingshot was any round pebbles a boy could find, approximately the size of a marble. With such an outfit, he could bag birds, ground squirrels, cottontail rabbits, and similar-sized quarry.

With a modern commercial slingshot, and the uniform ammunition available, a high degree of accuracy can be attained with practice. For practice, pebbles or lead fishing sinkers may be used. For hunting small game, special ammunition is available at a reasonable price. Most manufacturers of slingshots sell extra rubber bands.

Steel Traps

Cottontails, snowshoe rabbits, and jackrabbits are especially easy to trap where they occur in appreciable numbers. And the easiest way of trapping them is with a steel trap. A single-spring steel trap, size #1, weighs under a pound. It comes equipped with a short length of chain with an integral spike at the end, which may be driven into a log or tree to anchor the trap. In addition to this, it is wise to bend onto the chain ring a 3-foot length of ordinary baling wire with which to anchor the trap to a stake or bush.

Trapping an animal is an art employing deception. The trap must be so placed that the animal in its normal course of travel will pass over the trap without suspecting its presence, step on the pan, and set it off. This normally requires concealing the trap; and for animals with a keen sense of smell, it means that all traces of human odor must also be removed.

Rabbits, however, pay little attention to human odor, and not much more to visual signs left by people; hence trapping them is easy. The trap is usually concealed in a runway, trail, or entrance to a burrow. To set a runway trap, a spot must be found where rabbits move about considerably. This is often a trail through underbrush or along a stream bank. In heavy desert sagebrush, jackrabbits make numerous trails between high sages. A study of the tracks will indicate both the quantity of game and those places where the bunnies travel most. The place for the trap is where tracks are thickest.

First, hollow out a place in the dirt deep enough to lay the set trap without its jaws protruding above the surface. Next, sift small quantities of the scooped-out dirt into the

Setting trap in ground: 1. Trap is set in shallow, scooped-out spot in trail where tracks are numerous. 2. At areas X in figure 1, dirt is carefully sifted between jaws and trigger-pan until a cone-shaped elevation is made just higher than the pan. Be sure no dirt gets under pan, as this will prevent tripping. When dirt cone is just higher than pan, light twigs and tiny sticks (like toothpicks) are laid across dirt-cone top. Leaves are laid on these, and the set is lightly brushed so covering looks natural.

1

2

trap, between open jaws and pan, to build up a tiny inverted cone. When the top of the cone is above the level of the pan, lay tiny needle-like twigs across its top, forming a trap pad. This keeps the covering of leaves from sinking in and tripping the pan. Lastly, scatter leaves thinly over the entire trap, and cover the leaves with a thin layer of dust. By brushing the entire surface lightly with a leafy branch, the set may be made to look like a natural part of the forest. The chain is anchored to a bush, tree, or log, and similarly concealed.

When snow is on the ground, the trap is set and placed in the bottom of a small scooped-out place in the snow. The bottom of this hollow should be flat so the set trap won't tilt. Next, lay a block of snow, or a piece of snow crust slightly larger than the hollowed-out area, over the trap. With a knife shave the entire top portion of this snow block, little by little, until only a thin shell of snow remains. This prevents the trap from freezing and makes a bridge of snow over the trap thin enough so the foot of a rabbit or other animal will break through and trip the pan. The anchoring chain is similarly concealed under the snow. Sprinkling the surface with snow, or brushing it with a twig, removes all evidence of the set.

Such a snow-set is used in the Arctic for white foxes, which are far more wary than rabbits. On a trip inland from the coast, an Eskimo hunter will poke a piece of driftwood into the snow on top of a small knoll. On the next trip, he will return to the spot and observe whether a fox has left tracks and urinated on the stick. If so, he makes a snow-set close by. Owing to the scarcity of trees in the area, the fox will return to the stick for the same purpose and be caught in the trap.

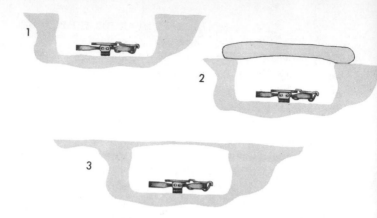

Setting trap in snow: 1. Trap is set inside small, scooped-out hole in snow. 2. A slab of snow is found, or shaped, large enough to fit across the opening. 3. With slab in place, surface is shaved with edge of knife carefully so that it becomes very thin (as thin as the strength of the packed snow will permit) over the trap's pan. Trap should be set deep enough into hole so that there is air space enough for jaws to trip without hitting snow covering.

When baiting a trap, place the food in a position so that the animal must get under it to eat. The trap is set beneath. For rabbits, suspend bits of lettuce, a carrot, or a piece of cabbage on a piece of string from a foot to 18 inches above the trap. During winter or after heavy snowfall, a bunch of grass dug beneath the snow and hung in this way makes a good bait. As with any set, a baited trap should be placed where evidence of the game is greatest. Its success is largely determined by the amount of game and the scarcity of the food supply.

Box Trap

A baited box trap will catch squirrels, cottontails, and other small game—if you have sufficient patience. The box is set precariously on the end of a small stick which rests on some hard surface, like a flat rock or tiny chip, and a string is attached to the bottom end. The string, concealed by leaves or dirt, leads away to a place of concealment. With the trap set, bait is spread far enough under the box so that the quarry will have to get under the box to get it. When and if this occurs, the person in concealment at the other end of the line jerks the stick out; the box falls; and he is left with the task of catching the game a second time—inside the box.

Snares

Metal snares may be bought from several companies advertising in the trapping magazines. They are made of

Baited box trap

flexible wire and feature a device which locks the loop after it has been drawn tight.

In my own early days in a rural area, we used to unravel chicken wire and use it for making snares. At that time, hordes of jackrabbits, white hares, and cottontails would nibble at the haystacks and girdle the bark from the trees of the young orchard. We'd bend a tiny loop in the end of 3 feet of straightened chicken wire, form a lasso, and drape it near the bottom of a ditch, along a fenceline, or in a trail in the snow by a young apple tree. Nearly every morning we'd have a strangled jackrabbit, which we skinned and fed to the chickens.

In an emergency, even nylon monofilament line or fishing line may be used similarly. The 10-yard coil of line recommended for the emergency kit will be strong enough for cottontail rabbits, or a coil of light flexible wire may be taken along especially for the purpose.

Well-traveled trails, patches in the snow, and entrances to holes and burrows are all good places to set a snare. The loop should be approximately twice the diameter of the animal and hung so that it drapes over the patch with its center the height of the animal's head. The running end of the snare is led off to some form of anchorage and tied.

The pull of a struggling rabbit will tighten the wire loop, and subsequent twisting will lock it in place. When using nylon or thread line, the same result can be achieved by using a hangman's knot to form the loop. With a nylon monofilament snare, don't use the hangman's knot for the main loop, but rather use it for the small loop through which the running end of the line is threaded to form the lasso loop.

The best anchorage for a snare is a twitch-up, made by bending a flexible sapling and holding it under a forked or notched stick driven into the ground. The snare is tied to the end of this bent sapling, and the loop draped over the trail. When the animal is snared, its struggles free the sapling from beneath the forked stick, and the animal is jerked into the air. This prevents its chewing through a line snare.

In placing a snare over a trail, the more naturally it can be hung from adjacent brush, the more chances it has to succeed. Often these chances can be improved along some narrow spot in the path by casually moving a log into such a position that a natural-looking entering V is created in the foliage. Most game prefer to follow the easiest route and will enter such an unobtrusive passageway. As rabbits, racoons, and other small game move considerably at night, and a snare is less visible after dark, it is likely that the game will be caught after sunset. All care should be used with both traps and snares to see that they are continuously tended, and that caught game doesn't suffer. On leaving an area, all traps and snares, without exception, should be picked up.

Skinning Small Game

To prepare small game for the pot it must be skinned, dressed, cooled, washed, and cut into serving pieces. A young jackrabbit is the easiest small game animal to skin. The job can be done in thirty seconds with no tools—not even a knife.

If you are right-handed, grasp one hind leg between the foot and the hock joint in the left hand. Then completely

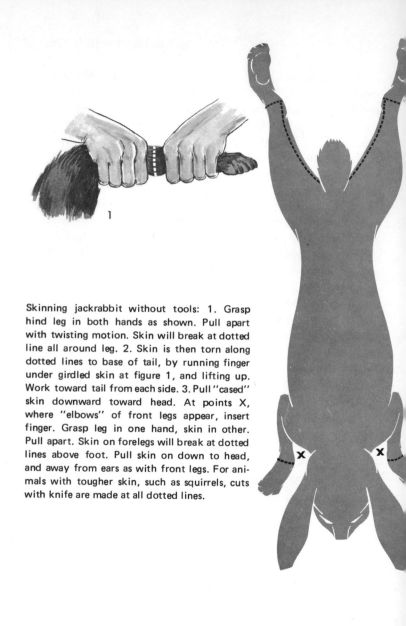

Skinning jackrabbit without tools: 1. Grasp hind leg in both hands as shown. Pull apart with twisting motion. Skin will break at dotted line all around leg. 2. Skin is then torn along dotted lines to base of tail, by running finger under girdled skin at figure 1, and lifting up. Work toward tail from each side. 3. Pull "cased" skin downward toward head. At points X, where "elbows" of front legs appear, insert finger. Grasp leg in one hand, skin in other. Pull apart. Skin on forelegs will break at dotted lines above foot. Pull skin on down to head, and away from ears as with front legs. For animals with tougher skin, such as squirrels, cuts with knife are made at all dotted lines.

circle the leg just above the hock joint with the thumb and index finger of the right hand. The hands, in this position, will be close together. Bring them up before the chest, and pull hard. This breaks the skin of the leg at the hock, in a complete circle, and allows it to be stripped down against the rabbit's thigh. The skin of the opposite leg is pulled up against the body in the same way.

Next, insert a finger into the broken skin at one hip, poke it across the rabbit's back at the root of the tail, and bring the finger out the opposite opening in the skin. Grasp the skin thus held by the finger, and pull hard. This pulls all hide away from the back, strips the hide off the tail, and breaks the skin completely across the rabbit's rear end.

Then turn the rabbit over and grasp the underside of the skin all the way across, at the edge of where it has been broken, and again pull. This strips all skin away from the hind part of the rabbit, except a small patch over the genitals.

With that done, grasp both hind legs in one hand, and pull on the skin, toward the head, with the other. A continuous pull will peel the skin over the shoulders. At this stage, both front legs will be partially skinned, with the hide folding downward toward the feet and showing an elbow of skinned flesh. Poke a finger between the hide and bone at each elbow, grasp the hide with one hand and the leg with the other, and pull apart. This will peel the leg all the way to the foot, where the skin will break off. Each front foot comes out with a "mitten" of fur left on.

Another pull brings the hide down over the head. As at each elbow, a finger may be pushed between skin and rabbit at the base of the ear. A pull between cartilage and skin strips all hide from the ear. A final pull strips all remaining hide from the head, and the job is done.

Many persons are afraid of handling wild rabbits for fear of contracting tularemia. Any rabbit showing signs of logyness or disease should never be touched, although wearing a pair of rubber gloves during skinning is still a good precaution.

Other small game animals are skinned in the same way. When the animal's skin is too tough to break at the legs and rear, cut it with a knife at these points. This means that the skin must be girdled at the two hind hocks, a cut made from these to the tail, and the skin girdled above each front foot.

Dressing Small Game

In dressing any small game, unless the entire hide is wanted for taxidermy, the animal is only skinned to the base of the skull. The head is then twisted away or cut off and left with the discarded hide.

To dress a rabbit or squirrel, place the skinned animal on its back on a flat rock surface, and with a sharp pocketknife make an abdominal cut from the tail to the throat. Also cut through the pelvic bone, separating the hips; and cut through the rib cage, opening it for cleaning. When splitting the pelvis, care should be used not to cut into the genitals and anus. These are girdled in the process, left attached to the internal organs, and pulled with them through the pelvic opening. Finally, wash out any remaining blood or intestinal fluids.

The best time to skin and dress small game is immediately after it has been killed. If the animal has been killed close to camp, cleaning and skinning it immediately is no problem. Where game must be carried for an hour or so before reaching camp, it should be dressed immediately but the skin left on to protect the meat from dirt. The abdominal cut is made as before. Then, grasping the hind legs, whirl the carcass around the head, quite like a sling, giving a jerk at the termination of about the second swing. The viscera will pull free and be thrown clear.

A grouse or other gamebird is cleaned in a similar manner. Girdle the leg skin with a knife above the hocks; pull off the skin, girdle the tail and anus; cut an abdominal incision from tail to rib cage; and pull the insides free. Finally, sever the neck and pull the windpipe from the body cavity in the same operation; cut off the legs and wings at the hocks and elbows.

If birds must be carried for some time before reaching camp, they should be cleaned without removing the feathers. A simple way is to cut fully across the abdominal wall just ahead of the pelvic bones, so the intestines droop out. Then, holding the bird by the wings, make a practice shot for the sling. Remnants may be finished off with the knife and fingers.

Any game, large or small, should be cooled thoroughly before cooking. Body heat gives a nauseating flavor to meat, which, if eaten, induces diarrhea. Grouse may be eaten the same day, once they are thoroughly cooled. Rabbits and squirrels should be hung for one to four days before cooking. With any tough animal, this also breaks down the muscle fibers and helps to tenderize the meat.

A good way of cooling small game, and removing any traces of blood at the same time, is to soak the meat in a pan of salt water. Small game may be soaked a full day in cold salt water without damage, then hung where air will circulate or placed in a camp cooler.

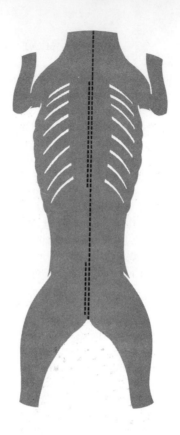

Dressing small game such as rabbits and squirrels, after skinning. As shown in this belly view, make incision all the way from anal vent to throat. Split pelvis and rib-cage, shown by double dotted lines. Girdle around genitals and anus, leaving these attached to viscera. Pelvis and chest is best cut by placing strong knife blade under bones, and lifting upward. With incision complete from tail to throat, insides may be pulled free with fingers, or flung out by throwing carcass around head and jerking. Remaining blood is wiped out, or washed with clean water.

162

Cooking Small Game

Anyone who takes to the hills should know the fundamentals of cooking and a few basic recipes. Small game can be prepared in camp in various ways, from the primitive to the elaborate, depending on time, equipment, ingredients, and the skill of the cook.

The simplest method of cooking a grouse, squirrel, or rabbit is to roast it at the end of a stick held over the fire. This takes time and patience, and the meat must be constantly turned to prevent scorching. It helps if strips of bacon are attached to the game to baste it. Otherwise, the meat has a tendency to dry out on the outside and remain raw within.

Another method is to roast the game spitted on a wire stretched taut between two stakes driven into the ground on opposite sides of the fire. The position of the game over the fire may be regulated by sliding it back and forth, and it may be turned at times with a stick and propped with a forked branch so that all sides cook evenly.

A simple way of preparing small game is to boil the meat, after it has been cut up, in a cooking pot. The addition of a single vegetable, such as a carrot, onion, or potato, improves the dish considerably and turns the recipe in the direction of a full-fledged stew.

Frying is basically a poor form of cooking, as it coats food with hard-to-digest fats. However, frying is a quick way for the outdoorsman to prepare food, and as he is usually active and in good health, his digestion will not suffer. Also, modern cooking oils have increased the digestibility of fried food, and if only a part of the meal is fried, the normal person should have no difficulty.

To fry small game or birds, simply cut into serving pieces and place in a skillet containing butter, bacon fat, or cooking oil hot enough to sizzle. The pieces of meat should be as uniform in size as possible. They should be left in the hot fat only a couple of minutes to sear, then turned over and seared on the opposite side. This seals the surfaces and retains the inside juices.

With both sides seared, the skillet should be covered with a lid and cooked over less heat to prevent burning the meat. The tighter the lid the better, as this helps save the moisture steaming up, causing it to baste the meat as it cooks. Ten to fifteen minutes is enough for grouse and rabbit.

The best utensil for frying is a heavy Dutch oven. It keeps the heat constant, will cook after the fire lowers, and has a seal sufficiently tight to save most of the moisture.

Here's one of the choicest recipes for grouse, if a Dutch oven is available: Split the bird into halves with an ax, through the sternum, and sauté in 1/8th pound of sizzing butter. Sear quickly on both sides, then cook slowly until the halves are golden brown. Salt and pepper to taste. One grouse per person makes a fine serving.

After learning the simplest methods of roasting, frying, and boiling camp meat, you will want to graduate to more difficult and better tasting recipes. Here are some tested recipes for small game:

FRIED SQUIRREL

Soak the cut-up pieces in salt water overnight, and drain. If the squirrel is tough (hide will come off the same way), parboil pieces for 10 minutes. This means simply to boil for 10 minutes, throw the water away and save the squirrel.

Roll pieces in flour. Fry in butter, bacon fat, or cooking oil until tender.

FRIED RABBIT

Prepare as for squirrel, except add 2 tablespoons vinegar to the soaking water, parboil in salt water, and save the broth. After rabbit pieces are fried until tender, add 2 tablespoons flour to the skillet, stirring until it browns. Add broth, stirring constantly until brown sauce boils. Sauce may be poured over pieces, or used as gravy for slices of bread. Similar brown sauce may be made for fried squirrel.

FRIED GROUSE

Soak overnight in salt water. Dredge pieces in flour containing salt and pepper. Dip into slightly beaten egg. Fry in deep fat, in Dutch oven, for 7 minutes.

FRICASSEED GROUSE

Rub soaked and drained pieces with salt and pepper. Brown in hot fat in Dutch oven. Add 2 cups of water, cover, and simmer slowly until grouse is tender. Remove pieces. Thicken remainder with a little flour and cook until smooth, after adding bay leaf and celery seasoning. Serve over meat or bread slices.

SQUIRREL STEW

Put serving pieces in saucepan together with 1/2-cup vinegar, 1 teaspoonful mixed spices, 1 diced onion, and 6 celery leaves. Cover with water. Let stand 3 hours. Drain and place in Dutch oven. Brown pieces. Salt and pepper. Add 2 diced onions and 2 diced carrots. Cover with water. Put on cover and cook slowly until tender. Thicken broth with flour to consistency of thick cream, and serve with watercress salad.

RABBIT PIE

Cover serving pieces with boiling water. Add onion, bacon, salt, and pepper. Cover Dutch oven and simmer until meat is tender. Thicken broth with flour in ratio of 2 tablespoonfuls to each cup of liquid, and pour over rabbit. Make thick dough of ready-mix biscuit flour. Pat into sheet 1/4-inch thick. Cut slits for steam to escape. Place over contents in Dutch oven and cook in hot coals for 30 minutes.

GROUSE WITH DUMPLINGS

Put serving pieces in saucepan. Cover with boiling water. Add salt and pepper and simmer until meat is tender. Prepare dumpling dough with 2 cups flour, 4 teaspoonfuls baking powder, 2 tablespoonfuls shortening, 1 teaspoonful salt, and canned milk to thicken. Mix flour, salt, and baking powder. Add shortening to mixture by cutting it in with 2 knives. Add canned milk until a thick batter results. Drop batter, a teaspoonful at a time, into the boiling broth with grouse. Cover Dutch oven and boil 12 minutes. Serve at once.

GO-LIGHT STEW

Cube the meat into 1-inch cubes. Cube 1 raw potato into similar size. Cut 1 onion into sections, and slice 1 carrot

into 1/2-inch slices. Mix and season with salt, pepper, and
savory salt. Wrap the contents into two thicknesses of foil,
bend edges over to make a good seal, and cook in hot coals
for 20 to 30 minutes. Foil isn't large or strong enough to
cook more than one serving at a time. The above proportions serve one.

Preparing Big Game

The enjoyment of the outdoors is often connected with
the sport of hunting big game, and many of the best camp
dishes are made of those portions of a game animal which
can't be successfully packed out of the hills but in order to
be utilized at all must be served at camp.

Deer, elk, and moose liver is good to eat; antelope and
caribou liver isn't so good; and bear liver should not be
eaten. The best way to prepare liver is to soak it in cold salt
water overnight, cut into strips half-inch thick, and fry in
butter or bacon grease with sliced onions. It should be
served piping hot.

The heart of deer, elk, antelope, moose, and caribou (except during the rutting season) all make fine eating. Heart
may be sliced half-inch thick, dredged in flour, and slow-
fried until done; or baked with dressing in a Dutch oven. A
good dressing is made of 2 cups stale bread cubes, half a
teaspoonful chopped watercress if available, 2 tablespoonfuls melted butter, salt, pepper, dried sage, 3 tablespoonfuls
diced celery, 1 teaspoonful chopped onion, 2 teaspoonfuls
poultry seasoning, and water or broth enough to make the
dressing pack well. The heart is stuffed with this dressing,
and a ring of it is laid around the meat in the Dutch oven.

The oven should be prepared with 2 tablespoonfuls melted butter and 1 cup water, to prevent sticking. Cook until tender; baste occasionally.

The choicest cut of an elk or moose, the tenderloin, is often wasted, owing to the difficulty of cutting up the huge quarters and transporting them. Tenderloin of elk or moose should be immediately cut out in a continuous strip, cooled overnight, and eaten at camp. A fine way of preparing it is to cut the tenderloin into pieces 1-inch thick, across the grain, and saute in butter in the Dutch oven. Add salt and pepper to taste after cooking.

HUNTER'S STEW

One of the most famous of all camp meats is hunter's stew. This, too, may be built around a discarded cut of big-game meat. There is no better meat for a stew than that section of the neck of an elk, just behind the ears, cut in small chunks half the size of a fist. Pieces of bone may or may not be included. The meat pieces are cooled at camp overnight in salt water. Next, the pieces are put in a large kettle or Dutch oven, and slow-boiled for two or three hours over the campfire. The broth from the boiling meat is occasionally skimmed. The kettle should remain covered.

With the meat nearly done, vegetables are added. The best vegetables are carrots, onions, cabbage, beans, and potatoes. However, any vegetables available at camp, and in any combination, may be used for a hunter's stew. They should be added according to the length of time it takes to cook them. That is, any dried or quick-soaked beans or peas should be added first, then carrots, cabbage, onions, and potatoes. The main idea is to have all ingredients tender at about the same time.

Lastly, a can of condensed tomato soup should be added. If tomato soup isn't available, a small can of stewed tomatoes, may be substituted. Add salt, pepper, and savory salt just before serving.

The virtues of a hunter's stew are that the longer you cook it the better it gets, and it may be reheated several times until it is all used.

10

Fish for the Pan

In addition to natural baits that may be found on the spot, or artificial lures that may be carried in the duffel, an outdoorsman can catch fish for the pan with emergency lures made in the outdoors with nothing except meager equipment, lots of imagination, and a modest degree of skill. Everyone going into wilderness country should, in case of emergency, have some knowledge of how to make such lures.

Shirt-Tail Flies

A logical place to start is with artificial flies, because both trout and bass are widely spread throughout North America and both take artificial flies. Moreover, artificial flies will take other species of fish as well, and the material for making them can be found *anywhere.* The necessary hooks, thread, and line weigh next to nothing and are handily taken along. It's a broad statement to make, but give me a hook, a yard of thread, and some nylon leader material and I can make an artificial fly, regardless of the situation, which will take trout.

My interest in emergency flies began many years ago in the Cassiars of British Columbia, where Doc Ernie Wygant and I were fishing for Arctic grayling at the inlet of Cry Lake. No matter what fly we put on, those beauties would nail it. As an experiment, Doc took twelve flies out of his book and laid them on the canoe seat. These flies ranged in size and variety from a #16 Red Ant to a hulking #6 wet nymph. We tied on those twelve flies, alternately, one fly for one cast, then we'd change. We even took turns casting. We caught twelve of the grayling feeding in the current of the inlet in twelve casts, with twelve separate flies.

"Doc," I said, "I believe if anyone was caught up here in an emergency, he could catch those fish on anything."

This gave me an idea. I was wearing a blue woolen shirt at the time. I took my hunting knife and cut off a worm-like strip from the tail of the shirt, threaded it onto a bare fly hook, and cast. On the second cast I hooked a grayling! Since then, experimenting with creations which could be used for survival situations, I have made and tested trout flies of almost anything you can name.

The accompanying photo shows examples of flies I have tied with odd scraps of material:

1. A fly made from a single grouse feather, plus a strip of aluminum foil used to wrap camera film. The tail is of

Emergency flies fashioned on the spot from materials found in the outdoors. All have been tested by the author and have proved to be excellent trout-takers. See accompanying text for tying details.

fibers from the grouse feather. Aluminum was wrapped on as a body. Hackle is remainder of feather.

2. This streamer fly was made of nothing more than a string of cloth cut from my red shirttail and hairs cut with a hunting knife from my chest.

3. This fly is similar to No. 1, except it was made from one domestic hen feather. A few fibers were tied on for the tail. Other fibers off the butt end were bunched together, rolled around the hook into a rough body, and wound with thread. Hackle was made from the tip end of the soft feather.

4. This fly was created out of nothing more sophisticated than a piece of a cloth shoelace, a length of white twine, and some deer hair picked up at the campsite. The lace, wound on, formed the body. The twine made the body ribs. The deer hairs were tied on as a streamer.

5. This fly was tied of several elk hairs and a strand of burlap unraveled from a potato sack. The strand was wound onto a 4X-shank hook. The hairs were tied on at the front end as a streamer. In the water, this material looked extremely natural. The burlap, after wetting, gave the fly a lifelike, translucent body like that of a real insect. In the water, the brownish elk hair had just the right coloration to resemble wings, and could be made to pulse back and forth just like the wings of a dying bug. The finished creation looked so good, I promptly gave it a name—Ormond's Bull-'N-Burlap Fly—and started fishing with it. The trout on the Yellowstone River really nailed it!

Enthused with the results, I created similar Buck-'N-Burlap flies out of burlap and deer hair, and Bear-N-Burlap flies with the streamer hairs of three separate species of bruins—all with the idea of using materials found in widely scattered areas.

Under extreme necessity, all these flies and dozens more like them can be tied out of nothing more than materials at hand, with no vise, bobbin, varnish, or wax. You need only a hook, a yard of sewing thread, and something that looks like fur or feathers. Hooks may be stuck into the tip end of a sharpened sapling in place of a vise, or simply held in the hand. Without varnish and wax, a camp-made fly will soon unravel and wear out. By then it will have served its purpose.

Emergency Lures

Other types of emergency lures can be made for other types of fishing. As an example, a neighbor boy had so

How to make a plastic-spoon wobbler: Obtain a red or yellow plastic spoon (1) and cut off the handle by carefully notching it at the points shown (2). Drill a hole at each end by twisting the point of a knife blade back and forth (3), but be careful not to shatter the plastic. Attach a snap swivel at the front, if one is available, and either a single or a treble hook at the rear (4). If you lack a snap swivel, tie the line directly to the spoon.

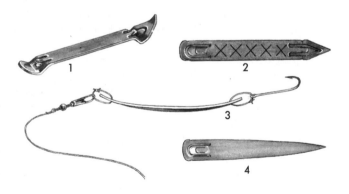

How to make a trolling spoon from a beer-can opener: Take an ordinary beer-can opener (1) and pound it flat with an ax or hammer. Also hammer it along center X's to make it slightly concave (2). Then pound it into a mild crescent shape (3) to give it a fluttering action in the water, and attach monofilament loops for line and hook. If a file is available, opener can be tapered at end to give a minnow-like shape (4).

much success with wobblers he had made out of pop-bottle caps that he considered making them commercially. He hammered the caps flat into various shapes, threaded a barrel-swivel into a hole at each end, and attached a trailing hook to the lower swivel. He removed the cork from the

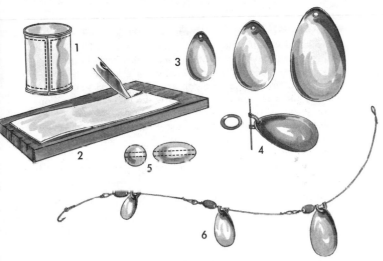

How to make a multiple-blade trolling spinner: (1) Cut a tin can along dotted lines, lay it flat on a wooden surface (2) and cut out blades in graduating sizes from 1 to 2 inches (3). Pound blades in center with a rock until they are slightly concave, and punch holes. (4) Cut ellipse-shaped clevices from tin. These, when folded in half, must fit through holes in blade. (5) Shape wooden beads, which help blades to rotate freely, from small branches and burn out centers with a hot wire. (6) Assemble blades, clevices, and beads on lengths of fine wire 5 to 8 inches long. Tie loops for line and hook.

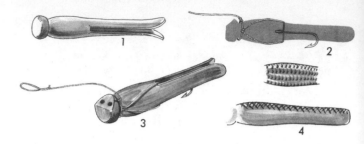

How to make a clothespin bass plug: (1) Start with an old-fashioned wooden clothespin. (2) Flatten top of knob and burn a small dent at partition center with hot wire to keep hook from slipping. Tie hook between prongs with monofilament, bringing it from top and bottom and knotting it along the side. Then loop it around the neck (3) and tie on top of plug. Burn eyes into head. Plug should be charred along top to simulate shading, and "scales" can be added by chipping lightly with a knife blade (4).

underside, leaving brass on one side and the painted lettering on the other.

I have seen fish caught with a spinner made from the bowl of a plastic spoon, a wobbler made from a metal beer-can opener, and a multiple-blade trolling spinner made from a tin can. It is the pride of oldtimers to be able to whittle a wooden plug from a clothespin, attach a hook, paint it with fingernail enamel, and catch bass with it.

For anyone who must travel light in wilderness country, it is wise to include in the minimum tackle the makings of emergency lures—hooks, a few swivels, a spool of thread, and a coil of nylon leader.

Emergency Tackle

Emergency lures not only can be made on the spot, but fished with a minimum of tackle. Spoons and wobblers may be used with nothing except a length of line attached. The line may be loosely coiled near the water's edge; a length held in the hand and swung around the head like a sling; the lure thrown into a river pool or into a lake, and hand-lined in rapidly enough to make it wobble.

Another method is to wrap the line around the bottom edge of a coffee can and hold the can by the other edge. I know an old river hermit who swears he invented spincasting by this trick. He even nailed a short handle to the bottom of a pound coffee can and tied the end of his line to the handle. Next, he wound the line around the can and affixed his bait and sinker to the end. Then, holding the handle in his left hand, he threw the lure with his right. The line, of course, would peel off the can like monofilament off a spinning reel, to be wound on again as he retrieved.

If you have a reel and line but your rod has been broken, you can make a temporary rod of a long willow, alder, or even a tiny, dry jack pine. The reel can be wound onto the butt end with fishing line, cord, or a shoelace. Guides may be cut off the damaged rod and wound on in the same fashion. If no guides are available, you can make them from a couple of paper clips, pot bails, or even tiny twigs that angle abruptly. Tie one at the rod tip and the other midway on the rod.

Again, with only a line, hook, and some natural bait located on the spot, you can still get fish for the pan by setting a bait overnight. The lure may be tossed into a river or lake and the other end of the line tied to a springy bush. If, during the night, a fish gobbles the bait and becomes hooked, the springiness of the bush keeps it from breaking the line.

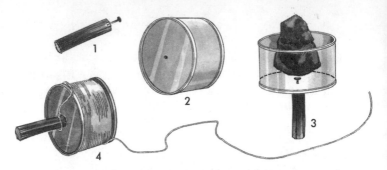

How to make a coffee-can spinning reel: The handle is a short piece of stick (1) and the spool an ordinary coffee can (2). Drive a nail a quarter of the way into the end of the handle, then remove it and punch a hole in the bottom of the can. Stand handle on the ground and with a rock drive nail through hole in can into hole in handle (3). Tie end of fishing line to handle and wind it around can (4). Holding reel in left hand, throw lure and line with right so line "spins" off

Snagging game fish is usually against the law in most areas, though often trash fish may be snagged. However, in an emergency, most people would consider snagging a fish to prevent starvation the lesser of two evils. With patience, fish can be snagged in pools and eddies of a stream. Tie several hooks to a line about 6 inches apart, and tie a sinker—a nail or small pebble which can be half-hitched several times—to the end of the line. Then toss or lower the rig into a pool and leave it on the bottom until you see a fish cross above it. An upward jerk usually snags him.

A trick to get a lure well out into a stream when no rod is available is to put the lure on a wooden chip, let it float with the current from above the desired spot, then jerk the lure off the chip. Another stunt, when no thread is available to tie an emergency fly, is to unravel the seam of a pants' cuff and use the thread.

If you have no fish hook, a usable hook may be made from a length of tough stick such as a thorn. Taper the stick at both ends and sharpen the ends to points. For average-sized fish, the hook should be about 1½ inches long. Next, cut a groove exactly at the center, so that the leader can be tied snugly around the stick. Push the hook into the mouth of a grasshopper or work it carefully into the length of a worm so just a point protrudes. When a fish bites, allow it to swallow the bait, then jerk the line quickly but not too hard. This pulls the end of the stick into the flesh of the fish's mouth, tilting it so it lodges crosswise in the mouth. Such a hook will hold sufficiently long for a small fish to be landed.

Cleaning Fish

Since gamefish represent an important part of the wilderness diet, and since the farther from civilization one gets the easier fish are to catch, every outdoorsman should know how to clean them and at least a few basic ways of preparing them. The easiest way to clean a small fish is first to slit the abdominal wall from the anal vent to the apex of the angle formed by the cartilage under the gills. This V of hard cartilage will join, by a thin membrane, a larger V—the lower jaw. A second cut should be made, crosswise, through the membrane between these two V's, and forward until the knife severs this lower V cartilage loose from the lower jaw. With this cut made, the lower jaw will be left intact with the fish's head, as will the outer gill plates. The V of cartilage should then be grasped with the fingers of one hand, and the fish's lower jaw with the other.

By pulling the cartilage and lower jaw apart, the gills, pectoral fins, and intestines will be stripped free. Occasionally the gills will fail to pull free at their upper edge, where they join the spine. Pinching them at this junction with the thumb and index finger will break them off, after which the stripping motion is continued.

With the insides pulled out, the layer of blood lying against the spine is scraped out with the thumbnail. A small notch is cut and the anus removed, and the fish is washed in cold water to complete the job. The head may be left on or removed. Fish with heavy scales should be scaled before cleaning with a sharp knife, scraping from the tail toward the head. If the fish is fresh, the scales will come off easily. Older fish are more difficult to scale.

No-Utensil Cooking

Perhaps the simplest, quickest way of preparing trout and other small fish is to rub them with salt, skewer each fish on a peeled hardwood stick, and cook them before the hot coals of a fire. Sharpen the bottom end of the stick and shove it into the ground at an angle, so the fish is held at an appropriate distance over the heat.

Another fine way of preparing fish with a minimum of utensils is to roll them in a double thickness of tin or aluminum foil and cook them in the hot coals of a diminishing fire. The whole fish, sections, or filets are first salted and peppered, and a tablespoon of butter, if available, is spread along the full length of the fish. The foil is rolled and placed in the fire so that no joints are on the bottom, or else the butter will run out as it melts. Cooking time is twenty minutes for 10- to 12-inch fish.

Finally, when no cooking utensils are available, a simple way of preparing fish is to "plank" them. First filet the fish, or split them into halves with the skin left on. Then prepare a plank of wood by smoothing one side of a slab cut from a log. Pine isn't a good wood for this, as it gives a strong flavor to the cooked fish. Grease the plank well with butter or bacon fat and place the filet skin side down on the plank and fasten it solidly by nailing or tacking the upper edge of the skin. Prop the plank at a steep angle before the fire and allow the fish to bake. If possible, drape strips of bacon over the fish as it cooks, as this bastes the meat and keeps it from burning.

If no timber is available for a plank, a flat slab of rock may be substituted. This will have to be used at a milder angle, since it will be impossible to fasten the filet to the rock.

Planked fish may be salted either before or after cooking. Careless cooking, or not tending the fire, can easily result in a ruined fish. With some cooks, it's better to throw away the fish and eat the plank.

Frying Fish

Small, pan-sized fish may be fried whole. The butter or fat should be hot enough to sing when they are placed in the pan. The fish are cooked on one side until partly done, turned over, then slowly cooked until done with a lid on the skillet. Some prefer to salt the fish first, others just before eating. Freshly caught fish will curl up when fried.

To avoid this, open the fish its full length and lay the halves, which remain joined along the dorsal side, flat in the pan.

Another fine way to fry small fish is first to roll them in flour which has been salted and peppered. Flouring the fish helps prevent burning them.

Larger fish must be cut into pieces before frying. These pieces may be several inches long, of steak thickness, and are made by cutting across the fish. Salmon and steelhead are especially good when cut this way, and fried or sautéed in butter.

If a Dutch oven is available at camp, one of the finest ways of cooking fish is to fry them whole, in 1/8-pound of butter, for eighteen minutes (in a hot bed of coals) without removing the lid. This will cook them through without the necessity of turning them, and the tight lid of the oven holds in all juices and flavor. One of the best meals my wife and I have ever eaten was a half-dozen golden trout cooked this way by the outfitter, just after we'd got into camp from an all-day horseback ride in a rainstorm.

Fileting

Fileting is another fine way of preparing larger fish. To filet a fish, lay it on its side on a flat surface and girdle it all around with a sharp knife at points just ahead of the tail and just behind the pectoral fins and gill coverings. Then make another cut lengthwise along the backbone, connecting these two cuts. Next, beginning at the back, cut the halves of flesh away from the ribs and spine. The shaving-like cuts are made just over the bones, all the way down to

How to filet a fish: First, girdle fish with a sharp knife just ahead of the tail. Cut down the spine outside the ribs on each side and girdle around behind the gills. Then peel off filet in one piece, leaving entire skeleton of fish intact.

the abdominal incision, and the flesh is lifted away. The result is two halves of meat, leaving the fish's skeleton intact. All fins are cut away from the halves, which may then be cooked as is, or again cut into smaller filets.

183

During hot weather, fish in some waters have a strong or gamey taste. This taste is most pronounced in the skin and cartilege surrounding the fins. Fileting is a fine way to cook such fish, but it is advisable to skin them first to remove the gamey taste. A fish is skinned after the two girdling cuts and the cut along the spine have been made. A corner of skin is cut away until it can be grasped in the fingers. Then a hard pull will strip off the skin on some species. With others, grip the skin with a pair of pliers and pull hard, while holding the fish down with the other hand.

Fileting, incidentally, is the best way to prepare fresh sturgeon. The flesh is first sliced into sections by cutting across the fish. These sections should be 4 inches long. Each section is then cut into filets by cutting lengthwise along these chunks to get rectangular pieces 1-inch wide, 4 inches long, and 5/8-inch thick. These filets are then cut free of any fat, which in a sturgeon is the red, stringy meat, and slow-fried in melted butter. Allow forty-five minutes for the filets to cook through and turn golden in color. There is no better delicacy.

Baked Fish

Fish may also be baked at camp in a Dutch oven, or by using two "dripping-pans," one inverted over the other. If the fish is not too large, it is baked whole. Salt and pepper before cooking, and lay strips of bacon, if available, over the top to baste as it cooks. Baked fish is excellent with tomato sauce. Ten minutes before the fish is done, pour a can of condensed tomato soup over it and cook until the soup thickens.

Another way of preparing baked fish is to fill the body cavity, and make a ring around the fish, with poultry dressing. A good dressing is the one suggested for grouse: dry bread crumbs to which several spoonfuls of raisins have been added.

Leftover fish which has been fried or baked can be made into chowder; or it can be made into a fishloaf. Here is a good recipe for fishloaf:

FISHLOAF

Two cups flaked fish. 2 well-beaten eggs. 2 tablespoons melted butter or margarine. ½-cup cornmeal. ¼-cup bread or cracker crumbs. ½-cup canned milk. Combine the fish, eggs, butter, cornmeal, and crumbs. Add milk. Season to taste. Mix lightly with two forks. Form into loaf and bake for 20 minutes in a well-greased Dutch oven. Thicken condensed tomato soup into heavy sauce and pour over baked fishloaf.

Smoked Fish

Often in wilderness country you will be confronted with the problem of having caught a number of large fish which you cannot eat before they spoil. Such a situation is ideal for smoking fish.

The outdoorsman can build several types of smokehouses with material available on the spot. The Indians in the Far North, for example, often make smokehouses of large strips of birch and aspen bark shaped into a small wigwam. Racks of green alders are erected inside, on which the fish are laid.

Smokehouse of green alders or willows laid across two cross-bars which are supported by four stakes. Canvas draped around rack contains smoke from small smudge fire just inside edge.

The smokehouse is erected on a cutbank, and a small fire is built below. The smoke is piped from the fire to the house by means of a trench dug up the side of the cutbank and covered with green bark sections, like shingles, over which dirt has been placed.

One of the simplest temporary smokehouses consists of a rack of green alder saplings 2 to 3 feet high wrapped in a canvas tarp, with a tiny smudge of fire kept going just inside one edge. With this arrangement, the canvas can be kept open enough at the top to provide just enough draft to keep the smoke rising inside. Such a simple house requires almost constant attention to see that the fire doesn't blaze up.

A better smokehouse can be made of two lengths of stovepipe and a large pasteboard carton. The alder frame is made of four uprights. To these, crossbars of alder are tied or nailed, and enough green alder sticks are laid across these crossbars to make a platform. These sticks for the platform should be laid about 1 inch apart. As the fish smokes and cooks, it softens, and will drop through if

A more elaborate smokehouse, also of green alders, but having several levels and covered with a cardboard carton. Stovepipe (bottom) funnels smoke from smudge fire built in rock cairn.

the sticks are too far apart. Two such shelves will hold a large catch of fish.

The "house" is simply the large carton turned upside-down over the framework. A small draft hole in the top of the box is made by cutting three sides of a rectangle, leaving it hinged on one side so the draft can be regulated.

The lengths of stovepipe are used to pipe the smoke from the fire up the cutbank and into the bottom of the smokehouse. The fire itself is built in a small rock cairn several feet down the cutbank. The fire may be covered with green bark strips or foil so that the smoke leads into the pipe. Covering the cairn also keeps the fire from blazing up too much. A small pit can be dug in sandy ground if no rocks are available for making a cairn.

To start the smoking process, clean the fish and soak them overnight in a strong solution of salt water. Wipe them dry and lay them on the shelves of the alder rack. Invert the carton over the framework and build the fire. Once the fire is started, it is fed with green wood, which will smoke continuously.

Apple wood is one of the best for smoking fish but is seldom available in the woods. Green aspen is nearly as good and is usually found in wilderness country where enough fish for smoking purposes are apt to be caught. Small trees of 4 to 6 inches in diameter are fine. Cut these into lengths which will fit into the cairn or pit and split them into quarters. Such green aspen logs will burn if just enough dry twigs and small branches are periodically added to keep a fire going. It takes a bit more fire to burn smaller, unsplit branches, which are also fine for the purpose. If the fire can be tended only a few hours each day, it can be allowed to go out overnight and started again the following day.

It takes seven hours or more to smoke fish properly, depending on their size. When the fish become brown, wrinkled, and look like old moccasins, they are usually done. They may be tasted occasionally to check on the progress.

11

Edible Plants

North America's inventory of cultivated plants has traditionally been so extensive that we are unaware of the many nutritive wild plants that can sustain the human organism. There is hardly an area of the entire continent where some of these edible plants are not found, and the outdoorsman should be able to recognize them and know how to use them as emergency foods.

In traveling over the more remote areas, there won't be many occasions when a total dependence on edible plants will be necessary. Exceptions to this generality are such misfortunes as being lost from a camp or source of supplies, being in an airplant crash over wilderness country, or being capsized with a boat on inland waterways. It is comforting to know that in such emergencies food in some form lies all about. It should be added assurance to realize that an entire race of people, the early American Indians, thrived on the edible plants that nature provides.

In changing from accustomed foods to wild edible plants, some judgment should be used. In the main, it is best to make as gradual a change as the situation will permit. That is, one should not, if possible, change abruptly to a complete diet of wild plants.

When for any reason the supply of domestic food runs low, the remainder should be rationed to last as long as possible, and complementing amounts of wild edible plants and fruits should be added. This can usually be done, except in dire emergencies, by simple forethought and planning.

Mixing the remaining food gradually with the wild plants and berries which nature provides accomplishes several vital purposes. First, the change to strange, less palatable foods is made more easily. Secondly, there is less shock to the digestive system. Some wild foods tend to act as emetics or cathartics; but by gradually introducing them into the system, the body will accommodate them without trouble. Perhaps even more important, if by mistake one happens to eat a toxic plant, a small amount is far less apt to cause trouble than a full portion.

If you accidentally eat a wild food that is toxic, the best remedy is to get it out of your system as fast as possible. This is accomplished by vomiting. If soda or dry mustard is available in the grub box, quantities of either diluted with warm water and drunk to excess will generally induce vomiting. Perhaps the simplest way is to drink an excess of warm water and poke a finger down your gullet.

Another good procedure to follow when you are thrown upon edible plants and fruits for survival is to eat small amounts of wild plants as they are found. This, too, helps the system to adjust. As an example, if you are moving through wild berry country, it's better to pick and eat the fruit as you travel rather than to sit in one place and eat until you are full. Of course, if you come upon a food supply in one area and suspect that other areas are sparse, you should take a quantity of food along. You can carry edible roots and wild greens in your pack and cook them at night over the campfire. Cooked tubers and roots are temporarily preserved and may be carried until a new supply is found. Just as you mark a spot in strange country until you find a new landmark, so you should mark areas of edible plants and fruits, preferably on a field-made map, until a new supply can be reached.

Emergency Foods

When traveling in wilderness country, the gradual change from an accustomed food supply to wild foods can be accomplished more easily if you always carry some form of emergency food. Dehydrated fruit, carried in a plastic refrigerator-bag to keep it clean, is a nourishing emergency food. Dehydrated soup, assuming there is anything to cook it in, is another. A half-pound package of raisins or chocolate candy bars are good emergency foods for short trips.

Pinole

The ideal emergency food should be light, dry, and contain as much energy in proportion to its weight as possible. One of the very best is pinole. It is easily made, is indestructible, won't spoil, and has great food value for its weight.

A pound bag of pinole will, under dire necessity, sustain a person for a week. If even small amounts of wild fruit, plants, and fish or small game can be added, it will keep one going for several weeks if necessary. The simplest form of pinole is parched corn. With a small bag of this food, Indians have crossed vast regions of wilderness country with nothing else save what they could glean from the land.

A more palatable form of pinole is made with a combination of kernel corn and brown sugar. Spread a pint of dry, sweet garden corn in a shallow cake pan and place in a hot oven (about 350 degrees), which will parch the corn without burning it. When the corn is a mild brown all over, sprinkle two tablespoonfuls of brown sugar evenly over the top, and heat again until the sugar just begins to melt. Cool the mixture and grind it in a home food-grinder.

The pinole should be put in a plastic refrigerator-bag, which in turn is sewed into a small canvas bag. The double bag will protect the contents and can be stored anywhere in the duffel without spilling.

When it is necessary to use this food in an emergency, small amounts totaling two tablespoonfuls are placed in the mouth and washed down with drinking water. This meager portion, supplemented by a few handfuls of wild fruit, will keep a person going all day. The corn, soaked to bulk by the water in the stomach, gives the sensation of at least a degree of fullness.

Threshed Wheat

Another simple concentrated food is threshed wheat. Dry wheat kernels, which can be carried in a pocket or small bag, will never spoil, have lots of food value for their bulk, and are pleasant to nibble on. A pound of wheat kernels will sustain life for a week, in an emergency. They are easily obtained from farmers or stock-feed stores in agricultural areas. Make sure that such wheat has not been treated chemically, but is the kind that has been stored as food. A fair substitute for threshed wheat is cracked wheat, which is put up as a bulk cereal.

Edible Plants

Arrowhead

Sometimes known as arrowleaf because of the pointed shape of the leaves, arrowhead is an aquatic plant whose leaves reach the surface of the water. It is found in the wetlands and swamp areas from central Canada to the Gulf of Mexico. The root, a starchy vegetable, is edible and may be prepared by boiling or roasting.

Barrel Cactus

This formidable-looking plant grows in desert regions. Shaped like a watermelon, it has a spiny surface and reaches a height of approximately 2 feet. The plant may be broken open with an ax or heavy knife for the moist pulp inside, which can be eaten or chewed for the moisture it contains.

Burdock

Widely distributed in the United States and Canada, this plant is regarded in agrarian areas as nothing but a weed and a nuisance. The leaves resemble rhubarb leaves and grow on long tough stems. The plant grows from 3 to 7 feet in height, and blooms with numerous hooked flower heads. It is simple to locate burdock in an area if any livestock are near, as the hooked flowers cling to the wool of domestic sheep and the manes and tails of horses. The roots of burdock are edible in their first year, as are the young shoots. The roots are either boiled or roasted, and the young shoots may be boiled and salted as greens.

Camas

A plant of the lily family occurring in the Northwest, camas, or quamash, grows with slender dark-green stems and has blue blossoms. Adult camas have bulbs like small onions, and these bulbs are edible. Eaten raw, they have a flavor similar to a turnip. Before the Indians were driven from the prairies, they would dig whole fields for the camas bulbs and dry them. They were a staple of the Indian diet. The little railroad settlement of Camas, Idaho, was named after this plant. The western camas should not be confused with the death camass, which is poisonous and occurs in all the western states and most of the Southwest. The flowers of the death camass are yellow-white and grow in clusters.

Cattails

Often called tule, this plant is one of the family of bullrushes. It is found throughout temperate North America and reaches into southern Canada. It occurs both in freshwater and saltwater marshes, alongside ponds and quiet streams. Cattails grow from 3 to 8 feet high, and are common to waterfowl country. The name comes from the compacted seed-aggregations at the end of the long stem, which resemble a cat's tail. The edible portion is the tuberous root, which may be cooked as a starchy vegetable or in vegetable soup.

Century Plant

A member of the cactus family, this plant is widely scattered over the desert areas of the Southwest. The spiny plant grows to a height of 2 feet or more at the base, with a long pole-like stem carrying the bloom. The spike-like spines may be chopped away, leaving a pulpy base which looks like an overgrown pineapple. This may be roasted or boiled as one would prepare squash. The century plant played an important role in the southwestern Indians' long war with the whites. While the white soldiers had to extend their food lines wherever they chased the Indians, the red warriors lived to a large extent off these plants. Squaws would casually go on ahead, over the slow lines of retreat, roast great quantities of the plant in huge pits, and have food for the warriors when they arrived.

Chicory

Also known as succory, chicory was introduced from Europe into the eastern part of the United States and Canada. Its root is often used as a coffee substitute or to adulterate coffee. The root may also be used as a herb.

Chokecherry

Large alder-like shrubs often growing to well over the height of a man, chokecherry bushes bloom with long, tapering blossom-stems having numerous small, white blossoms. These blossoms are succeeded by tapering clusters of red berries which turn nearly black when completely ripe. The fruit is well named. The first cherries you eat pucker your mouth so that it is difficult to breathe without whistling a concerto. You will soon get used to this extreme tartness, however, and will find the fruit pleasant to nibble on. Each fruit has a large stone. There is no better jelly than chokecherry jelly, which is especially fine to garnish the meat of waterfowl. Chokecherry juice won't jell of itself, but must be added to apple juice. The pectin which apple juice contains will cause the combination to set. Chokecherry bushes have a wide distribution over southern Canada, northern United States, and in spotty scatterings considerably farther south.

Chufa

One of the family of grasses, having a bearded-tuber root system, chufa ranges all across Canada and reaches southward into the tropics. The tubers may be roasted or boiled as a pot-vegetable, or roasted and beaten into a flour. Where cooking utensils are not available, the tubers may be rolled into wet leaves and roasted in the coals of a fire. The wet leaves help keep the tubers from burning.

Clover

Various parts of clover can be used as an emergency food. The dried heads can be pounded and used as bread food. The young leaves can be used as a salad or cooked herb. Tea purportedly having medicinal properties can be made from the dry flower-heads.

Dandelion

Widely distributed over the continent, dandelion, like burdock, is considered a nuisance. It is known also as lion's tooth because of the jagged leaves. Dandelions have a bright-yellow composite flower which grows on a long, bare stem. These stems, when broken, bleed with a milky fluid. The bloom has often been used in the making of dandelion wine. The young plants make good greens, somewhat bitter to the taste. As with other wild greens, dandelions should first be boiled or scalded in hot water. The water should then be drained off, and the blanched plants boiled again until thoroughly cooked. This takes away part of the bitter taste. Served with salt and pepper, and a bit of butter if available, dandelion greens taste something like spinach.

Dock

There are approximately fifteen species of dock, some of which are scattered throughout temperate North America, reaching well into southern Canada. The young leaves are used as cooked herbs or in greens. Most species of dock are short, stout plants, with leaves from 6 inches to a foot in length growing out of stout leaf-stalks. The leaves are elongated. Dock lives near swamps and alongside roadways. It has a range from southern Canada southward over the temperate parts of the United States.

Fireweed

As its name suggests, fireweed follows the great forest fires of Canada and Alaska, and occurs southward into the northern tier of the United States. It also grows in cleared areas in the same regions, and, because of road-clearing operations, now occurs along the borrow-pits of much of the length of the Alaska Highway. The plant grows to approximately 3 feet, and is characterized by the bright lavender-colored flowers. The new shoots are cooked as a pot vegetable, and Indians use the pith from the large stalks in making soup.

Groundnut

Indian potato or wild bean are other names for this plant. The groundnut is a twining vine growing close to the ground and having elongated seed pods. Its range is from central Canada to the Gulf of Mexico. The roots of this plant are a series of tubers, or root enlargements, which sometimes reach a length of 3 inches. These tubers can be roasted, boiled, fried, or even sliced and eaten raw quite like Irish potatoes. Seeds from the pods are sometimes used as dry beans.

Hog Peanut

Like the groundnut, the hog peanut grows with a long twining vine, and has underground fruits occurring in tough pods. These pods are boiled, which softens the skin so the seeds can be removed. The seeds, or fruits, are cooked similarly to dry beans. The range of the hog peanut is from southern Canada to the Gulf of Mexico.

Indian Cucumber

This plant grows with a long, slender stem, which has a circle of several leaves branching out from the stem near the top. At the stem's top is a smaller circle of fewer leaves near which are the black-purple berries. The root is a small tuber approximately an inch in diameter. This is the edible part and can be eaten uncooked. Indian cucumbers are common to eastern Canada, the Great Lakes, and southward to Florida.

Jerusalem Artichoke

A member of the sunflower family, this plant is native to the central portions of North America. It has a tuber root similar to the Irish potato's, which is the edible part. It may be boiled, baked, or roasted. If fire isn't available, the tuber may be sliced and eaten raw, with salt.

Lichens

These are tiny plants that grow on rocks and sterile ground. They occur in the barren regions north of Hudson Bay, into the Arctic, and southward, and are often mistaken for moss. They have been known to prevent starvation among explorers. They can be picked off rocks and boiled into a jelly-like substance.

Mallow

Usually occurring in the cultivated areas about farmyards and in fields, mallow is generally considered a weed. The young plants may be boiled and used as greens.

Marsh Marigold

Sometimes called the American cowslip, this is not a true marigold but one of the buttercup family of plants. It ranges from Alaska southward to the southern states, and is found in rich meadowlands. It has a bright-yellow, waxy-looking bloom. The edible part is the plant's top, and only the tender tips should be used. These are prepared by double-boiling, draining off the first water, and as greens or pot herbs. Extreme caution should be used in eating marsh marigold not to eat any of the raw plant. *The raw plant is poisonous.*

Milkweed

There are approximately forty varieties of milkweed common to North America. The most abundant is the common milkweed. The plant is light green in color and grows to a height of 2 to 4 feet. When the stems or leaves are broken off, the plant bleeds with a milky substance which gives it its name. In agricultural areas milkweeds are a nuisance. After the plants get a good start, they are hard to destroy. The seeds grow in pods reaching 3 inches in length, which have long, silky fibers attached, often giving the plant the additional name of silkweed. The edible part is the young shoots just after they emerge from the ground. These are prepared like asparagus or greens.

Mushrooms

Members of the Fungi family, mushrooms grow in damp shady places in the soil and in dead or decaying plants, mainly rotting tree trunks. There are several thousand known varieties of mushrooms, many of which are poisonous. Only botanists or people skilled in plant differentiation can tell the edible plants from the poisonous ones. There is no true distinction between mushrooms and toadstools, as many people believe, though amateurs generally consider that mushrooms are the edible forms, while the toadstools are poisonous. While incorrect, this may save many people from eating poisonous varieties. There is, unfortunately, no simple guide to help the beginner determine the edible from the poisonous mushrooms. His safest course is to reject all mushrooms unless he definitely knows them to be safe.

Here are some warning signs to look for when picking mushrooms:

Mushrooms having white or pale milky juice.

Mushrooms in the button stage.

Mushrooms having a scaly bulb or membranous cup at the base (the poison amanita or death cup is one of these).

Mushrooms having underside full of minute pores, and which grow from the earth.

Decaying mushrooms.

Woodland mushrooms having flat reddish tops and white radiating gill-spokes.

Mushrooms of yellow-orange color coming out of old stumps and having broad gills extending down the stems, and with surfaces which phosphoresce in the dark.

Such species as the *meadow mushroom*, the *shaggy mane*, and the *morel* are edible, but again one should be absolutely certain of the species before attempting to use it. Edible specics are baked and slow-simmered in butter.

Mountain Sorrel

This plant grows in wide areas in the Arctic, Canada, and along the spine of the Rocky Mountains. It is a small plant with rounded leaves, resembling a small rhubarb plant. It has been used by Arctic explorers as a scurvy preventative, and for this reason named scurvy grass. It is prepared as a salad or cooked herb.

Mustard

Black and yellow mustard plants are of European origin but have become naturalized in North America and are common in farming country. It grows vigorously, to a height of 3 or 4 feet, and interferes with harvesting. The young mustard plants are edible, if made into greens.

Pigweed

The lowly pigweed grows throughout the temperate parts of North America and is common in gardens, barnyards, and along ditchbanks. In some areas it is given the more aristocratic name of lamb's quarters, as it is also called in Europe. In some regions it is also called goose foot. Under favorable conditions of fertility, the plant will reach 10 feet in height. The leaves of the young plant are used for greens, and are prepared in the same way as dandelion greens.

Pine

The inner bark, or cambium layer, of pine trees was used by early Indians as emergency food. It can be eaten fresh as it is stripped off the tree, cooked as a herb, or dried and later mixed with other plants as the flour for famine bread. The white pine is considered the best species for the purpose.

Pokeweed

This is a smooth perennial herb with large petioled leaves, that is, leaf and stalk are in combination. The plant grows to a height of between 5 and 9 feet. It is often seen along the roadside in the United States and Canada. Pokeweed blooms with a white flower, which is succeeded by purple berries. The roots of pokeweed are large and branching, and are also poisonous. Only the young shoots of the plant should ever be eaten. These are prepared by cooking in two waters, as asparagus tips are prepared.

Prairie Turnip

The prairie turnip, or wild potato, is native to the Great Plains and the West. It derives its name from its shape, which is similar to the cultivated variety. The Indians used it extensively because of its starchy root, which was

prepared as a vegetable. Some attempts were made to cultivate the plant as a potato, hence the name wild potato.

Purslane

The Purslane family comprises several species which are
common throughout the United States and the warmer
areas of Canada. Its location is often spotty. One of the
best-known members of the Purslane family is the bitterroot plant common to Canada and the Northwest. This
plant grows in mountain country and blooms with a single
rose-colored blossom. The blossom will open only in sunlight. The roots of the plant are long and tapering. These
are wholesome to eat, but have a bitter flavor which gives
rise to the name. When the plant is cooked it gives off an
odor like tobacco, and for this reason the plant is sometimes called tobacco root. So popular was the plant in the
Northwest that the Bitterroot Range of mountains, separating Idaho and Montana, was named for it. The bitterroot is
also Montana's state flower.

Sego Lily

Also called mariposa, this small lily grows in mountain
and semidesert areas, reaching a height of 15 inches or so.
It grows on a long thin stem having the same light-green
color as the plant. The plant itself has a small bulb which is
edible when boiled.

Silverberry

This is a small shrub bearing light silver-colored berries
which are dry and pulpy to the taste. It is common to

western United States, western Canada, and Alaska. In Alaska it is also known as wolfberry, while farther south in the Yukon it is called the donjekberry, after the Donjek River along which it is found in abundance. Like rolled oats, good for man or horse, the donjekberry was, in the early days of Yukon horse-packing, picked in quantities and packed into the back country to feed horses, in lieu of grain. The silverberry has a small kernel of nutrient inside each berry.

Reed

This is a coarse kind of grass, growing from 6 to 10 feet high, and having jointed stems averaging about a half-inch in diameter. Its leaves are similar to thin corn-stalk leaves. The plant lives in shallow water, bogs, and marshes, and is found near both fresh and salt waters. The range is spotty inland, but generally covers from central Canada to the Gulf of Mexico. The roots may be dug and prepared in the same manner as potatoes.

Slippery Elm

The inner bark of this tree, like the bark of the pine, has been used as emergency food. It is either eaten raw or boiled with fat into a stew. The tree grows from the Great Lakes region southward and eastward to the Atlantic Coastal States.

Sorrel

There are several species of sorrel, which in appearance is like small dock. Its range is principally in eastern

Canada. The plant is used as a herb, to nibble on, and to quench thirst.

Sow Thistle

This plant is a prickly-leafed thistle, common to cultivated agricultural lands, and is considered noxious because it is so difficult to eradicate once it has become started. The flowers are yellow, and the plant has a milky juice when it is cut or broken. The young plants can be boiled in two waters, as with dandelions, and used as emergency greens.

Stinging Nettle

This plant is widely distributed throughout the temperate regions of the United States and Canada. It is both an annual and a perennial herb. The entire plant is thickly covered with fine, needle-shaped hairs. When the plant is accidentally brushed or hit with the hand, these tiny hairs prick the skin, depositing a mildly poisonous fluid which causes the sting. This can be avoided when handling the plant by pressing the fine hairs downward against the stem. As with milkweed, the young shoots of stinging nettle are edible as greens.

Sunflower

The seeds of the sunflower, common to the Great Plains region, were long useful to the early Indians for making flour. The seeds of the larger plants were first parched, then ground. Later they were used in the making of bread and in soups.

Water Cress

One of the few wild plants which may be picked and eaten on the spot, water cress is an aquatic whose leaves grow above the surface. It is perennial and of the mustard family. Water cress has a tart, tangy flavor which adds to the palatability of salads. It may be eaten as a salad, or used as a filling for bread-and-butter sandwiches. The plant grows in clear creeks and springs in the more temperate and mountainous areas of North America, and is best to eat before it flowers. The plant may be cut just below the surface of the water or simply pinched off with the fingers.

Water Hyacinth

This plant is a transplant from South America and now appears in the sluggish streams of the South, where it has become a nuisance. In emergencies, the young leaves may be cooked and eaten as an herb, but the plant should not be eaten raw.

Wild Grape

Wild grapes grow in mountainous areas, and are tart, dark-blue little fruits usually growing in bunches. The leaves of the plant are light green in color and short.

Wild Onion

The wild onion grows with a straight stem and long, thin leaves. The bloom occurs at the tip of the stem. The plant may be recognized by its onion-garlic odor and flavor. The small bulb from which the plant grows is the edible portion, and cooking by boiling destroys some of its objectionable odor and taste. In their trek across the Great Plains to the Salt Lake Valley over a century ago, the Mormon pioneers ate large quantities of wild onions, usually adding them to stews.

Wild Parsnip

Usually occurring where seeds from the cultivated variety have been scattered, wild parsnip can be prepared and eaten in the same way as tame parsnips. There is, however, a real danger connected with their use, which should never be ignored. That is their similarity to the water hemlock, which is probably the most poisonous plant in the United States. Both adult varieties send up their thick stalks having seeds in an umbrella-like cluster at the top. The stalks of the water hemlock, when cut longitudinally, show a number of transverse chambers which contain the poisonous substance. The poisonous water hemlock grows along streams, usually in wet meadowlands. In the United States it is widely distributed across the country.

Wild Rice

Most of the Atlantic coastal states from Maine to Louisiana, as well as southern Canada, the Great Lakes region, and the upper Mississippi Basin have areas of wild rice. It is found in tidal rivers and marshes, and is a favorite food of waterfowl. The plant grows from 2 feet to well over the height of a man. Seeds form in a tassel at the ends of the stalks, and ripen during late August and September. The seeds may be eaten raw or cooked.

Wild Berries

The bloom of many wild plants is edible. This includes the blossoms of wild berries and fruits such as strawberries, raspberries, huckleberries, etc. The blossoms of wild roses, buttercups (if cooked), wild geraniums, sweet william, and prickly pear are all edible. So is the bloom of wild white clover and red clover.

It is not safe to eat the bloom of plants which are known to be poisonous to livestock. Among the plants poisonous to livestock are the loco weed, larkspur, jimson weed, death camass, lupine, greasewood, and water hemlock. Also, several plants are poisonous to stock when certain parts are eaten, whereas man may eat other parts (usually after cooking) and find them not poisonous. Among these are the milkweed (mature plants and leaves) and chokecherry (leaves). These are both toxic to livestock.

The senses of taste and smell offer some guidance in the matter of detecting poisonous blossoms. For example, the jimson weed, a member of the Nightshade family, grows tall and rank; and the entire plant is highly poisonous. Its big, white, trumpet-shaped flowers, as well as the leaves of the plant itself, have a disagreeable odor. This should be a natural warning. If any bloom has either an objectionable odor, or upon being tasted has a sickening or unpleasant taste, it should be left alone.

The following wild plants produce berries that are edible:

Bearberry

Often called kinnikinik, this is a red berry which grows from the Arctic regions to the Southwest. It is useful only in emergencies. The berry is dry to the taste and about as appetizing as a piece of red cork, but it does contain some nourishment. It is said to be better cooked than raw.

Blackberry

There are scores of species of wild blackberries, which are so called because of their coloration when ripe. The blackberry is an aggregate-type berry which grows from a brambly bush and is often called brambleberry. It thrives well in the temperate parts of North America, with a range extending into central Canada. The berry resembles a wild raspberry except for the darker color. Most varieties are sweet and luscious.

Blueberry

Widely distributed over northern United States, Canada, and Alaska, the blueberry falls into two general classifications. On one type, generally spread over the eastern areas of North America, the berries grow in terminal clusters. On the other, found in the West, the berries grow singly on bushes, like western huckleberries. The berries of the western type are dusky blue in color and grow on bushes ranging up to 2 feet in height. After the first frosts, these bushes turn red, making the large patches look like scarlet splashes on the landscape. The plants like the high ridges and sidehills, and often grow in patches of several acres. The berries are very sweet and juicy.

Dewberry

A species of blackberry that grows close to the ground.

Elderberry

Growing on large tree-like shrubs, this plant has a wide distribution in mountainous country. The blossoms and fruit form in large clusters at the ends of branches. The tiny blossoms are cream-white in color, and are succeeded by fruit which is dark blue, turning even darker when ripe. Hermits living in wild mountain country often make elderberry wine and jelly. Both are excellent. The stalks of the shrub are virtually hollow in the mature plant, and filled with pith. If the pith is poked out, the dry stalk can be made into an elk bugle. I have personally "bugled up" several bull elk on elderberry bugles.

Gooseberry

This plant is found in the northern tier of states and across southern Canada. The fruit grows on prickly bushes ranging up to 3 feet in height, and turns dark blue when ripe. When completely ripened, it is palatable raw, and excellent when made into jam or jelly. The dried blossom ends should be rubbed off the fruit before eating.

Ground Juniper

Grows on the open hilltops and slopes from Alaska to northern United States. The small juniper berries they produce are poor eating, but do have some value as an emergency food.

Haw

This is the fruit of the Hawthorn tree, which is native to Europe and Asia but has become naturalized in North America. The trees reach a height of 15 to 20 feet or more, having thorns protruding from their branches. The ripened fruit is blue-black in color, and reaches the size of a fingernail. The fruit resembles large serviceberries, with each growing on a stem of considerable length. Inside it is yellow, pulpy, and full of seeds. The ripened fruit often hangs on the tree after the leaves have fallen. Haws are not palatable but are edible. The thorn apple is a variety of hawthorn.

Cranberry

The high-bush cranberry is common to the northern States and Canada. Another, the mountain cranberry, is native to Newfoundland and Labrador. Still another species, the low-bush cranberry, grows in the muskeg areas of Canada and Alaska nearly to the Arctic. These berries grow close to the ground on vinelike bushes whose waxy, stiff leaves are evergreen. Each berry of the low-bush variety averages about the size of a small garden pea. The berries are yellow-green until they begin to ripen, when they turn bright red. They have a fine tart flavor and can be eaten raw. If sugar is available in camp, they can be made into jam by cooking equal parts of sugar and berries. The jam is wonderful as topping for hot cakes or as garnish for wild meat.

Huckleberry

Black huckleberries are native to the eastern part of the continent, and range from Georgia into Canada. They are characterized by their black color and the hard seeds of the fruit. Western or blue huckleberries grow throughout the mountainous areas of western North America, have tiny seeds, and are more allied to the blueberry. Depending on the species, the shrubs of this western variety reach a height of from 10 inches to 2 feet. They like the high ridges in conifer-timber areas, and the northern slopes of high mountainsides. Some species have tiny red fruit. Others bear dark blue-black fruit which is luscious and sweet. There is no better fruit eaten as is, fresh from the shrub, nor is there any better pie than a huckleberry pie. Bears love huckleberries. One way for the outdoorsman to locate the patches is to keep a sharp lookout for the bruins or their spoor. If the dung of a grizzly is blue, there are blueberry patches near. Similarly, if the dung of a black bear is purple, huckleberries are within his circuit of travel.

Mossberry

These small, nearly black berries grow on a low evergreen type of bush similar to that of low-bush cranberries. They are found in the muskeg regions of North America. The berries average about quarter-inch in diameter, and are very juicy and sweet to the taste. Many times they will be passed by because of their dark coloration, which, amid the dark-green leaves, blends well with the ground.

Mulberry

The edible mulberries are of the black or red varieties. The red mulberry is native to North America, with a distribution from New England to Florida and Texas. The black mulberry is an import from Asia, and is currently cultivated in the South and in California for the delicate sweet fruit. Mulberry trees bear abundantly. The fruit, too tender and delicate to transport well, is fine when eaten raw or made into jams.

Pawpaw

This small, deciduous tree or shrub, also called papaw, is native to the United States in the area east of the Mississippi River. The tree blooms with purple blossoms, and bears a banana-like fruit of pulpy texture, which is good to eat after the first frosts. In Mexico and other tropical areas of the continent, the tree is known as the papaya. In appearance, this tree resembles a palm, with a tall trunk ending in a top of yellow leaves. The fruit, too, is yellow in color, and tastes something like a ripe melon or pear. It is one of the best-known fruits of Mexico and the American tropics, and is generally eaten fresh.

Persimmon

The persimmon tree is a transplant from Asia, and was brought into the South shortly after the Civil War. It is now cultivated in areas near the west coast for its use in making furniture. A native variety of the same tree grows in a region just south of the Great Lakes, all the way to the Gulf of Mexico. This native tree grows to a height of over 50 feet, and bears a fruit that resembles a plum. The fruit is bitter to the taste, and like the fruit of the pawpaw, must be ripened by frost before it is palatable.

Raspberry

Wild raspberries grow in the temperate parts of the United States, over wide areas of Canada, and in Alaska. They grow on small spiny canes, which give them their name. The wild variety is comparable to the domestic raspberry except that it is smaller and generally softer and more hairy. Like blueberries, wild raspberries grow in great profusion in many parts of Canada, and the natives there still gather them when they ripen in August, to can for winter. The fruit is sweet and juicy and is best when eaten directly from the bushes. Both grizzly bears and black bears love raspberries and gorge on the fruit. They can pick off each berry neatly with their mouths, without getting the spiny canes.

Serviceberry

The serviceberry grows on bushes often reaching 10 feet in height, and has a distribution from the Gulf of Mexico to Alaska. The bushes have dark purple-red bark and dark-green leaves. Each fruit grows on a long stem, is purple outside and has a white meat, purple-stained, inside. The fruit has numerous large seeds, is somewhat mushy in texture, but has a fine flavor. In Canada the serviceberry is often called the saskatoonberry During the early settlement of the West and Canada, this fruit was picked in large quantities and canned, either fresh or mixed with apples, and made into jam for winter consumption.

Strawberry

Wild strawberries are similar to the domestic varieties in the general appearance of bloom, plant, and fruit. Both plant and fruit are smaller in the wild state, with the plants being more spindly and pale. They are found in the temperate areas of the continent, and generally grow in wooded mountain country, often in shaded areas.

Edible Nuts

In addition to the fruits, many trees bear nuts that may be eaten raw or pounded into flour and made into nutbread when needed as emergency food. Among the edible nuts are beechnut, butternut, chestnut, hickory, peanut, pecan, pine (pinion), sweet acorn, and walnut.

Emergency Drinks

Many of the edible plants or fruits have some portions which can be made into emergency drinks. Some of these are the following:

Chicory. The tubers are roasted, ground, or pounded, and brewed like coffee.

Chufa. Prepared in the same way as chicory.

Dandelion. Roots may be ground and brewed into a bitter drink.

Elderberry. Hot water poured over ripe elderberries and allowed to stand, then cooled, makes a refreshing drink, especially if sugar is available to sweeten it.

Goldenrod. Both the young leaves and the flowers of this plant are brewed into tea.

Labrador Tea. The leaves of this small, lacey-leafed plant, also called mountain tea and Hudson Bay tea, may be brewed into a delicious tea.

Mint. The leaves of such mints as spearmint, peppermint, and Bergamot may be crushed, hot water poured over them, and made into flavorful drinks.

Mulberry. Crushed and immersed in water, and allowed to stand, mulberries make a tasty fruit beverage. Other wild fruits such as blueberries and huckleberries may be used similarly.

Sassafras. In early America, sassafras tea was given to all members of the family for the medicinal qualities it was thought to contain. The tea is made by brewing the roots of the sassafras tree.

Sweet Birch. The dried leaves of this tree can be used to make an emergency tea.

12

Knots and Lashings

A knot is formed by intertwining parts of a rope or two ropes to hold them together. A hitch is the fastening used to join a rope to a solid object such as a tree, log, or pole. A lash is the binding used to hold one or more objects in place.

The common material used to do all this is rope or cord. Often other materials such as leather thongs, nylon filament, or string are used for the same purpose, either alone or in combination with rope.

Hemp and Nylon Rope

Before getting into the tying of knots and hitches, it is helpful to understand a few facts about rope. The two most common ropes used for outdoor purposes today are hemp rope and nylon rope in braided form. The size of either should be matched to the intended purpose; and size, in the use of rope, usually means strength. The strength of any rope also depends upon the material from which it is woven, and its age.

A basic formula for determining the breaking strain of new hemp rope is: diameter squared multiplied by 7200. The safety load is considered to be one-quarter of the breaking strain, in pounds.

As an example, a quarter-inch rope, or ¼ X ¼ X 7200 pounds, would break if subjected to 450 pounds of strain. The safe load would be 112 pounds. A half-inch rope of Manila or sisal hemp would break at about 1800 pounds, and could sustain a safe load of around 450 pounds.

Braided nylon rope will support approximately three times that amount. A safe load for quarter-inch nylon rope would therefore be 336 pounds, and for the half-inch size, 1350 pounds.

A factor to remember is that ropes generally do not break along their length, but at knots, assuming that the rope's strength is uniform. Any knot causing a sharp angle to the direction of strain weakens the rope at that point.

Generally, hemp rope is used for rough purposes, such as lashing duffel on pack stock, lashing bundles and other cargo, and for tent guys and pole lashings. Nylon rope is neater in appearance, and is used for lashing packboard loads, and for boat painters, outdoor clotheslines, etc. Nylon is slicker, and tends to give under some of the simple knots which would hold, by friction, with hemp rope. New hemp rope is hard to handle in lashing gear. Wet hemp

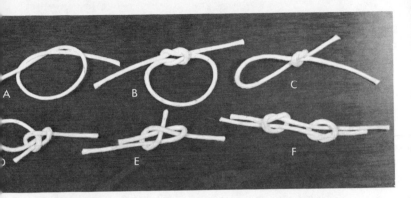

Fig. 1. Useful knots for the outdoorsman: (A) overhand knot; (B) square knot; (C) slip knot; (D) bowline; (E) sheetbend; (F) water knot.

can't be tied as solidly as when dry. And frozen hemp rope should be avoided like a plague.

Stopper Knot

Either type of rope, hemp or nylon, will fray or unravel at the cut end. For this reason, some type of knot, or stopper, must be used. The simplest stopper to use with hemp rope is a single overhand knot at the running end of the rope. Hemp rope is formed of three twisted strands, which are then twisted together in the opposite direction. To tie a satisfactory end knot, untwist the strands for a few inches, but do not untwist each individual strand, otherwise the knot will be too soft for practical use. With the strands separated and laid lengthwise together, an overhand knot (Fig. 1A) should then be made so that after it is pulled as taut as possible the knot itself lies snugly against the

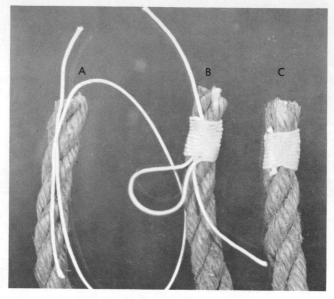

Fig. 2. Whipping the end of a rope.

untwisted part of the rope. The finished knot should be laid on a hard surface and rolled back and forth beneath the foot. This makes it snug and smooth.

Whipping and Burning

A good way to "stop" a braided nylon rope is to whip and burn the end. To whip the end of a rope, lay the ends of a length of strong cord oppositely along the rope end so they overlap for 3 or 4 inches (Fig. 2A). Then, while holding down the two cords along the rope, begin winding the loop around the rope, and back along its standing part (Fig. 2B). When about 1 inch has been wound as taut as possible, each end of the cord is pulled tight from opposite

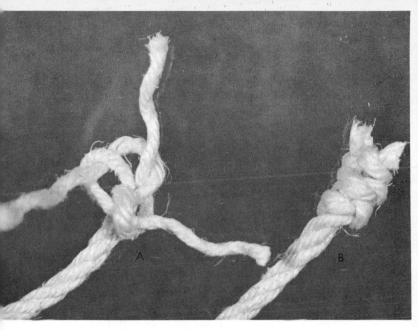

Fig. 3. Turkey-head knot.

ends of the winding. It will be seen that both ends pull under the winding. When pulled free of loops, the unused ends of the cord are cut off snug against the whipping (Fig. 2C). A lighted match, held for a second under the cut end of the rope, will fuse the nylon threads together, further keeping the rope from unfraying.

Turkey-head Knot

If you want to be fancier, or to use a hemp rope for such purposes as threading through small-diametered rings on horse hackamores, a turkey-head knot (Fig. 3) may be made in the rope's end.

To make a turkey-head knot, untwist the three strands from each other for about 6 inches, for a half-inch rope, but don't untwist each individual strand. Next, bend the strands downward so they look like spokes of a wheel running out evenly from the solid part of the rope. Mentally number the strands 1, 2, and 3, beginning at the right if you are right-handed.

Now take 1, loop it loosely under 2, and bring it up to vertical. Loop 2 around the adjacent 1 and also under 3, then bring it to vertical. Lastly, bring strand 3 under the adjacent 2, and also under the loose loop formed by strand 1, then up to vertical (Fig. 3A).

You now have a woven knot. Pull this as tight as possible and down against the untwisted portion of the rope. Make three more similar knots, pulling each succeeding knot taut against the under portion.

The result is four layers of woven strands, each lying tightly on top of the other (Fig. 3B). To finish, the knot is laid on the floor or hard earth and rolled firmly back and forth under the foot. The finished knot won't untie and is small enough in diameter to thread through tight places.

Braiding

Often similar sizes of rope or cord are not available for joining. Rope often has to be joined to string, leather thongs, or cord. Many times rope breaks and unravels, leaving only individual strands which could be used if they were strong enough.

For such reasons, anyone using rope should know how to braid. Many is the time I've seen the "straw strings" of threshed wheat bundles, and the twine used around hay bales, braided into emergency rope.

In the simplest braiding, three strands of material are knotted together with an overhand knot, and the knot hung onto a nail solidly set in a tree. Braiding is begun by taking the right strand over and across the center strand; then the left strand is passed over and across the center strand (originally the right strand), as in Fig. 4A. This motion is repeated until the desired length is reached.

When a strand runs out, it is spliced by laying another length alongside it, holding or whipping the two together,

Fig. 4. Two methods of braiding: (A) three-strand braid; (B) four-strand braid.

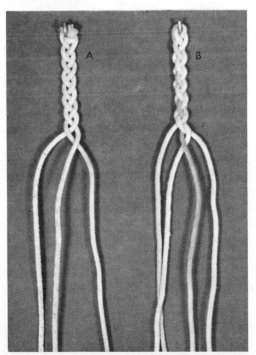

and braiding in the overlapping ends as a single strand. The ends, or fuzz, are later cut off the finished braiding. The finished product is a flat rope.

A far better rope is made by braiding four strands of material. To braid four, fasten all strands together with a knot, or whipping, and hang the knot onto a nail as before. Next spread the four strands and mentally number them 1, 2, 3, and 4, beginning at the right.

To begin, bring strand 1 down under 2 and 3, then up over 3, holding 1 solidly upon 3 with the thumb and index finger. Next, bring 4 down under from the opposite side, and under the two middle strands, bringing it up between them and the now-right strand taking the place of the original number 1; and firmly over and upon the middle strand next to it (Fig. 4B).

In other words, the strand numbers will change as each takes the place of another. But their positions won't. The procedure is to braid first with the right-hand strand, then the left-hand strand. Each in turn is brought under *two* strands, up between, over and across the strand adjacent to it. That's all there is to it, and the technique can be learned in sixty seconds, with four lengths of shoelace or fishing line.

If the tension is kept tight and uniform as the braiding continues, the result will be a neat round rope, which should be finished by rolling it between the palms. Rawhide or leather thongs braided this way can be made into fine emergency rope or stock halters of the hackamore type.

Knots

Most knots depend for their holding power on the friction created by two ropes, or the strands of a single rope, binding against each other. Simple knots will suffice for rough rope such as hemp, while slick rope material such as nylon requires more involved knots in order to hold. Often a combination of two knots is used for slick rope.

A half-dozen basic knots and their variations will suffice for every purpose. If the average outdoorsman will learn that many, and the specific purposes for which each is most suited, he will be better off than trying to memorize numerous specialized knots which he will soon forget because he has no use for them.

Square Knot

One of the simplest knots is the square knot (Fig. 1B). This is made by tying two overhand knots, one upon the other, but alternating the direction of the second half. To tie a square knot, take a rope end in each hand. Put the right rope under the left rope. Bring it full around, and point both ends upward. Next, take the now-right end (it was the left before) and bring it *over* the other end, down under and around, and tighten. If the knot is made by tying both parts identically, the result is a granny knot, which won't hold.

The square knot is useful for joining rope ends where mild tension must be kept on both ropes while the knot is tied. It is the knot used to tie your shoes, except that the loops are not pulled completely through.

In tying a square knot upon angular packages, it helps keep the tension to tie the knot, if possible, upon a corner. Often a variation called the "surgeon's knot" is made in order to hold all tension. This is done by making two turns around for the first part of the square knot instead of one.

Slip Knot

Another simple, usable knot is the slip knot (Fig. 1C). This is made by doubling the end of a rope back against itself, and tying a simple overhand knot with the rope end around the standing part of the rope. The noose will slip tight when the knot is tied around a tree or pole. The slip knot, plus a single half-hitch, is the best way to tie a saddle horse to a tree when it must be left for some time. The slip knot holds the rope against the tree so it won't slip down where Dobbin can step over it and entangle himself; and the half-hitch keeps the slip knot from untying, especially in new hemp rope or in the "hard twist" common to lariats.

Sheet Bend

For joining two ends of rope, no knot surpasses the sheet bend (Fig. 1E). To tie a sheet bend, form the end of one rope into a small loop. Poke the end of another rope up through this loop, bring it around both parts of the other rope, and tuck the end under where it came up through the loop, but over both parts of the opposite rope.

If one rope is smaller in diameter than the other, use the smaller as the end to push up through the loop, and tie as before, except make one complete turn around the larger rope before threading the smaller under itself. Leather thongs can be joined to larger rope by this method, which is useful in tying rope to saddle strings, etc.

Even after wetting, or considerable strain, a sheet bend can usually be quickly untied by bending the loop end downward over the standing opposite rope.

Bowline

The very best knot for making a loop that won't slip is the bowline (Fig. 1D). To tie a bowline, make a loop around a tree and grasp the end in the left hand. Next, make a loop in the standing part of the rope between you and the tree, tipping the rope forward so that the part next to the standing end is on top. Lastly, poke the end downward through this loop, bring it under and around the

Fig. 5. Simple clove hitch for tying tent guy ropes (A). Looped end (B) makes it easy to untie in wet weather.

standing part of the rope, and back through the loop from beneath.

The bowline is useful in any circumstance where a non-slipping loop, which may be easily untied, is desired. You can, for example, fit a loop formed by a bowline over a rock, ledge, or heavy branch; lower yourself down the rope to solid footing below; then flip the loop off the rock or branch and take your rope with you.

Clove Hitch

The clove hitch (Fig. 5A) is one of the most useful knots for tying a rope to a pole or log. To tie one, toss the end of a rope over a horizontal branch or pole. Bring the end down, under, and up at the left side of the standing part. Cross the end over the standing part, make another turn down around the pole, bringing the end up again, and under its own loop to the right of the standing part of the rope.

Water Knot

A useful knot for joining rope together is called the water knot (Fig. 1F). It is made by laying two rope ends together so they overlap for a foot or more. Then an overhand knot is tied in each of the ends so that it encloses the standing part of the other rope. When pulled tight, the knot holds well, but it is hard to take apart.

Timber Hitch

The timber hitch is useful when working with logs (Fig. 6). It is made by looping the rope around a log, crossing the

Fig. 6. Timber hitch for hauling logs.

end over the standing part and back against itself, where it is then wound round and round that portion of the loop. When pulled tight, friction prevents it from unwinding.

Ring Hitches

Where medium-diametered hemp rope must be used to tie onto iron rings, such as halter rings and cinch rings, an overhand knot should be tied at the end of the rope, and the rope tied to the ring with another overhand knot. This simple knot will hold in any hemp rope, once the rope's initial stiffness has worn off.

For attaching small-diametered rope to small rings, which tend to cut the rope easily, it's best to make two or three turns around the ring, then finish off with two half-hitches, and again bring the knot at the rope's end snugly up against the finished knot. This type of knot distributes the strain evenly.

Looped Knots

Often knots must be tied so that they may be easily untied, even after they have been wetted by storm or water; and often when your fingers are half frozen. "Hard knots," such as a plain slip knot, should not be used where they must be quickly untied. Examples are tent ropes guyed to poles, or lead ropes tied to horses' tails in packstring work.

Usually any type of knot can be finished off, not by threading the end completely through at its final stage, but by looping it through. Half-hitches may be looped, either for the second part or for both parts by doubling the end. A bowline can be completed by looping. So can a sheet bend. So can a square knot, as in the loops left when tying your shoes. A clove hitch can be looped in its final stage, instead of threaded—and this, incidentally, makes a fine sour-weather hitch for tying tent ropes around a side pole.

Fig. 7. Two wraps and double half-hitch, end looped.

When rain or snow wets such looped knots, they are handily untied simply by jerking the final loop, which loosens the tightest part of the knot and makes untying easy. Looped knots will hold as firmly as otherwise, if used where constant tension is applied.

Tying Rope Under Tension

Often the ideal knot for a purpose cannot be tied because it is necessary to apply tension to the rope during the tying. The best hitch for tying a rope under tension to a solid object is to make two wraps around and two half-hitches (Fig. 7). For example, in hoisting a weight with the rope over a branch, tension is held while two turns of the rope are made around the pole; then two half-hitches hold that tension and finish the hitch. Again, when steadying the heavy ridgepole of a large tent with a guy rope, you can quickly take two turns around the stake, finish off with half-hitches, and not lose an inch of slack. If, in such cases, both parts of the double half-hitch are made with looped rope, the entire hitch can be quickly jerked free.

Lashings

Knots and lashings used to join poles and small logs together are somewhat different than knots used to join two lengths of rope or tie a rope to an object.

Shear-Pole Lash

One of the most common lashings is the one used for joining two shear poles for erecting tents. Lay the two poles side by side, attach the rope end with a clove hitch to one of the poles, and make three overhand turns around both poles. Make two turns with the rope around these loops at right angles and between the poles (called frapping); and finish off with a clove hitch around the opposite pole. When the poles are spread, forming the shears, the twisting tension will bind them firmly together.

A similar binding for shear poles can be made without the use of the two clove hitches. Simply make three turns around both poles, two more turns of frapping between the poles and around the loops, and join the rope ends with a square knot (Fig. 8).

If enough rope is available, this same type of hitch can be used for joining any number of poles together, as in making a raft or a pole tripod. The rope is looped around all poles at the desired position. A couple of frapping turns are made between each pair of poles and finished with a half-hitch, and the two ends are tied with a square knot.

Fig. 8. Shear-pole lash.

Fig. 9. Diagonal lash.

Diagonal Lash

The other basic lash is for tying one pole at right angles to another pole. This may be done in two ways. The simplest is to make three turns with the rope around both poles, diagonally, at the junction; then finish with frapping. Pulled tight, this takes up any slack and pulls the binding tight to prevent slipping (Fig. 9). If you are lashing a pole frame, each corner should be lashed in the opposite direction; otherwise, because the tension is the same at both ends, the frame will sag into a parallelogram. In other words, make one diagonal binding pointing to the right, the opposite one pointing left.

Square Lash

A second way of binding a crossbar to another pole requires more rope but is more solid (Fig. 10). Attach rope

Fig. 10. Square lash.

with a clove hitch to the crossbar. Next wind the rope
down under the lengthwise pole, up the opposite side, over
the end of the crossbar, down under the lengthwise pole
again on the opposite side of the crossbar, up over the
crossbar to its other side . . . and repeat for three or four
turns. Finish off with two turns around the rope itself between the poles, and another clove hitch around the
opposite pole.

Lashing Poles Side by Side

Often you will want to join several small poles side by
side, as in making a pole bed frame or table top. The poles
need not be secured as firmly as when making a raft
(Fig. 11).

Fig. 11. Lashing poles side by side.

First, lay all the poles side by side. Loop the rope at the middle and, beginning at one side near the ends, place the loop around the first pole. Then, push one end down between the first and second poles, the other end up between them. Secure the second pole by pushing the end of the upper rope down again through the space between the second and third poles, the opposite end up between them. It's just like stiching a double overhand-stitch in cloth with two needles. Finish at the opposite side by pulling the rope tight, and tying off with a square knot. A similar lash at the opposite end of the poles will secure them.

Weaving Stitch

Where several crossbars are to be laid upon siderails, but with space between them, they may be secured by a weaving "stitch" made in this way: Tie the rope with a clove hitch to one end of a rail. Place the rope under the first crossbar, up and around it in a half-hitch, and bring the rope under the siderail to the next crossbar. A similar half-hitch is made around the second bar, but on the opposite side of the siderail. The turn around the third bar is made as for the first. When all crossbars have been lashed, the rope is drawn tight and finished off with another clove hitch. Tension on the rope binds all cross members downward against the rail, and longitudinally against each other (Fig. 12).

Express Hitch

The lashing of duffel and gear into compact bundles which won't spill their contents and which may be handled easily is vital for most outdoors travel and camping. Containers that fit the larger items represent the best packaging; but for the inevitable and numerous small items, the best

Fig. 12. Weaving stitch.

Fig. 13. Express hitch.

single way of packaging is to wrap them securely into a canvas manta (a 6-foot square of canvas) and tie them up with an express hitch (Fig. 13). Smaller bundles may be wrapped in smaller pieces of canvas and hitched similarly.

First, the items are fitted together as compactly as their shapes will allow, and placed in the middle of the manta. Next, the sides of the canvas are folded over. If the side is longer than the bundle, it should be folded under itself rather than extended over and onto the opposite side. With both sides folded in, the bottom is folded over. The top should always be folded last, so that the flap covers the other folds—this to prevent rain or snow from wetting the contents.

To begin the express hitch used in securing the package, make a slip-knot loop, or a lasso-type loop with the smaller loop tied with a bowline knot. Loop this around the top part of the package, with the knot resting over the folded top-flap. Pull tight, and while holding the tension, make a half-hitch around the package at its center. Pull and hold this tight, while making a third half-hitch around the package near its bottom end.

You now have three loops around the package. Next bring the rope down under the package, and up to the first loop at the back. Make a half-hitch around this cross-loop; continue to the second cross-loop and make another half-hitch; do the same at the third loop, then bring the rope over the package's top, down to the first cross-loop, and tie off with half-hitches around that part of the rope leading downward from the first loop.

Rectangular packages are easy to tie with an express hitch. Odd-shaped bundles may be tied up in the same way, however. A good way to increase the rigidity of the hitch, with odd-shaped bundles, is to make two turns around each cross-loop instead of a single half-hitch, when bringing the standing part of the rope around the package after the three loops are made. When drawn tight, the rope twists these turns diagonally, so no part of the rope slips in any direction.

Such an improved express hitch is often used for tying a rock solidly enough to be used for an emergency boat anchor. Another hitch for tying a rock for the same purpose, if a long rock can be found with a straight or thin middle, is a slip knot and a half-hitch. When pulled tight, and the rope wetted, such a combination will hold well.

Packboard Lash

Packboards have a series of screw eyes anchored solidly into the standards. To bind a packboard load, first attach a 6-foot length of heavy cord or light rope to each of the opposite top screw eyes. Next, lay the wrapped load on the packboard so that the top flap is outside and pointing down. Place the load an inch higher than it is intended to ride, to accommodate for sagging during travel. Then lace the load alternately across with the cords, just as you lace your shoes (Fig. 14).

To finish the tie, place your knee upon the rope binding on the load, so it won't slip, and tie a bowline knot in one rope, shortly after it has passed through the final screw eye. Thread the opposite rope through the loop formed by this,

Fig. 14. Packboard lash.

and pull the two ropes tightly together. Finish with two looped half-hitches. Tension may be kept by doing this, while some would be lost in finishing off with a square knot.

The same lashing is used for a toboggan load, except that the ropes at the toboggan's sides become the screw eyes of the packboard.

Care of Rope

Rope is valuable outdoor equipment; in some cases, life-saving equipment. Care in its use and storage will insure its being usable when needed, and certain precautions and rules should be observed.

First, never cut a length of rope unless it is absolutely necessary. Cut rope will unravel unless knotted, and unraveled rope is ruined rope. Short lengths are never as useful as longer lengths, and knotted or spliced rope is never as satisfactory as unknotted rope. It is far better to coil up unneeded rope, after lashing, and leave it long enough for another purpose.

Another good way to preserve the length of a rope, is to "knit" the surplus. This is done by beginning at the final knot of any job, making a slip knot, reaching through the loop formed and bringing in another loop, making still another loop through this one, just as in crocheting. When the surplus rope is all knitted, pull the end through the final loop so it won't unravel, and tie it in a coil to the final knot of the lash.

After using a length of rope, it should be coiled neatly and hung off the damp earth away from gnawing animals.

One way of coiling rope is to grasp the end in the left hand, raise that hand to vertical, then wrap the rope around the uplifted elbow and between the thumb and fingers until it is all coiled. With the coil finished, the loops are knotted snugly together with two or three half-hitches around all strands

Where larger rope is used, it may be coiled into longer loops by holding one end in the left hand and making successive loops of the desired size with the right hand, which are hung over the left forearm until all rope has been coiled. With these coils completed, three turns are made around the entire coil, drawing all strands together tightly against each other. The end is then drawn through the coil just above these lateral turns. This will hold the coil in place until the rope is needed again.

Where possible it is best to hang coiled rope inside to protect it against weather and rodents. When this is impossible, rope should be placed on something high, and canvas draped over it. Like canoe paddles and the handles of camp tools, rope accumulates salt from the perspiration of humans or pack animals. Animals like porcupines will gnaw and ruin rope for the salt contained in this perspiration.

Occasionally you can be *too* careful in your consideration of good rope. A young fellow in Wyoming found it necessary to "tail" his packstring—that is, he tied one loaded animal to the tail of the beast ahead of it. One of these horses was a beautiful buckskin, with a long, nearly white, magnificent tail.

Because of the arroyos through which the string passed, tension was hard and often abrupt on the tails of the animals. Back on level ground again, the young fellow tried to untail the beasts, but found the buckskin's tail so tightly twisted in the rope that he had to cut the hairs. He really did a good job, with the result that the animal's long flowing tail was cut off square and short.

At camp, the owner and outfitter was understandably angry. "I suppose it didn't occur to you to cut the rope, instead of Buck's tail?" he asked.

The youngster was unapologetic. "A horse's tail will grow out again," he assured his employer. "A rope won't."

13

The Ingenious Outdoorsman – What He Can Make

The farther one goes into the wilderness, and the longer he remains there, the greater becomes his need for improvising certain items of equipment. Basic items of gear become damaged or wear out. Equipment for every purpose cannot usually be taken along owing to weight and difficulties of transportation. And often specialized pieces of equipment cannot be purchased but must be made, often on the spot, to fill special needs. Tap an experienced outdoorsman and you find an ingenious and inventive person. Following are some of the ways outdoor living can be made easier by improvising camp equipment.

Camp Lights

The best camp lights yet developed are the gasoline lantern and the battery-operated flashlight. Emergency lamps help to prolong the life of these types of lighting and serve as independent means of illumination when the need arises. The most inexpensive and portable are wax candles. A half-dozen candles of half-inch diameter should go along on any lengthy outdoor trip.

Candles may be used in many ways. The simplest is to light the candle, then tip it so that several drops of melted wax will land on a table at the desired spot. Set the candle base into the soft wax and hold till it cools and sets. The lighted candle then won't tip over. Another way is to push the candle into the top of a bottle and use the bottle as a lamp base. Again, one blade of a pocketknife may be shoved into a tree, the blade at its other end pulled to an upright position, and the candle impaled on the uplifted blade.

It is possible to focus the light from a candle by making a simple lantern. Cut two inch-long slits, one across the other, on one side of a #10 tin can midway along its length, and fit a wire or cord bail to the can's opposite side. The right-angle corners of tin formed by the cuts are pushed inward so that the candle can be shoved through. To hold the candle snugly, bend the points of the tin in or out.

In use, the can is held longitudinally, the open end focusing the light into a beam. As the candle burns down, it is shoved farther up into the can. This type of tin-can lantern is called a "palooser," because so many were once used in the Palouse country of the Pacific Northwest.

Three simple candle holders that can be made in the outdoors
with only a pocket knife and a tin can.

Surplus wax from candles and butt ends should not be
thrown away. They can be melted and used for a tin-cup
light. This is made by cutting down a small tin can to one-
half its height, but leaving an inch-wide strip along the
seam. Bend over the raw edges of this strip as well as the
circular cut-edge of the can. Then bend the rimmed strip
into a handle, as on a tin cup. The wax pieces are melted
in this cup around a wick made either of cotton cord or
three strands of string braided together.

The sheepherders of the Northwest made an even simpler light with melted bacon grease and a wick. The melted grease was put in a saucer, and the wick was made by braiding together three small strips of an old cotton bandana handkerchief, and running one end of the resultant cord or wick up through the center hole of a metal burr from the wagon-box, so it would stand up out of the melted grease. The resulting smoky light was known, inelegantly, as a "bitch," a "greasy bitch," or a "smoky bitch." All three applied.

Potato-sack Pack

Packs for lugging duffel about are not difficult to improvise. One of the simplest for small items is made by sewing a seam across the open end of a 100-pound potato or seed-grain bag, then cutting an 8-inch hole through the exact center of both parts of the flattened sack. To finish, tie a short cord or light rope to each of the four corners. The items of duffel are placed through the center hole, into each side of the sack, and the sack lifted over the head and set down over the shoulders. Part of the load rides at the rear, part of it in front. The corners are tied at each side by the four cords.

This emergency pack will carry reasonable loads. The seam across the bag's end can be sewn with any available string. A usable needle can be made by straightening one of the metal keys used for opening canned meat; or the cord can simply be threaded through the mesh of the bag with the fingers. Wearing such a pack makes one appear

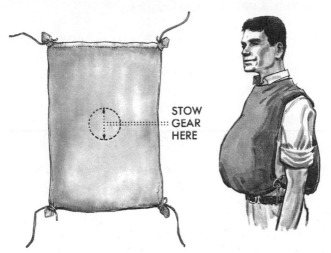

Potato sack with hole cut in middle becomes an emergency pack.

somewhat bosomy, but for temporary use, for loads up to 15 or 20 pounds, it is quite comfortable.

Camp Table

A camp table for comfortable outdoor dining can be built on a framework of four posts set solidly into the ground 30 to 34 inches high. These posts should be set on the smokeless side of the fire. Dry pine posts 4 inches in diameter are ideal. They should be placed at each corner of a rectangle forming the desired size of the table, say, 3 feet by 5 feet.

Next, attach a pair of crossbars to each pair of end posts so their upper surfaces are just even with the post tops. They may be attached with spikes, if available, or lashed with rope, buckskin thongs, or wire. Onto these crossbars, small poles or saplings 2 to 4 inches in diameter are laid closely together and hitched solidly with the weaving hitch. It helps to get the straightest saplings possible, and to smooth their upper surfaces to prevent utensils from slipping through the finished table top.

A fine addition to such a table is to make seats integral with it. This can be done by spiking or lashing another pair of crossbars to the legs, long enough to extend about 18 inches past each side of the table and approximately 14 inches off the ground. Next, flatten the upper surfaces of six poles having diameters of about 4 inches. Lay these lengthwise along the table's sides, three on each side, on the protruding ends of the lower crossbars and lash or spike them close together. In a large, permanent camp, such a table-bench is often built first, then a large wall tent pitched over it.

Camp Bed

Some sort of framework should always be made at camp on which to place your bed. Today's bed is apt to be a good sleeping bag laid on an air mattress. This combination, as well as beds of blankets and boughs, should be raised off the ground. Moisture will soak up into the bed, and even though a rubber air mattress keeps it off the sleeper, moisture clings to mattress when it is rolled up, subsequently getting into the bed itself.

One simple arrangement for a bed frame is to lay two 3-foot logs at either end of the bed, allowing an extra foot of bed length. That is, lay them 7 feet apart for a 6-foot bag. Onto these, lash 4-inch poles alongside each other until a 3-foot width is covered. The outside poles, one on either side, should be of larger diameter than the others to prevent the sleeper from rolling off. If sufficient cord or rope isn't available for lashing the poles, they may be laid into shallow notches cut into each end log. When the weight of the bag is on them, they will not slip out of place.

Camp Cot

A camp cot on the same order may be built easily at camp if some additions are made to a 6-foot canvas tarp beforehand. Two strips of the same 8-ounce canvas are sewn lengthwise, along both edges of the strips. These strips should be 8 inches in width, and double-sewn along all edges for sufficient strength. The strips are sewn to the tarp three feet apart, down the central part of the tarp. The strips in no way will hinder other uses for which the tarp might normally be used.

At camp, two straight poles, such as lodgepole pine, are shoved through the loops formed by the two strips. The poles should be 3 inches in diameter, and a foot longer than the length of the tarp; and both larger ends should be at the same end of the tarp, towards the head of the cot.

The two poles are then spiked or lashed solidly to two lengths of logs, as for the camp bed above. The end logs should be of large diameter, so that when the bed on the cot sags, the sleeper will still be off the ground. The sleeping bag is then placed on the cot, and the remaining "flaps" of the tarp folded across.

Raised Fireplaces

For cooking at a semipermanent campsite where no stove is available, it is practical to raise the fireplace off the ground to a comfortable cooking height. This may be done in two ways: One is to stake off a 2-foot square of ground with 30-inch stakes of green wood—like a picket fence enclosing a square. Six inches below the top of the stakes, lash four crossbars, one on each side, to keep the stakes

Burlap bag slipped over orange crate makes an efficient camp cooler. Shallow pan of water feeds moisture through cloth wick onto burlap.

from spreading. Into this space, dirt is shoveled to the full height. Gravel or rocks are then laid over the dirt top to make a foundation for the cooking fire, which is built on top.

A second method is to build a miniature log cabin enclosing an area 2-by-2 feet square. The logs are notched on their undersides and laid on a pair of cross logs. This is continued until the desired height is reached; then the enclosure is shoveled full of earth. If enough green logs are not available, dry logs may be used except for the top layer.

Camp Coolers

The easiest way to improvise a cooler is to dig a pocket in a spring and place the food containers into the small pool. In a creek, it's best to form a cairn of rocks at the edge of the water, leaving just enough opening for the water to come in. Cans set directly into the creek are apt to float away.

A lid for such a cooler can be made from a large, flat rock. If none is available, the split half of a thick log, with the flat side down, makes a good cover. A heavy cover keeps direct sunlight out, and keeps any predator from getting into the cooler.

You can make a simple cooler by tying all canned goods into a burlap sack putting it into a creek, and anchoring it with a strong rope to a stump on the bank.

Many foods, such as bacon, butter, fruit, and meats, cannot be kept cool in this fashion, however. But if a burlap sack and an orange crate are available, a fine cooler for all foods can be made. Stand the crate on end and attach a

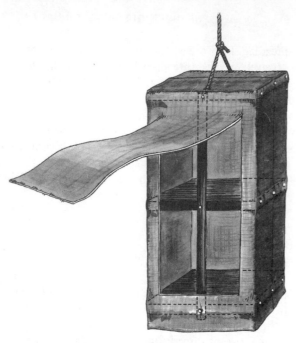

Cooler can be made of wooden slabs cut from a log and inserted in burlap bag which has an opening flap cut as shown. Cleat nailed to slabs keeps them from tilting.

rope to the upper end. Cut a hole in the sack's bottom and thread the rope through. Food packages are placed on the two shelves of the box (middle partition and bottom end), the sack is lowered over the crate, and the cooler is suspended by the rope from a high limb. Sprinkle water over the burlap sack and set a tin can full of water on top of the box. If a small strip of burlap or cloth is then placed in the filled can with one end draped over the edge and onto the burlap sack, it will siphon enough water to keep the sack moist. Evaporation of this moisture will cause the container to remain cool, even during the heat of mid-day. Additional water may be sprinkled on, if needed.

If no crate is available, a cooler can be made by slabbing out four boards from a section of log. Make each board a foot square, if a log that size is available. Then cut a strip about 10 inches wide out of the sack, leaving it "hinged" at the bottom. The boards are placed inside the sack and nailed into position like the shelves of an upright cupboard—one at the sack's bottom, the others spaced below. The bag becomes the sides and back of the cupboard. The rope is tied to the upper board. A willow cleat nailed to all shelves at the face, or open side, keeps the shelves from tipping and joins them solidly together. In use, the food is placed in this upright cupboard, the flap is closed, and water is sprinkled over the bag. A can of water with a cloth wick on top, as with the orange-crate cooler, will keep the burlap moist.

Washstands

A simple stand for the wash basin can be made by driving three saplings firmly into the ground just far enough apart so they will catch the under rim of the basin when the tops are "sprung" a trifle.

A fancier washstand can be made by lashing three saplings together a foot or so from their tops. The bottom parts of the saplings become the legs, which are spread apart to form a tripod. This also spreads their tops into a triangle of three pole ends on which the wash basin is set.

Another good washstand is made by slightly flattening two opposite sides of a large tree at a height of 34 inches,

Three ways to support a wash basin at camp: (1) on stick platform lashed to flattened sides of a tree; (2) on three saplings driven into the ground; and (3) on tripod of three saplings lashed halfway down.

and nailing or lashing two saplings, one at each side, which will stick out horizontally for 15 inches in front of the tree. Onto these saplings poles are lashed, making a small table having its back edge against the tree. The wash basin is set upon this. This arrangement is also fine for shaving, since the mirror can be handily hung on the tree above the stand.

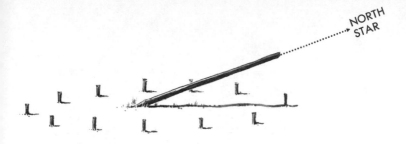

Clock-compass that tells time and indicates north can be made in camp of a pole and twelve stakes.

Clock-Compass

You can build a combination clock-and-compass with only a small pole and some stakes. Choose a small spot of ground exposed to the sun at all times during the daylight hours. Smooth the surface until it is level. Next, wait for a starry night and take an 8- to 10-foot straight pole, and drive into the ground at an angle so that its tip points directly at the North Star. At noon some day as you loaf around camp, drive a stake into the ground near the far end of the shadow cast by the slanting pole. That's 12 o'clock on your woods clock. Drive stakes similarly for each hour of the day and you have a permanent sun dial.

Emergency Snowshoes and Binding

During winter travel, a broken snowshoe presents a problem. If the break isn't too bad, a repair often can be made by splicing a light slat to the broken sidebar. However, an emergency shoe in the shape of a board can be slabbed out of a 3-foot length of dry log. Roughly shape the board to size, cut out a semi-circular hole for the toe, and with a

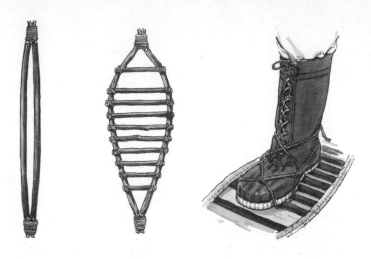

Emergency snowshoe improvised from two saplings and a number of short sticks.

knife bore two holes, one at either side of the toe hole. Thread a length of rope through these holes, around both snowshoe and pac, for an emergency binding. The lightest possible wood should be chosen, and the snowshoe shaped according to the width and strength of the wood, and only large enough to support one's weight. Cedar is the best wood for this, as it slabs easily.

A different type of emergency snowshoe can be made of green alders or willows. Two sidebars of suitable length are placed side by side and bound at both ends with fishing line or cord. The saplings should be flattened with a knife at the ends to prevent them from slipping. Next, lash an alder crossbar tightly at the position where the ball of the foot normally rides over the standard snowshoe lacing, spreading the sidebars sufficiently to get the desired width. Lash smaller crossbars behind this one, an inch apart, across the space where the foot will ride, and a final crossbar just forward of the toe opening. Finally, a burlap bag or a piece of clothing, such as a leg of a pair of Levis, should be sewn around the frame to cover the bottom of the shoe.

An emergency snowshoe binding, either for the above shoe or for a commercial model, can be made of a length of cotton clothesline, cord, leather thong, or rope. Cotton clothesline and sash cord are best, as they won't stretch when wet. Double the length of line at the middle and place this loop around the heel of the pac. Bring each end forward, and under the crossbars at either side of the toe; then up and across the toe, and back through the cords on either side of the arch. Crisscross them over the front of the foot, and tie them at the back of the pac. This emergency binding is easily twisted out of, if necessary.

Birchbark Kettles

Birchbark kettles are made of birchbark that has been soaked in water until it becomes soft. One of the best is the basket-kettle shown in the illustration. For sewing cord you can use spruce or tamarack roots, leather thong, or nylon cord. Holes are punched with an awl, if available, or a knife blade. A rim of bent willow or birch is sewn all around at the kettle's top in a continuous overhand stitch, to give rigidity and a carrying rim to the finished vessel.

All seams are waterproofed with emergency glue, which can be made in the outdoors by boiling together 15 percent bacon fat or animal suet and 85 percent resin found in such conifers as spruce, balsam fir, and pine. The addition of the animal fat makes the product less brittle. Fish

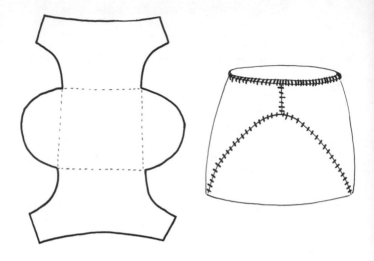

Pattern for cutting birch-bark kettle and completed kettle laced with thong or strips of root fiber.

glue can be made by boiling in water the heads, fins, and tails of fish, until nothing except a sticky gelatin-like substance remains.

Camper's Soap

Soap is a necessity for trips into the woods, especially for prolonged stays. If you exhaust your supply, you can make your own by pouring scalding water several times over wood ashes, and using the resultant liquid in the wash water for washing clothes. Pioneer women in the West often had no other form of soap for the purpose. They would keep all ashes from the kitchen stove in a wooden barrel. Hot water was repeatedly poured through these ashes and drained off through a hole at the bottom of the barrel. The lye of the ashes, largely potash, was the cleaning agent.

Another recipe calls for boiling this same liquid, strong as it can be made, with small amounts of bacon grease and other animal fat. The mixture is boiled until most of the water is evaporated, and then allowed to set overnight. The soap will rise to the surface and can be skimmed off.

The tallow of a freshly killed deer can also be used to make soap. Pour 2½ gallons of scalding water over 2 gallons of wood ashes. Stir occasionally, and let the mixture set overnight. Skim off the froth, and drain or pour off the clear liquid as needed. Meantime, render a half-pound of deer tallow, and boil down the melted fat in the wood-ashes liquid, in a small castiron, enameled, or galvanized container. When the approximate 3 quarts of liquid has been slow-boiled away with the tallow to the final pint, allow the remainder to set overnight. The soap will rise to the top as a crust.

Bacon rinds, surplus grease, and other animal fat can be made into a better soap with the addition of ordinary household lye. Add four pounds of such cracklings, rinds, or grease to 4 quarts of cold water and 13 ounces of lye and let soak for three days in an enameled kettle or pot. Next, add 5 quarts of cold water and cook the mixture over a fire for thirty minutes, or until all cracklings dissolve. Allow the mixture to stand overnight, after which the soap will rise to the top and can be cut away in bar-sized cubes. These are set upon a log to dry.

Deer tallow can be combined with lye to make a fine-grade soap which will rival the commercial product. Dissolve 1 can of lye in 7 cups cold water. While the mixture is still hot, add 4 pounds of clean deer tallow, broken or cut into small bits; ½ cup borax; ½ cup household ammonia; and 1 cup Chlorox (this particular product must be used, not a substitute).

Let the mixture stand for a couple of days, or until it granulates, stirring once in a while with a wooden paddle (not metal). During the stirring, the large lumps may be broken up. The resulting soap is like cheese curd and may be further granulated, after it has completely dried, by running it through a food grinder.

Preserving Animal Skins

The skins of game animals may be used in a variety of ways, either as rawhide or as buckskin leather, for fashioning articles of use to the outdoorsman.

Deer skins and similar hides should be worked on when they are fresh. Otherwise, they must be salted well and dried out to preserve them until they can be tanned. Before tanning a dry hide, it must be loosened by soaking. This is done by immersing the complete hide in a solution of salt and water (1 pound of salt to 2 gallons of water), for from six hours to two or three days, depending upon the stiffness of the hide.

Making Rawhide

For making rawhide, the hide must be fleshed of all remaining meat and fat. Pare off the larger pieces, then scrape the flesh side of the hide with a blunt knife, horse rasp, or similar implement, holding the skin firmly over a

First step in making rawhide or buckskin from an animal hide is to scrape off remaining meat and fat with blunt-edged tool.

smooth log set at a workable height. This should be done in the shade, as full sunlight tends to "burn" the hide.

The next step is to remove the hair. This can be done in several ways. One is to stir a gallon of wood ashes into a tubful of hot water, allow the water to cool to room temperature, and soak the hide in the mixture for several days. Periodic testing will show when the hair is loose enough to slip easily.

Another way of loosening the hair is to use slaked lime. Place two pounds of caustic lime into a wooden tub or barrel and slake by *slowly* adding small amounts of cold water. As the lime slakes, add up to a gallon of water, then cover the container and let it stand for a day. Next add 10 gallons more water, stir thoroughly, and immerse the hide in the mixture. Often it is necessary to weight the hide down with a rock to keep it completely covered.

After hide has been treated with lime solution or buried in the earth from two to six days, most of the hair can be easily removed.

Several times each day, churn the hide around in the mixture with a wooden bat, so that the lime keeps well off the bottom of the barrel. Do this without getting the hands into the solution. Normally, within four to five days the hair will slip easily from the hide.

The Indians used to loosen the hair by simply burying the hide in the earth while it was still fresh. Depending upon the "greenness" of the hide and the temperature, this takes from two to six days. The hide should be buried 6 to 8 inches deep, and spread out completely flat. A good way to determine how long to leave the hide buried is to dig up a corner each day and test the hair by pulling on it with the fingers. For this reason, it is best to bury the hide with the hair side up. When the hair slips easily the hide should be dug up and the hair removed immediately.

After loosening the hair, the damp hide should be placed over the log and all hair pulled out, or rubbed and scraped away. Use the edge of a sharp rock to do this, as well as to remove the dark, filmy layer of "scruff" which covers the skin itself.

If lime has been used to loosen the hair, the hide must next be de-limed in a solution of 1 quart vinegar to 6 gallons of water, and in sufficient quantity to cover the skin. Soaking the hide in this solution for two days will get rid

Remaining bits of hair are then scraped from hide with edge of a sharp rock.

of the lime. During this time it should be churned about periodically. Afterward, the hide should be washed repeatedly in clean water to remove all traces of the acetic acid in the vinegar.

To finish such a cleansed hide into rawhide, it is then stretched tightly and allowed to dry slowly in the shade where air will circulate around every part of it. This can be done by stretching the hide inside a frame made by lashing four poles together. The hide is sewn to all four poles through small holes made in the outside edges. If a board platform is available, the hide can be stretched as tight as possible and tacked along its edges to the board. The board is then stood up on edge. When it dries, rawhide will be extremely hard, but it can be softened by soaking it overnight. This will leave it soft enough to be worked into articles.

Rawhide is useful for making chair seats and backs, ornamental drumheads, knife and ax sheaths. Some cowboys still use a rawhide lariat for catching horses and mules inside a corral, where a quick, stiff loop must be snaked out to catch a skittery animal on the first try, and there is no time for a soft lariat to build a loop. All professional steer ropers use a rawhide "burner" instead of a metal honda for the tiny end loop in a rope lasso. These burners are shaped of wet steer rawhide, formed inside the loop and allowed to dry out. Rawhide has long been used as the covering for the horns of stock saddles. I have a riding saddle which was custom-built for me half a lifetime ago, and the rawhide around its horn is still in good shape. This, too, is steer rawhide.

When rawhide lacing dries out it is almost transparent, and makes a substantial and good-looking lace for leather sheaths to enclose sharp-edged tools. Laced in while still wet, it can be shaped with the leather to take the form of the tool. When dry, it provides a hard protective cover for the cutting edge of the tool.

Making Buckskin

For most uses, however, it is better to finish the hide by tanning it into buckskin. This involves two more steps: tanning and softening the raw hide.

When hide has dried after soaking in tanning solution, it is softened by working it over a blunt-edged post set in the ground at a convenient height.

A simple tanning solution is made of household white soap-chips. After the hide has been cleaned, oil the flesh side lightly with deer tallow and hang it over a pole in the shade for a day. Next, dissolve 3 pounds of soap-chips in 10 gallons of warm water, and soak the hide in this solution (kept at room temperature if possible) for from three

Hide is finished by smoking it over a smudge fire. Here smoke was piped upward into basket which contains hide suspended upon two saplings shoved through slits. Basket is raised off hot pipe; shield over fire regulates draft.

days to a week, until the hide will permit the soapsuds to be squeezed through it. At this stage, rinse all the soap from the hide by repeated washings in clean water. When the hide has dried to the stage where it is still mildly damp, it is ready for softening. There are also commercial tanning preparations available today. Any taxidermist can direct you.

Finished buckskin, having been smoked and softened, is darker than original hide and waterproof. Light film of Neatsfoot oil may be rubbed onto flesh side.

To soften a hide into buckskin, it must be worked over a thin, blunt surface to break down every fiber. A good implement at camp for doing this is a 5-inch post set into the ground at a workable height—18 inches is just right. The top of the post should be thinned down to leave a blunt edge like a shovel blade or the end of a boat oar. With a movement much like polishing shoes with a cloth, the hide is pulled back and forth across the wooden edge, flesh side down, until it is soft all over. This takes considerable effort.

To finish, the hide is smoked slowly over a hardwood smudge fire. One way of doing this is to use the softened hide as the "wrap" for a small smokehouse. Another is to pipe the smoke upward from the fire into a box or basket in which the hide is loosely suspended. The hide should be shifted occasionally so it will be evenly smoked, and care should be used that it never gets hot. Smoking darkens and softens the hide, as well as making it more waterproof.

Lastly, a very light film of Neatsfoot oil may be rubbed onto the flesh side of the hide, but it isn't really necessary for good buckskin.

Tanning Skins With Hair

Often the outdoorsman will wish to tan small skins with the hair on. The procedure for tanning small hides with the hair on is similar to the steps followed in making buckskin. The hides are softened and fleshed in the same way, but not de-haired. The hides are then put into the tanning mixture. A good one for small skins consists of 1 pound alum dissolved in 5 gallons of boiling water, to which is added 2½ pounds of table salt.

When this is dissolved and cooled, the skins are immersed and left from five to ten days, depending upon the size and thickness of the skins. Coyote skins, as an example, require about five days. During the tanning period, the skins are moved about periodically in the solution.

When the hide is the same color all the way through (as tested by slicing a thin strip off one edge), it is tanned. The skin is then hung to drain, and all of the solution washed out by repeated rinsing.

The skins are then hung in the shade to dry completely. They are next softened again by sponging warm water over the flesh side, then rolled up overnight to sweat. After sweating, the skins are softened by breaking the fibers over a blunt edge.

A final step is to rub a dressing of some kind of warm animal fat into the flesh side, to keep the skins soft. All excess oil or fat is then removed by rubbing sawdust over the skins. They are then ready for use.

Cutting Laces

Both rawhide and buckskin are used for lacings to braid rope and cord, or for leather thongs. The neatness and uniform strength of the lace depends upon an even width.

The best guide I've found for cutting continuous uniform lengths of lacing from leather or damp rawhide is simply two knives stuck solidly into a flattened log or table top. One knife does the cutting, the other guides the width.

The cutting knife, which should have a razor-sharp edge, is stuck firmly into the log at about an angle of 80 degrees. The knife used as a gauge should be set the desired width of the lacing from the cutting blade, say, a quarter-inch, and at

Two methods of cutting a lace from a circular piece of leather. In camp two knives stuck in a flattened log serve as a gauge for cutting lace in continuous spiral. At home two boards may be used as shown below.

the same angle, but with its edge in the opposite direction. It is best if the guiding blade is of greater width than the cutting blade. A butcher knife and thin pocketknife make a good combination.

The lacing is cut in a spiral around the edge of a piece of leather which has been trimmed so it is fairly round in contour. To begin, cut a 2-inch length of lacing with another knife, starting it from the left side of the leather, for a right-handed person. This length of lacing is placed between the two knife blades. Holding the end in the left hand, and the leather in the right, both are pulled against the sharp edge, which cuts it as the other blade gauges the width. By working fairly close to the blades, and keeping the uncut leather flat as it goes between, a continuous spiral length of lacing of uniform width can be quickly cut.

Where nails and flat boards are available, a similar gauge may be made by nailing a 1-inch board on a half-inch board so that the edge of the top board is over the center of the bottom board. A sharp knife is then shoved up through the bottom board at the desired width from the edge of the upper board. The edge serves as a guide as the lacing is cut by the blade.

Preserving Snake Skins

Snake skins are difficult to tan, but may be preserved by a salt-alum solution similar to that used for small skins. The snake skin is softened, then soaked in the lime solution used for de-hairing deer hides until the scales come loose. These are scraped or brushed off with a stiff-bristled brush, then the skin de-limed as above. It is then soaked for three or four days in the alum-salt solution used for small skins which has been diluted to 50 percent strength with water.

Next, to the alum-salt solution, 5 grams of sodium carbonate (dissolved in warm water) are added slowly, a drop at a time. The skin is kept in this solution five to six days, and periodically stirred.

The tanned skin is then drained, and soaked twelve hours in a solution of 1 part sulphonated oil to 3 parts water.

Lastly, the snake skin is removed, squeezed dry, stretched gently, and tacked in shape on a flat surface. When completely dry, it is removed and gently worked over a blunt board until it is pliable. It may then be ironed into shape with a warm flat-iron, and painted with liquid celluloid to give it a gloss.

Preserving Fish Skins

The best way of preserving fish specimens is, of course, to have them mounted. This entails at least a fundamental knowledge of taxidermy.

The skins of fish, however, may be preserved by a rather simple process. First, the fish is wiped off with a solution of alum (1 teaspoonful to a gallon of water) to remove the mucous, or slime. Next, the fish is skinned completely by making only one incision in the hide along midships of the unwanted side, running from the tail to gill coverts. Fins and tail are left integral with the skin, and are cut off at their base. The head is also left with the skin, with the eyes, cheek muscles, and all meat around the gills removed.

Next, the skin is fleshed with a dull knife, scraping toward the head, and the cleaned skin is dipped into a strong solution of grain alcohol (2 parts alcohol to 1 part water). This solution is drained off, then a weak formaldehyde solution is painted onto the fins, tail, and head, but *not* onto the skin. For preserving the skin itself, a deadly poisonous solution of 1 ounce of sodium arsenite to a gallon of water is swabbed onto the flesh side of the skin and allowed to soak in.

Lastly, the skin is shaped as desired, and allowed to dry. During the drying process, the fins and tail are spread to position between flat pieces of cardboard, and held there with paper clips. This preserves their natural shape, without letting them split.

Eskimo Tanning Methods

Often other parts of game animals, besides the hide, can be used in making outdoor equipment. One such part is the leg tendons of large game animals such as caribou, elk, moose, etc.

Leg tendons are prepared and used in the sewing of hides and skins, and make good emergency and permanent "thread." As an example, I have a pair of Eskimo-made mukluks whose inner boots were handsewn with a curved needle and split caribou tendon. The sewing, done by my Eskimo guide's wife, rivals machine sewing in evenness and delicacy of stitch, and the tendon thread is as strong as when the mukluks were made many years ago.

To give you an idea of how these tendons were prepared, as well as how the Eskimos, who have few outside materials to work with, go about tanning hides, I'm going to quote from a recent letter from this same Eskimo guide. With this man's limited opportunities to learn and use English, he writes remarkably well. I'm simply setting it down verbatim, to preserve the full flavor.

Dear Clyde.

I'll do my best to answer your questions. First we do have three ways of tanning and making leather of seal skins.

1. For bleaching a seal skin. You prabably see some white seal skins hanging on the outside racks while you was up here. In order to make a bleached seal skin here is what they do. After skinning a seal they don't bother to wash the blood or oil off the skin, but they do rub more oil on the hair and roll the skin in small roll and place it in a can or any container and cover the skin with blubber and place the container where the heat will reach the container (with skin in it) and leave the skin in the container for about a week. In a week's time the hair will slip off the skin as long as the container is in a warm place. After the hair slip off the next move is to get wooden pegs and peg and stretch it and freeze dry, and keep it outdoors all the time. This is done in winter only. And in about three weeks the skin is completely dried and white, and this leather is used for mukluk lace's and mukluk bottoms and tops.

2. This is done for making waterproof mukluks. In order to do this, after the skin is dried, first they get a piece of lime stone (which is plentiful near by) and place it in a burning stove in order to get it softer to grind it in powdered form (today some women use Dutch Cleanser for this purpose) and spread this powdered stone all over the skin just so it get

between hair and to the skin and they get a sharp edged rock and use it as a scraper and work it back and forth till the hair is scraped off. And the next thing is to get a metal skin scraper and scrape the access fat off as well as softening the skin. Then the skin is ready.

3. Tanning the skin for jackets, pants and mukluks not getting the hair off. After the skin is dried scrape the access fat off as well as getting it soft after scraping is done, get a handful of flour and place it in a bowl add water and mix it till it is thin and spread this flour on the skin and fold the skin and let it lay for over night and as the skin is drying it is worked with hands in order to get it soft and thats that.

And for the sinew and tandons. First clean the meat off the sinews, after cleaning them get a can or bowl of water and soak the sinews for about overnight or till the sinew turned white and blood off then it is time to get a piece of board and stretch them and place them to dry. After dry place them in cool place, when overdried will break off when they are bended. same to tendons. And for splitting, start on from the thinest part and peel off the desired size you want. And for using this sinew for sewing, place the thinest part in the eye of the needle that way the sinew will not split while sewing . . .

Obviously, these types of "native tan" are most useful in cold weather and climates when there is less danger of putrefaction. However, hair seals are nearly one-half blubber, or fat, and this fat is the tanning agent. I happen to know, also, that many Eskimos, for a more permanent tan for all seasons, use human urine as the tanning solution.

Catgut

Commercial catgut is made, not from the intestines of a cat, but from those of sheep, horses, and burros. Processing is an involved and tedious series of steps including the removal of all fat, soaking in alkaline baths, scraping, smoking in the fumes of sulfur, and drawing the ribbons of gut through a metal aperture to get a uniform size in the finished strings. These are used for stringing musical instruments, and for tying off incisions in surgery.

A simulated catgut can be made of the intestines of deer, elk, moose, and other game animals by somewhat the same process. The gut is scraped with a blunt knife until all fat is removed. Next, the intestine is soaked overnight in a solution made by pouring 3 gallons of boiling water over a gallon of wood ashes, and cooling. The gut is next drained and cleaned by washing in several changes of clean water, then placed for three days into the alum-salt tanning solution used for small hides. When the tanning is complete, the gut is washed again and cut into thin ribbons. These may be used as is, or twisted and dried into string suitable for sewing buckskin, leather articles, and canvas. Smoking catgut, as with buckskin, improves the product.

Leathercraft

Very often an outdoorsman will want to make his own knife and ax sheaths. These should be made of stiff, heavy

Samples of designs that may be cut with tools made at home
from heads of spikes.

steer hide for the protection it offers cutting edges during
rough handling. Heavy, factory-tanned leather may be laced
with rawhide or buckskin and decorated to suit one's
taste.

Begin by laying out a full-sized pattern on paper. Brown
wrapping paper makes a good design paper. Some experimentation may be necessary to get exactly the right size.
This is done by fitting the paper around the tool and cutting to shape, allowing for a lacing edge or seam.

Tooling a Design

Next comes the matter of the design itself, and here the
artistry of the individual has full play. In general, any design should be in keeping with the shape of the article. For
a long sheath or case, the design should be long, such as a
trailing vine and leaves, not a series of polka-dots.

The design need not be a realistic depiction of anything
in nature. The best designs are abstract, and often in the
form of flowing leaves, flowers, and stems. The best way to
get a good design is to practice a few times on a piece of
paper the same size as the finished work. When a good design is made, keep it for transferring to the leather. Don't
leave too much "background."

279

Generally speaking, the leather item is tooled on only one side—the side exposed when the item is worn or used. The design must fit this space.

Having created a suitable design, your next step is to transfer this design to the full-sized pattern. This is done by

Pattern for a holster has been cut from a piece of leather and design traced from original sketch on paper. Swivel knife was used while leather was still wet to cut around all outside lines to separate the design from the background area.

blacking the underside of the paper on which the design is drawn by rubbing the edge of a soft lead pencil all over the paper. Next, the paper is laid in place on the pattern, and the lines retraced with a pencil. This will transfer the design onto the paper pattern.

The next step is to transfer the pattern onto the leather. First, lay the flat leather on a smooth surface. Professionals use a marble slab, but this isn't necessary for the beginner. Next, sponge off both sides of the leather with water until they are damp but not wet. Make sure there are no pencil marks on the back of the paper pattern, then lay it in place on the face side of the wet leather. Once in place, it can be held by taping the edges with cellulose tape. Now go over all lines of the pattern with the pencil, bearing down quite heavily so as to leave the imprint in the leather. Make sure that every line of the design is traced. A dry ball-point pen makes a good tool.

Next, while the leather is still damp, cut around every outside line of the design with a swivel knife. This is a knife which can be made to revolve in the fingers while being held solidly with another finger. It has a blunt taper to its edge, so it will cut only a shallow groove in the leather. It is the only tool the beginner actually needs to buy—if he's good at improvising others. Cutting around all marks of the design outlines the pattern, forms a border, and separates the design from the background areas.

The next job is to stamp in the background. This is done with some pattern of background tool. It may be a cross-hatch pattern, basketweave, simple dots or a stipple. Any number of tools that can cut background designs are available from most hobby stores or leather-working companies which advertise in the outdoor journals.

The most fun, however, is to make your own. This is a simple job. Take a 40-penny spike, or 60-penny spike, and file or grind the head perfectly flat. The spike head may then be ground along the edges into a square, triangle, or thin rectangle, depending on the desired design. For working into corners of the leather background, at least one tool should be triangular in shape.

Next, take a triangular file and cut a crosshatch pattern on the flat head of the spike, making all cuts about 1/16 inch apart. Then cut off the spike's sharpened end so as to leave a tool of about 3 inches long. If you set this tool on a dampened scrap of leather, and hit the end with a hammer, you will be surprised to see what a pleasing design it leaves embedded in the leather.

Other designs may be filed or punched into spike heads. Another good one for backgrounds leaves a series of closely-set dots of raised leather. This one is made by driving the sharpened end of a center-punch into the spike head, making the punch marks in a crosshatch arrangement and as close together as possible. This head, when punched into wet leather, leaves raised dots which make a pleasing background design.

With a suitable tool, the background area all over the design is then stamped into the leather. Professionals use a mallet and machine-built tools for the job. The beginner needs only his own spike tools, a hammer for pounding, or even a wooden "mallet" made by cutting off a section of a tree branch having a smaller branch growing out of its side for a handle.

As you stamp in the background, the leather will dry. Before it gets too dry, sponge off the surface again and

Design has been completed by stamping in background with homemade tool and modeling the edges to give embossed, three-dimensional effect. Holster will then be laced with leather thong.

continue the work. Sponging occasionally, until the surface is just damp, prevents watermarks in the finished item.

When the background has all been stamped in, the shape of the design is modeled in. A modeling tool may be purchased, but the handle end of a small spoon can be made to serve. Briefly, in modeling, all edges of the design are smoothed down so they appear to raise gradually, from the level of the stamped background, giving an embossed, three-dimensional effect.

When all design has been modeled into the best possible shape, so that it appears to stand out from the background, a final border all around the entire design may be made if desired. One good design for this is simply a continuous row of tiny dots. These are made with a spike tool which has been ground or filed to a very thin strip of metal, into which are punched tiny holes, with the center-punch, at uniform distances from each other. The border mark is laid off by running the tip of a stylus, or blunt point, along a straightedged ruler around the border of the design, keeping the leather damp. The border of holes is then stamped in with the thin tool. Fancier bordering tools can be made as desired.

Lacing the Work

When the entire design is finished, the leather is allowed to dry out. The edges of the leather are cut to fit the outline of the intended sheath or case. The item is then folded into shape, and laced. If it is a knife sheath, two vertical slits should be cut in the leather at a point where the belt will go, each slit finished at both ends with a punched hole to prevent tearing. Otherwise, a separate belt loop can be riveted onto the sheath.

Lacing stitches vary from simple to involved. A good one for the beginner is a simple overhand lacing, with the lace going around and around the doubled edges of the sheath, through holes punched at uniform distance inside the edge. Where the leather edges come together, as in a knife sheath, the holes should not be punched opposite each other in the opposite edges. If this is done, the finished article will twist. Instead, the holes should be punched so each hole in one edge comes between two holes in the opposite edge.

Rawhide thongs processed as described, and soaked until they are soft enough to be workable, make good laces. Buckskin also makes fine lacing for many leather articles used in the outdoors. If you want to be real fancy, get a lacing leather known commercially as tooling calf.

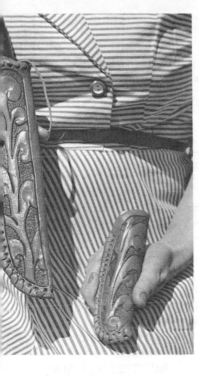

These two knife sheaths were
fashioned of homemade leather
and designed with spike-head
tools. Ends of lacing were
properly concealed.

In lacing, beginners don't know what to do with ends. A
good way to handle the beginning end is to lay 2 inches of
it, before it enters the first hole, between the edges to be
laced; then lace around both edges and the lace itself. This
way the lace end will be concealed in the finished item. The
remaining end lace may be similarly concealed. To do this,
lace the final 2 inches of the article loosely with, say, a
half-inch of slack in each overhand stitch. Next, bend the
end of the lacing down through this length of loose lacing
and between the edges to be laced together; and lastly, pull
the lace's end through between two lacing stitches. Then,
by starting where the lacing is tight, and pulling tight each

stitch, the end will be concealed except for a loop at the end and the tip of the lace itself. By pulling on the lace end, it can be drawn through, pulling the loop inside the laced work. The lace can then be snipped off close and its edge tucked under. This, in addition to making a neat job, prevents the lacing from coming loose.

With any single overhand lacing stitch, it is best to punch holes of considerably smaller diameter than the width of the lacing, and to space such holes exactly the lace's width apart. In use, the small holes contract the lacing tightly, but the lace outside the holes spreads flat and covers the entire edge, making a neat, smooth seam.

The final step is to dye and finish the leather. Steer hide may be dyed any desired color with leather dye, then waxed to finish. One of the finest and most appropriate finishes for outdoor items such as knife sheaths is a product named "Antique." This brown stain is smoothed onto the finished article, allowed to stand for a half-minute, or until the desired depth of the brown color is reached, then quickly wiped off with a clean cloth. The longer Antique remains on the leather, the darker it will stain. To preserve the finish, buff the leather occasionally with any good shoe polish or wax.

14

Tree Identification

Trees furnish the outdoorsman with fuel for his campfire, boughs for his bed and shelter, logs for his raft and his cabin, timber from which to slab out camp furniture, shade for his rest and travel, and even some edible food for his stomach. In addition, the woods furnish cover for the game he may seek, and slow down the moisture in watershed country so that he may have clear, stable, and fish-populated streams.

But in a deeper way, the magnificent forests of America give inspiration, meaning, and courage to the outdoorsman. There is nothing more straightforward or honest than the unvarying reach of a great fir tree toward the heavens. There is no greater lesson in courage than that given by a mighty oak, buffeted by all adversity, carrying its scars with dignity, and silently living on. And what could better depict evenual achievement and accomplishment than a 6000-ton redwood tree fourteen centuries old?

A tree is defined as a plant having a central trunk, which at maturity reaches a height of 10 feet or over. In the light of this definition, there are over 800 different kinds of trees in the United States alone. It is next to impossible for the average person to know them all. It does, however, add to our enjoyment of trees to be able to call some of the better-known species by their first names.

Classification of Trees

Trees may be broadly grouped in several ways. One way is to classify them as either broadleaf trees or conifers.

The broadleaf trees are generally hardwood trees, and, as the name suggests, have large leaves. They include such species as oak, maple, and basswood. The conifers have small leaves, or needles, suited to enduring cold climates, and are so named partly because of the shape of the tree. Conifers have a large central bole, and branches that reach out horizontally. As these branches rise toward the tree's top, they shorten in length, giving the entire tree a cone-shaped appearance. This, plus the fact that most conifers are conebearing trees, gives them their name. The seeds grow in these cones, which are produced by the branches. When the cones have ripened, the heavy scales open and the seeds are distributed by wind. The conifers include such species as pine, fir, spruce, and yew.

Most conifers are evergreens; that is, the tiny green leaves stay with the tree throughout all seasons of the year and shed gradually. At least one species of conifer is not an evergreen—the larch, or tamarack, which sheds its leaves annually like deciduous trees.

America's Forest Areas

To get an idea of the general forest areas of North America, imagine an ellipse of area roughly one-fifth the width of the United States, lying in a north-south direction, and covering the Great Plains region of the United States from the Mexican border well into the Prairie Provinces of Canada.

Such a broadly defined area is the relatively unforested region of the continent. So far as the United States is concerned, this belt of plains separates the forested parts of the nation into two major areas—the eastern forests and the western forests. Generally speaking, the eastern forests have been depleted to a greater extent than have the western forests, and the greater part of the cut timber today comes from the western area.

Going back to the above ellipse of plains area, it will be apparent that the western forests and the eastern forest belt tend to join northward beyond the plains region. Also, the lower end of the Pacific and Rocky Mountain forests tend to meet the end of the eastern-southern forests toward the Texas area of the Gulf of Mexico.

In effect this divides the continent into several broadly separated regions of forests. In a broad way, the trees of one region will differ from those in another. There is, of course, considerable overlapping of species; and within each general belt of forest there is, further, an admixture of species. However, by separating the continent into different regions, and considering the trees of each region separately, the identification of individual species becomes easier.

Northern Forest Belt

One of these divisions is the northern belt of forests, and the trees there are largely coniferous. This vast division of the continent covers parts of the New England States, and in a westward direction covers the upper Great Lakes area to Minnesota. From there the region is principally northward, covering a great share of Canada, and joins above the Canadian prairie country with the western forests. From there the northern belt of conifers continues into Alaska and covers a major portion of this new state.

The major species in this extended belt include the pines, firs, hemlock, larch or tamarack, spruce, and the arborvitaes, commonly called cedars.

There are several species of pines, including the famed white pine, red or Norway pine, jack pine, and pitch pine. The most important fir is the balsam fir. The three main species of spruce are the white spruce, the red spruce, and the black spruce.

Mixed in with these major species are, of course, numerous hardwoods and aspens.

Rocky Mountain Belt

Generally south and westward from this belt is a belt of forests coincident with the Rocky Mountains. This forested area broadly includes all the country along the chain of mountains from Mexico well into Canada where the overall region joins with the northern coniferous forests.

In the Rocky Mountain region there are four major kinds of trees—the firs, pines, spruces, and larch, which is the western brother of the eastern tamarack.

The principal fir here is the Douglas fir. Two other firs are the Colorado fir and the white fir. Pines may be divided into white pine, yellow or ponderosa pine, and lodgepole pine. There are two main species of spruce, the Englemann spruce and the Colorado, or blue spruce. As with the northern belt of forests, there are numerous other species of trees mixed in with the major trees of the Rocky Mountain region.

Pacific Forest Belt

Farther west than the Rocky Mountain belt is the Pacific region of forests. As the name suggests, this is a coastal region extending generally from the Mexican border along the Pacific and well into Alaska. The timber here is largely coniferous. Trees include such species as Douglas fir, redwood, pine, hemlock, fir, spruce, and arborvitae. Douglas fir is the main fir in this region, but noble fir, grand fir, and red fir are also found in the Pacific forests. Pines include ponderosa, white pine, and sugar pine. The principal spruce is the Sitka spruce.

Central Hardwood Belt

East of the Great Plains area in the United States is a broad belt of forests reaching southwesterly from the New England States all the way to Georgia and Texas. This general belt joins the northern belt of conifers to the south of the Great Lakes, and includes parts of Canada east of the Great Lakes. It covers also the lower Mississippi Basin, extending into the eastern parts of the Great Plains States themselves. This vast area is principally an area of hardwood trees.

The hardwood forests include numerous species including oak, chestnut, beech, hickory, birch, walnut, elm, gum, tulip, maple, locust, sycamore, basswood, wild cherry, ash, willow, and poplar. Oak is the most important tree of this hardwood group, economically speaking. Oaks are of many species, but are classified into two major groups, the red oaks and the white oaks. White oaks have rounded leaf-tips, while those of the red oaks are pointed. Elms include the American and the slippery elm. Maples include several species such as the silver maple, boxelder maple, and the hard or sugar maple, which is the most important maple for lumber. Ash includes several species, generally according to color. The white ash is most important.

Southern Forest Belts

To the southeast of this wide hardwood area is another belt of conifers. This area reaches from Virginia to Florida, and westward along the Gulf of Mexico inland, as far as Texas to the west. It includes major portions of the states of Mississippi, Louisiana, Georgia, and Alabama. The trees of this region are principally pine, cypress, and red cedar. Pines include the longleaf pine, shortleaf pine, slash pine, and loblolly pine.

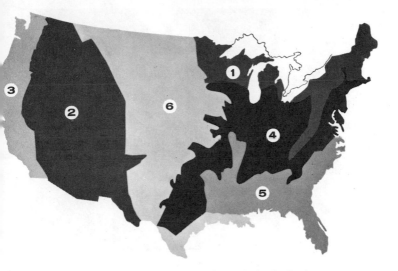

America's forest areas: 1. Northern forest belt, 2. Rocky Mountain belt, 3. Pacific forest belt, 4. Central hardwood belt, 5. Southern forest belt, 6. Plains belt.

A final forest belt is that of the evergreen hardwoods found in the subtropics. This area includes parts of Florida and the Gulf Coast States. Trees include mahogany, cedar, rosewood, citrus, and pine.

Mexico has only a small fraction of its land area forested. Trees include mesquite in the desert regions, the hardwoods in higher low-country, and pine along the higher crest of its spine.

The following section contains many of North America's most important trees, alphabetically arranged. All photographs courtesy of the U. S. Forest Service, unless otherwise credited.

White Ash

Ash

Swamp ash, blue ash, red ash, and white ash are all native to North America. The best known and most useful is the white ash, which might well be called the "baseball tree." More baseball bats are made from this species than from

Gray bark of the white ash has deep, diamond-shaped fissures and narrow, forking ridges. The leaves (above), which grow opposite one another, average 6 inches long with usually seven on a stem.

White ash is a heavy-limbed tree, the largest of which grow to a height of 100 feet or more and a butt diameter of 5 feet. It is broad and rounded in open country, straighter and taller in forest areas.

any other tree. The white ash grows to a height of 70 or 80 feet, with graceful, drooping foliage. The trunk is often free of major branches up to a considerable height. The majority of the leaves occur at the ends of the branches. These leaves are compound, with each set of leaves growing out of the central stem opposite to each other, with each individual leaflet averaging up to 6 inches long. The winged seeds average from 1 to 2 inches in length. The white ash is found from southeast Canada to the Gulf States, and as far west as Minnesota.

Aspen

The quaking aspen, as it is often called, is a member of the poplar family, and is well named. The round leaves of

Nearly round leaves of quaking aspen are 1 ¼ to 3 inches long, shiny green above and dull green beneath. The fruit, maturing in May and June, is light green in color and nearly ¼ inch long.

Quaking
aspen's
smooth,
thin bark
is green-
ish-white.
With age
it darkens
and be-
comes
furrowed.

297

this tree will move and flutter even with no detectable breeze. The tree grows over much of the continent, and though normally short in height, will, where it must compete for sunlight among the conifers, often reach a height of 60 feet or more. In Canada, where it is abundant, it is often called silver poplar. The aspen is short-lived and multiplies by sending up root stalks at considerable distance away from the main stem. With the first frosts, aspens turn a beautiful golden color, and are most striking when seen among evergreens. The aspen is important to the outdoorsman. The smoke from dry aspen splits has a pleasant odor which is one of the joys of the outdoors. Living aspen trunks are pale green with nearly black markings.

Basswood

The American basswood is also called a linden, or lime tree. Basswood grows over a wide area including southeastern Canada and the eastern half of the United States. Mature trees will reach 100 feet in height and reach maturity in about that same number of years. The tree has upward-spreading branches which flower with yellow-white blossoms containing honey. The dark-gray bark has deep furrows; the inner bark was once used by Indians for making rope. The wood is light in color, and is used where a light, soft wood is necessary for making furniture and toys.

Mature basswood has gray, furrowed bark with scaly ridges. Heart-shaped leaves, 4 to 8 inches long, are coarsely toothed; fruits are nutlike in appearance, ½ inch round.

Beech

This is a deciduous tree native to Eurasia and North America, and is found in the southeastern part of Canada and the eastern part of the United States. The trunk of the beech is statuesque in appearance and covered with a smooth silvery bark. Its leaves run from 3 to 6 inches in length and are shaped like a pointed ellipse. They are sharp-toothed at the end of their veins. Beechnuts form in small husks and, when ripe, drop to the ground, serving as food for several species of wildlife. Beech buds in the spring are long and pointed. Mature trees reach a height of 100 feet. The wood is useful for making boxes, novelties, and

Beech leaves have parallel veins ending in sharp points, are dark blue-green above, light green beneath. The blue-gray bark is thin and smooth.

furniture. The beech is often used as an ornamental tree.

Birch

There are several species of birch. Two of the most important are the yellow birch, found in the northeastern part of the United States and adjacent Canada, and as far west as Minnesota; and the white birch. The yellow birch has

Paper Birch

Leaves of the paper birch are oval, 2 to 4 inches long, coarsely and usually doubly toothed. They are dull dark green above, light green and sometimes hairy beneath.

played an important part in the making of furniture, boxes, and veneer wood for interior finishes in buildings, but the supply is diminishing. The white, or paper birch, so called

Bark of the paper birch (left) and yellow birch (right) curls in thin, papery strips. Paper-birch bark is white and smooth; yellow-birch bark yellowish or silvery-grey, turning reddish-brown on old trees.

302

because its bark peels off in light-colored, paper-like strips, has a range from Maine to Minnesota as far south as the tip of Lake Michigan and north to Canada. The paper birch is sometimes mistaken for an allied species, the gray birch. The paper birch has had a long romantic past in that it has been the principal material for covering birchbark canoes. In temperate climates birch trees will reach a height of 60 feet. But as the tree is found northward into the severe climates of northern Canada and Alaska, this height greatly decreases. The birch there is called the arctic birch, and in North America is the tree farthest north before all trees give way to tundra. I have hunted in arctic birch regions of both Canada and Alaska where the trees were not over 3 feet tall, and the small, waxy leaves were about the size of a thumbnail.

Cedar

There are several cedars, some which are called cedars but which are really arborvitae or juniper. One is the northern white cedar, or arborvitae. This tree grows in much of Canada and the United States, in the same general region as the white pine. The white cedar grows to a height of over 50 feet. The heavy foliage is in the form of flat sprays of leaves, with tiny leaves "braided" along the small branches. Another similar species is the southern white cedar, which grows in wet ground from the Northeast States to the Gulf of Mexico. This is sometimes called the swamp cedar. Still another cedar is the red cedar, spread widely over most of the United States. This species is not a true cedar but a juniper, and is identified by the clusters

Red cedar (left), a towering western tree, has reddish-brown bark that is thin and fibrous (below). Bark of white cedar (bottom) is also reddish-brown but has narrow connecting ridges.

Leaves of red cedar (left) are shiny dark green, scale-like, 1/8 to 1/2 inch long. Atlantic white-cedar leaves (right) are shorter, dull blue-green in color.

of small bluish berries which grow along the branch-tips. Another is the common juniper, which grows in semi-arid soil and rolling hill country over much of North America. This species has very sharp, short needles, and bears the typical blue juniperberries.

Cedar wood is light, but in some species splits badly, making it difficult to use as length-lumber. Cedar wood is, however, highly resistant to damage from soil and weather, and for this reason makes good fence posts and shingles for buildings. For a comparable reason, Port Orford cedar of the West Coast has long been used for making boats. The red cedar of western North America is highly prized as a wood for making fancy furniture, ornaments, and especially for making cedar chests.

Chestnut

The chestnut is a species closely allied to the beech. The American species was once common to the hardwood belt of forests, principally coincident with the Appalachian Mountains. The tree grew to a height of 70 to 100 feet, with long leaves having very sharp edges. The

chestnuts were formed inside big burrs that had sharp stickers on the outside, which would open after frosts. An Asiatic blight has decimated the American chestnut, and recent attempts to rehabilitate it, or to produce disease-resistant strains, have not been successful.

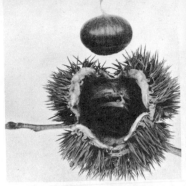

Fruit of the chestnut is a spiny bur about 2 inches in diameter (left), containing two or three edible nuts. Leaves are narrowly oblong, 5 to 9 inches long, parallel veined, with slightly curving teeth.

Dark-brown bark is irregularly fissured into broad, flat ridges.

Eastern Cottonwood

Cottonwood

There are three main species of cottonwood: The eastern cottonwood found in the eastern half of the United States; the swamp cottonwood, which was once found over the central part of the Mississippi Basin, along the Gulf to the north end of Florida, and up the Atlantic seacoast; and the black cottonwood, found principally in California and in the Northwest, and northward into Canada.

The species is fast-growing and will mature in less than two decades, reaching a height of 100 feet. The cotton-wood tends to follow river courses. The leaves are triangle-shaped, glossy, pale-green in color, and have toothed edges. In the fall after frost, when the leaves turn golden in color,

Bark of the eastern cottonwood is yellowish and smooth in young trees, becoming gray and deeply furrowed with age. Leaves are triangular, 3 to 6 inches long, coarsely toothed, smooth, light green, and shiny.

Smaller than the eastern species, black cottonwood has heart-shaped leaves and grayish-brown bark.

a row of cottonwoods along a river course makes a sight which is nothing less than spectacular. The name comes from the way the seed is formed and matures. The cottonwood tree produces strings of seed capsules whose small seeds have white, cotton-like attachments. These are blown from the tree during wind, and scatter the species. Wood from the cottonwood is light but warps badly as lumber. It does, however, make good excelsior, and light containers. It is also useful as firewood. Standing cottonwoods are highly useful as shelters in open country against wind.

Cypress

The cypress is a swamp species having needles for leaves, and bears round cones having woody scales. The bald

Bald cypress has reddish-brown or gray bark with long fibrous or scaly ridges. The yellow-green leaves, which are shed in the fall, are crowded feather-like on slender, horizontal twigs. Cones are ¾ to 1 inch in diameter and have hard scales.

cypress, like the western larch, sheds its leaves annually. The cypress ranges southward from the lower New England States to Florida, across the lower portions of the Gulf States to Mexico, and over much of the swampy areas of the Mississippi Basin. The cypress grows in water or mud along the shores of swamps. Its massive trunk flares like a fluted cone. Cypress trees will grow to over 100 feet in height, and reach 10 to 12 feet thick at the base. Some species have a large spreading top, others are shaped like a conifer. The wood is yellow or orange in color, and is highly impervious to water and decay. Doors and arches in Europe which were made of cypress have endured for a thousand years. In America the wood is used for outdoor purposes where resistance to weather is required.

Elm

Of the half-dozen species of elm which grow in North America, the American elm and the slippery elm are the best known. The American elm is classic in shape. Trees sometimes reach 100 feet in height and 6 feet in diameter. The trunk remains undivided for the first 20 to 30 feet, then the branches sweep upward and outward, drooping downward similar to the shape of an umbrella. The leaves are roughly elliptical in shape, having pointed ends and toothed edges. The leaves are not symmetrical at their bases; the larger half is on the convex side of the curving stem.

The slippery elm is named because of its slippery inner bark. Its range is not as broad as that of the American

Leaves of the American elm are not symmetrical in shape. Dark-green and smooth above, leaves are pale and usually hairy beneath. The flat, single-seeded fruits (right) are 3/8 to 1 inch long.

313

Gray bark of American elm is deeply furrowed, with long, forking, scaly ridges.

elm, but is limited to the eastern half of temperate North America. Its leaves resemble those of the American elm, but are considerably larger.

Fir

The firs were once considered in the same family of trees as the pines, though they differ in two respects.

The cones of firs have scales with flat, rounded apexes; and their leaves do not grow in bundles, or clusters, as do the true pines. Firs range in distribution from eastern Canada nearly to Alaska, and from the Northwest almost to the Arctic Circle. Two of the most important species are the balsam fir of the northern belt of forests, and the larger Douglas fir (not a true fir) which reaches its greatest importance in the Pacific coastal forests. The balsam fir is a typical "Christmas tree," with thick spreading branches beginning shortly above the ground. It reaches a height of 30 to 50 feet, and has shiny blue-green needles which, when crushed, give off a pleasant "piney" odor.

The Douglas fir ranks at the very top for lumber in North America, and in the West represents more than one-half of the standing timber. Douglas firs are among the tallest trees, with exceptional specimens reaching over 350 feet. Some trees are 15 feet through at their bases. The tree grows tall and stately, having relatively few branches for a considerable distance up the trunk.

Bark of balsam fir is gray or brown with many resin blisters. Needles are flat, rounded at tip; cones are upright.

Balsam fir (above) has thick, spreading branches starting near the ground. Douglas fir (right) is taller with few branches near the ground.

Bark of Douglas fir (left) is reddish-brown, thick, deeply furrowed into broad ridges. Needles (right) are short-stalked, flat, dark yellow-green or blue-green. Cones are light brown with thin, rounded scales.

Blue gum, or eucalyptus, trees shed their brown bark in long strips, exposing the grayish bark underneath.

Gum

Two species of gum are among our more important trees. One is the sweetgum, or red gum, which is distributed over the eastern part of the United States, from the lower New England States to central Florida, across the lower Mississippi Basin, and as far west as Texas. Other areas also occur in Mexico and Central America. Sweetgum trees reach a height of 90 to over 100 feet. The blue gum, or eucalyptus, is an imported variety now found in California, the Southwest, and along the Gulf States to Florida. The tree is an evergreen, with brown bark and willow-like leaves averaging up to a foot in length. The brown bark strips off in shaggy lengths, exposing the grayish underbark beneath, and makes the tree appear to be constantly molting. The leaves and fruit of the eucalyptus give off a sweet-smelling odor.

Hemlock

The eastern hemlock is a pyramid-shaped evergreen which may reach 100 feet in height and over 3 feet in diameter at the base. The short, flat, linear leaves occur on opposite sides on the branchlet, averaging about a half-inch in length, and give a lacey, soft appearance to the foliage. The foliage is dark-green on top, with the underside of the leaves being a silvery-gray. The eastern hemlock grows on rocky hillsides, and ranges in distribution from Nova Scotia southward to Alabama and Georgia, and from Nova Scotia westward as far as Minnesota. The western hemlock occurs in a coastal belt from Washington, along the coastline of British Columbia, and into the southeastern part of Alaska. This

Western hemlock's bark is reddish-brown, deeply furrowed into broad, flat ridges. The dark-green needles are short-stalked and flat.

Bark of eastern hemlock, smaller of the two species, is brown or purplish and deeply furrowed. Needles are similar to those of western hemlock.

species is larger than its eastern cousin, with trees often reaching well over 200 feet in height. Western hemlock likes cool, moist areas. A fast-growing tree, it often grows in large stands exclusive of other timber. It is becoming important as a pulp wood.

Hickory

There are several species of hickory, most of which are distributed along the Mississippi Basin and eastward. All species can be identified by their compound leaves and the nuts the trees bear. Differences among the species are

Shagbark Hickory

Shagbark hickory gets its name from gray, shaggy bark which curls away from trunk. Leaves, usually five, are long, elliptical, ginely toothed. The thin-shelled nuts are edible.

found in the bark, nuts, and number of leaflets. The shagbark, a common hickory, is so named because of its coarse, shaggy bark, whose individual bark-plates curl away from the trunk like long scabs ready to peel off. The shagbark grows to a height of over 100 feet. Beneath its rather disheveled exterior is a heavy wood of tough quality. Your ax and shovel probably have hickory handles. The leaves of the shagbark usually have five or seven leaflets, while those of other species of hickory may have seven or nine.

Larch

The American larch, or tamarack, grows from Maine westward beyond the Great Lakes, and over a northward range which covers most of Canada. It is common to wet, boggy ground, but also grows on adjacent hillsides. The average-sized tree is apt to be 50 to 70 feet tall, though like the birch, the tree dwindles to almost shrub-like stature at the northern limit of its range in Canada. The leaves of the larch are shed annually; otherwise it resembles the evergreens. These inch-long leaves appear in tiny knots or spurs along the branches, and number from 6 to 16 from each spur. The small half-inch cones look like miniature rose

The tall, stately larch is an important lumber tree, the wood being used for poles and construction. Stand above is 185 years old.

Bark of the larch is reddish-brown, scaly, deeply furrowed into flat ridges with many overlapping plates. The needles, which are shed in the fall, grow in clusters at the end of stunted branches.

blossoms. The trees at a distance often look meager of foliage because of the intermittent arrangement of the leaves.

The western larch, the tallest and most important North American larch, grows in the Rocky Mountain Northwest as well as in the eastern part of the Pacific belt of forests. It is an important lumber species, yielding a heavy softwood which is very durable.

Magnolia

The magnolia goes by several names such as swamp magnolia, sweet bay, swamp laurel, and laurel bay. The species is evergreen, having tough slick leaves 3 to 6 inches in length which are glossy-green on top and gray underneath. The trees grow to a maximum of around 60 feet, but are shorter in the northern extremities of their range. This range covers a strip of the east Atlantic Coast from the

southern part of North Carolina down to central Florida and around the coastal area of the Gulf of Mexico well into Texas. Spot areas appear much farther north. The coastal strip extends inland only approximately 100 miles, though farther up the Mississippi Basin. The bloom of the magnolia, which has been immortalized in song and story, is a creamy-white, cup-shaped flower averaging 2½ inches across, and has from 6 to 9 petals which are shaped like spoon blades. The tree is striking in appearance. For 30 feet or more the trunk may be free of branches. From there on up the branches are bunched to give a bulky compact appearance.

Sugar Maple

Maple

There are numerous species of maple in North America, with at least six species reaching commercial importance as lumber. These are the sugar or hard maple, black maple, silver maple, red maple, boxelder maple, and bigleaf maple. The maple has three distinguishing features. First, the leaves tend to grow opposite each other on the branchlets. Secondly, many species of maple such as the sugar maple, Norway maple, and silver maple have leaves which are deeply indented, and have five distinctive and sharp-pointed lobes. The lobe separations on some species such as the

325

Leaves of the big-leaf maple are very large, 6 to 12 inches in diameter, dark green and shiny. The bark is gray-brown, thin, smooth.

boxelder are barely separated. The third identifying characteristic of the maples is the pair of two winged seeds which grow together, and which resemble the winding keys of wind-up toys. These seeds are often called "keys" for this reason.

The sugar, or hard maple, is the most important of the group. It is found in every state east of the Great Plains, and in the southern parts of adjacent Canada. The sugar maple, in addition to its value for lumber, also yields a sap which is boiled down into maple syrup and sugar. Adult

Leaves of the sugar maple are 3 to 5 inches in diameter, dark green above, light green beneath. . Bark is gray, furrowed.

trees will occasionally reach 100 feet in height, and many will yield 20 gallons of sap per year. Of all the lumber produced by maples, bird's-eye maple is perhaps most valuable and is used in fancy woodwork and gun stocks.

Other species of maple have identifying characteristics. The red maple gets its name from its red buds and twigs of winter, and its scarlet leaves in the fall. The bigleaf maple of the Pacific slope has leaves which often reach a foot in width—hence the name. And the silver maple is so called because its leaves, though dark green on the upper surfaces, have a silvery-green under-surface.

Oak

Just as maples are identified by their winged seeds, so are the oaks characterized by their acorns. Of all the

White Oak

hardwoods in North America, the oak is most important, partly because of its quantity, and largely because of the wide variety of uses to which its tough, long-lasting wood may be put. The variety of uses for oak wood ranges from timber for ships, mine tunnels, and boats, to furniture, boxes, and crates. There are over sixty species of oak in North America, with at least one-third of the species important in a commercial way. The commercially important oaks are found eastward of a line extending from Texas to the northern end of the Great Lakes.

For lumber purposes, oak is divided into two groups, the "white oak" and the "red oak." White oak, chestnut oak, and swamp oak furnish white-oak lumber; and the marketed red oak consists of such species as northern red oak, swamp red oak, and southern red oak.

Acorns of the northern red oak (left) are 5/8 to 1-1/8 inches long and nest in shallow cups. Black-oak acorns (right) are smaller, 5/8 to 3/4 inches long, and are half enclosed by deep cups.

Acorns of the white oak (left) are 3/4 to 1 inch long and have a shallow cup. The bark is light gray and fissured into scaly ridges.

For purposes of identification, the white oaks have lighter bark, rounded leaf-tips, and the acorns are borne on first-year wood. The red oaks have darker bark, pointed lobes on their leaves, and the acorns are borne on second-year wood.

Some of the more important oaks are the white oak, live oak, black oak, and northern red oak. The white oak is the most important oak for lumbering. The tree reaches a height of 60 to 100 feet, is slow in growing, with full maturity coming after several hundred years. White oaks may reach 8 feet diameter at their bases.

The live oak of the Southern and Gulf States is a wide-spreading tree having the tradition of being the ship-builder's tree. The angular, knee-like timbers necessary to ship construction were made from the limb-tree junctions of this massive tree.

The black oak, actually one of the commercial red oaks, is named because of the dark color of its bark. Perhaps the black oak's best-remembered asset has been the use of its bark in the tanning of hides. The northern red oak began to receive serious attention from lumbermen when the supply of white oak began diminishing. Its strong, close-grained lumber makes railroad ties, posts, and furniture.

Scrub oak, which often reaches no more than 10 to 15 feet in height, is found in many places in the West and Southwest, where it grows in thick patches, often covering an entire mountainside.

Pine

The pines are one of the most important trees of the conifer group. In North America there are nearly three-

Sugar Pine

dozen species of pine. Pines grow largely in the mountainous regions of temperate North America, but in the colder areas are found at lower elevations. In the tropical parts of the continent, they are found only at the higher spines of elevation. Pines are identified by their hard, woody cones and by their leaves. The leaves, which are needle-shaped, are often referred to as "pine needles." Unlike the spruce and the fir, which bear single needles, pine leaves come from the branches in bundles or clusters of from two to five, with the lone exception of the singleleaf pine. Pine leaves vary in length with the species from an inch to 1½ feet. Among the important pines of North America are the lodgepole, long-needle, pinion, ponderosa, red, southern, and white pine.

Lodgepole Pine

Tall, straight, free of branches for most of its height, lodgepole pines grow to a diameter of from 8 to 12 inches. The bark is gray-green, with numerous small chip-like scales on its outer covering. The species ranges over the Northwest, along the Pacific Coast, and into adjacent Canada.

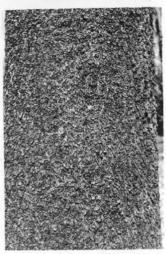

Bark of the lodgepole pine is brown and thin, with many loose scales. The stout needles, which grow in clusters of two, are 1 to 3 inches long, yellow-green in color.

331

*Long-
needle
Pine*

The most important of the southern pines, the long-needle is distinguished by its long leaves, as the name suggests. Needles will reach up to 18 inches in length. The

Needles of the longneedle pine grow in clusters of three. They are very long, 10 to 15 inches; the cones are 5 to 10 inches long, dull brown and prickly. The bark is orange-brown, extremely coarse and scaly.

332

wood of the longneedle pine is strong and is used in abundance for heavy construction purposes. This pine is also known as the turpentine-and-rosin tree, for its production of these items.

Pinion Pine

Scattered throughout the more arid hills of the Southwest, this is a small, bushy-type tree averaging 15 to 20 feet in height. It is known mainly for the "pine nuts" it produces, which have long been a staple part of the diet for Indians in that area. Even today, in spot areas, the local Indians still gather the small, sweet nuts in autumn, and sell them to stores within the region.

Ponderosa Pine

As the name indicates, this is the big, or ponderous pine. Adult trees will reach a height of 200 feet and a diameter of 6 feet at the base. The ponderosa has deeply furrowed bark of orange-russet color, with a bole generally free of branches for a considerable distance above the trunk.

Needles of the ponderosa pine grow in clumps of two or three and are 6 to 10 inches long, dark green in color.

Western Wood Products Ass'n

Ponderosa pines are tall and straight, reaching 200 feet in height. Bark is brown or blackish, furrowed in deep ridges, becoming yellow-brown on older trees and fissured into large, scaly plates.

Western Wood Products Ass'n

Needles are in clusters of two or three, and will grow from six to ten inches long. The cones of the ponderosa are brown-colored and grow to five inches in length. The range of this species is comparable to that of the western lodge-pole pine, though more extensive.

Red Pine

This is a medium-sized pine which grows in the north-eastern part of the United States and Canada. Its name was taken from the reddish-colored bark. The wood of the red pine contains more resin than that of the white pine, and is classed as a "hard pine," as against the soft wood of the white pine.

Bark of the red pine is reddish-brown, with broad, flat, scaly plates. Needles grow in clusters of two and are stout, twisted, 3/4 to 1-1/2 inches long. Cones are small, light yellow in color.

Loblolly Pine

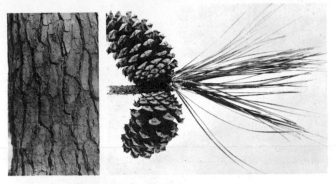

Bark of the loblolly pine is reddish-brown, deeply fissured into broad scaly plates. Needles grow in clusters of three, are 6 to 9 inches long, pale green. Cones are reddish-brown, 3 to 5 inches long, with stiff, sharp prickles.

Southern Pine

Southern pine, or yellow pine, is a name given collectively to the four major species of pines found in the southeastern part of the United States—the shortleaf, slash, longleaf, and loblolly pines.

White Pine

The white pines may be divided into two widely-separated species, the eastern white pine and the western white pine. The range of the eastern species includes the northeastern part of the United States, around the Great Lakes, and into adjacent Canada. The once-large forests of the eastern species have been largely decimated. The eastern white pine has long slender cones and sweet-smelling needles which grow in bundles of five. The western white pine grows mainly in the Northwest and adjacent Canada, with Idaho having the largest remaining stands. Mature

Western white pine (right) and eastern white pine (below) are both important lumber trees. Bark of western tree is gray, smooth, becoming fissured into large, flat scaly plates. Bark of eastern pine is gray or purplish and more deeply fissured. Needles of both grow in clusters of five.

trees reach several hundred years of age, and up to 175 feet in height. Leaves of this species also come in clusters of five. Because of its soft texture and easy-working qualities, western white pine lumber is in much demand for paneling and woodwork. Rustic knotty-pine is a choice lumber for cabinets.

Redwood

The giant redwoods, or sequoias, of California are not only our largest trees but are considered to be the oldest and largest living things on earth. Some specimens are estimated to be over 4000 years old, with individual trees reaching up to 6000 tons in weight. The trees are named for the russet color of their wood. A smaller species of redwood, growing within the same area, is used for shingles,

Redwood trees grow to enormous heights, 200 to 300 feet, with record tree measuring 364 feet. Bark is reddish-brown, thick, and deeply furrowed. Needles, 1/4 to 3/4 inch long, grow in two rows.

chests, doors, and furniture. The wood is brittle but very resistant to weathering and age.

Saguaro

The saguaro is a cactus, but grows to such prodigious size and height that it may be listed here. It is often called the "Joshua tree" because of its "arms," which extend from the main trunk, seeming to implore the heavens as did the Biblical character. The plant takes up water after a desert

rain and hoards it for dry weather beneath its spiny covering. As drought increases, the saguaro wrinkles. The species is found in Mexico, scattered in California, and principally around Tuscon, in Arizona. Mature plants may stand up to a height of 30 feet or more.

The ribbed trunk of the saguaro is spined with sharp needles. Reaching 2 feet in diameter, the trunk hoards water in its internal cavity for dry weather.

Spruce

Several species of spruce are common to North America and are found over wide areas of Canada, northward into the Yukon and Alaska, and southward into the northern tier of states. Spruces are generally dark in color and have short stiff needles which grow all around the branchlets. These needles are four-sided and in cross-section are nearly square, as against the long, rectangular shape of a cross-section of fir needles. The needles are slightly curved. Eastern varieties of spruce include the red, white, and black spruce. A spruce imported from Europe, the Norway spruce, is now widely spread in Canada. Two western

Bark of the Englemann spruce is grayish or purplish-brown, thin, with loosely attached scales. The needles (above) are 5/8 to 1-1/8 inches long, dark or pale blue-green. Cones are 1-1/2 to 2-1/2 inches long and pointed.

Norway spruce is a straight, cone-shaped tree reaching 150 feet in height. Branches rise at the tips, have many offshoots.

Blue spruce of the Rocky Mountain region has gray or brown bark furrowed into scaly ridges. Its dark leaves have a silvery sheen and branches curve upward at tips.

White spruce rarely exceeds 60 to 70 feet in height. Branches are long, densely clothed, sweeping out in graceful, upward curves.

species are the Engelmann spruce and the Colorado spruce. The Engelmann grows in high mountainous country from the Southwest to the Yukon, and is a most important lumber variety. Its wood is light but strong, and is much used in airplane construction. The Colorado, or blue spruce, is native to Colorado, but has been transplanted into other areas, largely as an ornamental tree. It has a silvery sheen to the dark color of its leaves.

Sycamore

Unlike the pines, the sycamore likes low, open country, and is found from the Northeastern States westward to the Plains States and southward to the Gulf of Mexico. The leaves resemble those of some maples in that they have five

Sycamore leaves are heart-shaped, 4 to 8 inches long, and coarsely toothed. The bark is smooth, peeling off in large flakes, showing patches of brown, gray, and green on the trunk.

lobes and are sharpedged. The leaves grow alternately along the branches, not oppositely as do the maples. Perhaps the most distinguishing feature of the sycamore is its bark. Due to flaking off of old bark, with patches of new bark appearing beneath, a combination of brown and cream-colored areas make the lower trunk appear speckled like the rump of an Appaloosa horse. The sycamore is one of the largest of broadleaved trees.

Walnut

Two species of North American walnut are the butternut and the black walnut. Both occupy the larger share of eastern United States, though the limit of range on the south is somewhat inside the Gulf coastal area. The butternut tree has a short trunk and low sweeping branches, with trees running to 40 or 50 feet in height and 2 feet or over at the base. The leaves are compound, with eleven to seventeen leaflets. The black walnut is one of the more important woods used in furniture, cabinets, and principally in gun stocks. It is a fine-grained wood, doesn't split easily, and

Black Walnut

takes a high finish. Black-walnut trees are larger than butternut trees, often reaching a height of 100 feet. They have umbrella-like crowns, compound leaves, and bark of dark-brown color. Mature nuts of this species are round in shape, reach up to 2 inches in diameter, and are enclosed in an outside husk.

Bark of black walnut (left) is dark brown to black, thick, with deep furrows and narrow, forking ridges. Leaves are compound, 12 to 24 inches long. Bark of the butternut (right) is light gray, furrowed into flat ridges.

347

The butternut, smaller than the black walnut, has a short trunk and low sweeping branches.

Leaves of the butternut are compound, 15 to 30 inches long, with 11 to 19 leaflets, which have no stalks.

Butternuts grow in clusters of three to five fruits. Egg shaped, with thick husks, they are edible, having a sweet and oily taste.

348

Weeping Willow

Willow

There are over 100 species of willow in North America. In addition, willows form hybrids easily, which adds to their total numbers. In general, willows are fast-growing trees which grow into large spreading shapes from short trunks, or from trunks which tend to separate. They are identified usually by long slender leaves which grow

Bark of the weeping willow is grayish-brown and fissured. The leaves are lance shaped, 3 to 6 inches long, and grow on long stems.

349

alternately along the branchlets, and the flowers which grow in catkins. Three of the best known willows are the black willow, the pussy willow, and the weeping willow. The black willow grows across southern Canada, and the eastern half of the United States with the exception of the extreme southeastern part. Pussy willows are found in the same overall region, and are identified by their soft, grayish buds resembling tiny rabbit tails, which grow on small trees reaching 15 feet or so in height. The weeping willow is found in most of southern Canada, and southward to the Gulf States, and likes moist ground. This species is noted for its exceptionally long branchlets, which droop often

Black willow has irregular, spreading branches and a dark trunk. It grows in eastern half of the U.S.A.

Bark of the black willow is dark brown or blackish, deeply furrowed, with scaly, forking ridges. Leaves are long, slim, pointed, finely toothed, shiny green above, pale beneath.

nearly to the ground, giving the tree its "weeping" appearance. As an example of how fast this and other willows grow, we planted a weeping willow on our acreage twenty-eight years ago by simply planting a cutting into moist ground. This tree now reaches 35 feet in height, and its diameter 6 feet up the trunk is 30 inches.

Pussy willow grows as a shrub or small tree. Branches are gathered in March and April for furry, gray buds which are valued for their decorative qualities.

15

Signs of the Animals

In his travels through the woods, and along streams and seacoasts, the outdoors lover sees only a small percentage of all the animals that inhabit the wilderness. There are many reasons for this. Many of the smaller wild animals are prey for larger animals; and consequently, in order for a species to survive, it must be furtive in all movement and activity. This semiconcealment keeps it from the eyes of man. Again, many of the smaller animals are nocturnal and do much of their moving about after man has gone to sleep. A bigger reason why man sees only a portion of the animals about him is the fact that man's activity and noise are interpreted by animals as evidence of an enemy. To protect themselves, they remain concealed.

To the more observing person, the signs that animals leave record their habits and their numbers. The fresh burrow, earth, and tracks in the sandy desert is a printed record of the jackrabbit, ground squirrel, or badger, depending upon the characteristics of the spoor. The felled aspen tree, teeth marks, drag trail, and wet "slide" into the mountain creek all tell the alert that fall is coming, and the beaver is storing green, succulent branches near the underwater entrance to his pond home, against the coming freeze-up. And the scarcely audible *tick-tick* in the trees above, on a still morning, means that somewhere in the leafy branches a squirrel is sorting seeds and nuts from the cones.

These and the many other signs of the animals tell the alert observer of forest activities, a cycle of living and true industry, and give him a sense of belonging. And since man himself is but an animal of a higher order, an awareness and

Elk tracks can be identified by their size and roundish shape. Dewclaws register when animal is walking in soft ground or snow.

an understanding of his woodland brethren add not only to his enjoyment but to his own significance.

Elk

A handsome, majestic animal with tremendous antlers and awesome bulk, the elk, or wapiti, is now native only to the West. He spends his summers high in the mountains and his winters at lower altitudes where the weather is not so harsh. Most of his signs are visual, but there are audible ones as well.

Tracks of a mature elk are large, up to 4½ inches long, and roundish. Dewclaws usually only register in mud or snow or when the animal is running. When walking, the elk leaves tracks that seem to be more in a line than when he's galloping.

Elk feed on grass, twigs, leaves, and bark, the bark of aspens being favored winter fare. You will often find these trees well scored where the animals have stripped off chunks of bark with their lower incisors. If you happen to come to an area where aspens have grown blackened trunks as far up as an elk can reach, you can be assured you've stumbled on a spot where elk have spent the winter year after year; their repeated gnawings have caused the trees to develop these rough, darkened holes. Also in winter, elk browse on shoots and twigs of trees, cleaning the branches as far up as they can reach.

Broken branches and torn bark are other tree signs to look for. These are left by the bull elk when he rubs his antlers against tree trunks and bushes to scrape off the velvet that has been covering them since they started growing

Aspens with black patches on their trunks are a sure sign that elk have stripped bark during winter feeding.

in March or April, and to polish and sharpen them in preparation for battles with other bulls in defense of his harem. Sometimes saplings used for this purpose are killed. Why aren't winter-dropped antlers a good sign of elk wanderings? Rodents, and sometimes elk themselves, usually chew them up in short order.

Patches of flattened grass in high country are often evidence that elk have bedded down there during summer.

In winter, elk paw sizeable holes in the snow to get to food, and you may even find their beds in the snow as well. In summer, look for areas where the grass has been depressed if you want to see places where these animals have been sleeping.

During the summer, when elk are in the high country, it will pay you to keep an eye on the banks of shallow ponds and lakes. Often you will find tracks there where the animals have come to drink, swim, and enjoy themselves. During the rut, before these tremendous deer have started for the lower country, the bulls frequently cool off their fiery enthusiasm by pawing away the wet ground and

357

Winter droppings of the elk are pellet shaped, similar to those left by other members of the deer family.

thrashing around in the mud. Sometimes these old wallows collect water and are visible for several years. Like deer and moose, elk often dig up the ground for minerals, and only your knowledge of tracks will tell you for sure what animal has done the excavating.

Elk droppings vary according to time of year. In summer they're flat, tending to be circular and about 5 or 6 inches across. In winter, they take on the pellet-like form common to those of the rest of the deer family.

The elk makes a variety of noises, most well known of which is the bugling of the bull in the fall. It is like a musical arpeggio of four distinct tones rising to a virtual whistle, then sliding downward to end in a series of grunts. It can be heard at dusk and at daybreak for nearly a mile in hushed wilderness country. It is the challenge cry of the bull during the rutting season.

Another sound associated with the rut is a horrendous one. It is the noise made when two of these many-tined monarchs join in battle, something that happens when one bull is trying to protect his harem of up to thirty cows from another bull with acquisitive ideas. The noise is a clashing and crashing of antlers that drowns out all other sounds of the forest community. It is accompanied by grunts, groans, and bellows of outrage. After a time, one of the animals calls it quits and looks elsewhere for female companionship.

Other sounds made by elk are a soft bark as the mother calls to her calf and sometimes a squeal or two as mother and youngster converse. A sharp, loud bark usually is a sign of alarm, and a lot of squealing and rumbling indicates that a startled band of mothers and young is trying to get back together, each parent with the proper offspring.

Whitetail Deer

This handsome animal ranges from southern Canada down through Mexico and Central America, and west to the Rockies. He is also found in parts of Idaho, Colorado, Wyoming, Arizona, and New Mexico. He varies considerably in size, from a maximum of up to 400 pounds for a large northern whitetail to a minimum of about 100 for the little Coues deer. The tiny Key deer of Florida are less than half of that and are extremely rare.

The Coues deer, who lives in southwestern Arizona, Mexico, and parts of Texas, is also referred to as the fantail, the Sonora whitetail, and the Arizona whitetail. Unlike his northern cousins whose coats change from reddish brown in summer to grayish in winter, the Coues keeps his brownish gray all year.

The study of a whitetail's tracks will tell you a lot about what he is doing. When the animal is walking, it places the hind foot practically on top of the heartshaped print of the front one, and the groups of two are slightly staggered. Dewclaws do not show. When galloping, the whitetail makes a separate and distinct print with each hoof, the toes are spread out so that the familiar heart shape is gone, hind feet print in front of front ones, and the dewclaws show,

This is classic whitetail country—the fringes of thick forests where deer can feed on bushes and saplings.

those of the hind feet being farther behind the hoofs than those of the front ones. In this gait, the prints also show as a staggered line. When bounding, this deer brings his four feet down closer together, and they form a rather triangular grouping. As in the galloping gait, hoofs are spread and dewclaws show.

Generally speaking, but this is by no means infallible, a buck, particularly a big one, shows more of a drag mark than a doe. This can be noticed in snow or in the disturbance of dead leaves on the forest floor. Furthermore, it is

Drag marks behind tracks in snow may mean a large whitetail buck has passed by.

quite natural that a larger animal will leave a trail that shows prints farther apart from the center line than will a small one. Another indication that a set of prints might have been made by a big buck is in the tracks themselves; those of a large male tend to toe out, but, like the other ways of telling the sex of a deer by its track, this is not always 100 percent accurate. In all of nature, each animal within a species has its own individuality, and just as there are women with big feet and men with small ones, so some does leave big prints and some bucks do not. Generally speaking, if you're following the trail of a herd of deer and you see the tracks overprinted by a conspicuously larger set of tracks, you can be reasonably sure a large buck has been bringing up the rear of a group of does and fawns.

Look for tracks at deer crossings, which are usually relatively narrow areas through which deer regularly pass in their travels from place to place. A saddle, or notch, in a ridge is a favorite deer crossing, for deer, like humans, tend to choose the easiest route across rough terrain.

There are many other signs of the whitetail, some of them varying by season. For instance, if you're hunting and see that the soft bark has been scraped and gouged from a small cedar or willow sapling, you may assume that there are bucks around. These marks are made in late August—usually well before hunting season—when the buck tries to scrape the velvet off his antlers. A more valuable sign to the hunter, because it is made in the fall, is evidence of brush and small growth that's been broken, stripped, and

361

generally beaten up. Bucks violate bushes in this manner by hooking them and sparring with them with their antlers in the general pugnacity of the rutting season. It is a sure sign you're in buck territory.

Another seasonal sign is the wallow. Like elk, whitetail bucks will occasionally wallow in mud during the rut, but

Whitetails often browse in winter on the bark of cedars, stripping the trunk to the limits of their reach.

they're by no means as addicted to the habit as are their larger relatives. If in doubt about which animal made the wallow you're looking at, check for hair, and don't forget to look over the surrounding tracks.

Antlers are usually shed sometime in January or February, and, as is usually the case with cast antlers and horn, they're chewed up by rodents for their calcium and lime. However, the deer themselves also gnaw cast antlers. If you find the remains of an antler, check the tooth marks; those left by the rodents are smaller than the mouthings left by deer.

Food of the whitetail is enormously varied. In spring and summer it is made up of grasses, buds, berries, mushrooms, fruit, many green leaves and shoots, water lilies, and, occasionally, a fish stolen from an angler's camp or actually caught. A deer catches a fish by stabbing at it with a hoof until it is so battered and bruised it can be picked up in the animal's mouth.

In fall, twigs, acorns, apples, leaves, and low-growing plants are consumed. In winter, where the snows are deep and the weather severe, deer yard up, perhaps several bucks as well as five or six does and their young. They stay together in a small area browsing on sprouts and twigs of cedar and spruce, suckers, and what shrubbery they can find. Edge areas along meadows and woodlots, where trees meet open spaces, are favorite feeding spots owing to the low bushes and second-growth saplings that usually grow there. Deer usually feed in these areas during the night, climbing into the high ridges at dawn and bedding down for the day. If the winter is hard, many deer will perish of starvation. In southern climes and areas of mild winters, whitetails generally do not yard up.

In the fall, broken saplings and trampled ground tell the passerby that two bucks have fought a battle.

When the low-growing feed has been eaten, the animals reach up to nibble away the twigs of the overhanging branches. Since a big buck can reach up higher than a small deer, the young and the does are the first to feel the pinch of hunger, many of them eventually dying. Also, in rearing up on their hind legs to reach a succulent branch, a deer can get his neck caught in the fork of a limb and hang or strangle himself.

Scats of deer are the familiar pellet variety, tending, however, to be softer, larger, and more shapeless when the animal is eating his soft summer fare.

Watch for deer beds in winter as well as summer. In summer they appear as depressed spots in grass or leaves. In winter, they are depressions in the snow. Usually you'll find them on hillsides where their makers can keep an eye out for danger.

Most common sound made by the whitetail is a sort of whistling snort, emitted when the animal is alarmed.

Contrary to the belief in some circles, both bucks and does snort and can be heard for considerable distances when they do. Another sound, rarely heard at any distance, is the low conversation between a doe and her offspring.

A deer noise that occasionally can be heard in the fall woods is the clashing of antlers when bucks fight over does. During the rut, bucks fight furiously among themselves, and the clashing of antlers, low grunts of indignation, and the thrashing around in an area of perhaps a half an acre is as readily recognizable as is the sight of the terrain after the fight is over.

Don't forget that deer like water lilies, and they wade out in ponds and lakes to get them. While you're sitting around

Winter droppings of whitetail (above) and mule deer (below) are pellet shaped, generally under an inch in size.

camp on a still evening, keep an ear cocked toward the shore; you may hear a deer pulling up the succulent stems.

Baby deer, usually twins, are born in May or early June, but by that time their father has long gone. He will stay by himself throughout the summer while his antlers are growing. By late August they're formed, and, in the north at least, the buck goes into the rut sometime in October. By this time, the young are weaned, but they generally stay with their mother until the following spring.

In November, the rut is in full swing and lasts about a month for each individual buck. He seeks a female but only stays with her a few days before dashing off to find another.

Mule Deer

The muley lives in the Rocky Mountain area from Canada to Mexico, and in parts of his eastern range he is found at the western limits of the whitetail's range. He is also very similar in habits and life history to his eastern cousin.

The mule deer is a somewhat bigger animal than the whitetail, about 475 pounds being tops for this brownish-gray creature. Also, he is more of a mountain animal, spending his summers at around 8,000 feet and migrating seasonally into the valleys where the winter weather is less harsh. These two ranges may be as much as 150 miles apart but are usually closer to 50. Certain mule deer, however, live in the southwestern deserts.

The trail of a galloping mule deer shows one prominent difference from that of the galloping whitetail. The muley bounds in high leaps, but when he comes down his hind

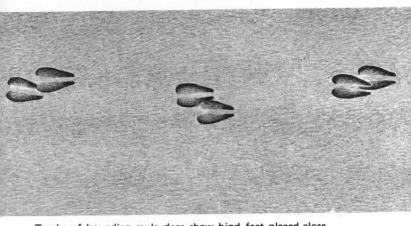

Tracks of bounding mule deer show hind feet placed close
behind forefeet. Prints are larger than whitetail's.

feet are behind the front ones. The galloping whitetail puts
his hind feet down in front of the front ones when going
all out. This leaping, bouncing-ball gait of the muley permits him to look over the countryside and spot danger
when in high midstride. He might cover 4 feet vertically and
20 feet or more horizontally in a single leap. Walking, his
track is similar to that of the whitetail, but his hoofs are a
bit bigger. Also, a muley that spends much time on rocky
ground is apt to have the points of his hoofs more rounded
than will an animal who has spent more time on less
abrasive soil or sand.

The muley doesn't fight as much as the whitetail, and
you're not going to hear the clashing of antlers as much
among this species during the rut. During courtship, a buck
may get together a harem of three or four females, but if a
larger male drives him off, he'll shrug and wander away in
search of other does.

A frequent sight in the southwestern desert—a jojoba tree with its branches stripped of foliage by browsing mule deer.

Watch for salt licks. Like all deer, the muley loves salt, and the clay in which it's deposited will be worn and eroded by many tongues.

Diet of the mule deer is varied, but he commonly eats more grass and herbs than does the whitetail. Twigs and leaves of all sorts of brush and berry bushes are eaten greedily as well as the leaves of aspens, oaks, mountain ash, bitter-brush, and willow. These deer are also fond of mushrooms, fungi, and mistletoe where available in their range.

An observant autumn hiker might note the velvet clinging to a rock and know that a mule deer scraped and sharpened his antlers there in late August.

In winter, the branch tips of juniper, mountain mahogany, and fir are nipped off and chewed up.

By the end of January in the north, and a month or so later in the south, the bucks lose their antlers and settle down for the winter. Small groups—a buck, a doe, yearlings, and fawns of the season—now get together to form large herds. With the coming of spring, the animals start for their summer quarters, munching the new grasses as they wander along. Fawns, usually twins, are born in late June or early July, after the does have reached the summer range. Bucks wander off by themselves until the two-month rut begins in October.

The muley, along with its many similarities to the white-tail, also makes a snorting whistle when alarmed. It emits a coughing grunt when fighting and now and then lets out a low, growling noise.

Blacktail Deer

There's little to distinguish the signs of this animal from those of other deer. Tracks, droppings, tree and bush signs,

369

all are just about identical. Range and some personal habits, however, differ.

The blacktail lives in a narrow coastal belt that goes from about central California north to the southern tip of Alaska and east to the western slopes of the Sierras and the Cascade Range. This is the area of heavy spruce and redwood forests, and its undergrowth is dense. Because it is so dense and so high, the blacktail makes his escape from enemies by stealing through it on well-known trails rather than by bounding off as do frightened muleys and whitetails.

Northern and inland animals tend to migrate to a certain extent from the high alpine meadows in the summer to the more hospitable valleys in the winter. Those living in the dense forests of the lowlands feed on the same sort of shrubbery enjoyed by the mule deer and on moss, mistletoe, fungus, and acorns. There's no grass in these dense forests. Leaves and twigs of alder, cedar, hemlock, and other trees are eaten in winter. Sometimes, when winter food becomes unbearably scarce, blacktails will forage along the shore for kelp and various seaweeds.

These deer are splendid swimmers, and those living along the coast of their range often swim from island to island in water that also has icebergs floating in it.

The blacktail mates in November in the north, a month earlier in the south.

A walking blacktail leaves well-spaced tracks.

In the North Woods country, water is apt to mean moose.
Here he finds his favorite food—aquatic plants.

Moose

This tremendous animal, weighing from 900 to 1,800
pounds for a huge Kenai specimen, is known, of course,
for his huge, palmated antlers, the 4- to 10-inch "bell"

that hangs under the base of his jaw, and his rubbery-looking snout.

His tracks are similar to those of an elk, but they are larger (up to 7 inches or so) and are more pointed, with a tendency to splay. Sometimes dewclaws show, particularly when the animal is trotting. Usually a bull's tracks are toed out, while those of a cow are straight. A moose trail shows staggered prints.

Moose love aquatic plants, so if you're in an area of ponds and marshes anywhere in his range (Maine, some of the western and northwestern states as well as wooded Canada and most of Alaska) keep your eyes open for tracks and signs of torn-up water lilies and ploughed-up pond bottoms.

Another visual sign of the moose that's concerned with his feeding is the mess he leaves of fir trees, aspens, and willows in winter. He strips branches as far up as he can,

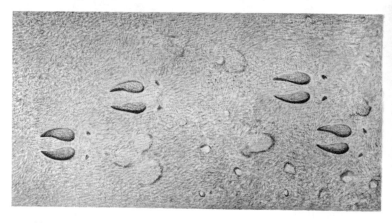

Moose tracks are large, up to 7 inches long, and form a staggered trail. They are more pointed than the elk's.

During fall rutting season, bulls often leave torn-up ground and broken trees as evidence of furious battles.

often standing on his hind legs and reaching up as high as 18 feet or so. Sometimes, when he is particularly interested in the branches of a sapling, he will jump on it, force it down by sheer weight, and nibble away at its top. Watch for small trees broken this way and also by the moose's having pulled the branches of such small trees until the trunks have snapped. This winter activity is accompanied by numerous tracks, usually within an area of several acres, showing that a bull, a cow, and a couple of young have yarded up there. Practically all the trees in the locality will be found stripped to a surprising height.

Moose chew on aspen bark, as do elk, and the only way you can tell for sure which animal has done the gnawing is to have a knowledge of wintering habitat and other signs. Their browsings on twigs do not show the neat, clipped-off ends left by rodents with their sharp teeth.

In winter, scats of moose are in the familiar pellet shape of the deer's, though more pear-shaped, and they are much larger and more numerous than are those of deer. In winter, these droppings are very dry and somewhat smooth. In summer, scats may be without recognizable form and resemble those left by a milk cow. As winter comes on again, however, and food becomes dryer, scats become more pelletlike.

Beds in snow or grass can be confused with those of elk because of the size of the animal that made them. Look for tracks and droppings to verify any beds you come across.

Other signs to look for in moose country—droppings over an inch long, tooth marks on aspen trunks where animal has chewed bark.

With his enormous reach, the moose strips willow saplings
10 feet tall of their foliage. He'll bend even taller trees to
the ground and clean them bare.

Another sign, one that can be smelled as well as seen, is the moose wallow. At a time when he is interested in attracting a lady friend, the bull paws a shallow pit perhaps 4 feet across in the soft ground. Then he urinates in it and wallows in the soggy mess. These wallows aren't hard to identify because of the tracks around them and the stench they exude.

Bulls drop their antlers around midwinter, to start new ones in early spring. Shed antlers are, of course, another sign, but so many members of the woods fraternity chew on them that they are rarely seen.

Another visual sign would be a quarter of an acre or so of woods torn up and scarred from the battle of two rutting bulls. The rut begins along in September, lasts about six weeks, and results in many battles that leave the trees, brush, and ground looking as if they'd been attacked by a maniac on a bulldozer.

When two bulls fight for the favors of the cows, they clash their antlers, shatter the foliage, and grunt with the efforts they're making to drive one another away with their heavy headgear. If you hear such a racket thundering through the fall woods in moose habitat, tread warily.

Listen too for the splashing of water and the showering of spray when you're in wet moose country. The animals wade out into lakes and ponds to get the floating vegetation, but for underwater plants moose go beneath the surface and come up snorting and blowing with mouthfuls of the stuff.

During the rut, the bull grunts as he wanders around in search of female companionship. The cow bellows, bawls, or whines as she tries to attract a bull. When cow and calf converse, the noises are quite low.

Caribou

With his towering, regal sack, snow-white neck, and beautiful dark-brown body, the caribou is perhaps one of the world's handsomest animals. On this continent, he ranges throughout most of Alaska, the tundra and forests of Canada, and a very small part of northern Minnesota. These creatures are divided into the woodland caribou of

A sign of caribou in the north country—antler velvet clinging to broken bushes in the fall.

eastern Canada, the mountain caribou, inhabiting the Rockies, and the Barren Ground variety, which lives in the far North.

There are many visual signs of the caribou, not the least of which is his very distinctive track. Hoofs are rounded, and the crescent-shaped halves spread when the animal puts his weight on them. Front hoofs tend to spread a bit more than hind ones and, at about 4 inches across for a good bull, are a little bigger. When the animal is walking, dewclaws, or pasterns, of the front feet show quite far behind the hoofs. Hind hoofs are put down just a little bit short of the front ones, and the dewclaw marks look as if they belonged to the hind feet rather than the front ones.

Males and females both grow antlers, though those of the females are not the least bit impressive when compared with those of a handsome buck. Mature bucks shed theirs sometime in November, and the does and immature bucks lose their racks in spring. By September, the bucks are getting rid of the velvet on their new antlers by cutting and slashing at bushes and young trees. The stuff hangs in the scarred and broken brush as another visual sign of the caribou.

It's long been a popular belief that these animals use their palmated brow tines, called shovels, for scraping snow

Full-grown caribou leave crescent-shaped tracks about 3 inches long. Under animal's weight, hoof halves spread wide apart.

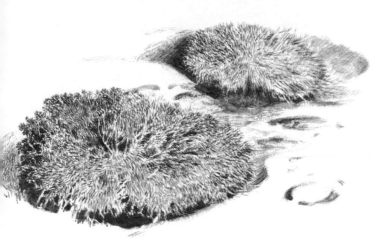

Exposed lichens in snow-covered terrain show where caribou dug holes with their front feet to get at favored food.

away from the lichens of which they are so fond. This is not true. In the first place, antlers have usually been shed when the snow is on the ground, and in the second place, their position in relation to the noses of their owners would make scraping with them extremely difficult. They paw the winter covering away with their front feet, and you'll often see areas in caribou habitat where they have dug large holes in the snow to get to moss and various grasses as well as lichens.

Winter droppings of caribou, similar to those of other deer, are pellet shaped and usually under an inch.

Caribou love lichens and eat them year round, but grasses, willow limbs, aspens, blueberry bushes, and other shrubs are also consumed. Look for stripped limbs and evidence of chewed-off twigs on bushes. Look also for signs that fungus has been nibbled at. Caribou are very partial to it.

Scats of these 300-pound animals are often in the pellet shape of other deer, but they can be soft and in a mass when the creatures have been eating juicy greens.

If you're wandering around in the north country in winter, keep an eye out for a cloud of vapor in the distance. This will indicate that a herd of caribou is on the move.

Strange winter sight in caribou country is cloud of vapor caused by body heat and breath of a traveling herd.

Depressions in the snow indicate that caribou have bedded-down during winter feeding.

The cloud is caused by the body heat of the animals and by the vapor of their breaths.

Watch too for beds in the snow and for caribou hair. The animal sloughs off his winter coat in huge tatters and shreds, usually in spring.

Caribou migrate seasonally from summer to winter feeding grounds, and the sight of a tremendous herd of the moving animals is not one to forget easily. Neither is the sound. When a caribou walks or trots, there is a definite *click* in his ankles, and when a large herd is under way the sound, mingled with occasional grunts and groans, is audible for some distance.

During winter, bulls begin to leave the cows, and by late spring the latter are in separate groups. Young, usually one but sometimes two, arrive in June or late May. In the fall, however, the bulls have their fighting equipment back, and an audible sign of this is the crashing made when they polish their antlers and occasionally engage in battles among themselves in defense of the harems they're beginning to acquire.

Caribou are not particularly vocal, but now and then you might hear a low grunting. This is generally used as communication between a doe and her offspring.

Some say the caribou is not very bright, and certainly his occasional, helter-skelter dashes from one direction to another defy reason. But be that as it may, his high, springy lope, his magnificent antlers, and his distinctive, clicking walk are part of the wilderness that is shrinking too fast.

Antelope

Often called the pronghorn, this animal of the arid plains regions of the western United States is among the fastest-moving creatures on earth and one of the most graceful. He likes the company of his fellows and is usually seen in bands of up to 100 animals, though in early fall the bucks begin to get together small groups of does as a harem. Twin fawns are the rule, and they're usually born eight months after the mating. Mature bucks rarely weigh over 125 pounds, and does are somewhat smaller.

Antelope tracks are rather heart shaped and deerlike, front hoofs being slightly longer than the hind ones. There are no dewclaws. When going full speed—and it has been estimated an antelope can hit 70 miles an hour—leaps can be as much as 20 feet or more.

Antelope uses white rump patch of erectile hairs to flash warning signals to herd when danger is near. These signals are tip-off to distant observer that antelope are in the area.

The pronghorn is mainly a weed eater rather than a grass eater, the bulk of his diet being dandelions, chicory, and other range weeds along with nibblings of desert shrubs such as sagebrush and juniper. Scats vary from pellets to longer masses.

The white rump patches on these basically dark-tan animals consists of erectile hairs, and when pronghorns are alarmed the patches stand out like huge fluffs of white cotton. At the same time, the startled creatures release a scent that a hunter can smell hundreds of feet away. By the

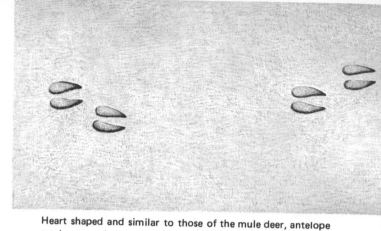

Heart shaped and similar to those of the mule deer, antelope tracks never show marks of dewclaws; the antelope has none.

Antelope droppings are either pellet shaped and less than an inch in length, or soft and elongated, depending on the season.

time he smells it, however, the antelope are well on their way to safety.

These swift animals are not particularly vocal, though when alarmed or ill at ease they sometimes make a loud, snorting whistle like that of a whitetail deer. When a doe is calling to her offspring, she may give a low bleat.

One of the great peculiarities of the antelope is his branched, hollow horns, which he sheds annually, usually in late winter. He is the only hoofed mammal with such horns known to shed them. Once dropped, they're munched on by rodents and even by the antelope themselves for the calcium they contain. If not chewed up, they disintegrate quite quickly. Both sexes have horns, but those of the female are seldom over 5 inches long while those of mature bucks average 10 or 12.

Rocky Mountain Bighorn

Great, brown, blocky animals with long coarse hair nothing like the wool found on domestic sheep, these nimble-footed creatures live in the high, windswept mountains of North America from southern British Columbia and Alberta south through the Rockies. Because of their magnificent, close-curled horns, they are at, or near, the top of every trophy hunter's list.

The Rocky Mountain ram weighs about 200 pounds, but large ones can reach 300. Ewes are smaller.

Tracks of the bighorn are rather like those of a whitetail deer, but the edges are straighter and the tips tend to be squared off rather than sharp. Hoof print of an adult male may be 3½ inches long, and when the animal is walking he

The resounding crash of two rams in a head-on charge may be heard in sheep country during the autumn rutting-season battles.

puts his hind foot on the print left by the front one. Bounding, he comes down with all four feet together. Not quite so sure-footed as the mountain goat, the bighorn is, however, faster as he leaps around the rocky cliffs and shale slides of his habitat.

There are other visual signs of the bighorn. Between feedings during the day, these beautiful creatures lie down to contemplate their domains and to chew their cuds. Their beds at this time are informal affairs, often prepared simply by scratching a few times in the ground with their forefeet. Their night beds, however, are another story. Usually on the lee side of a ridge, they are shallow, platterlike depressions about 3 feet long, and the rams often use them for a long time. If you come across something like this and don't recognize it by sight, just sniff and look a bit more closely. Bighorns often urinate in the beds when leaving them in the morning, and they leave their accumulated droppings around it. These latter, incidentally, tend to be pelletlike when the animals are feeding on dry food, massed together and softer when the diet is soft and succulent.

Sheep also use caves, particularly when the weather is very bad. Aside from the obvious visual signs, use your nose when exploring a cave suspected of having harbored sheep. And anywhere in sheep country, look for coarse, long hairs that have been caught in the rocks.

Sheep love salt, and they will gravitate to salt licks, particularly in spring and early summer. They can be recognized by the maze of tracks and trails leading to them and by the holes and smooth spots worn in them by the tongues of the countless animals using them. Sheep also get salt by eating decomposed rock with a high salt content.

Bulk of the bighorn's diet is grass and herbs, but the creatures occasionally browse on the buds of willow,

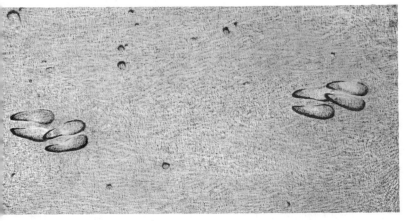

Bighorn's tracks are similar to those of whitetail but the edges are straighter; tips are square rather than sharp.

Shallow depressions on lee side of ridge are sheeps' night beds. These are usually deeper than animals' daytime resting places.

spruce, fir, and aspen. Where the snow is not too deep in winter, look for evidence of pawing. The animals in the central Rockies have to get grass in winter, and they'll paw through almost a foot of snow to reach it.

The bighorn is not a very vocal animal, but in summer there is much conversational bleating between ewes and lambs. Mature sheep snort to warn one another of danger, and when rams get angry they gnash their teeth.

Rams stay by themselves during the summer, usually in small bands of animals of the same age. About the middle to the end of October, however, they start looking for the ewes. By the middle of the following month, the rut is going full blast. Some rams assemble harems of up to seven ewes, and some of these harem masters are belligerent in the defense of their womenfolk if a strange ram appears on the scene. It is then that the spectacular battles between the rams take place.

A battle starts with the two combatants snorting at one another fairly close together. Then they walk away from each other 30 or 40 feet, turn as if on a prearranged signal, and charge each other head first. The crash when their massive horns meet can be heard for a mile or more. If you are in sheep country in the late fall, you might be lucky enough to hear this sound and even to see a battle in progress. The repeated chargings may last for a few minutes or a couple of hours. Both rams are usually on their feet when it is over, and sometimes the two wander off together as if nothing more serious had taken place than a mild difference of opinion. Occasionally, however, a few rams that have nothing better to do join in the fight, and the result is a pitched battle during which horn tips get broken, nose bleeds occur, deep gashes are given and received, and a contestant or so may be killed by being pushed over a cliff or getting his skull fractured.

Desert Bighorn

This animal is a southern extension of the Rocky Mountain bighorn, and he inhabits the hottest, most arid, most rugged country the southwestern United States, Lower California, and Mexico have to offer. He is also hard to spot because his gray-brown coat blends perfectly with the brown, rocky hills in which he lives.

A traveler on the arid southwestern desert is apt to see the decaying skulls and horns of desert bighorns baking under the torrid sun.

The desert bighorn is a bit smaller than the northern variety, and he probably weighs, on the average, about 50 pounds less. Because he lives in an area of burning heat, his hairs are shorter than those of the cold-weather bighorn. He also has a more slender neck, and his rump patch isn't quite as white as that of his somewhat bigger cousin.

Since the desert sheep lives in a climate so vastly different from that enjoyed by other sheep, it is natural that some of his habits would be different too. In the main, however, signs of him are similar. He makes a similar bed, he leaves his droppings around it, he battles in conventional sheep manner, his tracks are the same, and he also wanders into caves.

One difference, however, is that the rut gets under way earlier in the desert, usually around the first of September, and the lambs are usually born around the first of February. Another difference is in watering habits. Northern sheep have plenty of water, but the desert variety lives where it is not only scarce but somewhat nonexistent. Where there are no holes of accumulated rainwater, the southern sheep depends on dew, fruit of cactus plants, and the water stored in such cacti as the barrel cactus and the saguaro. It is a mystery how they do it without getting skewered, but they will nibble as much as 6 inches into the

Signs of bighorn sheep, both desert and mountain, are few, but one may occasionally see wisps of their hair clinging to a rock.

Like those of deer, the shape of wild-sheep droppings depends on available forage. This is type left by animal on thin forage.

huge saguaros for the moisture. Since grasses aren't as plentiful in the desert ranges, the sheep there are mainly browsers, living chiefly on such shrubs as mountain mahogany, buckbrush, and Mormon tea. They travel great distances, however, for the succulent greenery that springs up briefly early in the year.

Because rain is so scarce in this rough country, tracks can be very confusing. You can see one that looks as if it had been made only a couple of days before you came across it, but in reality it may have been made months before.

Also due to lack of moisture, the desert bighorn's horns—which are also of the close-curl type—tend to be drier. As a result of this, they crack and flake, and it is not uncommon to find pieces of them in ram beds and where the animals have been fighting or have bumped against rocks. Watch for this sign of the desert bighorn.

Dall Sheep and Stone Sheep

The Dall sheep is one of the handsomest of North American game animals. He is pure white with yellowish-brown

Ranging high among the northern peaks, the pure white Doll sheep often surveys the world from a bed outside his cave.

horns that flare out more than do those of the bighorn. Also, he is a smaller creature by far. Horns tend to be slenderer and rather triangular in cross section.

Range of these truly majestic animals is from the northern reaches of Alaska south and southeast through parts of the Yukon into northern British Columbia. Like all sheep, they tend to travel extensively, to seek less snowy altitudes for their winter ranges, and to have a sweetish odor about them that is well recognized by outdoorsmen of the north.

Food of the Dall is principally grass and sedge, though many other lichens and plants are nibbled at now and then.

Tracks of the Doll sheep are slightly sharper than those of the bighorn and are more tapered toward the front.

Bighorns broom their horns—rub the tips until they wear them off—so the ends will not obstruct their vision, but this is not done as frequently among the Dalls because their horns flare out more and do not tend to block the animals' vision as much as do the close curls of the massive bighorns.

As soon as the wilderness traveler gets south of Alaska and east of the Dalls' Yukon range, he begins to see the Stone sheep. This animal ranges much farther down into British Columbia than does the Dall, of whom he is such a close relative that he is a subspecies. In spite of that, however, he looks quite different. This beautiful creature is the darkest of the sheep, though his colors vary tremendously. He can be anything from a practically black animal to one that is light with a dark-brown saddle. Where the ranges of the Dalls and the Stones overlap, the sheep tend to be lighter with some darker markings, but in the southern part of his range the Stone is quite dark.

Stones average smaller than the bighorns, as a general rule, but a bit larger than their white cousins. Horns are similar in shape to those of the Dall, being outward flaring and more slender than those of the bighorn. Instead of being yellowish like those of the Dall, however, they are dark brown.

Both of these varieties of sheep have habits and leave signs like those of the Rocky Mountain animal. They fight

394

like them, leave similar tracks and droppings, make similar noises, and generally do not leave any evidence that marks them strongly apart. As a wilderness wanderer, you should pay careful attention to the ranges of the four types of sheep if you wish to interpret sheep signs toward identification of the kind of sheep trail you may be following.

Rocky Mountain Goat

One of the few animals on this continent that remains white all year, the Rocky Mountain goat is known in the United States as a dweller of the highest crags in the western mountains. This creature with the needlelike, back-curving horns, which are found in both sexes, is also at home in parts of western Canada.

Goats—occasionally come down off their windswept, rocky pinnacles in early summer when they're shedding, and the sign of a shedding goat's passing is unmistakable. He leaves huge gobs of white wool draped all over the brush. When he's got rid of it all, he looks much thinner than he will in winter when he has his hairy pantaloons, beard, and great shaggy coat back again.

Because the goat lives in an environment that's largely perpendicular, his concave hoofs have a hard outside and a softer inside. He can hook the horny edge over the smallest of rocky protuberances, thus getting a foothold as he picks his way slowly and sedately along the face of a cliff that would make a bighorn sheep shudder with apprehension. Besides this, his toes open at the front, giving him double purchase. Because the cloven hoofs tend to spread when the animal is moving along, tracks appear squarish and are

A sure sign that a goat has passed by: as they descend from the rocky heights during their summer shedding, they often leave bunches of white wool draped on bushes.

usually over 3 inches long in a mature billy. On the trail, prints usually show in groups of two when the animal is walking. In snow, foot drags are often apparent. When he bounds, the goat's tracks show all four prints closer together.

Tracks of the mountain goat in snow show foot drags behind the hoof prints, which are spread and somewhat squarish in appearance.

Goats sometimes seek refuge in caves, making snow beds outside. Look for traces of hair, tracks, and droppings.

In summer, goats feed on grasses, herbs, and flowers, and at this time their droppings are in 4- or 5-inch masses. In winter, when goats eat twigs and what dry grasses they can find, scats are in hard, separated pellets.

To see more signs of goats, look for mineral licks in the animals' range, dusty beds, and also for hollows in the dust where these 150- to 300-pound creatures have rolled and wallowed. Sometimes they make beds in snow, and occasionally they take refuge in caves. Tracks, droppings, and perhaps a few long, white hairs within should be the tip-off.

Mature male goats are usually solitary animals, but in November they get the mating urge. In late April, May, or June, young are born. Twins aren't rare, but one is the usual number of offspring. Mother and kid then join a group composed of other nannies and kids, young males, and young females to browse on the mountain slopes.

One last sign. If you're way up in the high country and see what you think is a patch of snow high above the timber line, get out your spotting scope. That patch of snow may be the goat you're looking for.

Droppings of the mountain goat are generally smaller than those of deer and sheep. Soft pellets like these indicate later summer feed.

Black Bear

This animal is the smallest of our bears—200 pounds on the average though 500-pounders have been taken—and the one with the widest distribution, from Alaska throughout Canada and most of the United States.

Tracks of this bruin are strangely human in shape, and frequently the little toe doesn't show up, making the animal seem to be a four-toed creature, which it is not. Sometimes the claw marks don't show either.

Feet are put down in such a way that the longer (up to 7 inches) hind foot leaves its print several inches in front of the front foot, which may be 5 inches long and is usually rounder than the hind one. Tracks show up as a double row of prints, one side being those left by the right feet and the other being those put down by the left ones. When the animal is loping, all tracks are more close together.

Blacks leave many visual signs besides their tracks. One of the most common is the markings left on what most persons refer to as a bear tree. Bears rub themselves on trees, usually pines or firs, and as they rub this way and that, some of their hairs remain clinging to the bark. Frequently, while rubbing, a bear will reach up to claw and bite the tree. Often evidence of this will be at such a height that you'll realize the bear was standing on his hind feet when he did it. Watch for hairs, claw and bite marks, and oozing pitch for indications of a bear tree.

If you should see an aspen with scabs on its bark quite a way up the tree, suspect the black bear. This facile climber often goes up aspens, and in so doing his claws gouge the soft bark. The tree grows scabs over these cuts that remain as long as the tree is standing.

Black bears often strip the bark near the bottom of pines, spruces, and firs to get at the syrupy juice beneath.

Still another tree sign left by the black bruins is one that can result in the death of the tree. These bears strip bark off pines, spruces, and firs near the bottom, sometimes girdling them, to get at the syrupy juice just beneath it. Look for vertical tooth marks when you see this sort of tree damage.

Watch too for turned-over rocks and old logs torn apart. Bears like ants and many varieties of beetles, and they look for such tidbits beneath stones and in rotton or decaying wood. Ant hills are frequently torn apart and their makers

A torn-up berry patch signifies a recent bear visit. Bruins strip the branches, eating twigs, leaves, fruit and all.

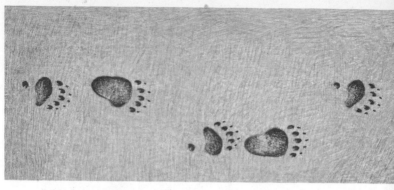

A black bear leaves a trail of paired sets of tracks, the longer hind-foot print appearing in front of the forefoot.

eaten with relish. These animals also like roots, bulbous plants, seeds, pocket gophers, ground squirrels, and other small, ground-dwelling creatures; so keep an eye out for prominent diggings where such tasty morsels have been sought. Big holes, flung dirt, and claw marks should be an easy indication of the lumbering beast that did the excavating.

Black bears also climb trees for birds' eggs and nestlings. They are fond of honey too and never miss an opportunity to raid a bee's nest. In fact, blackie likes pretty much of everything that he doesn't have to work too hard to get.

Scats of this creature tend to be rather uniform in diameter and often appear as disjointed sigments consisting most frequently of grasses, roots, wood shavings, pine nuts, and berry seeds when berries are ripe. If the animal has been dining on another animal (carrion, usually) scats will be mostly hair. Some berries, notably strawberries, will produce a semiliquid mass.

If you are in bear country and find your garbage can tipped over and the contents scattered over the countryside, look for a black bear somewhere in the vicinity.

402

A bear bed is a rather hastily constructed affair. When tired, the animal simply scoops out a depression and flops down in it. The long winter sleep, however, is another matter, at least for bears with a modicum of interest in their own comfort.

When cold weather comes along, they den up in caves, under ledges, in hollow stumps, beneath the root structures of blown-down trees, or in holes they have dug themselves.

Black bears like to rub against trees, leaving traces of their hair as well as claw and bite marks. Pitch oozing from a tree is a good sign to look for.

Scats of the black bear are often in disjointed segments, about 2 inches long, usually containing traces of vegetable matter on which the animal largely feeds.

Often the den faces south. Lazy bears, and there are lazy bears as well as lazy people, simply wander into some thick brush and pass a dreary winter shivering with the cold.

The bear usually sleeps till April or May. While sleeping fitfully, the female gives birth to any number of cubs up to four. She awakens long enough to bite the umbilical cord and lick her children clean, but as they struggle up to the milk that awaits them on her underside, she goes back to sleep and slumbers for another couple of months.

Black bears don't make much noise, but now and then a mother bear will grunt or growl at her offspring, and they, in turn, will whimper if separated from her. An angry bear will roar and snarl with such volume that he can be heard half a mile away. A wounded or hurt bear will moan, wail, sob, and howl with all the anguish of a man in deep agony.

One sound you might listen for is the noise made by nuts as they rain through tree branches. Bears love acorns, chestnuts, and beechnuts, and they climb trees to shake the nuts to the ground where they later eat them.

Grizzly Bear

This huge bear with the dished-in face has been practically run out of the United States, being now only found in small numbers in the high, wild areas of Wyoming, Idaho, Montana, Colorado, and in Yellowstone Park as well as Glacier National Park. Farther north, in Alaska, British Columbia, and the Yukon Territory, he is far more abundant.

If you should be wandering around anywhere in the grizzly's range, and stumble over the half-eaten carcass of a deer, moose, or elk that has been loosely covered with leaves, twigs, or other forest litter, get away as fast as your legs can carry you. You are already a shoo-in favorite to get chewed up, because you've probably stumbled on the jealously guarded food cache of a grizzly bear. It is possible you've come across a mountain lion's larder, but don't bet

Grizzlies like to dig for marmots, tearing up large areas of earth and displacing rocks in search of burrowing prey.

on it. Get out. Likewise, if you smell decaying flesh, move away fast, unless you've put the stuff there in the first place as bait for a trophy bear.

The grizzly is a very large animal, averaging from 500 to 750 pounds, though they have been recorded at 1,000 or more. This bear has a big hump on his shoulder, and his color varies tremendously from yellowish brown to dark brown with light hairs along the back. This latter coloration gives the grizzly another name by which he is frequently known—silvertip.

His habits are very similar to those of the black bear, with, however, several important differences. For one thing, he eats more meat, though he is basically a vegetarian feeding on berries, grasses, buds, tubers, and roots. Like the black bear too, he is very fond of burrowing animals, and an area worked over by a grizzly digging for marmots is an area full of excavations big enough to bury a sofa. He

All bears leave similar tracks, but the grizzly's is larger than the black's, the hind foot often measuring 10 inches.

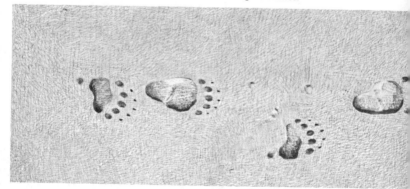

is passionately fond of carrion, and when he is after fresh meat he can kill an elk, deer, or moose with one blow of his massive paw.

After he has killed it—usually an old or sick one—he'll feed on it and then cart the remains off somewhere and cover them, as mentioned earlier, returning to dine on them until the carcass is completely consumed.

Unlike the black, the grizzly does not climb trees, but he leaves claw marks and telltale hairs on their trunks.

Grizzly tracks are similar to those of black bears. Prints of the grizzly bear, however, are generally larger. Hind prints may be 10 inches long by almost 6 inches wide.

A large hole in the ground near timberline may be a grizzly's den, which he digs in August in preparation for the winter.

Front ones are apt to go 5½ by 5½. Old, established trails are sometimes made up of zigzag pits on either side of the center line where the bears have been stepping into each other's prints for years. This trait is not as marked in the black and grizzly, however, as it is in the brown. Often an old grizzly trail is merely a deep set of parallel ruts.

When near salmon rivers of the West Coast, keep an eye out for the remains of eaten fish. The big bears come down to the rivers during the spawning runs and scoop the big fish out onto the beach where they devour them. Sometimes they grab them from the water with their powerful jaws. Nearby tracks should positively identify the anglers.

A grizzly usually dens near timberline, in a rocky cave, beneath the roots of a big tree, or in a self-excavated hole. He starts looking for a likely spot in August, and when the weather turns nippy he enters it, curls up, and sleeps until April. The sow gives birth in her den just as does the female black.

Occasionally the bear comes out of his den before the snow has gone, and this gives rise to something that has been reliably reported that might be considered a definite sign. Look for snow slides. Most bears have their playful moments, and on at least one occasion a grizzly was seen repeatedly sliding down a snow-covered hill on his broad rump. He appeared to be enjoying himself vastly.

Scats of the grizzly are similar to those of the black, but they are generally larger. During berry time, they might be semiliquid.

The grizzly makes noises that vary from grunts, snorts, growls, and coughs to full-fledged roars. Like the black, he carries on horribly when hurt.

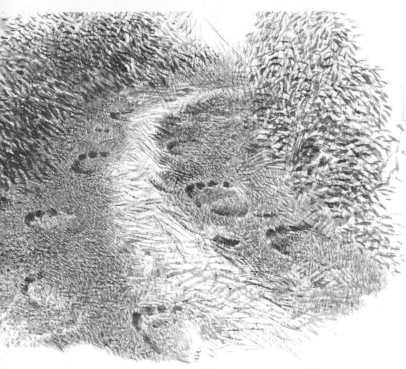

Brownies often tread in tracks left by predecessors, and their trail may appear as a well-worn path in the wilds.

Brown Bear

This truly tremendous animal is the largest terrestrial carnivorous mammal in the world. A full-grown bear may weigh 1,500 to 1,600 pounds and have a reach when standing of 12 feet. Basically his habits and diet are very similar to those of the grizzly, to whom he is closely related. In fact, where their ranges overlap, it is sometimes difficult to tell whether a given specimen is a brown or a grizzly.

The true brown, however, has a small range—the southwest coast of Alaska, including many of the islands and the heights of the coastal mountains. Some of these giant bears inhabit northwest British Columbia, but the largest animals are generally found in the Aleutians or on Kodiak Island.

The brownie's track is just like that of the grizzly, but it is much larger. The hind foot may measure 16 inches long. One interesting thing about an established trail of this animal is that it frequently appears as a series of zigzag pits sometimes as much as 10 inches deep. These are formed on a well-used trail because each bear steps into the same prints made by his predecessors. Another interesting thing about trails such as this is that they often follow a perfectly straight line and, where they go up a mountainside, are visible from a great distance. If a trail like this, particularly one in mossy tundra, has been abandoned for some years,

Brown bear leaves largest track. Hind foot, which he places in front of forefoot like other bears, may measure 16 inches.

Fisherman of the bear family, brownie visits salmon streams during spawning time, litters the bank with scraps.

it will grow up in clumps of grass, because seeds collect in the pits. This won't tell you where bears are, but it certainly will tell you where they've been.

You will find well-worn bear trails along salmon streams, because this variety of bear greatly enjoys fish and comes to the rivers during the June spawning runs. Look for uneaten fish as well as the streamside tracks. The animals customarily litter the banks with far more salmon than they can eat. Also along the streams, look for resting places scooped out among the alder thickets and willows. Sometimes you'll even find a mattress—a pile of moss 10 or 12 feet across that the bear has assembled to make his naps more comfortable.

The brown's diet is similar to that of the grizzly, but he frequently eats a lot of shoreside sedge. In spring he feeds almost completely on grasses, later digging up roots and feeding on berries. Regarding the latter, watch for berry patches that have been heavily torn up. Bears eat berries by stripping the bushes and eating leaves and twigs along with the fruit. Ground-burrowing animals are also game for the brownie, and any dead animal is much relished. He even eats dead whales that have washed up on shore.

Scats of the brownie are similar to, but larger than, those of the black. It is well to remember too that a fish diet, as well as one of berries, will make them loose.

Young brown bears can climb trees, but when they grow older they give up such nonsense. They do, however, rub themselves on trees, tear out bark with their teeth, and reach up to claw them as do other bears.

A brown usually goes to bed in late September in a den chosen much as the grizzly chooses his, and he doesn't reappear until about mid-April.

Females mate only once every two or three years, and it is only during the breeding season of a month or six weeks in May and June that the sexes show any affection for one another. Young are born in the den and stay with the mother no more than two years.

Polar Bear

This animal is the bear of the Arctic wastes and pack ice. He may run as large as the brown, but generally he doesn't. He ranges throughout the Arctic from northern Alaska, over the Arctic Ocean pack ice, and into Hudson Bay and the coastal areas of northern Labrador.

The polar bear has a long, slender neck and is generally a more graceful animal than is the brown bear. The only part of him that's not creamy white is the tip of his nose.

Padding across the snow-covered ice of his Arctic habitat, the polar bear leaves a massive trail—his only sign.

Five-toed paw prints are not easily distinguishable because the pads are covered with fur.

The ice bear is a terrific swimmer and a fantastic traveler. Sometimes he comes ashore where there's vegetation, but this is rare. Usually he gets his groceries from the ice and sea, feeding on seals, walruses, fish, porpoises, ducks, and marine vegetation. When these animals come ashore to catch spawning fish in the cold, northern streams, they will eat a lot of grass and land vegetation. The bears gather from great distances to feed on dead whales, and that's about the

Polar bear's tracks are difficult to distinguish because foot-pads are covered with fur, but a well-formed impression would look like this.

only time they tolerate one another's company except during the brief courting season in June or early July.

Chances are, unless you frequent zoos, that you'll not see a polar bear or even see a sign of one unless you are hunting him. If you are, watch for the massive trail in the snow-covered ice that could only have been made by a tremendous animal. He is the only tremendous animal in his range, and he travels alone.

Unlike other bears, the polar does not hibernate—with one notable exception. The female—who has young at two-year intervals—hibernates in piled-up masses of ice or in hard-packed snow, but only when she's expecting cubs.

Gray Wolf

In most of this country (Alaska excepted), you will look in vain for signs of this handsome animal. He's been harassed to the point where his numbers are limited to parts of Wisconsin, Michigan, and Minnesota. In sections of Texas, Oklahoma, the Mississippi Valley, and Florida, a smaller species of the wolf is known as the red wolf. In Canada and Alaska, the gray wolf—also called the timber wolf—comes into his own and may reach a length of 7 feet and a weight of 175 pounds.

Tracks of the four paws usually show fairly close together but are spread out in a staggered line when the animal is loping, are more closely bunched in a bounding gallop. They're very similar to dog tracks, though much bigger. The front tracks are larger than those of the hind feet, measuring 4 to 5 inches in length. Toes of the hind feet do not spread as much as those of the front ones. If you're doing your observing in the north country, you might easily confuse the tracks of a wolf with those of a husky. It's also good to remember that usually dogs do not have the same suspicious nature that a wolf has. When approaching an object, a dog will usually come up to it directly, but a wolf will advance in a devious path that takes advantage of

Wolf tracks resemble dog tracks but are much larger, sometimes measuring 5 inches in length. These were made in dry mud.

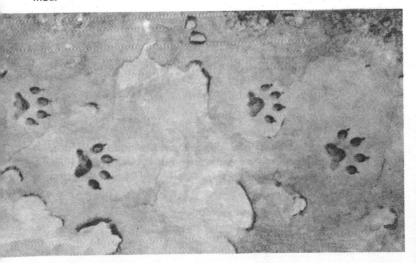

Trail of wolf track approaching a caribou across reveals the animal's wary nature. he advances from one point of cover to the next until he reaches his quarry.

every bit of cover. Watch for this pattern when trying to determine whether the tracks you are following are those of a dog or of a wolf.

In northern wolf country, watch for caribou. Where there are caribou, there will almost certainly be wolves not far behind. These predators, whose color vary drastically from light to dark, follow the herds on their migrations. Don't look for much in the remains of prey, however, which is a sort of negative sign in itself. These powerful creatures have jaws of almost unbelievable strength. If they pull down an animal of any size, they'll crunch up and swallow the biggest bones, leaving only blood, a few hairs, and horns or antlers. Big animals, however, aren't the staple of wolves. Their main diet is gophers, rabbits, and squirrels. Of the bigger animals, usually the young and aged are pulled down.

Keep an eye out for dens. They are usually dug in a bank of soft soil, and they may extend 25 or more feet to end in a roomy chamber. The male does not use the den but keeps

A wolf den in the bank of soft soil often extends 25 feet, ending in a roomy chamber.

Wolves also den in rock caves on hillsides which provide a wide view of the landscape—and approaching foes.

watch on its entrance when he is not out collecting food for his burgeoning family, additions to which are forthcoming any time from April through June. Six is the average litter, but there may be twice that number. Wolves also den in caverns, hollow trees, or enlarge an abandoned den of a coyote, badger, or other burrowing animal.

You may be in wolf country and never see one of the creatures. They're secretive and smart, but they're not above broadcasting signs of their presence vocally as well as visually. They have a sound that once heard can never be forgotten. It has all the loneliness of the wilderness in it and all the longing of a hopeless dream. This howl has none of the short, yapping bark. It is long and deep, and you'll usually hear it when you're back in camp snugged down for the night. Mating call of the male is throaty, and when he is chasing game he will utter a guttural note, the direction

418

of which is often hard to determine. A high, plaintive cry is often used near the den.

Fox

The most widely distributed fox in North America is the red fox, a graceful animal that has learned to adapt himself readily to the trappings of civilization and the conversion of the wild countryside to farmland. Areas of the deep

A hollow log may be a fox den. Telltale signs are hairs of the entrance or animal leftovers—tufts of rabbit fur or feathers.

Southeast, the Gulf Coast, and parts of the Southwest are the only ones in this country that he avoids.

Signs of the red fox aren't hard to discern. His tracks, almost in a straight line, are rather delicate, showing four claws and the imprint of pads. In winter, however, there's so much fur on the animal's feet that the individual pads may not show up in the snow. Prints of the rear feet are often superimposed on those of the forefeet.

The red fox sleeps out during the winter, but along about January or February mating takes place, and the female, called the vixen, digs or prepares a den. This might be one she has dug herself in the loose ground or it may be the enlarged hole of one of the burrowing animals such as the woodchuck. In any event, such fox homes are not easy to discover because the animals make sure there is no earth outside of them to indicate their presence.

If you find a hole 10 to 20 inches across, you may be looking at a fox den. Hairs around its entrance may be a giveaway, as may be nearby odds and ends of animal left-overs such as tufts of rabbit fur or inedible feathers. If a mild, skunklike odor is present also, you can be sure you've spotted a fox den.

The dog fox roams fairly far afield after the pups are born, but the vixen stays quite close to her den area, sometimes all her life. The dog fox barks in a short yelp, but the female is more shrill and yaps. During mating season, that yap is apt to be more of a scream.

While the red fox lives over much of the United States and Canada, the gray fox is native to the eastern section of the country and parts of the West and Southwest. This little creature prefers to roam at night more than the red fox, and he likes the brushy areas of the wooded lowlands and swamps more than does his more gregarious, red-haired cousin. He also climbs trees.

In the plains and dry areas of the West and Midwest lives the swift, or kit, fox. He is quite small and, like another desert fox—the long-eared fox—is rarely seen, spending much of his time below ground.

Coyote

At dusk or daylight in the desert areas of the West and Southwest, one may hear from his bedroll a sudden, eerie, high-pitched noise that sounds like a cry of anguish from some soul lost in hell. *Yip, yip, yip, yowroooooooooo*! This long-drawn-out wail, often taken up by another animal, is

Patches of earth showing through the snow in coyote country are often places where the animal dug for a warm bed.

the aria of the coyote. It is one of the most thrilling of wilderness sounds.

Tracks of the coyote—he weighs from 20 to 50 pounds—follow the canine pattern laid down by wolves and dogs, and, like them, the coyote has front feet larger than those in the back. The animal tends to pick out a prominent spot for his droppings, a spot that is sure to be investigated by

Coyote den is characterized by semicircle of dirt around entrance, formed by animal after digging hole.

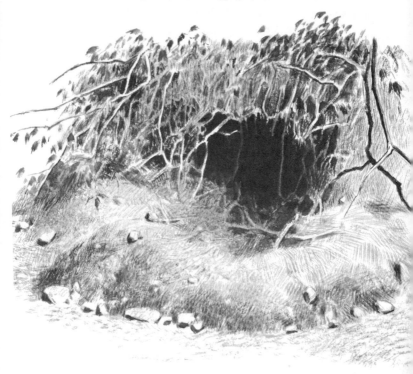

Coyote tracks follow canine pattern of wolf's. Heel pads of fore and hind feet are slightly different in shape.

other passersby of the same general family. This may be a trail crossing, rock, stump, or any place not easily missed by, say, a fox or another coyote.

Young are born in a hollow log, in the rocks, a cave, or in a burrow. This latter is dug in loose soil or is the remodeled home of a skunk, badger, or fox. A tip-off to coyote occupancy is that the earth pushed out of the entrance in digging or enlarging is pushed back to the entrance and shaped around it into a fairly low heap, usually somewhat fan shaped. Another tip-off is that the 5- to 30-foot burrow is apt to have a ventilation hole in the roof of the chamber at its end. If you are near a coyote den, you might hear the grown-ups inside barking.

Mating takes place in January or February, and about sixty days later the young are born in litters that range from three pups to well over a dozen. At this time the male does the hunting, dropping food at the entrance to the den for his mate and progeny.

Coyotes eat just about everything, but their favorite foods are rabbits and rodents, with generous helpings of carrion. They're very partial to watermelons.

In spite of being shot, poisoned, and trapped for their occasional misdemeanors among domestic stock, coyotes are surviving and extending their range east and north. They are now found in some Canadian provinces, a few of the western states, and Alaska.

Cougar

Not too long ago, while hunting deer on the Jicarilla Apache Indian Reservation in New Mexico, two of us heard the most horrible cry of anguish imaginable not over a quarter of a mile away. It was a highpitched *Ya-a-a-a-a! Ya-a-a-a-a!* dying in intensity and into silence, quite like a man screaming in the agony of death. Later we talked to the hunter who had shot the animal responsible for this death cry and found that it had been a large cougar, a beast long believed never to scream. It does scream, however, and the sound has been likened to a roaring, a howling, or the scream of a woman in mortal terror. This cry is not often heard, though, as these big cats—a huge one would go 200

Cougar tracks are easily identified by their catlike appearance. Even in soft mud, as here, claws do not register.

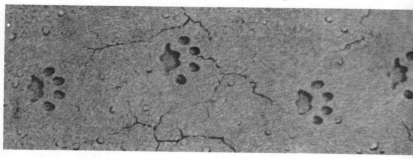

Deer carcass buried under sticks and foliage is sure sign that cougar has been in the area and will return to finish his meal

pounds—are almost entirely nocturnal and usually very quiet. They have to be, at least when hunting, as they are beasts of prey whose victims, principally deer, would be spooked by caterwauling and yowling. As cats, however, they do vocalize to some extent, making the same sort of sounds house cats do, only louder and deeper.

There are several visual signs of cougars, or mountain lions. Tracks are quite distinctive. Claws seldom show, and the widths of the prints vary from about 3 to over 4 inches. Front-foot tracks are larger than those of the rear feet, and the toes tend to spread when the animal puts on speed. In winter, tracks are apt to show foot drags in the snow, and there might be evidence of where the tail has brushed the white fluff on either side of the tracks.

Scratchings are another sign to watch for in cougar country.

Favored lair of the cougar, a cave offers shelter from the cold and a place for the mother to give birth in the spring.

During his nightly travels the cougar leaves another sign—scratchings. In common with other cats, mountain lions cover their droppings with earth, and these sign heaps, coupled with tracks, clearly show the trail a cougar has taken.

When one of these tree-climbing animals has killed a deer and eaten all he wants of it, he drags it to a spot of his own choosing and covers it with anything handy, such as sticks, leaves, branches, or other forest litter where it remains until he has finished eating it. If you should find a partially eaten carcass so buried, you can be sure a cougar is in the vicinity. But don't be frightened. These huge cats are timid and far more afraid of humans than humans are of them.

In this country these handsome, tawny animals range principally in the West, north to south, and in parts of Texas, Louisiana, and Florida. A full-grown male will stretch up to 8 feet, including its black-tipped tail. It kills by leaping on its victim's back and biting into the neck. The cougar occasionally kills farm stock, but deer are by far the preferred diet.

Bobcat

Living all over the conterminous United States, with the exception of sections of the mid-South and parts of the corn-belt region, the bobcat resembles an overgrown alley cat with a short tail and tufted ears. He is called variously the wild cat, bay lynx, and other local names. He is light with black spots and averages 20 to 25 pounds, though a really big one will go 10 pounds more. He leaves definite signs, and since he is thriving in a world of encroaching civilization, these signs are of more than passing interest.

His tracks are rather rounded, more so than those of dogs and coyotes, and there is hair between the toes in winter. His larger northern neighbor, the lynx, also has this hair between the toes when cold weather sets in. The bobcat shows no claw marks on the ground, and when the animal is really moving, the front toes tend to spread more than those of the hind feet. Prints are about 8 to 14 inches apart, unless the animal is bounding.

Bobcats often hunt by stretching out on a branch over a game trail, where they wait to pounce on some luckless animal passing below. When they do this, they approach the tree from the side away from the trail.

In summer, these cats, as do all of their tribe, bury their droppings by scratching dirt over them. In the case of the bobcat, however, this is apt to be a haphazard operation, so knowledge of the scats is of value. In very dry areas of the country, these droppings are likely to be marked by constricted segments, and sometimes they appear as pellets. Where the climate is more damp, the scats can be confused with the waste of dogs or coyotes. If you see claw marks around droppings, however, and signs of attempts to bury

The bobcat's tracks are slightly smaller than the cougar's. Absence of claw marks distinguishes them from coyote's.

Bits of bark at the base of a tree, as well as claw marks on trunk, are signs of bobcat's claw-sharpening habit.

them with earth are present, chances are better than good that a bobcat has been your predecessor on the trail.

Another sign of these animals can occasionally be seen at the bases of trees. Since bobcats sharpen their claws on trees and stumps, bits of bark are scraped off and drop to the ground. The claw marks themselves, of course, are another sign.

The bobcat is a noisy fellow during mating season, usually January or February. His howling and screeching at that time can be fearsome. At other times his noises are similar to those of the house cat, but with more volume.

This deceptively gentle looking cat is a rarely seen nocturnal wanderer who dens in the rocks, occasionally in a hollow tree, and once in a while in an abandoned fox's den. His basic diet consists of small animals such as rabbits and rodents, but now and then he'll pull down a deer, usually a fawn or sick adult. Sometimes he'll turn his attention to livestock and domestic fowl. But he is a sign of the wilds, and that he is increasing in numbers, in spite of the enthusiasm with which he is hunted, is an indication of his adaptability and courage.

Beaver

A thrilling night sound for the autumn camper near water—especially after ice begins to form—is the *slap-plunk* of a beaver at work. A noisier form of beaver communication can be heard when the animal is alerted—a sound like someone slapping water hard with the flat of a paddle. This warning tells all the beavers in the colony to dive for safety. To make this noise, the animal brings his flat, scaly tail over his back and slaps it quickly down on the water. The resultant *crack* can be heard for incredible distances.

The most common visual sign of the beaver is his dam. Of logs, branches, stones, and mud, it keeps the water behind it at a constant level. Here, in the center of the pond

Pile of chips and a partially cut tree tell the passerby that a beaver has been hard at work building a lodge or a dam.

backed up by the 3- to 4-foot-high structure, the one-chamber lodges are built. These lodges, which are 6 to 8 feet across, have subterranean entrances and house an entire family. Occasionally, these stick houses will be erected on the banks of lakes and streams.

To build his strong dams and lodges, and to get the branches on which he most often feeds, the beaver cuts down many trees. He can fell a tree 2 feet thick with his chisel-shaped teeth. The woodland wanderer who comes across stumps and chips bordering a stream or pond should recognize them as evidence of beavers.

Still another sign might be a canal. When trees are far from the water's edge, the animals dig canals from the woods area to the water. They are up to 3 feet wide and 18 inches deep. The beavers cut their wood to the lengths

An expert engineer, the beaver builds an efficient dam across a stream to protect his intricately constructed lodge behind it.

required—usually 2 to 6 feet—and float it down the canals to their building sites.

Any spot where beavers are working is crisscrossed with their tracks. The front feet are handlike, have long claws, and are not used when swimming. The large hind feet are webbed and used as paddles. When the animals are cutting wood, they often stand on their hind feet and use their heavy tails as supports.

Beavers are dark and squat, weighing up to 60 pounds or more. They have valves in their nostrils and ears that

When in danger, the beaver warns his colony by slapping the water with his tail. The noise can be heard far away.

close automatically when they submerge. Young are born in late April, May, or early June in litters of six. Favored food is the bark of aspen, willow, birch, poplar, and alder, slender branches of which they store under water for winter eating. When ice forms on the ponds, the animals travel from the dry chambers of their houses, via the subsurface

Canals leading to river are sign of beaver's ingenuity. When trees are scarce on river, he cuts trees inland and floats logs down.

entrances, to their food caches. Selecting a succulent branch, the hungry beaver brings it back and eats its bark by holding it in his front feet and chewing on it as a man eats corn on the cob.

Foot-wide holes in the ground, with piles of dirt around the edge, are signs of a badger's hunting trips into marmot dens.

Badger

This rather flattened animal with the white stripe running from its nose back over its head is the prime excavator of the western states. He favors the plains country from Mexico into southwest Canada, but he can occasionally be found in the woodlands where there's no heavy brush to impede his rapid digging. He also inhabits parts of the Great Lakes country.

The principal signs of this energetic creature are often encountered by horsemen. A badger digs goodsized holes, and a rider whose cantering mount steps into one is apt to have a bad fall. The horse is liable to break its leg.

Beginning to hunt late in the afternoon and continuing through the night, the badger seeks out prairie-dog villages, and pocket gopher or ground-squirrel dens. Boring like an

Badger tracks are characterized by a toed-in pattern. Front and hind feet appear close together.

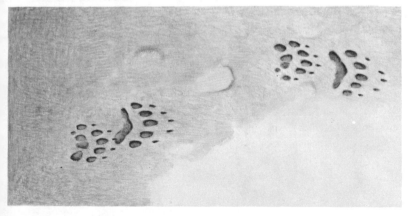

auger through the burrows of these little fellows in quest of his dinner, he throws huge quantities of dirt outside of the burrows and leaves an elliptical hole almost a foot in diameter behind him. Where the hunting is good, the badger will leave quite a few enlarged holes as testimony to his digging ability and his appetite.

The badger uses for his home one of the burrows he has enlarged, or else he digs one of his own up to 30 feet long with a chamber 2 to 6 feet below the ground at the end of it. He digs with unbelievable speed, and in the large pile of excavated earth outside of the hole his tracks are generally

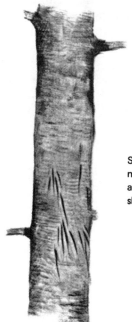

Series of cuts in bark of a tree might be a badger sign in certain areas. He hones his claws sharp this way.

visible. They're usually over 2 inches long, toed in, and the imprint of the long claws on the front feet is apt to be in evidence. When the animal is running, his hind feet, which have shorter claws that rarely show on the ground, are put down in front of the forefeet. In certain areas, you may observe marks left on trees where badgers have honed their front claws.

The badger makes little noise, at least little noise that would carry far enough to be considered a sign. He is a wheezy fellow, and if he is in a fight he hisses, growls, and emits a musk somewhat like that of a skunk but not as strong.

Besides dining on burrowing rodents, the badger eats insects in tremendous quantities, lizards, snakes, and ground-nesting birds. He loves honey and digs up many a nest of bees to get it. He likes rabbits too, and if he kills more than he needs to eat at any given time, he buries whatever is left for the future.

In the northern part of his range, the badger hibernates, often going below the frost line and plugging up his tunnel with earth to protect himself from the cold. Young, numbering anywhere from one to five, are born in spring.

Raccoon

This 15- to 20-pound animal with the masked face and ringed tail is native, in one form or another, to every state from the Atlantic Ocean to the Pacific and from the southern United States to the southern part of Canada.

His tracks, rather handlike in appearance with the five toes showing on each foot, are generally paired, left hind

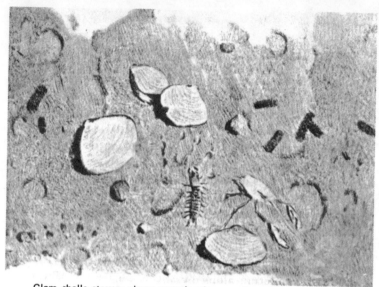

Clam shells strewn along water's edge may be evidence of recent raccoon feast. Animal opens them with claws and eats contents.

foot coming down beside the right front one. Hind feet are larger than the forefeet.

The raccoon likes woods, swamps, and partly cleared land, though he is fond of wet places like the edges of tidal creeks, swamps, marshes, and bottom lands. Coons favor hollow trees to live in, however, and you can often spot a coon's home by looking carefully for any tree, such as an old oak, elm, or sycamore that has a downward-sloping hole in it some 6 inches in diameter. These cavities are frequently caused by the butt of a broken-off limb having rotted out. Once you've found a likely looking hole, look for two other signs for positive identification of its occupant. Around the edges of the opening you should see some grayish-black or brown hairs, and if the hole is one used by a coon there will also be scratches that the animal has made in the bark with the claws of his powerful feet. Lacking a hole in a tree, a coon will sometimes live in a hollow log or a cleft in the rocks.

When wandering along by any water, keep an eye out for discarded clam shells and the remains of crawfish. Coons love the latter. The former they open dextrously, eating the insides with relish. If you should happen to see a duck's nest that has been torn apart, and bits of eggshell around, look for coon tracks.

Besides eggs, crawfish, and clams, coons like all sorts of fruits and berries as well as nuts, insects, and the various grains. They'll raid cornfields too, ripping off and partly eating the ears, which they leave strewn all over the place.

Raccoon droppings, like those of skunks and opossums, are granular. However, they are usually found on logs and limbs.

Rotted hole in a tree could be a raccoon den; to be sure, check entrance for traces of grayish-black or brown hairs, and claw marks.

Scats of this animal aren't easy to identify, though they tend to be even in circumference, granular, and may contain berry seeds. A better tip-off on the droppings, which may be confused with those of skunks and possums, is that often they're deposited on logs or the bigger branches of trees.

Coons don't knock themselves out vocally, but they do make gutteral chatterings. If you're in the woods at night and think you hear a screech owl, listen carefully. If the sound comes from ground level, it's probably the *hoo-hoo-hooing* of a coon setting out on his nocturnal search for sustenance.

Muskrat

A dome-shaped lodge bulking about 3 feet above the surface of a shallow pond or marsh is one sign that this

Shallow ponds or marshes often contain muskrat lodges, domes of mud and sticks with several underwater exits.

ratlike aquatic animal is in the area. Built of sticks, the roots and stalks of water plants, and chinked with mud, these houses have several underwater exits and contain a dry chamber inside. Near these houses will be found several feeding shelters—smaller, rounder, and more uniform in shape.

Another interesting visual sign of the muskrat, whose range extends over most of United States, is the breather, or push-up. This is found in more northerly areas and is a hole in the ice packed with roots and vegetation. The animal digs out a hollow in this packing and uses it as a

Breather hole in ice is unique muskrat sign.

Muskrat burrows along rivers often have entrances away from the bank camouflaged with small pile of vegetation.

breather or as a temporary shelter. The mass formed on the ice above the hole is about the size of a volley ball.

Muskrats living along the edges of watercourses dig burrows in the bank, but they're hard to spot unless you're looking for them. Occasionally, however, you might see a small pile of vegetation well back from the bank. This is the loose wadding that hides the surface entrance to the bank burrow.

Other visual signs of the muskrat are particles of chewed plants and stems floating on the water and possibly air bubbles under the ice. Tracks, of course, are a good identification, and the muskrat has a refinement to his that make

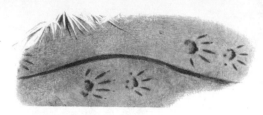

Muskrat's hind-foot tracks show partial webbing, and long, flat tail leaves drag mark half an inch wide.

evidence of his passage unmistakable. Hind feet, much larger than the front ones, are partially webbed, and the tracks are small and handlike. But more important, he drags his long, vertically flattened, scaly tail and leaves a continuous imprint with it half an inch wide.

The muskrat gets his name from a musky odor that is particularly strong in males at mating time—and three or more litters are born each year! Mature animals are 10 to 14 inches long with a tail that reaches almost a foot in length. They feed on aquatic plants mostly but occasionally grab off crawfish, crabs, mussels, and small fish not fast enough to get away.

Porcupine

This grunting, slow, and rather purposeful creature with the barbed quills lives over most of northern North America where there are woodlands that will support him. He makes his home in rocky crevices, hollow logs, or brush piles.

Tracks of the porcupine show short steps with the toes pointed in, and the prints themselves look like miniature bearpaw snowshoes with long claw marks quite far ahead of the main pads. If there is deep snow, or if the porky is walking on something soft, there will be marks on the trail as if someone had been following the tracks and wielding a broom lightly. These marks, of course, come from the stiff,

Bark chewed in large patches high on tree trunk, with edges neatly trimmed, is usually porcupine's work.

awkward tail as it swings back and forth with the animal's slow, plodding gait.

The generally bean-shaped droppings of the quill pig can be confused with those of deer, though often they are connected and sometimes somewhat irregular in shape.

Perhaps the most obvious sign of the porcupine's presence is the readily seen evidence of chewing on the bark of such trees as beech, maple, birch, pine, fir, and spruce. The porky eats only the inner bark, chipping off the outer layer with his beaverlike teeth and letting it drop to the ground. He generally chews bark in large patches, which are readily recognizable because they are too high for a nonclimbing animal to have made and because they show carefully trimmed edges with neat tooth prints. Frequently a porcupine will girdle a tree, thus killing it.

Porcupine's tracks are spaced about 6 inches apart, and toes point in. On soft ground or snow tail drag shows.

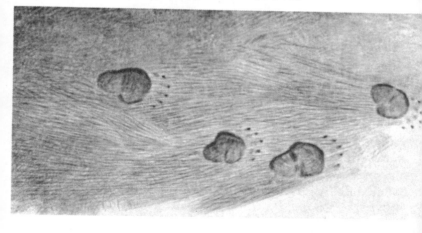

Signs the porkies leave on the ground are the cast-off bits of outer bark, droppings, and the cone-bearing twigs the creatures cut off and let fall.

Though porcupines gnaw trees, this is principally a winter activity. In spring this destructive animal eats catkins and flowers, and in summer he turns his attention to leaves and plants.

Another sign that porky has been around can be seen if you wake up some morning in camp and find that your ax handle or canoe paddle has been appreciably reduced in size. The animals love salt, and they will spend a lot of time working on any piece of wood that has been subjected to sweat.

Porcupines seem like quiet, dignified animals, but they can make a variety of noises. They bark, snort, and moan in a manner that occasionally sounds quite human. During mating season the male goes falsetto, and the female indulges in squalls.

Incidentally, porcupines cannot shoot their quills. However, an angry porky swings his tail with great vehemence, and any loose quills will sail through the air with high velocity.

A porcupine will not attack, but he is of danger to livestock and dogs, none of which seem able to resist taking a close look at him. A slap with that vicious tail will drive dozens of quills into the face of the curious.

Woodchuck

This brown, lumbering chap of the summer fields who hibernates in the winter is well known to farmers, country boys, and varmint shooters throughout the eastern half of the United States, extreme southern portion excepted.

One of the first signs of the woodchuck that most people see is the hole leading to his den. This orifice in the ground, 8 inches or so in diameter, may be in the woods or on a

Most obvious sign of a woodchuck is his den, a hole in a field or on a hillside and rimmed with excavated dirt.

Tracks of the chuck are placed close together. Hind foot
has five toes, forefoot only four.

hillside, but the animal who digs it prefers a spot on the
brushy border of a clover-filled field. Outside of his hole is
usually a huge pile of excavated earth. Actually, the chuck
digs several burrows, some distance apart. Aside from this,
each burrow has more than one opening. If you see a fairly
sizeable hole with no earth around it, look for one nearby
with the telltale earth mound. The holes without the earth
are plunge holes and are dug from underneath.

A woodchuck's tracks show four toes on each forefoot
and five on each of the hind ones. When walking, the
chuck, or groundhog, puts his hind feet down close to the
front ones.

One other visual sign of the chuck may be bits of the
chuck himself. Like most of the rabbit clan, the woodchuck
gets pretty violent in his courtship period, which occurs
right after he comes out of hibernation in early spring.
Males contend bitterly for the favors of females, and in the
ensuing fights the combatants often rip hunks out of one

In the West, a crevice in rock formation may turn out to be den of rockchuck.

another, and on occasion tails are bitten off to lie on the ground as mute testimony to the violence.

The woodchuck is also known as the whistlepig, and the reason isn't hard to figure. He whistles. Another audible sign of the animal is a chattering and gritting of teeth when he is disturbed.

The woodchuck's favorite diet is clover, though he also eats the stems of buttercups, daisies, and thistles as well as leaves and flowers. He relishes farm produce and often attacks melon patches with gusto.

Most people don't realize it, but chucks once in a while climb trees.

Cousins of the eastern woodchuck are the rockchucks of the West and the hoary marmots of the western mountains and the mountains of Alaska and western Canada. Tracks of all three are quite similar, though in the hoary marmot prints of the hind feet have a tendency to register in the prints of the front ones.

The marmot is about twice as big as the woodchuck, an animal reaching a maximum of only about 14 pounds, and he also gives out with a whistle, one that can be heard for incredible distances on a still day. He also is a hibernating and burrowing creature, and he digs shallow holes along his various pathways that serve as emergency shelters when danger threatens. Another visual sign of the hoary marmot is his slide. Before the snow has melted in spring, he likes to toboggan down steep banks and hillsides.

The rockchuck is similar to the woodchuck in habits, though his favored denning areas are rocky caves and crevices.

Gray Squirrel

This handsome little creature, who has a western cousin known as the western gray squirrel, is found throughout the eastern states from Florida to Ontario and west to Texas and the Dakotas. Rare is the person living in this area who has never seen one.

Tracks show long hind feet, with five toes, placed side by side in front of four-toed front feet when the animal is bounding. When walking, however, hind feet and front feet alternate.

Another visual sign of this prolific little rodent is his home. The gray squirrel likes oaks, hickories, and beeches, and his dens and leafy nests are usually found in stands of these hardwoods, though sometimes such stands are mixed in with pine trees. A den can be an abandoned woodpecker's hole or other suitable tree cavity. It is in this den that the female brings forth an average litter of four or five

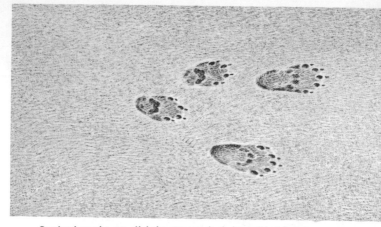

Squirrel tracks are slightly over an inch long; hind feet register in front of forefeet when animal is bounding.

young, usually during early spring in the North and a month or so earlier in the South.

The gray also makes two types of leaf nest, and they're readily seen in the woods when the leaves are off the trees. They sit on branches anywhere from 30 to 60 feet above ground. One type, constructed of bark, leaves, small branches, and built near the trunk of the tree, contains a chamber of about 16 inches across by about a foot high. This is used for warm-weather living, in emergencies, when parasites become too thick in the den, or, occasionally, to raise a summer brood.

The other type of leaf nest is usually farther out on a branch and has a side entrance. It is used for resting or loafing, usually by the male.

In his eating habits, the squirrel is somewhat of a slob, and he leaves many signs of his bad table manners throughout the woods. Diet fluctuates with the produce of the season, and clusters of tree buds and flowers, such as those of oaks, elms, and maples, are nipped off and eaten. At that time of year the denuded clusters form cuttings beneath these types of trees that may pile up several inches deep. Look for these signs where squirrels abound.

In summer, diet may include mushrooms, fruits and berries, tree seeds, and insect cocoons. Come late summer, early fall, and winter, the squirrel's intake switches to the type of food for which he is most noted—nuts. These may be butternuts, acorns, walnuts, hickory nuts, pecans. Look for their hulls at the bases of trees for an indication of what sort of animal has been dining above.

All squirrels bury nuts, but the gray, unlike the red, buries each nut separately in a fist-size hole. Evidence of the squirrel digging these holes in the forest floor is often

Telltale signs of the squirrel's dining habits are nibbled pine cones and acorns at the base of a tree.

easily seen. Also easily seen is the stirred-up appearance of the dead leaves in fall and winter when the animals are scurrying around digging their holes or scratching around trying to find the food they've already buried. Since these animals don't dig up all the nuts they've hidden, they can be considered responsible for much of the forest's new growth.

Another sign of the squirrel's thoughtlessness in eating is found in the mess he occasionally makes of young conifers. Grays, as well as fox squirrels and red squirrels, look for the sap and layer of cambium beneath the bark and chew lustily on limbs and trunks, often girdling young trees. Evidence of this can occasionally be seen at the root line. Porcupines munch bark too, but porcupine teeth are larger than those of squirrels. If you see a tree with eaten bark, check for the size of the dentures that have done the work. Droppings too should be a tip-off. Those of porcupines, while somewhat deerlike, are usually a bit larger than the rather similarly shaped scats of squirrels.

Squirrels have several signs that can be easily heard, and even the inexperienced outdoorsman can soon learn to identify them quickly. If you're wandering through the fall hardwoods and hear something like a small, intermittent rain pattering through the trees, you can be assured that one of these little rodents is nearby eating nuts and that the shells are filtering down through the branches.

Another sound, usually associated with fall, is the rustling of the dead leaves on the forest floor, made as the squirrels scoot here and there burying nuts.

The voice of the gray is deeper than that of the red squirrel and is commonly a loud, fast, chatter. The gray squirrel barks too, with a rather impatient sound at times and at times with a rather soft, questioning quality. Quiet chatterings take place when the animals are conversing with one another. When predators, such as owls and hawks, are around, the squirrels cry in terror as they streak for cover.

The western gray squirrel is much like his eastern counterpart, but he lives in the mountain ranges of the West Coast, mostly in the higher altitudes up to 8,000 feet. He sometimes journeys to lower reaches in the fall, however, when the acorns are about ready for him to harvest. This little chap is more readily at home in conifers than is the eastern gray.

The fox squirrel, though larger, is also very similar to the eastern gray, even to his tracks and his habit of storing nuts individually.

Two beautiful tree squirrels are the tassel-eared squirrels—the Abert (correct) and Kaibab—which are about the size of a big gray. The Abert lives from the Grand Canyon east to New Mexico and north to northern Colorado. The Kaibab is known only on Arizona's Kaibab Plateau.

Red Squirrel

Noisiness is perhaps the greatest sign of this redcoated forest busybody, who's also called the chickaree and pine squirrel in the West. Smaller than the gray squirrel, this almost unbelievably agile little rodent lives in the coniferous forests of North America from Virginia up through Canada and west to the West Coast and Alaska.

He leaves a track that shows repeated runnings back and forth, crisscrosses, and all the irregularities of an inquisitive, active, little animal. Prints, like those of the gray squirrel,

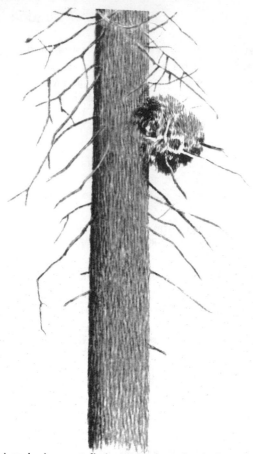

When red squirrel cannot find woodpecker den in hard-wood tree, he builds a leaf nest in a conifer.

show larger, five-toed hind feet tending to be placed parallel in front of the four-toed front ones. However, don't count on this placement all the time. Sometimes the red will alternate his prints. And sometimes, in snow, the tracks will disappear altogether. This is because the red frequently burrows along under the snow to get to his food caches and to poke around in the ground in search of food.

As far as his home grounds are concerned, the red likes his conifers mixed with hardwoods, and in the latter he prefers tree cavities, often taken over from a woodpecker, for his den. However, if no large-enough hardwoods are available, or if conifers are all he can find, he has to build a nest. This is usually some 30 to 50 feet up (though it may be much lower in areas of stunted trees) and is made of leaves, moss, grass, twigs, bark, or any useful ground litter. Built close to the trunk, it may be 20 inches across and up to a foot deep. The inside chamber is rarely more than 6 inches across. An individual family may build several nests in an area.

While the leaf nests are easy to spot, and the dens in trees aren't easily missed, the red makes still a third type of home, particularly where suitable trees are not available, that is not so easy to identify. It may be in a hollow stump, or the red may make an underground burrow beneath a stump or stone pile. This burrow may have as many as five tunnels leading from the surface to the narrow passages and small rooms that are used for the storage of food or material for the nest. Look for suspicious holes around stumps, stone piles, or stone walls, and be sure to check the tracks leading to them.

Food habits of the red give an observer a fine opportunity to check his knowledge of the squirrel's presence. For instance, these little animals are very fond of maple and black-birch sap. If you're wandering around the woods in spring and see shallow depressions on the upper sides of the limbs of these trees, you can be sure a red has hollowed out the saucerlike holes to get at the flowing juice. Mushrooms jammed under loose tree bark are a sure sign. These animals love them (even the poisonous ones, which seem to cause no harm) and either wedge them under pieces of bark or place them in the fork of a limb to dry out and be eaten later.

The red squirrel's diet is extremely varied. Besides mushrooms and sap, he likes roots, berries, and the seeds of various grasses. In spring, he nips seeds, flowers, and twig tips from pines, firs, spruces, and all the nut trees. Look for indications of this.

Another thing to look for in this little fellow's country is a midden. This is a pile of pine cones and cone scales—usually built around a rock, tree, or stump in a somewhat damp location—that may contain up to 10 bushels of fresh cones. When the squirrel dines on these cones, which he's cut from the tree, tossed down, and piled up later, he usually sits on the rock or stump around which the midden has been piled. The midden itself and the cone husks on the central protuberance are great tip-offs that a red squirrel is around. Over the years, a midden may grow to as much as 3 feet high and 25 or 30 feet across. Pine squirrels of the Pacific Coast area occasionally store cones in springs or creeks. The moisture tends to keep the cones from losing their seeds by drying out and opening. Damp area of the midden serves the same purpose.

In late summer, the red begins to scamper around in earnest as he collects his winter food. Twigs, nuts, and seeds are high on his list of favorites, and he almost goes beside himself cutting them down. Small seeds and nuts he piles up in various locations, and the cones usually go onto the midden. In the Rocky Mountain area, the pine squirrel often chews on the cast antlers and, when he can find them, the bones of large animals, frequently dragging them to the top of his midden.

The red makes a great deal of racket in the woods. He chatters constantly to himself while working, and if any stranger wanders into his territory, his sharp barks of alarm are interspersed with sputters and growls of indignation as he stamps his feet and scolds with an increasing fury. Should another red cross the boundaries he's laid out for himself, he flies into a rage and attacks without mercy. All these signs are easily heard and quite recognizable.

Another thing to listen for, particularly in late summer and early fall, is the thump made as the severed pine cones hit the forest floor and the rattle of seeds and twigs as they rain down through the trees.

Naturally, as in the case of the gray, the rustling of dead leaves is another tip-off.

Ground Squirrels

Ground squirrels are small, terrestrial rodents found practically all over North America except in the East. There are many species, and the geographic races number more than 100 living in such varying environments as the mountains and the desert.

Burrows of these little creatures, most of whom hibernate, form extensive tunnel work underground, from 6 inches below the surface to many feet down. If you're driving around in western country and suddenly find that one wheel has disappeared beneath the ground, check for a network of subterranean passages and chambers. Many holes in a given area—some with several bushels of dirt and debris in front of them and some with none—are another good indication. Horsemen should be extremely wary in such a locality.

Another sign, besides the holes and the animals themselves, might be a small landslide. The burrows sometimes funnel rainwater into small, underground torrents that loosen the soil and send it cascading downhill. Another visual sign would be a chewed antler or antelope horn.

Ground squirrels have claws that are longer than those of tree squirrels, and you may notice this in the tracks that have been put down on properly receptive ground. Also, there is a difference in the overall pattern. Tree-squirrel pattern is rather squarish, but that of the ground squirrel shows that the front feet are put down more in a line—one nearly behind the other—giving the set of four prints a roughly triangular look. There are other ways to determine whether the tracks you're studying are those of tree squirrels or ground squirrels. For instance, if you see confusing-looking tracks in the snow, you can be pretty sure they were made by a tree squirrel, since the other variety is usually sound asleep in wintertime. Furthermore, tree squirrels generally prefer woodlands, whereas ground squirrels like more open country where tree squirrels are not frequently found.

It is beyond the scope of this book to go deeply into the many races of ground squirrels, but following is a brief description of several of the more well-known varieties.

Columbian Ground Squirrel

One of the largest of this tribe is the Columbian ground squirrel, and he reaches a length of 11 to 15 inches. These animals live communally in areas of scattered trees and rocky slopes up to 8,000 feet, though they often wander into valleys where they do great damage to hay and grain. Besides eating such farm produce, they dig up wild-onion bulbs and also eat flowers and berries. Water for the Columbian is supplied by the succulence of spring grasses and plants, and when they turn brown and dry out from the summer sun, the squirrel starts to think of hibernation. He may get his winter fur as early as July, and then he goes to sleep in his den for seven or eight months, though in the uplands, where grasses tend to stay green longer, he may be abroad until early fall.

Watch for these animals, and listen for their chirping, along rocky hillsides where there's a scattering of trees. Entrance holes are readily spotted by the huge mounds of earth in front of them, though holes made on leaving hibernation are dug from below and show no such accumulation.

Thirteen-Lined Ground Squirrel

This squirrel is medium size for the species and is sort of buff color with alternating white and dark stripes running down its back. White spots run the length of the dark stripes. This squirrel eats more meat than any of the others—insects, worms, small mice, carrion. If you see the broken eggs and violated nest of a ground-dwelling bird, suspect the thirteen-liner. Aside from meat, this little fellow also consumes just about all kinds of seeds as well as cactus fruits, roots, and acorns.

Burrows of these animals are generally shallow, about 2 inches across, and usually have no earth around them. Most identifiable sound is a high-pitched whistle that can sometimes actually be mistaken for a bird call.

Antelope Squirrel

The antelope squirrel is a small member of the species, averaging about 9 inches. It loves the heat, lives in the hottest part of the Southwest, and generally does not hibernate, except possibly in the highest part of its range, which may be at an altitude of 6,000 feet. These animals are not numerous, and holes indicating the burrows of four or five creatures per acre would be a sign of antelope-squirrel country. Another sign is the shape of the hole itself. It is usually oval and not more than 3 inches across at its widest. Look for burrow entrances in rocky foothills that are near seed-bearing bushes and various greens. You might also find them at the bases of plants or bushes or alongside a big rock, but don't bother to look for an earth mound. The little animal generally carts the dirt away and scatters it. Seeds and grains are the main diet, but he also eats insects, carrion, leaves, twigs, and fruit. A super-cautious, highly nervous, restless little creature, the antelope squirrel can, and does, climb well. He makes a sort of chittering noise that is very rapid and shrill.

Golden-Mantled Ground Squirrel

The golden-mantled ground squirrel only makes a racket among his own kind, being very quiet when trespassers are wandering around in his territory. When among members of his own species only, however, he chirps and grunts. If in a fight, he is apt to scream, and just before he dives into his burrow in fright he emits a loud, sharp whistle. This little fellow looks something like a chipmunk, is 9 to 12 inches long, and makes a burrow entrance that's about 3 inches across. Look for such entrances in the western mountains at heights up to 13,000 feet. Preferred locations are edges of rock slides or gravelly hillsides. Diet is fruit, nuts, and various grasses. This squirrel also likes mushrooms, insects, and, to some extent, meat.

Prairie Dog

Prairie dogs are pale buff, sociable little animals living in large towns, each creature having its own home except when rearing young. He's fair sized—12 to 16 inches—and he digs a complicated and elaborate burrow with a hallway that may plunge down 16 feet. At the end of this are various passageways and chambers, sometimes even a bathroom. The entrance hole is 6 or 7 inches across and is surrounded by a rim of earth that can be 2 feet high and twice that across. Entrances to burrows may be close but are usually 40 feet or so apart. Only prairie dogs that live in the flatlands build the circular mound around their holes. They're dykes, actually, and serve to keep the water out in the event of hard rains. Dogs living on hillsides toss dirt from their holes downhill the way most digging animals do.

Because these creatures subsist almost completely on succulent grasses and forage, they've been harried and poisoned almost out of existence by cattle raisers. A very small part of the prairie dog's diet is made up of insects.

When conversing, the dogs chirp, chirr, and whistle, but when alarmed, they bark.

Oppossum

The possum, as he is more generally called, leaves very little sign. Perhaps that's why he's been around,

A sheltered spot like this rock formation may house a possum during his daytime sleeping hours. He prowls for food at night.

virtually unchanged, for somewhere around a hundred million years.

His tracks are quite distinctive in that the hind feet resemble human hands, complete with "thumbs" that can move at right angles to the other four toes. The middle three toes on the hind feet tend to be close together. The front feet have five slender toes and leave tracks that look something like those of birds. When the tail drag shows, it is in the shape of a curve.

Full-grown possums resemble giant mice. They are 2 to 3 feet in length, including the foot-long tail, and an adult can weigh up to 14 pounds. The range of North America's only marsupial, once confined to the Southeast, is expanding. He is now found in Canada and west as far as Colorado. Natives of California, Oregon, and Washington also know him. In fact, he is spreading so far north that occasionally members of his tribe have been found with frostbitten tails and ears.

The possum lives just about anywhere there's shelter, in hollow logs, between rocks, or in tree trunks. He sleeps all day, but in the evening he sallies forth, generally in swamps and wet bottom lands, for whatever is edible—fruits, vegetables, or the flesh of creatures dead or alive. A fine climber, he goes up persimmon trees in the South to feed on the ripe fruit.

Possums are very stupid, and, as every school child knows, play dead when frightened. Perhaps two other reasons why they have survived through the ages are that they smell vile and are very prolific.

Weasel

The first animal I ever shot as a boy with my first .22 was a weasel. On the farm where I grew up we always dreaded their appearance, accompanied by their strong musky odor, in the chicken coop, where the blood-thirsty little killers could destroy dozens of domestic fowl in a single night. This seems odd for an animal only 10 inches long and an inch in diameter, which looks like a loop of rope as it runs

Weasel trail shows animal's habit of burrowing under snow
for several yards, then continuing on the surface.

on the ground, along a log, or through the brush in a
loping bounce.

There are three basic species of weasel, the least weasel,
the short-tailed weasel, and the long-tailed weasel. The
long-tailed has the widest distribution, only southwestern
Arizona and part of southern California doing without his
presence. He has a long body, short legs, and small head.
Like most of his many subspecies, he turns white during
winter in his northern range. The tip of his tail remains
black, however, and this white-and-black tail was much
sought for the robes of royalty.

Tracks of the weasel aren't hard to recognize, because of the prints themselves and because the trail shows swift changes of direction, odd loopings, back tracking, and all sorts of irregularities that attest to the little creature's eagerness and curiosity. Though there are many variations in the weasel's print pattern, usual evidence of a weasel is a series of twin prints. This pattern is most often seen because a running weasel usually plants his hind feet in the tracks made by the front ones. In snow, a tail drag is occasionally seen. Often these animals take alternately long and short leaps.

Sometimes, when following a weasel track in the snow, you'll be astonished to find that it disappears in a neat round hole, only to reappear some distance farther along. This is because these agile little fellows frequently dive under the snow, proceed for some feet under it, then

Weasel places hind feet in tracks of forefeet; hence trail consists of series of twin prints. Remains of animal's recent kill are sometimes found nearby.

emerge once more. Weasels are mostly nocturnal, but now and then they are seen in daylight.

Many authorities believe a weasel kills just for fun, and it is not unusual to see the corpse of more than one small animal alongside his trail.

If you should ever have occasion to break open a bale of hay, and then find a pile of dead mice in it, you can be sure you've found a spot where a weasel thought he had enough privacy to indulge in his habit of strong food. Besides denning and storing food in hay, these graceful little mammals also live in hollow logs, rabbit holes, beneath rocks, or in the dens of small burrowing animals.

Droppings are another sign of the weasel. They are long, slender, and dark, and they usually contain fur, pieces of bone, and occasionally feathers. Scats are often dropped repeatedly in the same spot, frequently on stones or in easily seen locations beside the trail or even in it.

Another sign of the weasel comes not from the weasel himself but from birds. Birds occasionally attack him, and they make a frightful racket when they do.

Aside from an occasional propensity for cleaning out a hen house, the weasel dines mostly on small mammals—including rabbits—birds, frogs, and snakes. He is an energetic member of a large family, and generally he does more good than harm.

Marten

Also called the American sable, the marten is found in the northern coniferous forests and the western mountains of the United States. His signs are almost as hard to come by as is the animal himself. He has been extensively trapped, and because of this his numbers have declined, though in areas where martens are protected, such as New York's Adirondack region, they are making a comeback.

The main sign of the marten is his track, and the reason it is not seen as often as those of other animals is that this dark-brown creature with the pale-buff patch on throat and chest spends a lot of time in trees.

Footprints left by the marten are often rather indistinct, particularly in winter, as at that time of year the animal's feet are so fully furred that the toe pads do not show. The size of the tracks varies tremendously, measuring up to 4½ inches long in soft snow. Toward winter's end, the toe pads start to appear, and by summer they're easily seen in the prints. When the marten is going all out, hind prints are in, or slightly ahead of, those of the front feet, and the tracks may be 3 feet apart.

Scats are like those of minks and weasels. Martens, however, are very fond of berries, and the scats, often found with previous droppings, sometimes contain their seeds.

Walking tracks of a marten in late winter snow reveal toe pads clearly. In mid-winter, fur on feet conceal toe pads.

The marten often chooses a hollow tree for a den for the female to give birth.

These animals den in the hollows of trees and bring forth two or three young a year. Diet, besides berries, includes small mammals, especially pine squirrels, birds, eggs, nuts, and occasionally fish and frogs.

470

The marten's vocal sounds consist of screams and squeals, but these largely nocturnal creatures are seldom heard.

Mink

This lithe, sometimes playful member of the weasel family is dark brown all year long and has a white patch on his chin. Visual signs of the animal are quite numerous.

Prints of hind feet when animal is walking are almost on top of those made by the front ones. The male is larger than his mate, and the tracks show this. Also, tracks differ widely according to the substance on which they're made. In snow, they've been measured at as much as 2½ inches long. In mud, they resemble those of a house cat. Imprint of the heel of the hind foot, which is slightly webbed, is only sometimes visible.

Living in most of North America, with the exception of most of the southwestern United States, the mink prefers for his habitat areas along wooded streams, marshes—even tidal ones—and lakes and ponds. As a result, his tracks are readily discernible in the mud. Minks love muskrat meat and often rip apart muskrat houses to reach their

Tracks of a running mink appear in groups of four slightly spaced prints, with a foot or more separating groups.

Four-inch hole in a river bank is frequently a mink den, which sometimes extends a dozen or more feet into the ground.

inhabitants. Sometimes, indeed, they take up housekeeping in the dwellings of these animals after they've eaten them.

Minks also den in empty woodchuck holes that are handy to the water, holes in the rocks, hollow logs and stumps, muskrat burrows, and their own dens in the bank. These last are about 4 inches in diameter, and they lead to tunnels as long as 10 or 12 feet.

In winter, visual signs of the mink are more numerous. When traveling in snow, he will sometimes push himself along and leave a trough behind him, and once in a while he will coast down a snowy incline like a boy on a toboggan. He will occasionally dive beneath the surface of the snow, and his track will disappear only to reappear some feet farther on. He does this to see what's below the white layer of silence and also, some observers believe, just for fun.

If you happen to see a neat, round hole through the snow and ice of a pond, you can be pretty sure a mink has made it to go foraging underwater. Usually the hole is somewhat muddy, and there may be the remains of aquatic food, such as frogs, scattered nearby.

When the slightest bit upset, the mink lets go with an un-mistakeable odor, and it's sometimes evident at his burrow.

Adult male minks run to about 2 feet in length with tails of 6 to 8 inches. Young are born in early spring, and litters average five to eight kits. As they grow older, they play, often making slides on stream banks as they coast down to the water.

Sounds of minks are barks, hisses, deep-toned purrs, and screams. Their food is varied: muskrats, small birds, fish, small mammals, worms, domestic poultry, and turtle eggs.

Rabbits

Cottontail

The Eastern cottontail has the greatest distribution of all the nearly seventy species and subspecies of the rabbit family. He ranges to the Midwest, but other forms of cottontail complete the distribution to cover practically all the United States. His familiar tracks with their narrow prints and paired hind feet can be found almost everywhere.

Cottontails pass a lot of the daytime hours relaxing in their "forms," slight depressions in the earth which the rabbits dig themselves. When not in their forms, the creatures may be resting or sleeping in their dens or burrows. These are sometimes abandoned holes, such as those of woodchucks, or are in tangles of protective cover such as hedgerows, briers, or brush piles.

Generally nocturnal, though often seen in early morning and late afternoon, cottontails feed greedily in vegetable

In the fall and winter, fruit trees with their bark gnawed at the base are evidence that cottontails have been foraging for food.

gardens that contain leafy produce or practically any new growth, as irate gardeners can readily testify. In fall and winter, these rabbits chew the bark of bushes and fruit trees besides eating various grains and twigs. Bark gnawings are larger than those of mice, with which they are sometimes confused, and are above the snow. Also, bark alongside the chewings will be in strips. When a cottontail chews off a twig, the end of it will show evidence of many bites rather than a clean cut.

Another sign of the cottontail is the nest. In the North, these rabbits breed for about seven months, starting in January, and bring forth as many as five litters a year. In the South, they breed all year. The nests, usually in open fields, are shallow, somewhat oblong depressions, 7 or 8 inches long. The female digs these with her front feet,

The cottontail, like other rabbits, spends much of the day resting in a "form," a rounded depression in the earth which the animal digs under a bush or other shelter.

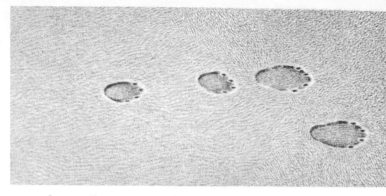

Cottontail's hopping gait leaves a trail of prints in groups of four with a foot or more of space between the groups.

often simply enlarging a cow track or the scratchings of some other animal. She then lines it with grass as well as with fur she has pulled from her underside with her teeth. If you don't see a nest, you may hear faint squeaks from the hungry fawns therein.

When two bucks, as the males are called, are vying for the favors of the same female, or doe, they may get into a real battle. Bits of fur scattered around are good evidence of this, as the combatants get pretty violent at such times.

Scats of the cottontail are round and smaller than those of the jacks.

Adult cottontails make little noise. They do, however, often indicate danger by thumping with one of their hind feet, and an injured rabbit will sometimes scream.

Snowshoe Rabbit

Unlike the cottontail, a rabbit that doesn't like deep snow too much because of his comparatively small feet, the snowshoe is in his element when the white fluff covers the ground. At that time of year, the 13- to 18-inch animal bounds over the snow using his tremendous, well-furred hind feet to keep him from breaking through. Also, the snowshoe turns from brown in summer to white in winter, a transformation that gives him his other name—varying hare.

Conifers stripped of their bark up to 2 feet above the ground are sign of snowshoe rabbit's winter browsing.

Snowshoe rabbit bounds across deep snow with aid of large hind feet, which register in front of forefeet.

The snowshoe inhabits the entire northern United States wherever there are forests, brush, and swamps, and his distinctive tracks are a familiar sight to woodsmen in these regions. The huge hind feet always come down in front of the smaller front ones, and, when the animal is going all out, the hind ones are not quite side by side and the front ones are staggered behind them. When the hare is moving at a slow hop, hind feet are paired and the front ones nearly so.

The snowshoe feeds at night and early in the morning. During the day he spends most of his time in a form. In summer this is a depression in the floor of his habitat, and in winter it is a dished-out spot in the snow. Seeing these, along with the tracks, should prove to you that you're in snowshoe country.

While this animal will eat carrion once in a while, his main diet in summer is made up of grasses, clover, and other greens. In winter, he likes twigs, conifer needles, and bark. When eating bark, he slices it from the tree with diagonal cuts of his large incisors, and when nipping twigs he makes clean, slanting cuts. Often a snowshoe will kill a conifer by eating all the bark off it to a height of about 2 feet, standing on his hind legs to get every last bit of it he can reach. This bark-eating propensity is, of course, a positive sign. Scats are round and larger than those of the cottontail.

As in the case of the well-known bunny rabbit, snowshoe bucks sometimes fight over coy females.

Young are born in a rather haphazard fashion, the mother then leaving them in some spot not easily found while she moves off. She feeds them regularly, however, and if danger threatens the young ones they make a low, gurgling noise.

Whitetailed Jackrabbit

This long-eared animal is mainly indigenous to the central Northwest, and he is the only jackrabbit with an all-white tail. He weighs from 5 to 10 pounds, and in summer his coat is grayish brown. In winter it turns white in his northern range.

This is a very fast-moving critter, and when he is really pouring on the coal his leaps may be as much as 20 feet, though such extreme spacing between tracks is not often seen. Prints themselves show fairly long hind feet, more or less paired, in front of front feet when the animal is speeding. At slower speeds, extreme length of hind feet doesn't always show. Also, tracks generally show a straight course rather than the zigzag one made by the smaller species.

The whitetailed jack lives in the open prairie as well as on the slopes of the open mountains, and, like most of his kind, feeds at night on just about any available greenery, including snakeweed and sagebrush. Also like others of his ilk, this animal rests in forms during the day. These are scooped-out places in the grass beside a rock or bush or are simply platter-sized depressions in the snow. Occasionally, if the snow is deep, the whitetailed jack will tunnel into it for protection from enemies and weather.

Blacktailed Jackrabbit

This fellow with the 8-inch ears and the blacktopped tail mainly inhabits the Southwest, though he is known also from the state of Washington south into Mexico. Grayish to sandy color, he does not turn white in winter.

Because the range of this rabbit and that of his white-tailed cousin overlap in some areas, their tracks can cause some confusion. Usually, however, the blacktail's tracks are somewhat smaller. Also, the blacktail has an interesting pattern as he bounds along. While his regular jumps may be 15 feet along the ground, he occasionally makes leaps 4 feet or so into the air to see what's going on around him. When he lands from one of these observatory take-offs, his front feet are usually in front of the hind ones. Also, this rabbit may leave a tail mark on the trail.

Somewhat smaller than the whitetail, the blacktailed jack feeds on the usual grasses as well as on field crops, sometimes causing widespread destruction. However, he also feeds on cactus plants, occasionally going after those with sharp spines. He gets at the pulp of these by chewing around the thorns, pulling them out, and then sticking his nose in the resultant hole. Watch for this sign on such cacti as the prickly pear. When feeding on desert bushes, he leaves a slanting cut on the small, nipped-off branches.

This rabbit, too, spends much time in forms near any rocks or shrubs that give a little protection. He does not occupy a burrow, but will go down a hole when hotly pursued.

The nests of all jackrabbits are oval, well hidden by grass or brush, and lined with fur. If you find one, you'll doubtless have little trouble recognizing it.

If you find patches of rabbit fur scattered around, you can come to the fairly safe conclusion that a pair of battling bucks has been trying to reach a decision about which will have the favors of some nearby female. When buck jacks fight, they don't fool around. The hind foot of a jackrabbit has a good set of claws, and if he connects with it he can disembowel his luckless opponent. Occasionally grunts and growls can be heard when rabbit battles are going on.

Skunk

Probably the most obvious sign that skunks are in the neighborhood—and their neighborhood is most of North America—is the vile-smelling musk they spray when they are injured or threatened. Once smelled it can never be forgotten. If it hits an eye, it hurts terribly and causes blindness for fifteen or twenty minutes. The fine spray will carry 15 feet or so if the wind is right, and it can be smelled through the woods for half a mile or more.

But evidence of skunks can be determined in other ways. Since the animals feed mostly on insects, look for small pits in the ground—some 2 inches deep and 3 or 4 across—where these nocturnal prowlers have been digging for them.

Hairs around den entrances are another positive sign. These quiet, bulky little animals den in any sort of natural hole or abandoned burrow. One dug by the skunk itself, however, is short and terminated by a round chamber.

Droppings also offer a clear sign of a skunk's passage. These are made up of berry seeds and the indigestible coverings of many types of insects.

A small opening in the rocks is a likely place for a skunk to make his home. Watch for traces of hair.

Tracks should give no trouble to the observant woods rover. The hind feet leave imprints in front of the forefeet; both show claw marks in the dirt.

The striped skunk, glossy black with white stripes, has the widest range of North American skunks. Besides him, however, there's the eastern spotted skunk and the hognosed skunk. The former weighs only about 1½ pounds, can climb trees, and has a white spot on his forehead as

Rooted-up area with small pits in the ground indicate that skunk was digging for insect food during nocturnal prowl.

Tracks of the skunk are under 2 inches long; larger hind foot with prominent heel registers in front of forefoot.

well as one under each ear. He lives mainly in the south and looks spotted because his narrow, white stripes are broken. The hog-nosed skunk. the only South American variety, has a piglike snout, short fur, and lives in parts of Arizona, Colorado, and Texas.

Javelina

The javelina, or peccary, is a bad-smelling, piglike little creature whose signs may be encountered by the outdoorsman in Arizona, New Mexico, and Texas. He is not a true

The peccary often dens in clefts in the desert rock formations of the southwest. The animal leaves a skunklike odor wherever it lives.

Chewed-up prickly pear cactus is reliable proof that javelinas have been feeding on their favorite plant.

hog in the sense that those of Asia and Africa are, but he
is the best we can do in the way of a wild pig native to the
United States. The "Russian" boars of Tennessee, North
Carolina, and elsewhere are from imported stock.

The little javelina—a big one would weigh 60 pounds—
is a gregarious chap traveling in noisy groups of up to sixty
or so animals. As the herd wanders along feeding, mostly
in early morning and evening, its members keep up a steady
grunting and yapping. To the experienced dweller of the
Southwest, this rumbling conversation is readily identifiable. If the herd is alerted and takes refuge in flight, some

485

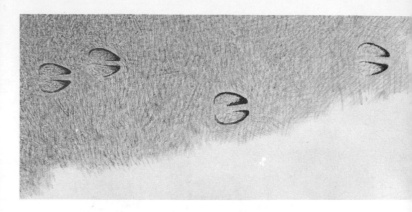

Javelina tracks, similar to those of pigs, are slightly cver an inch long. Hind foot registers behind forefoot.

of the more outraged animals will emit shrill grunts as they bounce away for safety.

Visual signs of javelinas have to do with their eating habits and their tracks, the latter being imprinted in pairs with the hind feet falling directly behind the forefeet.

The peccary will eat practically anything edible, including snakes of all sizes. His favored diet, however, is the prickly pear cactus, and an area of chewed-up prickly pears is sure evidence that javelinas have passed through. However, he also enjoys small animals such as mice and lizards, and with his long, flexible, flat-ended snout he digs up tubers and insects. Any spot that shows signs of this rooting around indicates that a band of the little pigs may have passed by. They like charcoal too, and will poke around where campfires have existed.

A very distinctive sign of the peccary is his odor, particularly pungent when the animal has been frightened. He has a gland on his back, about 8 inches up from his short tail, through which he emits his strong, musky smell.

Anyone in javelina country who wanders into a cave or cleft in the rocks and perceives a skunklike aroma in the enclosure can be sure javelinas have been there before him.

The peccary, or more properly the collared peccary, is the only member of his tribe living in the United States, but another species, the white-lipped peccary, lives from southern Mexico south. Our javelina is called a collared peccary because a band of light-grayish hair encircles his thick neck and stands out clearly against the darker gray of the rest of his body.

In spite of tales told with wide-eyed intensity about the ferocity of this big-headed, slender-legged little animal with the fearsome tusks, the javelina is peaceful and only fights when cornered.

Snakes

Though cursed by nature with a repulsive appearance, most snakes are actually beneficial to man, for they control many undesirable rodents and insects. A few species of snakes, however, do have a poisonous bite, and, as with the eating of wild plants, you should stay clear of all species until you are sure they're harmless.

Snakes leave very little sign. They will leave a trail in soft sand or mud that can either be an arrowstraight furrow, a series of curves, or, in the case of the sidewinder, a series of parallel indentations. Occasionally some types can be heard slithering over or through dry brush and leaves; some release a musky odor when frightened; and, of course, the rattler makes a distinct buzzing when agitated.

Most nonpoisonous snakes found in the United States have slender heads and round pupils.

All snakes shed their skins frequently, and these semi-transparent sheds are often found in snake habitat. All snakes hibernate too, and all are totally deaf. Incidentally, dens are usually on south-facing slopes. Colors of snakes vary tremendously, even among a given species. The more northerly and high the habitat, the darker, generally, is the specimen.

Black Snake

Also called the black racer, this reptile lives from New England to Florida and west to Ohio and southern Indiana. He averages 4½ feet long, lays eggs, is a plain black color, and eats small animals, frogs, eggs, and other snakes. This snake prefers dry, open places but is also found in woods, meadows, and around loose rock or brush piles. When hibernating, which he does with many companions, he picks stone crevices or the abandoned hole of a ground-burrowing animal. Certain members of his tribe can scoot over the tops of bushes. If you hear a suspicious rustling, look for this snake or any of his cousins—the racers.

Chicken Snake

This reptile lives in Florida and north to lower North Carolina. He averages 4 feet long and has four dark stripes— two on his back and one on each side—running the length of the body on a yellow or tan background. This fellow hunts in trees and the rafters of barns and chicken houses for rats and mice.

Garter Snake

Range is most of the eastern United States for this 20-inch serpent with three light stripes on a darker background running down its back. The common garter bears living young and lives in fields, meadows, gardens, and marshes. It rather prefers damp, open spots and is found from sea level to high mountain slopes. When caught, this snake exudes an unpleasant odor from its musk glands. Diet is largely worms, amphibians, and insects

King Snake

The common king snake ranges throughout most of the southern United States in three subspecies—the Eastern, the black, in the Ohio and Tennessee valleys, and the speckled, which lives in and west of the Mississippi Valley. Colors vary tremendously in these fairly long (up to 6 feet) snakes. All of them lay eggs, have relatively small heads, are constrictors, and live in the burrows of other animals. These reptiles are very valuable, eating rats, mice, and poisonous snakes, bites of which don't bother them a bit. When alarmed, they vibrate their tails and hiss.

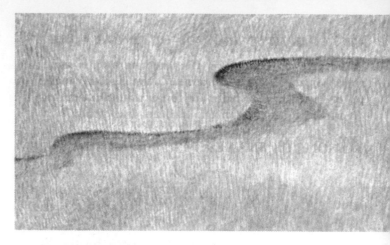

Path of a king snake in the dust leaves a long, undulating track, an inch or more in width.

Water Snake

The common water snake is aptly named. He loves water and commonly lives near it, often sunning himself on a branch hanging over a stream, swamp, or pond. He ranges from South Carolina to Canada and west to eastern Colorado. He is a blotchy-looking snake with crossbands on his foreparts and is sometimes confused with the moccasin. Diet is mostly made up of crawfish, fish, frogs and other amphibians, and occasionally small animals. It bears live young.

The Copperheads

The three subspecies of this reptile are well colored with chestnut-brown crossbands on their backs. Head is copper colored without markings. The southern copperhead ranges pretty much throughout the Southeast, the northern takes over for the Northeast, and the broad-banded operates from southern Kansas to the middle of Texas. These are highly poisonous, are members of the pit-viper family, and bear living young.

Coral Snake

This is a highly dangerous creature with bright red, yellow, and black rings. There are other snakes with the same coloration, but the poisonous coral is the only one with a black nose and the only one that has the red ring touching the yellow. This snake rarely exceeds 45 inches, lives from Florida to North Carolina, burrows, and generally keeps himself hidden underground in fields or, in some cases, near water.

POISONOUS SNAKES

Poisonous snakes—the coral snake excepted—have triangular-shaped heads, eliptical pupils, and evident poison sacs.

Water Moccasin

Called a cottonmouth in the South because of the white interior of its mouth, it is very fond of water and gives off quite a pungent odor when caught. Look for this creature near the quiet waters of bayous and swamps from Virginia to Florida and west to Texas. He resembles somewhat the water snake and is one of the largest of American poisonous snakes, reaching 6 feet.

Rock crevices are often the homes of copperheads and rattlesnakes. Sometimes several snakes congregate in same place.

The Rattlesnakes

These terrifying serpents come in many forms, but perhaps the best known is the diamondback. Characteristically, it has a diamond-shaped pattern on its back. The western variety lives throughout the Southwest, while the eastern one is known from Florida and Louisiana north to North Carolina. Average length is about 5 feet. As with all pit vipers, young are born live.

The timber rattler, which inhabits the Northeast from Maine to Alabama and Oklahoma, likes to live in timberlands where there are plenty of rocky outcroppings. He's got dark, V-shaped crossbands on his back. They're usually dark on a lighter brown or yellowish background.

The prairie rattler lives in the prairie states and is marked with brown blotches on a background color of anything from greenish yellow to olive. He lives principally in the burrows of other animals, often those dug by prairie dogs. This is the rattler of the Great Plains region.

Rattle of the rattlesnake is a series of horny cylindrical rings at the end of the tail which knock against each other.

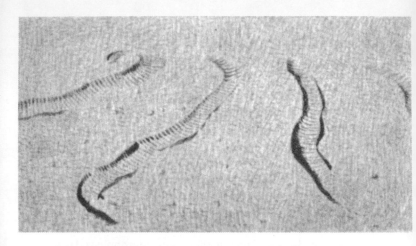

J-shaped tracks in sand show sidewinder's unique method of locomotion, different from undulating course of other snakes. Note clear prints left by belly scales.

The sidewinder is distinguished from other rattlers by the hornlike protuberances over the eyes and the distinctive track. Since he lives in the sandy deserts of Lower California, southern California, Nevada, Utah, and Arizona, this track is readily seen and easily identifiable. It is a series of J-shaped markings in the sand made by the snakes bringing his head through the air, setting it down, then looping the body after it. The snake does not drag its body, and a good track will show the imprints of every belly scale. You'll look a long time before seeing the maker of this track, however, as the sidewinder is nocturnal. He only averages about 18 inches in length, and females are usually larger than the males.

16

How to Handle Outdoor Pests

Nature had a purpose in creating outdoor pests. But the outdoorsman, plagued by them, sometimes fails to see their necessity or purpose. Despite this, the joys and benefits far outweigh the occasional nuisances, and one should never allow pests to spoil the enjoyment of the outdoors. There are ways to dampen or thwart outdoor pests.

Mosquitoes

One of the most tiresome of outdoor pests is the lowly mosquito. This little insect, which usually hums his presence, is found widely in the unsettled areas of Alaska, Canada, and the United States (lower). The insects breed and live in areas of shallow, stagnant, or slow-moving

495

water; in much of the "bush" country; in areas of meadow land; and in much of the timbered plateau regions.

The "hottest" mosquito season is from early summer to midsummer. With midsummer, and especially after the first few cool nights of the higher elevations, the number of pests tapers off. Therein lies the first secret of how to handle mosquitoes. Wherever possible, trips, and especially extended trips in heavy mosquito country, should be arranged for after the midsummer season.

When one must go earlier than this, and indeed at any time, camps and stopovers should be made in open, brush-less areas where any breeze can strike. This includes such areas as open river beaches, points of land extending out into water, or in the case of boat expeditions such as floats down Canada's Yukon or Stewart Rivers, islands midstream in the rivers. Breezes here will either blow away, or diminish the mosquito supply.

At night, any tent, cabin, house trailer, or camper should have mosquito proof mesh covers for the windows, doors, or tent-flaps. With the sleeping quarters made pest-proof for the night, any stray mosquitoes left inside may be killed with a spray of good insect repellant. This allows for a full night's rest free of their humming or bites. A good night's rest is imperative in mosquito country, if one must fight them during the day.

Good repellants are somewhat effective during the day-time also. Such products as "Off" will keep them off one's skin for a time, but must be used often in hot weather, as it "sweats off."

Finally, during unavoidable times of unendurable swarms of mosquitoes, some hardy souls still continue with their outdoor activities while wearing mesh head-gear, like the mesh veils which beekeepers wear while robbing bee-hives.

Black Flies

Another pest, occupying much of the same wide range of country, is the small black fly of the "bush" in the Far North. This tenacious little devil cannot be "shooed" or waved off like mosquitoes. Instead it will stick with a person, either on his skin or flying just a few inches from his face or body. Once upon the skin, the black fly likes to work its way into areas between skin and clothing, into ear orifices, and into nostrils. Once there, it bites and the sting, especially of many, becomes tedious and painful.

Many of the same techniques used for thwarting mosquitoes may be applied against black flies. By the middle of August, and the first heavy frosts of the North, the droves of black flies thin out. Trips, such as extended hunts, camping and fishing trips, and back-packing expeditions, made after that are far more enjoyable.

When moving about in black fly country, pauses for rest should be made on the higher, generally breeze-swept ridges, not down in thick bush. Any camps or stopovers should be made on the more open, brushless areas. As with mosquitoes, windows on campers, trailers, and cabins, as well as tent openings, should be fly-proofed; and repellant used inside to get the stragglers.

Where horses are used for travel in bush country, all corrals and rest areas for the stock should be well away from areas used by humans. Horses attract black flies, and will literally bring in hordes of them from the bush during bad fly seasons.

It helps to have sleeves that fasten tightly at the wrists, and pants that fit well down over the boots. Shirts also should be fastened at the front and throat. A small brushy twig, like a piece of Arctic Birch, used constantly as a fan about the face, will help to bat away most of the little black pests.

Other fly pests are the deer fly, the horse fly, and the big black ox fly. The deer fly is most numerous. The horse fly is larger and less numerous. It is dusky blue in color whereas the deer fly is black. The ox fly is the least numerous of the three, and is seldom seen except around horses and cattle. Its sting will send domestic stock into fits.

The best remedy for these three flies is to kill them by slapping them after they settle down, but before they bits. Or, if they are numerous, use insect repellant.

Yellow Jackets and Bees

Another flying insect that is troublesome around mountain camps is the yellow jacket, so called because of the coloration on its lanky, thin body. This wasp-like bug is attracted to camps because of the presence of food. The yellow jacket particularly likes any kind of exposed food with a sugar content. Most of the time in much of mountain country, when an outdoor table is set with sugar, fruit, jam, syrup, and so forth, these pests will appear. Their sting, if a person molests them, is immediate and painful.

The best remedy, when eating picnic lunches or any kind of outdoor meal, is to keep all foods covered when not in use. If the insects must be brushed off foodstuffs, use a twig or flyswatter, not the hand, as they often sting before one can move it.

Perhaps the biggest danger with yellow jackets is inadvertently disturbing their big woven nests. These big gray nests are made of chewed wood fiber, and engineered into cone-shaped nests running from a few inches to a foot in diameter. The nests are attached to dry tree limbs, tall brush, or even to sagebrush several feet off the ground.

If a hiker or horseman gets too close to one as he moves down little-used trails, the insects feel endangered, and will come out fighting mad. Before one knows it, he is surrounded by a virtual cloud of yellow bugs, stinging him with amazing rapidity. The sting is painful and somewhat poisonous. On a riding horse, the sting spots will swell immediately into egg-shaped lumps.

My first introduction to aerodynamics happened years ago, when I was riding a wilderness trail behind a pack-string. Suddenly, the mules ahead began bucking and jerking loose from the string. Before I could figure what was up, several yellow jackets swarmed over my own horse, and he came uncorked.

The pack on one of the mules had brushed into a "hornet's nest" of yellow jackets hanging from a clump of brush, and the rodeo was on. Both my horse and I were airborne, and came down some time later.

Another wild bee that is an occasional pest is the ground bee. This small insect is usually found in arid country and digs into the ground in a series of clean-cut round holes. Where one comes upon a single bee, there is apt to be a colony nearby. The best way of handling ground bees is to determine from their activity just where the ground colony may be, and then move away quickly without disturbing it.

Often today domestic bees are used for plant pollination near areas used for outdoor recreation, and one encounters these busy insects working. Like other bees, the domestic bee will sting, and the sting is painful. Certain factors will aggravate these bees, and make them sting. They sting more when it's windy. Further, beekeepers have found that the person who is most likely to be stung is the one who fears bees, and manifests it by waving off wildly any bee that comes near, and showing other evidence of fear.

The solution around bees is to stay calm, even though one or more may fly close to the face, and to move slowly. They usually won't sting.

Spiders, Ants, Ticks

The bite of some spiders is poisonous, and normally can be avoided. The female black widow's bite is more poisonous than that of the rattlesnake, per amount of injection. This is small enough so that not many fatalities result. This spider does not like being disturbed, and spins its web in dark, out-of-the-way places, such as old deserted buildings, forest cabins, unused woodpiles, and old privvies. Most bites can be prevented by taking care not to use bare hands around such places. Where any black widows are found, a spraying of Diazinon or Dursban will kill them.

Another spider found in many areas of North America's Southwest is the scorpion. Its bite is also painful and poisonous. Scorpions normally hide out under rocks and leaves by day and come out at night for food. They're best avoided by not handling rocks and other ground materials with the bare hands before ascertaining with a stick that such objects do not cover these insects. Going bare-footed in any suspected scorpion country is also dangerous.

Ants are another insect which, if allowed to, hinder the fun of outdoor picnics, camping, and similar activity. When ants are found, a few minutes' study of their movement will disclose that they are trading back and forth to the anthill, normally not too far away. The only real solution then is to move away from the infested area. "Ants in the pants" is fun to the comedian, but no fun in actuality.

In areas of the West, another seasonal pest is the Rocky Mountain tick, whose bite can cause Rocky Mountain Spotted Fever—often fatal. Generally this tick comes out shortly after the warmth of spring, and may be found on sagebrush, grass, and other low foliage. They are picked up by brushing against this foliage while engaging in activities such as spring chuck-hunting, hiking, and camping. The ticks contact clothing, cling to it and work their way onto human flesh, where within hours they will dig in.

Often these ticks will cause a slight itching as they crawl on the skin. They may be picked off, but often are ignored because their small, flat bodies resemble a tiny scab. Each evening, after one suspects that he's been in tick country, he should peel off his clothes, and carefully examine himself all over, paying close attention to hairy areas, where the insects dig in, and sometimes are not found for days. When a "dug-in" tick is found, it may be pulled off. Often this will leave its head still embedded in the skin. A drop or two of gasoline applied before the tick is pulled free will often make it loosen its grip. If any infection occurs afterward, or any sign of fever, one should always check with a doctor.

Plant Pests

The various species of cacti become pests in many regions of the continent. Most cacti are best handled simply by being aware of their presence, wearing strong leather shoes when walking in cactus country, and avoiding them.

One of the most miserable is the Devil's Club, native to parts of Alaska and its offshore islands. Its long, elk antler-like arms reach out and seem to grab one. Each arm is covered with myriads of fuzzy needle-like barbs which stick, penetrate, and fester. The best precaution is to watch for it, never let it touch you, and always be aware of its presence. This can be done by patient, slow travel, and constant attention to where one is going.

Several poisonous outdoor plants might be considered pests. One of them is the stinging nettle, which grows in green clumps along many streams. It's identified by slender stems reaching several feet in height, often thickly clumped together, and has long leaves coated with minute, prickly "fuzz." This fuzz penetrates when hit or touched by the hand, and becomes painful. It, like poison oak and other poisonous plants, is best handled by learning to identify it, and then avoiding it.

Snakes

Most snakes are beneficial, but some are poisonous. Three of the most common poisonous snakes in North America are the cottonmouth moccasin, the copperhead, and the rattlesnake. The rattlesnake is the most poisonous of the three, and can be found over the most widespread area.

Contact with a snake is almost always unsuspected and startling. Normally it is at close range. The best possible way of avoiding snake trouble is to travel slowly and carefully watching ahead when in any suspected snake country, such as in rocky regions, desert areas, along rock-bound streams, and in brushy, dry country. Visual detection of a snake is the best precaution. Again, never walk on or over brushy, dry, or rocky areas which can't be seen well, until probed with a stout stick. Nor should such objects be handled with the bare hands.

Rattlesnakes will often rattle when surprised. When a snake rattles, one should stop short in his tracks, and freeze to immobility until the reptile can be visually located. Usually the snake won't strike until the person moves again. When the snake, or its probable location, is determined, a quick long step in the *opposite* direction, usually from the direction the person has come, will put him out of immediate range. A rattlesnake can't spring from its coiled position to a distance exceeding two-thirds its total length. That is, a snake of three feet can't strike out for more than two feet. This makes the single quick leap backward a safety valve. Presence of mind and absence of body are both necessary.

Rattlesnakes won't always rattle when distrubed, especially during the hot days of August, so other precautions should be used in snake country. One of the very best is, whenever possible or appropriate, to wear thigh-length rubber boots. These gum-boots are ninety percent snakeproof, and will ward off most snake strikes, since they are aimed mostly at the legs.

When gum-boots are not used in snake country, the next best precaution is to wear loose pants. The folds of loose pant legs will absorb without damage a lot more snake-strike than, say, tight jeans over the calf of the leg.

When riding horseback in desert or other likely snake country, the rider should always stay alert. Horses hate rattlesnakes, and a saddlehorse, hearing the nerve-shattering *Buzzzz!* of a rattler near his legs will involuntarily "shy," or leap sideways. This represents a double danger—unseating the rider, and dumping him inadvertently upon the snake.

One intriguing thing about a rattler is that it often chooses the most inappropriate time to show itself.

One old-time riverman I know pulled his boat up on a sandy beach along the Salmon River, and walked to a nearby pile of dry driftwood. Gathering a quick armful, he started back towards the boat, expecting to make a fire and cook lunch. Suddenly one of the "sticks" he was carrying began squirming and rattling with an unmistakable sound. With the wood, he'd picked up a snake, sunning itself in the August heat.

The horrified man likely holds the current record for "broadcasting" firewood.

Game Animals

Some small-game animals and a few large animals are often considered pests, in that they can spoil the enjoyment of the outdoors. The skunk is one of these, and should be avoided at all costs because of the foul odor it sprays when threatened or injured.

This animal shades up by day, normally, then comes out to forage for food from dusk to daylight. It likes to burrow under old abandoned buildings, and shades for the day in the most brushy areas. Be very cautious when approaching brushy dikes, any old buildings, garbage heaps or cans, and places where a skunk might be stepped on without warning. Be constantly alert in any suspected skunk country, and move slowly. Also, keep the family dog away from such places.

Porcupines are lumbering non-aggressive animals which are pests to the outdoorsman only in that they can destroy camp gear. They live in timbered country and are easy to spot, whether up trees, which they girdle, or on the ground. The animals are armed with barbed quills, which they embed in a person or dog by flipping the tail sideways. The porcupine cannot throw its quills, as once believed.

The way to handle porcupines is to let them alone, and, at night, hang up or store in a safe place any camp gear, such as canoe paddles, axes, and shovels whose wooden handles contain traces of human perspiration. Porcupines will chew these, often to destruction, for the traces of salt remaining from the sweat. Saddles or other horse-rigging is often ruined, if left lying on the ground at timber country camps for the same reason.

Black bears can occasionally become pests around camps, especially buildings containing stored food and left unattended for long periods of time. They become more of a nuisance during years of short wild-berry supply, when they are more or less driven to it by hunger. They raid and dig up garbage heaps around vacant camps, eventually suspect or smell any foods stored inside, and somehow break in.

In any bear country, the outdoorsman should destroy any garbage as it accumulates by burying it deeply, or burning it. Vacation cabins and other such buildings should be shuttered with wooden shutters when not in use.

The trappers in Canada, which has an extensive black bear population, have learned how to solve the problem with their food caches, of necessity stored and left unattended in advance of the trapping season. They build high scaffold-like caches by sawing off the tops of three or four spruce trees growing together; building a flat overhanging log platform on top about twelve to fifteen feet off the ground; and storing food in a tiny "hut" on top. The cache is reached by ladder, which is then taken down. The cache's "legs" are covered by tin, often taken from empty 5-gallon gas cans, so marauding bears can't climb up them.

For tent, trailer, or camping travel in bear country, the presence of the family pet dog on leash, where regulations permit it, will normally keep any black bear pest away from camp. For some reason, the smallest dog, barking at a black bear, will send it scurrying or up a tree.

The magnificent grizzly bear should only be thought of as a pest in the sense that it occasionally endangers human life. The ways to prevent grizzly trouble is never come between a sow and her cubs, never startle or anger one seen at some distance, or never come upon one suddenly, if possible, along a trail or in the bush. In case of a sudden, unexpected contact, one should never make quick movements, shout, whistle, or wave the arms at the animal, or display visible fear. Any one of these actions is almost certain to induce a charge. And there is no running from a grizzly bear.

Foot travelers in known or suspected grizzly country should always make their presence known for some distance ahead by some kind of intermittent small sound such as low coughing, low talking to a partner, or gentle singing. Persons wearing pack-boards might attach a tiny turkey bell to the pack; its ringing can be heard by any grizzly for hundreds of yards.

This majestic animal is most wary of man in ninety-nine cases out of a hundred. Any of these sounds will disclose man's presence, and the naturally wary beast will move away from contact. The hundredth time keeps wilderness life interesting.

At any more or less permanent campsite, where any species of bear becomes a pest and periodically returns, you can rig up an alarm system in the tent area so that a bruin announces his presence. One way is to lay a row of empty tin cans in openings between trees. Another is to run a fishing line around trees near the tent, and place the reel by the bed. A sudden banging of the cans or the whirring of the reel during the night will alert you to the intruder. Yelling and throwing something in its direction will usually scare it away.

17

Where to Go

In the early days of our country, the supply of natural outdoor resources was thought to be "inexhaustible." This included the forests, the minerals, the fish and game, the water, and the land.

It didn't take thinking people too long to decide that the widespread and accepted exploitation which naturally followed could not last forever, and that the day was inevitable when non-renewable resources would surely become extinct, and the others would be depleted.

This gradual trend towards conservation influenced Congress to create agencies aimed at making these resources available to the greatest number of people, for the longest time, and for the greatest good. Such agencies as Fish & Wildlife Service, the National Park Service, and the Bureau of Land Management came into being under the Department of the Interior, along with conservation agencies such as the Forest Service and Soil Conservation Service, under the Department of Agriculture. It took time to put these federal agencies into operation, and they were continuously opposed by private interests.

Canada and Mexico developed comparable provincial and central legislative agencies.

The struggle between private and public interests, as regards natural resources, has never died and is currently stronger than ever. To a great extent it has been, and still is, revolving around the question of public lands. The government agencies manage these lands under the concept of multiple use. That is, when leasing the lands to private interests, or allowing the public to utilize the many attractions and resources, they consider the overall public interest—domestic stock grazing, lumbering, mining, winter sports, hunting, fishing, and other forms of recreational and scenic use.

Many of these overall uses are concurrent. As one example, the Bureau of Land Management supervises approximately 175,000,000 acres of grazing land in the lower 48 states, most of it west of the Mississippi, on which numerous recreational activities such as hunting and fishing are permitted. At the same time and in these same regions, sheep and cattle-grazing takes place. These uses are also regulated by state Fish & Game Departments in joint cooperation.

The Forest Service supervises such things as timber harvest, roads, fire protection, and the setting aside of areas for vacation-home building and campsites, while the state upon which the forest is located manages the fish and game.

The admission of Alaska to statehood has increased the controversy over federal versus state and private rights. Currently, the matter has reached the proportions, mainly in the West, of a national struggle and a legal battle is impending. The current controversy is erroneously referred to as the "Sagebrush Rebellion"—an attempt by several of the key western states to shift the public Bureau of Land Management lands from federal to state control.

The position of the federal government has always been, and is now, that these lands are national property, held in trust for the public in perpetuity; that they were acquired by purchase or settlement for all the public; that the status of ownership has never changed and will not change; that the desire for state ownership is motivated by greed; and that, if changed to state ownership, many of these lands would eventually change to private ownership, for purposes of personal exploitation.

The affected states maintain that the federal government has grossly mismanaged the lands (which in many instances they have); that the various states, with their local experience, are in a far better position to manage their lands than government bureaucrats located in offices 3,000 miles away; and that there are several legal interpretations of the Constitution to indicate that certain states rights, in this instance, may supercede federal rights.

One fact appears to be clear. In the event that public lands became state lands, many of them would eventually become private lands, subject to trespass laws.

The whole matter is of vital interest to today's outdoorsman and to the generations which follow. The fact is that there is never going to be any more land. Those who love camping, sightseeing, skiing, snowmobiling, hiking, backpacking, rock-hounding, or any other recreational activity, will be doing it mostly on these remaining public lands.

Whether one leans towards federal or state control of these lands, he should make his voice heard. Whether he likes or dislikes the present federal control of these lands, he should, and can, exert a personal influence. He can write his congressmen, who are influenced by his thinking. He can attend the various meetings of such agencies as the Forest Service and Bureau of Land Management, where most officials are eager for public opinion to guide them in making decisions and changes in current management.

As one example in my own area, numerous public meetings are being advertised and held, asking for public opinion on such matters as possible winter snowmobile trails on Forest Service lands, placing limits on the use of off-the-road vehicles (ORV's) to prevent possible damage to watersheds, and amounts of firewood to be taken from local public forests. Ranchers, prospectors, winter sports enthusiasts, and numerous businessmen, as well as interested outdoorsmen, attend these meetings.

Each of the various federal agencies cooperates with the different state Fish & Game Departments in the regulation and harvest of fish and game on public lands, since fish and game, with the exception of migratory waterfowl, is generally considered to be the property of each sovereign state. Waterfowl is managed federally.

In early days, the federal restrictions on the use of public lands were relatively few and basic. They dealt largely with forest fire prevention, grazing rights and over-grazing, access roads, illegal cutting of timber, and similar factors.

As westward movement and populations increased, the restrictive measures of necessity became more numerous and more complex. Problems had to be met as they arose, and enforcement and administrative personnel increased.

The end result is that today the rules and regulations covering the use of public lands for outdoor enjoyment or other purposes are many and involved.

A good example of this is found in the Salmon River country, in the primitive area of central Idaho, and its recreational uses. At one time, the public was largely free to float down the Rivers Of No Return (the East Fork and main Salmon Rivers), and enjoy the adjacent beauties of the country. These included the marvelous scenery, the thrilling steelhead and trout fishing, the huge herds of wild sheep, deer, elk, and goats, which could be hunted in season, and the once-in-a-lifetime thrill of riding a craft over wild white water—all in an area which few men had ever seen.

All it took to do this was a desire to go, sufficient and capable equipment to make the hazardous float, and the nerve to try it. The only craft that would stand the trip over these waters, including Salmon Falls, were huge timber rafts, manned by 20-foot sweeps, then scrapped for lumber after the long float, at a point where the tiny village of Riggins now stands.

The floats, the general magnificence of the land, and the abundant game were soon advertised, and the area became a national attraction. As the years passed, a better river craft was developed, such as the old City of Salmon—a huge wooden-plank boat, still manned by sweeps but capable of withstanding the battering of the white water and rocks and running the rapids at Salmon Falls. The craft would then be tediously truck-hauled several hundred miles, on the road which began at Riggins, back to where the float began. Later came specially designed fiberglass boats and high-powered outboard motors, especially welded to handle the rigors of the rapids.

With their advent, the old "river rats" found that the float need only be made as far downstream as Salmon Falls, then the combination of boat and power could be used to drive reasonable loads of people and gear back *upstream*, to in-put somewhat downstream from North Fork.

This was a turning point in the public use of that great recreational area. Outfitters began setting up shop in the area, people flocked in for summer and fall float-trips, and hardy private sportsmen and boatmen even began "running the river" on its upper reaches.

With the influx of people, the regulations naturally increased, aimed at preventing over-use of the resources of the country. Today, in order to float that wild stretch of river, one must have a Forest Service use-permit; and a quota of summer boating parties has been established. In order to get in, one must apply far in advance of the boating season, and when the set quota is reached, no more permits are issued. Also, this entire magnificent region, now made accessible by boat-floats, is rigidly monitored and inspected to make sure that people using the area leave the natural campsites and surroundings in as good shape as they found them.

This same basic regulation applies to most public lands available to the outdoorsman today, and the administrative regulations are bound to increase for future generations, and increased use of the land.

For this reason, people using public lands for recreational purposes will need to keep abreast of regulations for the areas they wish to use. This should be done well in advance of such intended use. The best way is to contact an office of the appropriate agency and ask for information, maps, and general restrictions. This may be done either by telephone or letter to the nearest office. Almost any large town or city adjacent to or within the area of jurisdiction of any of these agencies can give this information. Otherwise, a letter or telephone call to the capital of the state or province administering jurisdiction over the lands can provide any necessary data.

It is, for instance, discouraging to plan all year for a week's summer horseback trip into some wilderness area, trailer-haul a couple of horses a thousand miles or so to reach the jumping-off point, and then discover that the region has just recently been closed to horse travel because of the seasonal scarcity of horse feed. Similarly, there is no percentage in planning a summer vacation around hunting for garnets, opals, and other gems in some remote area only to learn after arrival that the region has been closed to rock-hounding because of too much public use.

In the West, some state lands (a small proportion of the entire land area), remain and are open to public use. Originally these lands (in Idaho, for example, sections #16 and #36) were granted to the states by the federal government, out of each township, for the establishment and perpetuation of the public schools. They were known as "school sections."

Many of these have been sold off at auction to the highest bidders, after advertising, at public sale. This has been done periodically, when the state felt it was to its advantage, and partly for the purpose of getting the relatively unproductive lands on the private tax rolls.

The remaining lands are administered under the supervision of the State Land Board. The restrictions on their use by the public have always been simple and basic. They were intended to prevent such things as range fires, and the destruction, in any way, of the property.

Any information needed about the intended use of these remaining lands may be had from any district office of the appropriate State Land Board, or from their central office in the state's capital.

The availability of the national parks for outdoor activities has taken some of the pressure off our public lands. These great sanctuaries or monuments are usually areas of great scenic beauty or unusual phenomena which are irreplaceable, such as Yellowstone's breathtaking geyser formations, the vast ever-shifting coloration of the Grand Canyon and its unbelievable space of emptiness, or the awesome glacial formations of Glacier National Park.

Their public use is intensive and increases from year to year. They offer opportunities for limited outdoor sports, such as trail-hiking, photography, sometimes fishing, and modified outdoor living. They are rigidly protected and supervised, and one's activities while enjoying them must of necessity be among groups of people. No private exploitation of these great monuments is ever allowed except for the lease arrangements necessary to provide living and travel accommodations for the visiting public.

Another specialized form of this type of public land use is provided in areas of the West, Alaska, and Canada by the popular dude ranches. These usually have been established by ranchers or other large landholders living close to scenic recreation country, such as mountains, forests, lakes, and streams. Their owners cater especially to those who like to "play cowboy," and ride horses; and to those who like their outdoor fun tailored so that the rough edges are eliminated, while the joys remain.

At a big dude ranch one may enjoy such recreation as horseback riding, miniature rodeos, hiking, rustic living conditions and accommodations, meals, and almost everything necessary to the full enjoyment of the scenic country—all at a substantial price per day or week. The dude is referred to as the "paying guest," and everything possible is provided for his comfort and fun.

A specialized form of this dude-ranch concept rapidly gaining in popularity in the West is the covered wagon trail-ride. These rides are organized well in advance of the summer season, usually by some big dude ranch near mountain, forest, or other scenic country, and often with lease-access to public Forest Service land. A party of several dozen interested people will contract to go by wagon-train from one scenic area to another, camping out at night under the stars (or in tents during bad weather), eating outdoor meals tastefully prepared in Dutch ovens by outdoor-cooking artists, listening to impromptu groups singing western songs around campfires in the evening, and riding gentle saddlehorses along the trails in scenic country.

Anyone who gets tired of riding horses may ride in one of the covered wagons if he wishes. It is interesting that these covered wagons are authentic in most details and give an air of realism, except that they are built on rubber-tired running-gears known as Hoover wagons—a holdover from the Great Depression when Hoover was President, and the farmers were so broke they had to build farm wagons out of their automobiles.

Texas provides an example of specialized land use for outdoor sports, catering to the well-fixed person who likes hunting. This vast state has very little public land.

In the years following the Great Depression, the big ranchers in this state found it almost impossible to survive on the domestic stock their lands produced. They realized that the arid land was suitable for such game as the white-tail deer, wild turkeys, and later, some of the exotic game animals found in Africa and Asia. So they made agreements with the state Fish & Game Department for an unusual arrangement.

The ranchers were permitted to fence their lands with high deer-proof fences, buy and install breeding stock, cultivate the game on their lands until it had propagated enough to support permit-hunting; then, for high fees, they sold hunting rights called "leases" to wealthy groups for exclusive and private hunting; or they sold permits to individual well-heeled hunters who could find no other places to hunt.

In this way, many of the huge ranches became virtual private game farms, and hunting for many species became a year-round possibility.

Some of these ranches advertise in the sporting journals. Others are kept well-utilized by repeat business. These special arrangements do help reduce the growing pressure for places to hunt.

The one remaining area which can support considerable amounts of public use and enjoyment is the privately owned lands of the country—largely agrarian lands used by individual farmers and ranchers. These diversified lands are in real danger of being lost to the public by the actions of the relatively few who have misused them.

The land on which I sit is typical. It was homesteaded in the West by my dad, who cleared it of sagebrush and put it into cultivation nearly a century ago. It has never had a "no trespassing" sign on it and hasn't now. None of my neighbors have posted their land against public enjoyment, and there are only a few such signs in this entire end of the valley.

With the settlement of this area, a spirit of neighborliness has grown up with the land. People started with few neighbors. They liked them. They liked company. If someone wanted to fish on your land, or hunt birds on it, or, later, to run his snowmobile over it in winter, the attitude was, "Fine. Help yourself. Just shut the gates, and don't shoot near the house."

This is a spirit hard to understand or believe by residents of the great urban centers; and it is rapidly being spoiled by those who have come to regard the use of "open" land as somehow a right instead of the privilege it really is. Those who yell loudest at the increasing crop of "no trespassing" signs are often those who neglect to shut gates on farm lands, shoot near, or even at domestic stock and buildings, run jeeps over growing crops, and refuse to show common courtesy by thanking the landowner after using his land; and they would be the first to sue the same land-owner if he were to go to their homes in town, camp on the lawn, strew tin-cans, and commit comparable offenses.

The way to preserve the remaining privileges the public enjoys on private land is to treat the landowner with the respect he and his property deserve. Ask well in advance of an intended visit, either by letter, phone call, or personal contact, for the privilege of using his lands. Thank him afterward. Send him a Christmas card or small gift. Invite him to come and see you. Such consideration will help offset the discourtesies of the few thoughtless ones who spoil the enjoyment of the many. This won't be true of all places. But in my region or state, I have never been refused access to private lands after showing the above courtesies to a landowner.

Large-scale experiments along this line are being tried in various areas. Landowner-sportsmen groups are being formed. The owners agree to allow their lands to be used at certain times and for specific reasons. Sportsmen are held to ground rules of specific conduct. Such experiments appear to be working well.

18

How to Choose an Outdoor Partner

A partner is essential in most forms of outdoor recreation. It is true that solo trips afield have their value, and there is much to be said for a quiet day alone in the woods or along a stream, when one can ponder and enjoy things without interruption. But for most outdoor activities, having a partner is best.

One reason is that enjoyment is somehow heightened when an experience is shared with someone. This mutual sharing of an experience does not always have to be with words. Indeed, many times partners of long standing will ride, move, or walk through outdoor wonders with little more than a gesture or word passing between them. They have learned quiet communication and its value. One person may gesture quietly towards the sudden sight of a buck deer standing immobile on a distant hillside, or nod towards a V of wild geese flying overhead. The other nods in return, they watch silently, then pass on, somehow the better for the short experience.

Another reason for a good partner is practicality. The knowledge and experience of one complement that of the other. Individual outfits and equipment may be shared, avoiding duplication. One jeep hauls two to the jumping-off spot as well as one. One lantern lights the tent. One bow-saw is adequate for the occasion. And companionship is shared.

But perhaps the greatest single need for an outdoor partner, especially for extended trips or wilderness activity, is safety. Real danger seldom enters into outdoor enjoyment, and one may spend most of a lifetime in the outdoors without experiencing any real emergency. But danger is always present, and always seems to crop up unexpectedly. The good, reliable partner is the best solution for getting out of any emergency without disaster.

Here are examples of what *might* happen:

Two men are hunting in unfamiliar, rolling, timbered country where canyons wagon-wheel off in every direction, and there are no natural landmarks. Due to some erroneous information they received, they misinterpret some old tree-blazes they have been told to watch for. Deciding they must be lost, they change direction, and subsequently become hopelessly turned about. No other people are in the region—they are on their own.

Hours later, after failing to get their bearings, the two decide upon a sensible course. They head downhill and walk for several more hours, eventually coming to a tiny creek. They follow this, and eventually come upon a wood-chopper, who tells them how to get to another water-course six miles distant, and that following this course upstream will get them back to their camp by midnight. By the middle of the night, the two have made it, after sixteen hours of steady walking, and thirty Forest Service miles, much of it up and down.

When one partner occasionally asks his partner, "Are you okay?" the other cheerfully answers, "Sure." The next spring he admitted that he'd had to wear overshoes instead of shoes all winter because the experience had nearly crippled his feet. But he hadn't gone to pieces.

Or consider the man in deep wilderness country, who suddenly came down with acute appendicitis in the middle of the night. Someone immediately had to drive him in a truck more than seventy miles, over treacherous mountain passes and switch-backs, to reach a small-town doctor.

Again, one might put himself in the position of a man who was going on a long-awaited Alaska hunt. He and his pilot were flying in a light plane to a wilderness hunting-camp. The plane suddenly developed trouble, and they were forced to crash land on a tiny mountain-rimmed lake. They were marooned without any equipment, and, to make matters worse, the weather suddenly turned sour, with fog and rain closing in.

After serious consideration, the two decided on the only possible course. The pilot would "walk it out," some hundred bush miles, to where he could get help and another plane, taking the only food—a few crackers and pilot hard-tack or biscuit. The hunter would remain with the downed plane, live off the land, and survive if he could. The search planes in the area quit after a week because of continued fog and no visibility.

They came out of it intact. The pilot reached help. The hunter hiked up the mountain and killed a wild billy goat, afterward wryly remarking, "I learned over one hundred ways to cook a wild billy goat. Every one of them tastes horrible."

These are not mythical experiences. All of them have happened to me or hunting friends. The point is that a good partner in all instances was the difference between a hazard and a real disaster.

Many small factors, if looked for, can indicate the difference between someone who might be a suitable outdoor partner, and one who might fall to pieces if the chips were down. The longer the outdoor experience or stay, the greater the need for a dependable partner.

A primary and important factor in choosing an outdoor partner is similarity of interest. The social acquaintance, business partner, or banker who admires your credit rating may not be the best fellow around a smoky campfire. One week spent in wilderness country usually brings out either the best or the worst in a person; and under stress, his lack of real interest will begin to show through and likely spoil the enjoyment of both.

Again, the casual friend who feels you might owe him a favor and talks you into taking him for a week's pack-trip to some wilderness lakes, might not, under normal hardship or unaccustomed living conditions, bring out the best in either of you.

A former deer-hunting partner gave an enlightening example of this. He was a good hunter and annually returned with his buck. Two of his teen-aged neighbors, knowing the man was the most accommodating neighbor in the world, and had his own horses and hunting equipment, coaxed him for several seasons to take them deer-hunting.

Being a good sport and really wanting them to enjoy the activity as much as he did, he finally agreed and took them into mountain country, provided a saddlehorse for each, and all camp equipment for a week's stay. On the way to deer country, they stopped at a country store and bought candy, knick-knacks they might enjoy, and several magazines to read if the weather turned sour.

The first morning of the hunt, they rode up canyon. After an hour, the man spotted a small herd of deer, unmolested and at considerable distance. He told the boys to ride behind him and not make any noise whatever. They would go as far with the horses as they could without being detected, and then they'd stalk the deer on foot. The good fellow fairly burst with the thought that the boys were surely going to have the immeasurable thrill of bagging their very first big-game.

After several minutes of riding, the man turned in the saddle to see how the boys were coming. Both had the reins draped over their horses' necks, and both were engrossed in reading comic books! Oblivious to any deer or deer-hunting!

For some reason, the man turned his horse around, gave the youths a day's "grand tour" of the country, and took them back home. It's wonderful to take a boy or boys into the outdoors. But they, in turn, must have that vital quality of similarity of interest, if things are to go well.

Relative affluence does not necessarily enter the picture when choosing a good outdoor partner. Many people reach middle-age before becoming well-heeled enough to take on extensive outdoor experiences. Many of them want to take wilderness floats, wilderness hunts, and other rugged outdoor activity; and they "take it up" because all their friends are doing it, and it's the thing to do. But they often do not make good outdoor partners. They tend to complain about any inconvenience or hardship. A good rule is that if a person reaches middle-age without having manifested any interest in the outdoors, he will likely not make a good partner for the person who has loved the forests, streams, mountains, and the unexploited wilderness all his life.

All this is not meant to indicate that the experienced outdoorsman should never take the novice along on outdoor recreation. Far from it. But such trips, for the sake of both, should be of short duration. It's far easier to come home from a single day's outdoor recreation, when one of the partners gets tired of it, than from a week's tent-living deep in some primitive area.

Except when a grown and experienced person takes his son or other youngster into the woods or hills, partly for his own enjoyment, but more to get the youngster started right, the ages of outdoor partners should be reasonably similar. Although this factor may be unimportant when one of the partners is more experienced and rugged, and can "keep up his end" with the more youthful partner.

The man whose wife loves outdoor recreation has a built-in partner for most of his activities, and is most fortunate. He should not expect her to take on the most rugged exertions, but today's modern woman is not the weak sex she was once thought to be. Also, the conveniences and development of handy outdoor equipment, such as the marvelous motor home and self-contained camper, have eliminated much of the bother associated with outdoor living that at one time didn't appeal to women.

As a consequence, today's athletic-minded woman enjoys all such major recreational activities as boating, hiking, horseback riding, rock-hounding, skiing, fishing, and the milder types of hunting—with all the conveniences of home living taken to, or into, the recreational area.

Similarly, one's son or daughter, if they show an interest in the outdoors, can be taught to love it, and can become a most pleasant and rewarding outdoor recreational companion. There is a great thrill in watching a youngster develop outdoor skills and an affection for the outdoors. There are few satisfactions which can surpass that of hearing a teen-aged son or daughter confide to a friend, "I like to go places with Dad. We always have so much fun."

Make it a point to choose an outdoor partner with whom you have had no difficulty or personality clashes in the past, and for whom you have personal admiration. This prevents minor difficulties and temporary aggravations from becoming serious.

The choosing of a good partner works both ways. Never expect anything or any more of a companion than you are able, or willing, to give yourself. If any situation afield ever becomes awkward, tense, or miserable, always be willing and eager to go the extra mile for the safety, happiness, or well-being of your partner. A good rule for partners to remember when afield is never to get angry at the same time. It's a most valuable trait, too, when field conditions threaten to become intolerable, to laugh at oneself, call it a day, and begin all over again.

Finally, there is the matter of health and condition. Each partner owes it to the other to keep in good physical shape before engaging in the more strenuous forms of recreation. It's no fun to begin a ten-mile pack-trip into the mountains, only to have one of the partners give out, after a half-mile, and want to go home.

Regardless of the situation, almost anyone can find opportunities for getting into good physical shape. Gyms, health spas, swimming pools, and exercise programs are available to any urban dweller. And the rural person can always find chances to exercise, especially if he raises a garden, mows and waters a lawn, has horses or chickens, or owns an acreage. Jogging and walking are two of the best forms of exercise, and these exercises are available to anyone who wants to get into good physical shape. The best way, of course, is to *keep* in good shape.

If one were to sum up the process of just how to choose and keep a good outdoor partner, it would be to choose someone of similar age who has a deep interest in the outdoors and with whom one has no personality clash; someone with an unshakeable dependability, a willingness to go the extra mile, good physical shape, and a sense of humor when things go wrong.

19

Hunting How-To

How to Make an Elk Bugle

One of the most thrilling forms of hunting is bugleing for elk. Bull elk will answer the call of another bull during the rutting season, and this call can be simulated with a bamboo bugle. To use a bugle effectively requires a knowledge of the bull's mating call and the behavior at this time of the year.

The best bugles are made of node-free bamboo, of a length and diameter that will produce the four, distinct, arpeggio-like tones of the bull's bugling. The ideal size is 17 inches in length with an outside diameter of 1 inch.

Cut the bamboo to length and scrape the fuzz from the inside with fine sandpaper on a dowel. With a fine-toothed backsaw make a cut approximately 1½ inches from the open end, to a depth of about one-third the bamboo's diameter. Then, with a knife, make a slanting cut an inch from the saw cut, forming a notch.

Next, make a wooden plug that will fit snugly into the notched end of the bugle. Make this plug of a relatively hard wood; soft wood will absorb moisture and ruin the tone. The end of a broom handle makes a fine plug. This plug should be the same length as the distance from the blowing end to the notch. It should be sanded smooth and fit snugly. Then shave the top of the plug flat along its full length. This permits air to be blown into the bugle. Shave the plug cautiously, cutting down only enough to get the needed air passage.

By continued trial—pushing the plug farther in or pulling it out a trifle—you will find that the bugle can be blown. This is accomplished by blowing into the plug end and holding the hand over the other end. If it won't whistle, push the plug in or back it out a little. At some point, if everything is right, the bugle will produce a whistle. If you blow harder, you can make higher-pitched notes or tones, just as a bugler can, by tightening his lips, produce several

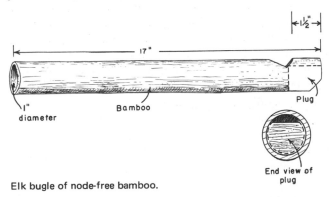

Elk bugle of node-free bamboo.

tones without any keys. You will find that you can make four distinct tones, like a musical arpeggio. If you can make only two or three, shift the plug, or flatten the top, or deepen the notch a trifle.

When you can make four tones, mark the position of the plug with a knife scratch so it can be replaced in the identical position. Then, if the blowing end is too big for your mouth, cut the lower edge on a slant—so that it resembles the top of a saxophone mouthpiece. Finally, coat the plug with airplane cement and replace it. It's smart at this stage to give it one more toot, to make certain it is tuned right, before the cement dries.

The finished bugle should sound something like this: "Da-da-da-deeeeeee-da-da-dum!" These four tones imitate the bull's bugling, with at least three-fourths of the time spent on note number four, the highest tone.

As good bamboo is becoming hard to obtain, an adequate bugle also can be made of 5/8-inch plastic garden hose. It won't have the same deep, mellow tone of the bamboo bugle, but will work fairly well, especially on bulls in primitive areas which haven't been overhunted. For a hose of 5/8-inch diameter, the correct length is 14 inches.

This bugle is made just as a bamboo bugle is, except that the end plug doesn't have to be cemented. It is shaped round, and should be friction-tight. The plastic seals it.

In an emergency, a form of elk bugle can be made of two empty cartridge cases of different size. One should be small The two cases are taped together with adhesive tape, edge-to-edge. The larger case is blown into first, since it will make the deeper tone. Then the smaller case is blown into for a longer period, simulating the high-pitched tone. A .38 Special revolver case and a .338 Magnum rifle case will make a crude bugle. It will often work on unalerted bulls.

How to Make a Moose Call

The Indians used to make moose calls of birchbark and the technique is useful today. The Indian call was made in the shape of a small horn or megaphone, ranging from 8 to 12 inches in length. The pattern for this resembled a fan, extended so that it covered one-third of a complete circle.

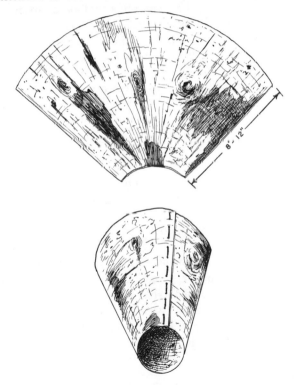

Birchbark moose call.

The edges of the bark were then overlapped and stitched down with cord, sinew, or buckskin.

To use such a call, place it over the lips and make a grunting sound—"Uh-waugh! Uh-waugh!" Rapidly expelling a lungful of air helps. This resembles the love call of a moose in the rut, and through the funnel-like call will carry for a considerable distance in calm evening air. You can make such a call of bark, or of a section of a cardboard carton.

Lacking either bark or cardboard, you can simply cup your hands over your mouth as when shouting. Each guttural sound is made with the cupped hands half closed for the first syllable, then opened widely for the second part—much as a trombonist opens the mute on the end of his instrument.

Varmint Calls

The purpose of a varmint call is to simulate the scream of a dying or caught rabbit and lure a varmint in the area within shooting range. You can make a simple varmint call from two slats of softwood, one or two wide rubber bands, and some adhesive tape.

The best wood for this call is a 3-foot yardstick available at any lumberyard. Such a yardstick is approximately 3/16 inch thick and of easily workable wood.

Saw two slats from the yardstick ¾ inch wide and 6 inches long. At the center of each slat, hollow out the face for 2 inches along the length to a depth of about 1/16 inch at the center.

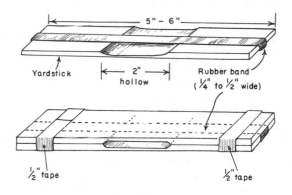

Varmint call made from two lengths of yardstick and rubber band.

Next, either one or two rubber bands of ¼ to ½ inch width (depending on the quality of tone desired), and 5 inches in length, are stretched tightly around the top slat When this top slat is placed over the lower slat, there will be a thin, eliptical opening at the center. The rubber band(s) will run across this opening. To complete the call, tape both ends of the slats tightly together about 1 inch from each end.

The finished call is held edgewise in the mouth, like a thin harmonica. The sound is made by blowing through it, against the edge of the taut rubber bands. With practice, and by cupping and opening the hands about the call as it is played, you can create the most unearthly yowls imaginable and can simulate the cry of a caught rabbit. The sound from this call will carry unbelievable distances, especially in still air. The point to remember is that the pitch of the sound is determined by the tension of the rubber bands, which in turn is determined by their length. For a higher pitch use a shorter, or tighter, band, and vice versa.

A simpler varmint call can be made with nothing more than a blade of large, tough grass. To make this call, place the hands with the palms together so that the two thumbs lie edgewise and parallel. The palms should be mildly cupped. With the thumbs in this position, they are bent slightly downward into the cupped hands. The blade of grass is placed edgewise between the thumbs, being held at one end between the nails and the first joint, and at the other end by the meaty portion at the second joint.

With the blade edgewise and taut, place the mouth over the opening between the thumbs, and blow hard. You'll make some weird and awesome screeches before you learn to regulate the tension of the grass blade and can simulate the cry of a trapped rabbit. The first coyote I ever called within rifle shot was coaxed with this type of varmint call.

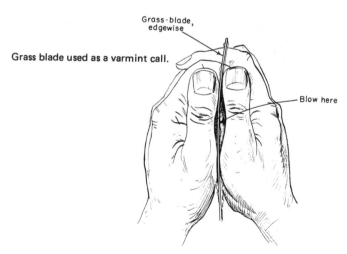

Grass-blade,
edgewise

Grass blade used as a varmint call.

Blow here

Rattling up a Buck

The best way to learn to rattle up a deer is to watch a buck rub off the summer's velvet, and polish his antlers, against a suitable tree. If these sounds—the swishing, banging, huffing, and rattling— could be put on tape, then somehow simulated, rattling would be comparatively easy. And, if the actual sounds of two bucks fighting could be heard, artificially duplicating those sounds would be simple.

First it is necessary to find a pair of shed deer antlers. Whitetail antlers should be used for rattling a whitetail buck. Old-timers at the game say that one-year-old antlers are best if they can be found, for they still have the crispness of live antlers.

Take the pair of antlers to a deer area, and station yourself in an opening in heavy foliage. One hunter can work alone, or two can be together—one to rattle, the other to shoot if and when a buck appears. Both should wear camouflage clothing to match the surroundings.

Holding an antler in each hand, bang them together as if two bucks charged each other head-on. Then twist and rattle them as if the bucks were disengaging their headgear. After a slight pause, rake an antler against a tree a few times. Then bang them together again. Next, rake one of antlers noisily over rocks. Repeat this sequence for up to a half minute, then remain silent, and listen. Naturally, you should be downwind from the direction you expect a buck might appear.

After ten minutes, if no buck shows up, move to another part of the opening (as though two fighting bucks might move) and repeat the performance. Always remain at the edge of the opening, not out in the open.

If there is a rutting buck in the area, and the rattling has authentically simulated two bucks fighting, or one scraping velvet off his antlers, he's apt to come out of curiosity or pugnacity.

I have repeatedly watch experienced hunters rattle for a buck in the whitetail country of Texas; and their performance, as they banged antlers together, moved off and raked them against brush, and got down on their knees to grunt and rake the dry antlers over patches of rocks, would rival the most imaginative Indian ceremonial show. But these hunters had rattled up bucks many times. One told me that once while he was on his knees, scraping on the rocks, "—a buck with horns like the Charter Oak jumped clean into the openin', and almost lit on top of me. I was so scared I couldn't shoot!"

Handling Guns Safely

There are many specific do's and don'ts about gun handling which, if followed, will prevent gun accidents. These rules, which have been time- and field-tested, are especially useful for the beginning shooter.

I have found a single rule which, if religiously followed, will prevent gun accidents. "Never point a gun at a human being."

But, this simple rule needs some explanation. It does not mean merely to avoid pointing a gun at a person when hunting. It means that even when handling and transporting guns they should not be pointed at someone.

Guns should not be carried so their muzzles point in a lateral direction—somewhere in the distance there may be a person. Instead, guns in the hunting field and elsewhere should be carried with muzzles either up or down. Similarly, guns should not be transported in vehicles on a seat in horizontal position. Guns should be transported in vehicles with muzzles pointed upward or downward.

Guns should not be placed muzzle up against a slender tree, post, or fencewire. They may fall over and point toward a person. This applies as well to the rifle carried in a saddle scabbard. It should never be carried horizontally alongside the saddle, but with the muzzle pointed either up or down.

If you examine this simple rule, in every aspect of its application, you'll find that it embraces almost every field situation; and that if the rule is rigidly applied it will largely do away with gun accidents.

There are of course many more gun rules dictated by common sense:

Do not clean a gun unless the action is open.

Keep ammunition locked up away from small children.

Don't try to shoot out obstructions from gun barrels.

Make certain the caliber or gauge of cartridges matches the gun to be used.

But the rule of never allowing a gun to be pointed at a human being, in all its applications, is the one rule that will cover most situations and prevent the most accidents.

Installing Scope Sights

The average shooter or hunter, if he is at all handy with simple tools, can install his own scope. Today's standard factory or custom rifles come already drilled and tapped for scope sights—that is, the receiver bridges and barrels are drilled for scope bases which have become standardized and will fit a variety of popular bases. These bases, in turn, will accept what have now become standardized diameters of scope tubes.

The tools needed for installing a scope are a couple of screwdrivers, an ordinary hammer, and a flat-ended punch.

If shop screwdrivers are used, make certain the ends are square and the sides are flat. This can be done by filing them, or grinding them on a small emery wheel. A screwdriver whose surfaces are not flat will jump from a screw head under tension and mar the looks of the job. One screwdriver should be small enough to fit the base screws and tightening screws of the scope itself. The other should fit larger screw knobs which hold the scope bands together.

Standard factory rifles come equipped with open sights. Some of these rifles will accept modern scope sights without removing the rear or the front sight, or both. Although the open sights protrude into a scope's line of sight, they will in actual use be blurred and will not interfere.

If it is necessary to remove an open sight, the hammer and small punch are needed. This punch may be a tiny brass plug about an inch long and 3/8 inch wide, designed for the purpose. Or a 16d nail, cut off to leave a 2 inch shank and filed square at the end, may be used. A square-end shop punch of suitable size is adequate. Place the punch on the base of the open sight as the rifle is held in a firm position horizontally. In this position, hit the punch sharply with the hammer, using a crisp, short stroke. It should move laterally in the barrel slot in which it has been fitted. A few more strokes with the hammer will punch out the sight base from the slot.

The important thing to remember in doing this is that such standard open sights are fitted into the barrel slots from the *right* side of the rifle, as the muzzle points away. Therefore, to remove the base requires that it be pounded out from the *left* side, since the barrel slots are midly tapered in dovetailing them.

The bottom of the scope bases, and that part of the rifle where they will be fastened, should be wiped free of all grease. If this job is completed with a slightly oiled cloth, all grease will be removed, but enough oil film will remain to prevent future rusting. The four tiny screws should be removed before doing this, and the tapped holes wiped free of all grease until perfectly dry. This can be done with a cloth on the end of a toothpick or match. Otherwise the base screws will tend to loosen with use.

The scope bases then are fitted and screwed to the receiver. Do not completely tighten the first screw of a base element before setting the second screw; then tighten both screws. The screws will withstand a firm turn with the screwdriver.

Next, fit the two scope rings around the scope tube and only partially tighten the setscrews, allowing the scope to turn within the rings. This allows positioning the scope correctly, but with enough tension so that it won't move unless desired. Now set the scope and rings into the bases, and partially tighten the large screws which hold the bands to the bases.

At this point, the scope rings and bases are firm enough so they won't move, but the scope tube itself will turn, under hand pressure, within the scope bands. This is necessary to adjust the scope so that its reticle will not cant, and to obtain proper eye-relief.

I have found the easiest way to rotate the scope so that it won't cant is simply to set the rifle in a solid position

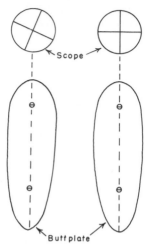

Align buttplate and scope reticle to correct cant. Scope at left is out of line.

as in shooting; then, with the eye just a few inches behind the buttplate, move it up and down between scope reticle and buttplate. If the line between the center of the reticle and the buttplate appears to be straight, there will be no cant. Also, it is a good idea to aim through the scope at this point along the verticle line of a building or door jam. Any deviation from true vertical can be detected, and this will also disclose if you tend to hold the buttplate a bit off vertical.

Eye-relief is the distance between a shooter's eye and the scope, in a position where he can get a full field of view. It averages in most scopes from 3 to 5 inches.

To get proper eye-relief, place the rifle at the shoulder in actual shooting position, with your face on the comb of the stock where it will be during actual use. With the

540

rifle, in this position, move the scope gently back and forth within the bands until a full field of view is achieved.

Occasionally, owing to the combination of rifle, scope, mounts, and individual shooter, it is not possible to get a completely full field of view. Also, with rifles of very heavy recoil, it is wise to move the scope beyond which a full field of view occurs, in order to keep your eye from getting bumped in an awkward shooting position. This is not too important—the rifle will shoot just as straight, but it's a little harder to shoot quickly.

One final important detail: In rotating and setting the scope, be sure that the elevation-adjustment knob is on top of the scope—not on the left with the windage knob on top. If this occurs, sighting-in will be extremely difficult.

With this done, tighten all screws in both scope and anchoring elements, each one a little at a time. Tightening all screws on the right side before tightening any on the left will cause the scope to rotate slightly to the right, producing a bit of cant.

Installing Sling Swivels

A sling on a hunting rifle is used ninety-nine percent of the time for lugging the rifle around, and one percent when actually shooting. For this reason alone, any hunting rifle should be equipped with a sling—it takes most of the drudgery out of carrying a rifle.

Almost all modern rifles come equipped from the factory with sling swivels. For those not so equipped, it is easy to put on sling swivels. The tools needed are a brace and bit and a large screwdriver.

After removing the stock from the barreled action, place it in some form of vise which will hold it solidly. Set the stock into the vise jaws between two strips of soft wood covered with cloth. This prevents marring the stock finish. The stock is placed upside down.

To set the rear swivel, mark a point with the end of a punch 2½ to 3 inches from the toe of the stock, exactly in the center. The distance depends upon preference, individual body size, and the overall length of the rifle. With a carbine or very short rifle, the distance from swivel to toe is less. This is where the rear swivel will be set.

A standard form of swivel, especially for the do-it-yourselfer, consists of a loop and screw as the rear element and a loop, screw, and nut for the fore-end.

The screw on the rear swivel tapers to a point and has deep, widely spaced threads. To set this swivel, it is only necessary to bore a hole in the stock with a bit whose diameter is slightly smaller than the swivel screw. When beginning to bore, make sure that the bit does not slip off the edge of the stock. Too large a bit will allow the swivel screw to slip out and loosen with use. And if the bit slips off, the stock will be marred. It is wise to experiment with the bit size on a piece of scrap wood. You then can tell if the fit will be snug enough, without splitting the stock. Bore the hole only a little at a time, testing the depth by pushing a match into the hole, holding a thumbnail at its depth, and comparing with the length of the swivel screw.

When the hole is the right depth, the swivel screw may be turned in until the base sets firmly upon the stock. Slip a screwdriver blade through the swivel loop to turn the screw flush.

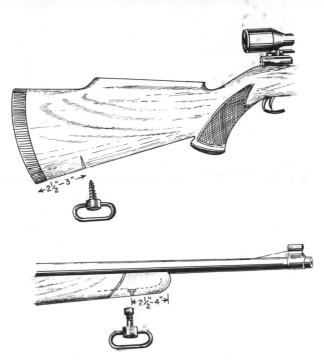

Installing sling swivels in stock and fore-end.

The fore-end swivel is set similarly, except that two holes are bored. The first hole is placed at a point 2½ to 4 inches down from the fore-end tip—this, as mentioned, according to personal preference and rifle length. This hole is bored with a bit of the same diameter as the swivel screw. The screw on this element will not fit into the wood itself, like the rear swivel, but into a nut inside the barrel channel. This is a round nut, of the escutcheon type, and will bind into the wood of a larger hole.

The first hole is bored through the stock's center, all the way into the barrel channel. Next, a second hole is bored, from the inside of the barrel channel, to a depth that will allow the nut to be countersunk far enough into the wood so that, when the barrel is refitted, the nut and the barrel will not touch. This is determined by boring a little at a time, and trial and error. If the two touch, the rifle will shoot high.

Care should be used in boring this counterunk hole to make sure it is concentric with the first hole. Otherwise, the holes will be off-center and the screw won't fit.

The final step is to place the nut firmly into its fitting hole, carefully pushing the swivel screw through from the stock's outside, and turning it down tight. The rifle is then reassembled.

Other types of swivels, having different styles of bases, are installed in a comparable manner. With any type, it is important to test the boring and fit first with a piece of similar scrap wood. It's hard to undo a botched job on a fine gunstock.

Installing a New Stock

There are several reasons why you may want to put a new stock on a rifle. You may wish to modernize a military arm or to restore an old or prized piece. Or you may accidentally break a stock while hunting and want to replace it.

The advent of machine-inletted stocks on a mass, commercial basis made it possible for the average person to do this, when previously it was next to impossible. At one time, stockmaking involved cutting the blank from suitable timber, seasoning the wood plank, marking out a design, and then tediously carving, whittling, gouging, and chiseling until the stock was complete. Today, when a stockmaker says that his inletted blanks are "ninety percent completed," he means just that. Some need only sanding and finishing.

It is best for the average person with ordinary skill with tools to begin by restocking a bolt-action rifle. He can then graduate to other types of stocks, such as the fore-ends of shotguns, stocks for lever-action rifles, etc.

It is important when ordering an inletted blank to obtain the correct size. Check the specifications from the maker. It is next to impossible to make over an inletted blank to fit a different rifle.

To begin, remove the barreled action from the old stock, using a screwdriver with the correct blade width. After this has been done, test the fit of the new stock. In most instances, if the stock has been purchased from a reputable maker, you will find that only a bit of snugness here and there prevents the two from fitting together. This is intentional. The barrel channel will be the most noticeable of these areas.

A round inletting rasp is best for working down these areas, although sandpaper around a wooden dowel will do nearly as well if you are careful. A sharp carpenter's chisel will be adequate for shaving down flat surfaces.

Before beginning to cut, however, you must determine just where the tight areas are. A good way of doing this is to mix a spoonful of ordinary vaseline or petroleum jelly with a small part of black oil paint, available in tube form from any hardware store or art shop. Lightly smear the metal areas where wood and metal should go together. Then, if the stock is temporarily fitted to the metal, the areas in need of working down a trifle will show plainly. Shave or sand these down a bit at a time, testing the fit as you go. One critical area in any stock is the recoil lug. This must fit snugly, and be perfectly square in the face. Otherwise the rifle won't shoot accurately.

When the stock is worked down so that all elements fit, it's best to fit the trigger-guard and magazine-floor section first. For this, use a pair of screws to situate that part in line with the receiver. Special ones are available at any large gunsmith shop, but aren't entirely necessary. Two small hardwood dowels, one for each guard screw, and of the same diameter, may be screwed temporarily into the holes, and will serve to line up the floor plate and action. The dowels may be whittled with a pocketknife. When the floor plate is temporarily in place, the dowels should fit into the holes of the receiver, through the stock.

The action and stock are then fitted together for a final testing. In cases where any alteration of the stock must be made to fit the individual shooter, it should be done at this stage. The barrel channel should be sanded down only to where a slight amount of pressure will remain at the junction of the fore-end and muzzle—say from 3 to 5 pounds. When the stock and barreled action fit, the stock is ready for sanding and finishing.

To sand the stock, start with a medium-grade sandpaper, gradually going to a finer grade as the work progresses, finishing with number 000, or as fine a grade available. Then wet the outside of the stock with a damp cloth or wet sponge, and dry it. You will find that a fuzz appears in the wood's grain. Sand this off with the finest sandpaper. Again wet the stock and dry it, and sand once more. Six such sandings and wettings will suffice for most stocks. At this stage, no more fuzz will appear. The stock is now ready for a finish.

Finishing a Stock

A good, old-time stock finish was ordinary boiled linseed oil, applied sparsely, a few drops at a time and rubbed with the palm of the hand until the oil disappeared. The stock was then allowed to dry for a few days, and the process repeated. After several treatments a walnut stock would take on a deep, smooth finish. This is still a fine way to finish a stock.

Modern finishes, however, will speed the job. One product is Linseed. This is basically a condensed linseed oil product, but can be applied much more rapidly. Another is Nu-Stock, useful for finishing a new stock or for touching up scratches and mars in an old stock.

The hard plastic finishes which now appear on many of the finest rifles can also be put on by the amateur. These finishes consist of epoxy resin, and are applied to the stock in one or more thin coats with a spray gun. Suspend the stock by two wires ending in hooks which go through the inlet of the wood and hold the stock in midair. Apply the epoxy several feet away, in a very fine spray, being careful not to get enough finish on at a time to cause it to run or sag.

If by mishap you inlet a stock too deeply, don't throw it away. It may be glass-bedded. Glass-bedding consists in gouging out the barrel channel and other areas even further, then applying liquid glass to the channel and allowing it to set solid. Manufacturer's directions will come with the product, and if followed, will save a bungled job of inletting. Many shooters glass-bed a rifle now and again anyway, to make a more perfect fit and make it shoot better.

Cleaning Guns in an Emergency

Once in a great while it happens to even the most careful shooter—he stumbles and pokes his gun muzzle into snow, mud, or dirt. The muzzle is clogged and must be cleaned before the gun can be safely fired. To fire a gun with an obstructed barrel is like bellying up to a buzz saw.

With a shotgun, the problem is usually solved without much trouble. The bore is large enough to permit entry of a stick or reed. The foreign material can be poked loose, then removed by blowing through the tube and wiping the inside with a handkerchief on a stick. Usually not over 6 inches will be plugged—it would take a mighty fall to plug a shotgun barrel more.

Cleaning out foreign material from a rifle barrel is much harder, but can be done with nothing more than what the average hunter wears. I learned this the hard way, years ago, when my wife stumbled and fell while on a deer hunt and plugged the end of her Model 99 Savage.

The first thing to do is to unload the weapon. Next, clean out most of the obstruction with a thin stick that has a tiny knot or hook at the end. A stalk of heavy beargrass, a small reed, or any stick that will fit into the muzzle without binding will accomplish this much. If no such stick can be found, the tough root of a plant, or the stem of a dried weed or flower, can often be used. Lacking these, a stick can be whittled out of some kind of available wood.

The next step is to remove one of your shoe- or bootlaces. Into one end of a lace, cut a slit approximately ½ inch long. This slit should not be too close to the end or it may tear. Then cut a patch of cloth from a handkerchief, coat lining, or shirttail which is slightly smaller than the patch you usually use with a cleaning rod. (The patch for a .30-caliber rifle is 2½ inches square.) Insert the patch in the slit.

If the rifle has a bolt action, remove the bolt and insert the lace from the receiver end, and work it through to the muzzle. Then grasp the lace above the muzzle and pull the patch through the barrel. Two or three patches will clean out the dirt, and the rifle will be safe to fire again.

A length of fishing line will serve the same purpose as a bootlace. Fold the line back upon itself at one end for 3 inches, then take the doubled end and tie a double overhand knot. Make two turns about, instead of one. The finished knot will then hang vertically with the patch, not at an angle which would make it bind. A half-inch loop formed in this way will hold the cloth patch. A nail tied to the other end helps in dropping the line through the barrel.

Sighting-In a Rifle

Until a rifle is sighted-in, it is just a combination of wood and metal that won't hit where it is aimed. Most rifles coming from the factory are roughly sighted-in. To shoot with precision, a rifle must be sight-in by the man who is going to shoot it. No one else can do it correctly.

The first thing to determine is the range at which the sight setting will coincide with the target. No rifle will shoot perfectly "flat" for any distance, and there are only two points in the bullet's arc of trajectory which will precisely coincide with the point of aim. Consequently, it is necessary to sight-in for an average range, then hold over or under for longer or shorter ranges. A .22 rimfire rifle may be sighted-in for 100 yards, but for shorter ranges it will be necessary to hold lower, and for longer ranges, higher. A good sighting-in range for a big-game rifle of the .30/06, .270, .308, or .284 class is 200 yards.

To sight-in for such a range with a rifle and cartridge of this power, it is necessary to have a target and a target butt of some kind to stop the bullet's flight, and some form of table or bench on which to hold the rifle firmly. A steep hillside, or a target butt (which will be described later), will safely stop the bullets. A bench-rest, or a table on which a rolled tent has been placed, or a rolled tent used with the shooter in the prone position, will all suffice to hold the rifle firmly.

With a bolt-action rifle, remove the bolt, set the rifle in a firm position and aim through the bore of the barrel so that the target appears in the exact center of the aperture. To maintain a steady position, hold the rifle butt with both hands.

With the target in the center of the bore, and the rifle held firmly, shift the eye until you can see through the sights. If the line of the sights, or the reticle of the scope, appears to be also on the target, the rifle is then sighted-in closely enough to get "on the paper," or somewhere near the bull's-eye.

If the line of the sights and bore do not seem to coincide, you must make adjustments in the sights until they do. To move the point of impact to the *right* with open sights, the rear sight must be moved to the *right*. To lift the impact *upward*, the rear sight must be shifted *up*. In short, the rear sight must be moved in the direction you want the shots to go.

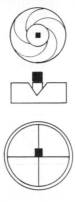

Sighting-in a rifle, showing bull's-eye centered in bore (top), and correct sight picture for open sights and scope crosshairs.

When sighting-in with a scope, or when bore sighting, if the reticle appears too far to the left in a trial shot, the rifle is currently shooting to the right and the windage dial must be adjusted "left." A crosshair or post which appears to be low when the target is centered in the bore indicates that the rifle shoots high. The elevation adjustment must then be made in the direction of "low." Some variation in this rule will be found, owing to barrel whip and other peculiarities of the individual rifle, but basically the generality will hold.

With the bore and scope adjusted so that both are on the target, fire a few trial shots, holding the rifle rigidly. A couple of shots will indicate about where the rifle is hitting. Then make the necessary windage and elevation adjustments.

For example, if a .30/06 cartridge using a 180-grain bullet of standard factory velocity hits exactly on the mark at 200 yards, that bullet in its flight will be about 2.4 inches high at 100 yards, on at 200 yards, 9 inches low at 300 yards, and 27 inches low at 500 yards.

It will be obvious that if a bullet starts from the muzzle below a rifle's line of sight, it must cross the line of sight, rise above it midway, then drop down to the exact line of sight in order to be "on" at, say, 200 yards. This means that a bullet will cross the line of sight at two places—one near the rifle, the other far out. With rifle cartridges of the 2,700–3,000 foot-second class, such as the .30/06, .284, etc., this first crossing occurs about 25 yards in front of the muzzle, when an average scope sight is used.

Because of this fact, and since some rifles of the lever-action or automatic class do not permit removing the bolt for bore sighting, you can get a rifle initially on target simply by shooting until it sights-in exactly at 25 yards.

A second way of sighting-in a hunting rifle is first to decide what outside range will be the limit at which you would ever shoot at game—say 350 yards. Then sighted-in the rifle as just described. For shooting at intermediate ranges, simply hold the sights lower in relation to where you want to hit. With some rifles, this may be as much as 5 inches. The first method, for this reason, is best for the average shooter.

Simple Shooting Bench

A shooting bench is a convenient aid for sighting-in rifles. The simple bench illustrated was made in a couple of hours from scrap material left over from a new building.

Four round fence posts approximately 4 inches in diameter and 30 inches long are used for the legs. These form the four corners of the bench: the front legs are 19 inches apart, the rear legs 44 inches apart. Nail two sets

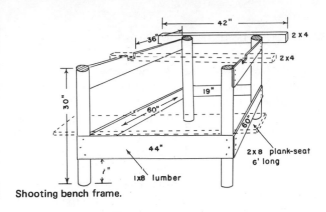

Shooting bench frame.

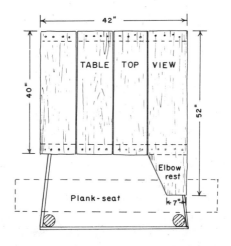

of 1-by-8-inch rails to the legs. To the ends of the bench nail bottom rails. The front top rail is a 2-by-4, 40 inches long, nailed flush with the post tops with its ends extended evenly beyond each of the posts. This supports the tabletop at the forward end. About 36 inches behind this 2-by-4,

553

nail another 2-by-4, 42 inches long, in two corresponding slots cut in the tops of the two side rails. At this stage, the framework resembled a four-sided pigpen.

The top, made from 1-by-10 lumber, is 42 inches wide and 40 inches long, with the exception of the right-hand board which is a 1-by-12, 52 inches long, and tapered to serve as an elbow rest. Nail these top boards to the 2-by-4 crossbars with 8d common nails. Place a 2-by-8 plank, 6 feet long, across the two side rails just inside the rear bottom rail, to make a seat. Do not nail the plank to the rails so that it can be adjusted to fit the individual shooter.

Fore-End Rest

An essential accessory for the shooting bench is a rest for the fore-end of the rifle. It should be solid to prevent barrel wobble and adjustable to fit individual shooters or different types of rifles. A good rest can be made from scraps of lumber and concrete.

First make a rectangular box of 1-inch lumber whose inside dimensions are 13½ inches long, 5 inches wide, and 6½ inches deep. In nailing the box together, allow the nail ends to protrude so they can be pulled with a hammer. Place an empty coffee can, with the lid on, in the box with half its diameter protruding. Hold it in place with a couple of nails at each side.

Mix a small batch of concrete in the ratio of 1 part Portland cement to 5 parts sand-and-gravel, and add water to a sticky thickness. Pour this mixture into the box and carefully poke it down around the can so that no air spaces remain. Fill the box level with the top.

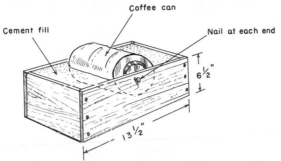

Fore-end rest made by pouring cement into a wood box.
Coffee can affixed in the center creates concavity for sandbags.

After the concrete has dried for two or three days, disas-
semble the box by pulling out the nails and remove the can.
Rub off the raw edges of concrete with a stick. You now
have a block of cement with a rounded depression in which
to place sandbags. When sighting-in, the fore-end of the rifle
is rested on the bags.

Sandbags

While getting the sand-and-gravel for the rest, it's wise to
buy a few shovelfuls of pure plastering sand for making
sandbags to put in the crescent-shaped opening. You can
make a sandbag from an odd piece of canvas 12 inches long
by 6 inches wide. Fold it over and run a seam along the
three open sides, leaving a 2-inch opening at one end. Pour
the sand through this hole (after turning the bag wrong
side out) and sew up the opening. With two bags you can
make adjustments in the height of the cement rest to
accommodate any shooter or rifle.

Backstop

The best possible backstop for a shooting or sighting-in range is a large mound cut away to leave a vertical face. If targets are placed against this face, bullets will be stopped safely. But for those who don't have mounds in their backyards, a safe shooting backstop can be made of 2-by-12-inch planking and 4-by-4-inch posts.

First cut sixteen 4-foot lengths of planking. Cut four 4-foot 4-by-4s for corner posts. Nail four planks to a pair of posts to make a panel. When you have made two panels, stand them up and nail on the remaining planks. The result is a square box, open at both ends.

Place the box at the end of the shooting range and fill with sand or dirt, tamping as you shovel. Not even a bullet

Wooden backstop for sighting-in range.

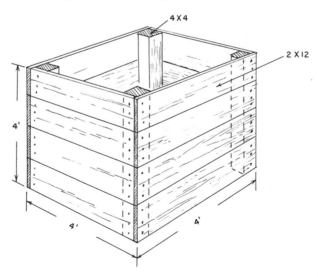

from .300 Magnum rifle will penetrate such a backstop. When the two middle planks behind the target become damaged after long use, pry them off with a wrecking bar and nail on new ones. Red pine planking, rough sawed, is the best wood for this backstop.

Sighting-In Targets

The best target for sighting-in a rifle is simply a sheet of yellow typing paper with a 2½-inch square of black paper (black film backing or construction paper) thumbtacked to its center. This simple target has many advantages. The best possible visual contrast is the combination of black on yellow, and thus the target is easier to see than other. The square bull's-eye gives more lineal distance in the area where the scope's cross-hairs are superimposed on the target, than would a round bull's eye. It is easier to "fit" the reticle on the target's edge. This is true for a post or crosshair, and for a hold at six o'clock or center.

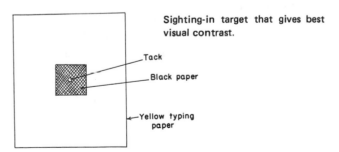

Sighting-in target that gives best visual contrast.

Tack

Black paper

Yellow typing paper

Shotgun Targets

Many shooters want to test their scatterguns on a target to learn what the pattern might be. In the past, this has been done mainly by aiming and firing at a 30-inch circle on paper at 40 yards. Gun manufacturers normally test their tubes and chokes on the basis of what percentage of the pellets will hit within a 30-inch circle at that range.

A far better target for the average shotgun shooter is a drawing of a game bird or waterfowl in flight. Such a test will give a far better indication of what is actually happening if the shooter casually walks up to within 40 yards of the target and fires quickly, as though field shooting.

Of course, the matter of lead must be disregarded in such a test, but it will plainly show any shooter where he is shooting in relation to where he *thinks* he is shooting. It will also show what pattern his shotgun will give. And it will additionally indicate if alterations in his shotgun should be made, to help him to "hit where he looks." Poor stock fit often adversely affects aim.

Bird targets are easy to sketch. Use black crayon, charcoal, or other plainly visible media. The targets should be drawn approximately life size. As examples, a life-sized quail, in flying position, will average around 9 inches. A mallard will be about 22 inches, a Canadian Honker nearly 36 inches, including wingspread. Newsprint is a good paper to use for these targets. It may be obtained from any big newspaper publisher in the form of roll ends left over from the presses.

After shooting, scribe a 30-inch circle around the thickest portion of the shot pattern. Mark the holes made by the tiny pellets with the eraser of an ordinary pencil which has

Shotgun target for testing the pattern of shot.

30" circle at 40 yds.

been inked on a pad. From such a pattern, you can see in which direction you miss your target and what kind of a pattern your gun throws. If the 30-inch circle encloses the bird, you are shooting well.

Shortening and Crowning a Rifle Barrel

Occasionally you may want to shorten one of your rifles. You may want to remodel a long-barreled military rifle, or repair a damaged muzzle, or modify a rifle for mountain hunting. This should be done before finishing the stock or sighting-in.

To shorten the barrel, clamp the rifle firmly in a vise (with padded jaws, as mentioned before), and cut off the extra length from the muzzle end with an ordinary hacksaw. A sharp blade will eliminate the need for extensive finishing-up work.

559

Even so, the cut made by such a saw will be rough, and in most instances slightly off "square." Before the rifle will again shoot accurately, the muzzle must be squared off at a true right angle to the bore, and the edges of the lands must be smoothed.

The easiest way to square off the muzzle is with a large, flat bastard file. The longer the file, the less it will wobble as you work. One who has done a lot of metal-work with a file will be able to file squarely across the muzzle without tilting the file.

To do a perfect job of flattening the muzzle, it is best to use some kind of guide. The simplest is a square of 1-inch board with a hole bored in its center exactly the diameter of the muzzle. The muzzle is shoved through the hole until the end of the barrel just perceptibly protrudes from the other side. If the board does not fit tightly around the muzzle, it may be wedged with a sliver of wood from the rear side of the board until it is tight.

Next, clamp the gun barrel in the vise with the muzzle up (most people can file better with a lateral stroke). With the muzzle in this position, file gently across the board. The file will touch only the metal if care is used, but if bits of wood are filed off it won't matter. The file will cross the muzzle squarely. The board won't allow it to tip, The result will be a barrel end which is perfectly flat and at true right angles to the axis of the bore. Unless this is accomplished, one or more of the barrel lands will extend imperceptibly farther than the others, and this will impair the rifle's accuracy.

The remaining job is to crown the muzzle. In remodeling a military rifle, or cutting down a barrel on an average rifle, it is not necessary to finish the muzzle with the type of

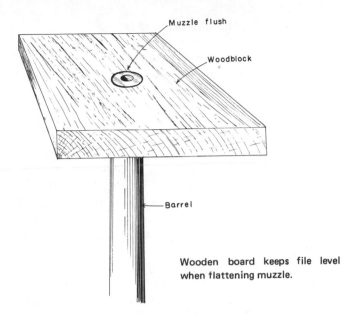

Muzzle flush

Woodblock

Barrel

Wooden board keeps file level when flattening muzzle.

crown found on factory rifles or expensive custom rifles. An adequate crown can be made by slightly countersinking the bore at the muzzle and smoothing it down evenly all around.

The simplest way to do this is with a brace and a large, roundheaded brass screw. Other materials necessary are a bit of ground emery and a few drops of olive oil.

Crowning the muzzle with roundhead brass screw in brace.

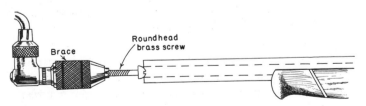

Brace

Roundhead brass screw

Clamp the sharp end of the brass screw in the jaws of the brace, put a mixture of the ground emery and olive oil on the head of the screw and, holding it lightly against the bore at the muzzle, turn it slowly. This will smooth and slightly countersink the end of the bore so that the land ends are precisely the same all the way around.

If a deeper countersink is desired, a sharp-angled countersink bit may be used first, before grinding with the brass screw-head. The bit should be held precisely in line with the axis of the bore, touched only lightly to the muzzle, and turned evenly. This will cut the lands to the desired depth, after which the screw and emery will impart the finishing smoothness.

Complete the job of crowning by smoothing down the sharp outside edge of the muzzle. If you are handy with a file, simply touch this edge lightly with the tool, and with an even turning stroke, touch away the sharp edge.

If you have a lathe, or other means of resolving the entire rifle barrel, you can do an even smoother job. As the barrel turns, hold the file lightly against the outside edge of the muzzle at a 45-degree angle.

After crowning the muzzle in this way, a touch of cold-blue, applied according to directions on the cut portions of the muzzle, will finish the job. Or the entire barrel may be reblued in a regular bluing tank.

Thwarting Condensation

The rusting of the metal on guns comes from the action of oxygen on water, particularly salt water. Anyone familiar with guns knows that water or snow must be removed within a matter of hours or rust pits will occur in the metal. This is ordinarily accomplished by cleaning the gun all over after moisture has touched it, and then coating the metal parts with a light film of good gun grease or oil.

A more treacherous form of water is moisture resulting from condensation. Condensation comes from rapid changes in temperature. Moisture condenses upon the cold metal, which violently cools it and turns it to water. This means that guns brought out of the cold into warm tents or cabins will have moisture condensed upon the metal parts. A scope sight used in cold weather will fog up when exposed to warm air.

The way to beat condensation is simply to avoid subjecting guns to quick changes of temperature. This is often difficult since hunters normally hunt in cold weather and bring their guns inside a warm tent or cabin at the end of the day. But when bringing a gun into a warm tent or cabin, you can wrap it in a hunting coat or parka. Then place the wrapped gun on a bunk temporarily, where it will gradually adjust to the room's temperature. The insulation of the coat will permit the room's heat to get to the gun gradually, preventing a sudden change in temperature.

A good way to wrap a gun in a coat is to poke the barrel into a sleeve, then wrap the body around all other metal parts so the receiver and scope are covered. Twist the end of the sleeve to shut off heat over the muzzle.

This is the way to prevent camera lenses from fogging. In the Arctic I constantly brought a pair of cameras into a warm hut when outside temperatures averaged around 26 degrees below zero without fogging the lenses. I wrapped both cameras in my down parka before entering the hut and left them that way for an hour or so.

At cold-season hunting camps, some outfitters leave their clients' rifles *outside* the tents during the night. After cleaning them, the hunters store them in a special rack built for the purpose. Both the rack and guns are covered for the night with a canvas tarp. No condensation occurs, since no quick changes of temperature take place.

When a horseback hunter carries his rifle in a saddle scabbard, the heat of the horse's body will cause condensation on the rifle whether the weather is warm or cold. A rifle carried for several hours, during the normal fall hunting season, will show condensation on the metal parts.

Moreover, the salt from the horse's perspiration will penetrate the best scabbard leather and rapidly rust the weapon. A cardinal rule in horseback hunting is never to leave a rifle in a scabbard overnight. Always clean the rifle, coat it with a thin film of oil or grease inside and out, dry out the sweat-soaked scabbard each night inside the tent or cabin, and do not replace the rifle in the scabbard until the next morning. One of the best commercial products for protecting a gun against condensation is the product Rig.

Finally, condensation can ruin a gun's metal, or the stock finish if the weapon is stored in an airtight case. It's always smart to loosen the zipper a few inches, or leave a solid case unlatched, during home storage.

Storing Guns at Camp

One place to store guns at camp is in an outside rack, as mentioned before. To make such a rack, find a pole about 3 to 5 inches in diameter which is long enough to stretch between two trees. Drive a number of 8d nails, at a slight upward angle, 4 inches apart, into the pole, then nail or lash it between the two trees at a 30-inch height. The length of the pole depends on the number of guns to be stored. Then smooth the ground beneath the rack and lay one side of a canvas tarp beneath the pole. The butts of the rifles are placed upon this part of the tarp and the balance is folded over the muzzles and back behind the pole.

A gun rack of this type should be placed where there is no hunter or horse traffic, and where rain or snow will not fall on it—such as under the branches of a big spruce tree near the tents. The weight of the canvas will prevent wind from blowing it off the guns.

When keeping guns inside a tent, don't put them on a sleeping bag or bunk that is being used. Condensation will inevitably form on the underside of the gun from heat remaining in the bag or in the ground beneath it.

One of the best ways to store a rifle inside a tent for the night is to hang it by the sling from a nail driven into the rear upright of a wall tent. The rifle may be hung either with the muzzle up or down. In a big wall tent which has a long wooden pole running along the top of each side wall, a fine place to hang a rifle is from a nail driven into one of these. But be sure the muzzle does not touch the tent fabric. Rain on the fabric will inevitably seep off and into the gun barrel. Also, the gun should never be hung so that any part of it touches the ground—it will accumulate moisture. For the same reason, rifles should not be stacked in a corner of a tent with muzzles against the canvas.

When storing any gun at camp, the most important rule of all is to unload that gun before entering the camp, keeping the muzzle pointed *downward* while it is being unloaded.

Rack for storing guns in camp. Tarp folds over the muzzles to protect them from rain.

Once in Wyoming I got off my cot and walked outside to see if a late hunter had bagged his elk. The hunter was dutifully unloading his rifle, but his muzzle was not pointed downward. Somewhere along about cartridge number three his finger got the trigger. He plowed a hole through the tent, the cot where I'd been five seconds before, and into a supply of groceries stored under the cot. The bullet would have hit me dead-center.

Reloading Ammunition

Among the reasons for reloading one's own ammunition are saving money, developing a better load for a certain gun, and experiencing the thrill of shooting a better target or taking the annual buck with a cartridge of your own making.

The equipment needed for handloading is minimal: a press, dies, loading block, powder scales, funnel, powder, bullets, and primers. The once-fired cases from factory ammunition are fine for reloading the same caliber. Complete reloading outfits cost from $50 up.

Before attempting to reload your own ammunition, study a good manual on the subject and carefully follow the instructions. Good manuals include *Lyman's Reloader's Handbook, Hornady Handbook of Cartridge Reloading, Speer Manual for Reloading Ammunition,* and Ackley's *Handbook for Shooters and Reloaders.* Besides detailed instructions, all these books include loading data for most popular cartridges. These are tested, safe loadings. *Never exceed the loads listed in these manuals, and always stay just a trifle below maximum loads until experienced in making up handloads.*

Handloading is divided into several simple steps: inspection of cases; case lubrication; resizing; decapping; priming; checking primed cases for fit, charging with powder; and bullet seating.

Inspection means to scrutinize all empty cases for flaws, and to throw away any case that is split, dented, or otherwise not perfect. Such cases are not safe to reload.

Lubricate the empty cases so they will enter and emerge from the constricting dies easily. Do this either by rolling them on a pad of heavy towel which has been oiled with a good commercial lubricant, or simply by wiping them all over with a cloth which has been lightly lubricated. Care should be used to see that no lubricant gets into the open mouth of the case.

Resize lubricated cases, either full length or only at the neck. New cases, unless factory resized, and empty cases fired in another gun, should be resized their full-lengths to give them perfect fit. A once-fired case may be only neck-sized, if it is to be shot in the same chamber.

To resize, set the empty case into the shell holder of the tool and actuate the lever. This pushes the case upward into the die, which resizes it to standard dimensions after the case has been expanded through previous firing. Also, as the case goes into the die, the central punch pushes out the old fired primer. Then, as the case is started from the die, place a primer in the tool's primer arm. This is placed under the empty primer pocket. As the case is further withdrawn, the live primer pushes into the primer pocket, and the primer arm is then flipped out of the way.

The sized and primed case is then totally withdrawn from the die. In doing this, an elliptical "button," which is integral with the central punch and on the top end, comes out the neck of the case. This button resizes the inside of the case neck as it emerges, so that the bullet will seat snugly.

With the case now sized and primed, inspect it again, and see if it will fit the intended chamber. Neck sizing, incidentally, is done by backing off the die in the tool for about half a turn, so that the die doesn't touch the case's shoulder.

To charge the sized cases, select a suitable type of powder, and weigh each individual charge on a powder scale which will weigh charges to one-tenth of a grain. The type of powder and number of grains is obtained from the loading data in the manual. I repeat: *maximum charges of powder should never be used by the beginning reloader*. Loads a grain or two under maximum will deliver almost as much velocity, and are safe to use. It's wise to remember that you're dealing with pressures up to 50,000 pounds per square inch or more; and that a difference of only a fraction of a grain over maximum will cause such pressures to skyrocket. The person who innocently decides to use a maximum load ("—surely a few grains more will make a better, faster load") is flirting with certain disaster.

Each powder charge, after being weighed, is funneled into an empty, primed case which is stood upright in the loading block.

When all the cases have been filled with powder, the bullets are seated. This is done with a second die, a part of the set, called a bullet seater. The seater is placed in the tool, the charged case is set into the shell holder, and a suitable bullet of the type, caliber, and weight recommended in the loading data is held on top of the case mouth. The tool's lever is again actuated, allowing the bullet and case to go into the die, which seats the bullet firmly inside the case neck.

In seating bullets, a good rule to follow is to seat any rifle bullet to approximately the depth of one bullet diameter. A .30-caliber bullet normally should be seated about .3 inch into the case neck.

With all bullets seated, the completed reloads are then taken from the loading block, wiped free of all oil, packed in cartridge cases, and labeled.

A good loading block, by the way, can be made with just a brace and bit and a 2- by 6-inch plank 18 inches long. Bore the plank in the pattern of a grid, with holes about 1 inch apart. A 5/8-inch bit is appropriate for .30-caliber cases, and all holes are bored nearly through—just to where the bit's point begins to protrude. Labeling should indicate the date and data of the load. For example: "May 5th, 1970. Speer 100-grain softpoint bullets. 47 grains #4831 powder. Winchester #120 primers. .257 Robers caliber. Seating depth .25 inch. Velocity 3,000 fs. Good antelope load."

Shells for handguns and shotguns are reloaded similarly, but with differences in dies and, with shotguns, somewhat altered steps in the process. Every good reloading tool will include detailed instructions for its operation.

Reloading for rifles will cut the cost about 50 percent. Shotgun reloading will cut the cost approximately 40 percent. To further reduce the cost, it is wise, as long as available supplies last, to use military surplus powders, available in bulk, which for hunting purposes are comparable to the commercial powders. Such powders currently cost a dollar per pound and under. Two of the finest are military powders #4895 and #4831.

When the beginning reloader reaches the point where he wants to reload faster, powder measures and turret-head reloading tools, as well as other specialized equipment, are all available. But the basic equipment described above will get him started.

Light Rifle Sling

Commercial rifle slings are usually too heavy for hunting, especially in mountain country. They are patterned after military slings designed for target shooting.

The hunting sling has two uses—to carry the rifle and to provide a quick, solid hold when shooting. The hasty sling is used in hunting, as against the arm-loop hold in target shooting. The hasty sling is assumed by thrusting the left

Light rifle sling made from latigo leather, riveted at fore-end swivel and laced at butt-stock swivel.

elbow (for right-handed shooters) downward through the space between rifle and sling at the bottom of the rifle, and placing the left hand around the forward portion of the sling and gripping the fore-end. Moving the hand backward produces tension and holds the sling tight. In that way, the sling helps hold the hunting rifle better in the off-hand, sitting, kneeling, and prone positions. The sling must be of proper length to do this.

Only a very light strap is needed to make a hasty sling. A length of latigo leather (meant for cinching a saddle) 1-inch width and 3¼ feet long is suitable. Or a length of 1-inch tanned buckskin may be used. A regular latigo strap may be cut to width if it's too wide.

To attach the front end of the sling to the rifle, fold it into the swivel from the outside, and fold it back 2 inches upon itself. Punch three holes of suitable size, in triangular form, through both sections of the strap. Rivet the strap together with three black rivets, the two-part type available at the 5-and-10.

If you can't stand the thought of metal rivets in a sling, you can lace the strap to itself with a length of leather thong or shoelace.

The lower end of the sling similarly goes through the lower swivel, then folds back over itself. Instead of riveting this end, lace it to fit your arm length. Punch a foot-long series of holes in the leather, approximately 3/16 inch from the edges and about 1½ inches apart.

Try the fit of the sling with a partner holding the lower end in place. A trial lacing will indicate whether the length is correct. It's wise to make the length about one hole too short at first since the leather will stretch somewhat.

I have a strap sling that was placed on a 7 mm rifle in 1941, and it still fits me today. That little rifle has taken deer, antelope, black bear, coyotes, and even elk over much of the western part of this continent.

The Rifle Scabbard

The stiff carbine-length military scabbards that are still available at surplus stores are unsuitable for sporting rifles. If you cannot find a scabbard to fit your rifle, have one custom made.

A scabbard for a scoped rifle should cover the rifle at least as far as the scope. Better ones cover the entire stock and fasten with some kind of flap or snap fastener at the butt end so that they may be undone quickly. The leather for a good scabbard should be stiff, but not exceptionally heavy. Otherwise the scabbard will pull too heavily on one side of the horse, causing galling, or otherwise crippling its back.

One position for a scabbard is on the right side, under the stirrup, pointing forward and down, with the butt high at the back of the saddle. When you dismount to shoot, you can grasp the butt over the horse's back as you swing down and to the left. The only trouble with this position is that the rifle may slip from the scabbard when you're riding up a steep hill.

A better way of carrying a scabbard is in the Northwest position. Here the scabbard rides on the horse's left side, beneath the skirt of the stirrup, with the butt forward and the muzzle down. In this position, the bolt is away from the horse, and the stock is easily grasped as you dismount on the left side. Also, when you spot game and neck-rein the horse, you are concealed by your mount as you pull the rifle from the scabbard—often avoiding frightening the game.

I have found that the best way to attach a scabbard to a stock saddle is to use a 2-foot strap with a 5/8-inch buckle at one end and holes at the other. To each of the straps encircling the front and rear of the scabbard—the scabbard loops—place a ¾-inch harness snap, obtainable at any hardware store. These snaps remain threaded into the loops at all times.

In use, the first strap and buckle is tied around the pommel of the saddle below the horn, through the opening in the saddle tree, and down around the left bulge. Twice

Method of attaching rifle scabbard to saddle in Northwest position.

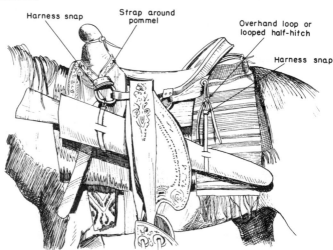

around is fine; then buckle down the strap tightly. This strap remains on the saddle for the entire trip. To put the scabbard on the saddle, the snap on the front scabbard loop is simply snapped through this strap around the pommel. The rear snap is then attached to a saddlestring, at proper height, at the rear of the saddle. To attach this snap, the leather saddlestring is looped with one half-hitch through the metal snap, and the loop pulled tight. There is little rifle weight on the rear loop, and such a string, pulled taut, will hold.

To remove the entire scabbard at night, or when leaving the horse to stalk game on foot, pull the rear saddlestring from its loop and unsnap the front buckle—a matter of five seconds. This type of attachment is also good in case of a fall.

The most important thing to remember about using a saddle scabbard is *never* to carry a chamber-loaded rifle. If there isn't time to chamber a cartridge after dismounting, there won't be time for a decent shot at game anyway.

Simple Duck and Goose Decoys

American Indians made simple waterfowl decoys of bunches of grass tied together to resemble sitting or feeding birds. To make them more natural, they often smeared mud on the bundles, giving them a mottled appearance similar to the female birds. After a bird was killed, it was set among the decoys with its head propped up in a natural pose. Today, waterfowl are more sophisticated and more natural-looking decoys are needed to bring them into range.

Simple decoys are easy to make. A stake silhouette decoy, made of ¼-inch plywood, can be painted to simulate either ducks or geese. Find a suitable picture of a live bird, either feeding or resting—the larger, the better. Such pictures can be found in most outdoor magazines or on calendars. Trace the bird on a piece of thin typing paper. Next mark a grid over the traced picture. For example, say that the picture is of a standing Canadian goose about 3 inches high. A good grid size would be about ¼-inch. To make the grid, rule off parallel lines with a pencil, horizontally and vertically, over the tracing. These may be numbered with letters in one direction, with numbers in another for later reference.

If you want the decoy to be 18 inches high, or about natural size, mark off a larger grid on the sheet of plywood from which the decoy is to be cut. The squares of this grid are proportionately larger. In this instance, the ratio of picture to decoy is 1 to 6, so each square will be 1½ inches.

Into each of the large squares on the plywood, draw the same line as in the corresponding square on the tracing. The result is a larger outline of the bird, in true proportions. Cut this out of the plywood sheet with a keyhole saw.

To paint the decoy, get some white paint and a tube of oil-black from a hardware store. The largest part of the goose will be a dull gray. Mix the color and paint the entire silhouette. Next paint the white areas with white paint, the black patches with black paint. With about three or four color mixtures, and some blending of the colors, plus a bit of dark daubing to resemble individual feathers, you can make a natural-looking goose. If you are more artistic, you can paint drakes and birds with more color.

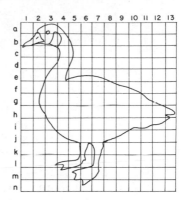

Draw decoy on paper ruled with a grid to aid in transferring the pattern to plywood.

There are two good ways to make stakes to hold the decoys in the water. One is to nail a length of wooden lath to the body, letting it extend 15 inches so that it resembles the leg of a bird, and sharpen the end. The other method is to use a wire stake. Bend a length of #10 galvanized wire into a short right angle at the top. Poke it through a small hole drilled through the decoy body about 5 inches from the bottom. To hold the wire in place, drive a small staple over the wire through the decoy. Or secure the wire stake with fine wire, wound through two pin-sized holes on either side of the stake. If a lath stake is used, it should be nailed to the body before painting, and then painted the color of a leg or as a part of the decoy.

Head decoys can be made from plywood and painted in the same way. Set the pointed lath stake at a slight angle off vertical to represent the bird's neck. Head decoys are very useful for attracting birds that feed in grain stubble that covers their bodies.

Estimating Bird Flocks

Have you ever wondered how many ducks or geese were passing overhead during migration time? There is a knack to estimating bird flocks with a fair degree of accuracy. As the flock flies by, quickly count a group of ten birds at one edge of the mass and make a mental picture of the space they occupy. Then superimpose that block on the rest of the flock and determine its number in multiples of ten. Even though individual birds change their position in a flock as they fly, this system is remarkably accurate. Just count the number of blocks and multiply by ten.

When counting geese flying in a wedge formation, there is time to simplify the blocking further. Count ten birds,

Estimate bird flocks by counting group of ten and visualizing number of blocks in the entire flock.

then get an image of a line of fifty birds, and superimpose this image on the entire migration.

You can estimate the number of elk, deer, or antelope in a herd with the same system ... taking a mental picture of ten animals and counting the number of blocks.

Blinds

Blinds are often necessary to allow a hunter to conceal himself from close-ranging birds. Such blinds take many forms, but they all should be made to blend with their surroundings by using natural materials. If such materials are not available, the blind should be constructed in advance to permit the game to become accustomed to it.

A good blind for waterfowl can be made from driftwood. Simply arrange a pile of driftwood along a river course where ducks pass so you can get inside it and huddle down. The less you alter the original pile, the better. Wear camouflage clothing to match the surroundings. With such a blind you will be indetectable to the wisest waterfowl.

Similar blinds can be made of down timber by crisscrossing lodgepole pines along deer trails and game runways. In the desert, blinds for hunting antelope can be made of sagebrush casually bunched into a covering at the edge of an alfalfa field where game habitually comes at daylight. The hunter gets there early and waits inside. I once used such a sagebrush blind to take closeup photos of "booming" sagegrouse. Some came within 20 feet.

During late fall along snowbound rivers, snow blinds are excellent for hunting geese and ducks. Snowdrifts at the water's edge, hollowed out to contain the hunter (who should wear white), provide good camouflage.

In the West, in bighorn sheep country, there are still the remains of rock cairns which the Indians built to hunt the wily animals. These cairns were made by piling up talus into a 3-foot "box" adjacent to a sheep trail. One or more hunters would wait, huddled inside a cairn, while others frightened bands of sheep from below. When the animals filed by, the hunters shot with bows and arrows. We once used this type of blind at the edge of a lake in lava country and took limits of ducks which skirted by, unable to detect us huddled inside the pile of rocks.

Camouflage clothing can be made easily and is one of the most effective blinds. In snow country, a bedsheet with a hole cut in the middle, worn like a poncho, is good camouflage. A large white handkerchief tied over your cap completes the deception. Another method is to use a 10-foot length of white cloth, 3 feet wide, with a hole cut in the exact center. Place the cloth over your head and tie the gaps at each side loosely together with cloth tapes sewed to the edges. This costume allows the arms enough freedom of movement for shooting.

I have found the best white costume for snow hunting to be a pair of white coveralls such as painters use, plus a white-covered hunting cap. If bought a size too large, such coveralls will conceal the hip boots ordinarily needed for waterfowl hunting. The garment should be bleach-washed in advance to take out the yellowish tint.

Camouflage garments are readily obtainable in mottled shades to match autumn foliage. Several yards of similar camouflage cloth can be carried along, worn as needed, or built into small hutlike blinds over brush framework. This kind of blind is particularly useful for varmint calling in desert areas where the location of the blind must be periodically changed.

A fine blind for goose and duck shooting in stubblefields is chicken wire stuffed with straw. Sit down and cover yourself with the "blanket"; you will resemble a small haystack. This blanket is also useful for pit-shooting in stubblefields. After digging a pit, cover the fresh earth with straw, lie down in the pit, and cover yourself with the straw blanket.

Perhaps the strangest blind of all was described to me recently by a Canadian friend who has learned how to outwit Canadian honkers in prairie stubblefields. He learned from long observation that his cattle and horses didn't frighten wild geese. So he cut from plywood a life-sized silhouette of a horse, painted one side, and attached a couple of hand-holds. When a flock of geese lands in his fields, he takes his shotgun and horse and wanders casually towards the resting birds. By taking only a step or so at a time, and artfully keeping the horse's painted side toward the geese, he can get within shooting range.

Hanging Heavy Deer

If you bag a heavy deer, and want to hang it to cool before getting it to camp, here are three practical methods:

Even if the deer weighs 300 pounds, you can hang it with three poles and a length of rope. The poles should be slender, about 7 or 8 feet long, trimmed of branches, and sharpened at the large ends. Lay the poles on the ground, with their tips together just above the dead deer's antlers and their butts extending outward like the spokes of a wheel. Lash the tips together, somewhat loosely so they won't bind later, and tie the end of the rope to the deer's antlers or head. Leave a foot or more of slack between the antlers and the poles.

Stand over the deer's head and lift his neck and head off the ground, raising the pole tripod enough so that the sharpened ends stick slightly into the dirt. Then push each pole, in succession, inward and upward, a little at a time. The tripod will gradually become erect, and the deer will hang off the ground to drain.

Tripod and pole for hanging a deer.

The second method of hanging a huge buck (or elk quarters) also requires a tripod. Before you erect it, tie a long, slender pole just under the lashing, about 3 feet from its large end. Tie a short nylon rope to this end of the pole, a longer piece to the other end, and drive a stake where the pole meets the ground.

Erect the tripod to full height so the sharpened ends of the three poles set firmly into the ground. Lift the buck's head as high as possible with one hand, at the same time bringing down the short end of the pole by the rope tied to its end with the other hand, and tie a half hitch around the antlers. Then pull on the hitch, holding what is gained, and bring the buck's head a couple of feet off the ground. Tie solidly. All that remains is to pull on the free rope at the pole's end, bring it down and tie it to the stake.

The third method is practical if a deer is killed on a hillside with trees. After cleaning the deer, drag it to a tree

Deer tied on uphill side of tree, allowed to swing to downhill side after branches have been cut.

and leave it on the uphill side. Lop off all branches on the uphill side, then tie the buck's antlers or head as high as possible off the ground. Next, cut off the branches on the downhill side so the carcass can swing freely. Shift the deer's body around the tree to the downhill side. Depending on the size of the deer, and the steepness of the hill, the carcass will swing freely. If it doesn't, tie a rope to one or both of the hind feet, pull it away from the hill, and tie the end to a bush or a stake.

Simple Game Hoist

A lone hunter can hang a heavy deer or elk quarters with nothing more than two small pulleys and a length of nylon cord.

The pulleys should be light, since they must be backpacked on the hunt. Two awning pulleys, about 2 inches long, of light metal, are strong enough to lift weights of up to 200 pounds and over. You also need a 30- to 50-foot length of 150-pound-test nylon rope.

To make the hoist, attach a yard of rope to the eye loop of each pulley. One rope will be tied to the deer's antlers, the other to a tree or tripod. Thread the remaining length through the pulleys, as shown in the illustration.

The leverage gained by this simple arrangement is 2 to 1. If you weigh 200 pounds, you therefore can lift a deer of well over 300 pounds. If you want to lift heavier loads, use pulleys with double blocks.

How to use two small pulleys as a game hoist.

Buttonholing a Deer

If you are hunting alone on horseback and kill a large mule deer, here is an easy way to bring it back to camp. After cleaning the deer, make an incision about 2 inches long just inside the meat of the belly at the point of the sternum. Then, using the game hoist previously described, lift the deer off the ground and lead the horse under it. Grab the deer by the legs and swing it across the saddle.

Insert the saddle horn in the incision. Tie the antlers back so they don't gouge the horse, and tie the legs on either side to the cinch rings. In tying the legs, it's best to cut slits just above the knee joints through which the ropes can be passed. Tie the ropes to the front of the cinch ring, otherwise the lashing tends to tip the ring into the horse and injure it. When leading the horse back to camp, avoid traveling through heavy brush that will catch the loaded animal on either side.

Packing Elk Quarters

The proper way to pack elk quarters out of the hills is to use a packhorse and packsaddle. However, if you are ever

Elk quarters packed on bareback horse.

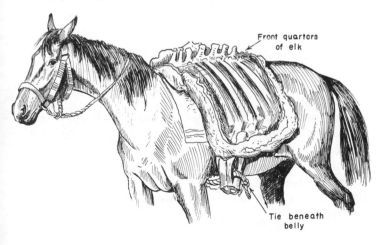

Front quarters of elk

Tie beneath belly

caught with an elk down and only a bareback horse or mule, you can pack half an elk with only a length of rope.

When dressing the elk, cut the carcass into halves instead of quarters—that is, leave the front and rear quarters together. Cut the meat and bone of all quarters through the dividing lines between them, but cut the skin only between the front and rear halves. This cut is made behind the third rib of the carcass. The result will be a set of front quarters and a set of rear quarters, with a skin hinge running the length of the halves.

Slip the halves onto the horse, hair side down, so that the right side of the elk rides on the left side of the horse. Cut slits above the knee joints on either side and tie the legs together at these points, running the rope under the horse's belly. Wrap a coat or shirt around the rope so it won't rub the horse.

Skidding and Travois

Besides packing, there are two ways of getting deer-sized game to camp. The carcass can either be skidded along the ground by two hunters or hauled by horse on an Indian-style travois.

The best way for two hunters to skid a big deer is with the aid of a sapling about 4 feet long and 2 to 3 inches in diameter. Cut holes in the deer's forelegs through the skin and between tendon and bone, just above the knee joints. Shove the sapling through these holes as the deer lies on its back. Tie the head, or antlers, between the forelegs against the sapling.

Each hunter takes an end of the sapling, lifts it till the deer's shoulders clear the ground, and walks away with the deer. Only the rear part at the hip bones will touch, and though this may rub off some hair, no meat will be damaged. I have helped drag deer like this for distances up to four miles without damage, on ground partially covered with snow.

If a horse is available, with harness only, a deer can be similarly dragged on snow without injury. It is dragged head forward. Always hitch the chain or rope to the deer's underjaw, never to the antlers. If the deer is antler-hitched, the tines will dig into earth and brush. Antelope can't be dragged this way because their hair will be rubbed off.

The Indians used a travois for skidding game to camp behind a horse. You can make a simple travois of two slender poles about 12 to 15 feet long. Tie the small end of

Using a sapling to skid a deer out of the woods.

each pole to the saddle rings above the cinch, allowing a short length to protrude so it won't pull out. Next lash a number of green saplings across the poles, far enough behind the horse to clear its hoofs, forming a simple platform. The deer is placed on this platform and tied down. When the horse is led toward camp, the butt ends of the two poles drag on the ground like runners. Use a martingale, or breast strap, with a stock saddle to prevent the saddle from being pulled back by the dragging poles.

Scalding Chicken or Grouse

Most hunters simply skin a grouse by cutting the skin at one leg, and tearing it off in strips until all skin is removed. The only cuts necessary are at the legs, the wingtips and front of the wings, and around the neck.

However, you may wish to pluck some species of upland birds, or exceptionally fat birds. The easiest way to do this is first to scald the bird. The feathers then come out with little effort.

Place the bird head first in a small bucket. In this position the hot water will go down against the base of the feathers. Boil enough water to cover the bird, and allow the water to cool for a couple of minutes. Then pour it over the bird, holding the legs and moving the bird in the bucket to get complete coverage. Swish the bird around until it is completely scalded. About two minutes are necessary for an average grouse, but a tough old bird takes longer. The right "scald" is at that point where all feathers become loosened, but before the bird becomes partially cooked. A freshly killed bird scalds easiest.

With the bird scalded, hold it by its feet and pull off the feathers in small tufts. (Pull the feathers toward the bird's head.) Singe off remaining pinfeathers with a lighted roll of newspaper.

Plucking Waterfowl with Paraffin

In a recent letter, Salmon River outfitter Don Smith told me how to pluck a duck or goose with paraffin:

"Get a 5-gallon can and put in 4 gallons of water. Bring the water to a boil, then shave in a couple of pounds of paraffin wax. When it melts, push the goose down through the paraffin. Hold it under like scalding a chicken. Then pull the goose slowly up through the hot paraffin. Let the

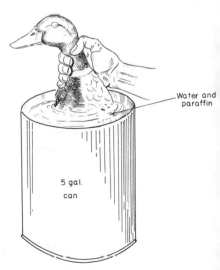

Waterfowl immersed in can of water and paraffin to remove feathers.

Water and paraffin

5 gal. can

goose drain over the can. Then head for the back door as fast as you can go, dripping only small amounts of paraffin on the kitchen floor. While the goose is cooling on the back porch, see if you can get the paraffin off the kitchen floor. After the goose cools, pull off the wax scab, and it is ready for the pot."

That's the basic technique, but here are a few suggestions.

It's easier to pull off bunches of the heaviest feathers before immersing the fowl into the water and paraffin. This leaves less area to pluck, and allows the melted wax to penetrate to the base of the feathers. Hold the duck or goose by the head or neck—there's less danger of scalding the hand. For a single bird, or a few small ducks, the proportion of water and wax may be retained but in smaller quantity—say, half as much solution. Finally, in warm weather (which is rare in duck season), the wax will cool quicker if the fowl is first dunked into a pail of cold water. The remaining pinfeathers can be removed by singeing with a lighted roll of newspaper.

Skinning Big Game for Trophies

If you want to make a wall trophy of a big-game animal you have killed, the worst mistake you can make is to rush up and stick the animal in the throat and cut off its head behind the ears. Good taxidermists can repair such field mistakes to some extent, but the trophy later will show "ropes" of bulging skin where these cuts have been made.

For deer, antelope, sheep, goat, caribou, elk, and moose, only two cuts in the skin are necessary to remove the cape in the field. The antlers or horns are later cut out as a "plate."

The first cut begins well back upon the animal's withers, and proceeds in a straight line up the center of the neck until a point between the ears is reached. From there a short cut is made to the base of each antler or horn, forming a Y in the neck cut.

The second cut begins at the withers, and proceeds down through the middle of one shoulder, around in front of that shoulder, well down below the brisket, and similarly up the opposite shoulder until the starting point is reached. In making this second cut, it is well to remember that "too much cape skin is just right." The taxidermist can cut off surplus skin far easier than he can locate skin to match a cape which is too short.

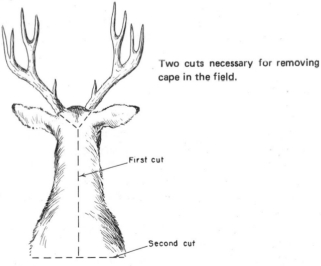

Two cuts necessary for removing cape in the field.

First cut

Second cut

From these two skin cuts, the neck and shoulders of the animal can be skinned out all the way to the medulla, or occipital protuberance. At this joint where head joins neck, the animal's head is then cut and twisted off, leaving the head inside the skin. In cool weather, or if the taxidermist can be reached within a few days, the head and cape will keep if it is salted well over the exposed flesh surfaces and inside the eye, ear, and nostril orbits.

If a taxidermist cannot be reached soon, it is necessary to skin out the head completely. This is done, without further cutting, by reversing the skin over the head as it is skinned away. Special care should be given to see that the ears are cut off very close to the skull, and that the lips and eyelids are not cut in any way. The caped skin should then be salted all over. The antler plate is now cut from the skull, as described in the next article.

Where even further delay is encountered, the ears must be skinned, or the skin covering them will slip. The ears are skinned by folding them wrong side out, and cutting delicately between the outside covering and the cartilage. After an ear is partly skinned, it is easier to finish if a mildly pointed stick is pushed up inside the folded ear. This brings the thin, delicate junction between ear skin and cartilage into position for separating it with the pointed blade. The ear must be skinned to its very tip.

It is only necessary to skin the outer side of each ear, leaving the cartilage integral with the inner side. A good salting of the skinned portion will keep it from spoiling. Many taxidermists leave the inside of the ears unskinned, and place the ear form between the outer ear skin and the cartilage.

Game animals which are not intended for head and shoulder mounts, but which are to be used as rugs or full skins, are field skinned in a different way. Here the entire skin is taken off with three cuts.

Place the animal on its back, and make the first cut lengthwise along the abdomen from anal vent to throat. At this point, you may either continue the cut up through the center of the chin or angle off to the corner of the mouth. With bear hides, the finishing cut to the mouth is preferable, since the seam that sews it up will show less.

The second cut begins at one hind foot, runs across to the base of the tail (just inside the thin skin of the inner hind leg), and across to the opposite hind foot.

Three cuts for skinning an animal for entire hide.

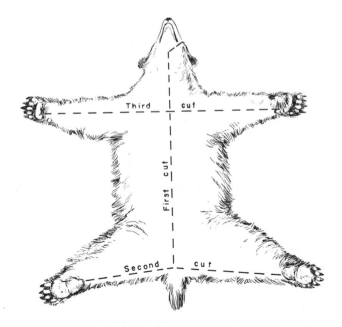

The third cut goes across the chest in a straight line from one front foot to the opposite front foot.

The four feet are either left integral with the skin, or the skin is girdled around each foot, leaving the feet with the carcass. With bear and other furred animals, the feet are normally left integral with the skin. When skinning a bear, first cut around the four foot-pads, but not the toepads, and then skin out each individual foot. Depending on the coolness of the weather, you can skin out all bones of the feet without making further cuts in the hide. This applies also to the animal's head. All flesh areas are then heavily salted.

Skinning Furred Animals

Smaller furred animals such as foxes, coyotes, and wolves often are used as full-hide trophies, but as cased hides to be hung on a wall instead of flat, rug-type mounts. The animal must be "cased" during field skinning.

To case a furred animal, make only one cut in the skin, from one hind foot across to the anal vent (just inside the thin, inner hair of the hind leg), and then across to the opposite hind foot. The hind feet are not girdled but cut off at the ankles, leaving the feet with the hide and the bones to be skinned out later. The tail is also left integral with the hide. (The technique for skinning the tail will be described later.) It is best not to cut the tail bone off at the base, at this point, since it is far easier to remove the entire bone from the tail skin if the bone is left on the carcass.

All skinning is done from this single cut in the skin between the hind feet. The skin is simply folded downward while the animal is suspended by its hind legs.

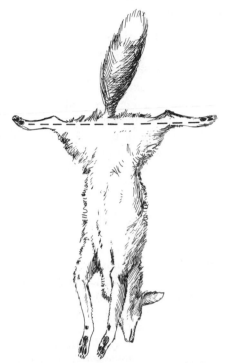

Single cut for skinning small, furred animals.

The forelegs are skinned down to the ankles, the bones of the leg severed, and the feet left inside the hide. The feet may be skinned later, usually by the taxidermist.

The head is skinned over the nose, care being taken not to cut the eyelids or lips. At the nose point, the nostrils are cut off where the gristly nose area joins the bony septum. This leaves the undamaged nostrils with the hide. All flesh areas are then heavily salted.

Skinning Birds

To prepare a game bird for mounting, the body must be removed from the skin, and the skin salted so it will keep until it reaches the taxidermist.

It is necessary to make two cuts in the skin. One goes from the anal vent up along the center of the belly line as far as the point of the breastbone. The other, shorter cut is made from the medulla of the bird down the center line at the back of the neck for a distance of 2 inches (for pheasants). These cuts are in heavily feathered areas and the subsequent seams necessary for sewing up the hide will not be visible in the mount.

The entire body of the bird is removed through these two cuts. The neck is cut, through the neck incision, and worked down into the body cavity. The legs are disjointed at the large end of the drumsticks, the meat pared away from the bones down to the junction of skin and lower legs, and the thigh bones left inside the bird's skin.

By carefully working the skin away from the body at the back and at the wing bases, the entire body can be removed through the belly incision. (After the wings are cut off at their bases.) All meat is removed from the skin, which is then heavily salted. Care should be taken to insure getting salt into the base of the skull, and the leg and wing areas. If a camp cooler is available, the skin may be wrapped in paper and kept in the cooler until the taxidermist can be reached.

How to Make an Indian Hide Frame

The Indians used a simple frame for stretching and fleshing hides. The frame was made just larger than the outside dimensions of the hide. The hide was placed inside and stitched to the frame with thong. With the hide roughly in place, the thong was tightened evenly, stretching the hide

Frame used by Indians for stretching and fleshing hides.

taut but not out of proportion. The frame was then stood on a slant in the shade. In desert regions, where wood was not available, the Indians pegged their hides to the ground.

The modern hunter could well use a hide frame for stretching his animal skins. Too often, he simply tosses his fresh deerskin over a pole and forgets it. The raw skin tends to curl at the edges and shrink. But if a deerskin is stitched to a frame soon after the kill, it will dry out quickly and remain in good condition until it is used for making wearing apparel or other articles.

Cutting Out the Antler Plate

Antlers or horns that are to be mounted on a wall plaque must be solidly attached to a section of the skull. This section is called the antler plate.

On some mounts, the skin of the animal is left on the antler plate; on others it is removed and the plate covered with velvet or other material. If you want to retain the skin, it must be cut away before cutting the skull.

The skull is cut with three separate incisions. One goes squarely across the back just above the medulla. The other two are made on each side so they join the first cut at the base of the skull, go down the face *through* the bony eye orbits, and join midway down the bone of the nose. Don't make the side cuts above the eye orbits. This will ruin the skull plate since the remaining section will not have the rigidity necessary for holding both antlers. Often an entire plate is broken by cutting in this fashion.

If the animal has been packed into camp, a saw is the best tool for this job. But for cutting out an antler plate

Two cuts for removing antler plate are shown here; the third goes across back of skull and joins the other two.

where the animal is dropped, a good ax will do. Hold the animal's head solidly, and keep cutting on the same lines until the bone is severed. Scrape away the remaining brain parts and take the antler plate to a taxidermist.

Skinning a Canine's Tail

In field dressing a coyote, fox, or wolf for mounting, the tail bone should be removed. Otherwise the tail will look unnatural. The best time to remove the tail bone is while skinning the animal, and the best tool to use is a length of willow or alder split lengthwise exactly through the center.

After making the cut in the skin from one hind foot to the opposite foot, the carcass should be skinned out for a few inches each way around the anus, the base of the tail, and the rump area. This makes room for working out the tail bone.

At this point, the skin of the tail is folded back over the tail itself and skinned all around with the sharp point of a small blade, much as in skinning out an ear. The folded-under fur of the tail will tend to bind it to the tail bone; and it is only possible to skin the tail, as it is folded over itself, for a few inches.

Next take the split stick and, with the boot toe held between the base of the tail and the skinned hide, place the halves on either side of the skinned tail, with their flat sides inwards. Grasp the sticks on either side of the tail bone, hold the toe firmly against the root of the tail, and pull, stripping the remaining skin from the tail bone. The tail bone will still be attached at its base, and the skin of the tail be left integral with the body skin. Finally, work salt into the tail opening.

Where willow branches are not available, a pair of pliers from a motor vehicle toolbox is a good substitute. Hold the tips of the jaws in one hand, the handles in the other, and pull hard against the folded skin at the base of the tail.

Keeping Meat in Hot Weather

Most big-game hunting seasons are timed for fall and cool weather, partly so meat can be kept without spoiling until it can be taken home. However, you will occasionally bag game during a period of hot weather, and unless you know how to take care of it, especially during the first critical hour, it will spoil.

Spoiled meat can be caused by animal heat, blowflies, or predators. To thwart animal heat, the game must be quickly dressed and the carcass cooled. This may be done either by quartering and hanging the carcass so that air circulates all around it, hastening the cooling process, or by using a substitute which will accomplish the same purpose. This applies to the larger game animals such as elk, moose, and caribou. Deer-sized game may be cooled without quartering, unless the weather is extremely warm.

A light game hoist, mentioned before, is suitable for hanging a carcass. Often, though, a large game animal will be killed away from timber, in an area where there are no suitable trees for hanging the quarters. In such instances, the meat may be quickly cooled if a can of black pepper and a brushpile are available.

First, dress the animal, being careful not to allow any intestinal fluid or urine to touch the meat, as they will taint it. Next, quarter the carcass. This hastens cooling and makes it easier to handle.

With the animal dressed, the next important step is to smear fresh blood over every part of the exposed flesh, being careful to coat those areas where skin meets flesh. If the animal's fresh blood cannot be saved for this purpose, in a small puddle, then it's best to smear all available flesh areas while the liquid blood is in the chest cavity, after dressing and before the final quartering. The meat areas remaining from the quartering may then be smeared with liquid blood before it coagulates.

Smearing the flesh areas with blood will cause a glaze, or seal, over the flesh, which will protect it against blowflies. In order for blowflies to lay their eggs, and for the eggs to turn to maggots and ruin the meat, the insects must have both warmth and moisture. The blood glaze will occur quickly, especially in hot sunlight, forming a seal against the blowflies and cooling the flesh.

Parts of the meat that cannot be covered with blood can be sealed by sprinkling the moist flesh areas heavily with black pepper. This will dry up flesh rapidly. A half-pound can is sufficient for four elk quarters. Black pepper on the flesh surfaces will not harm the flavor of the meat.

Next comes some real effort. From available foliage make a huge brushpile, large enough to accommodate all four quarters of the carcass without piling them on top of each other. More important, it must be bulky enough so that, when compressed by the quarters, it will stand about 18 inches high. This will allow the air to circulate completely around the quarters, accomplishing the same purpose as hanging the quarters by allowing animal heat to escape from all surfaces. For it is animal heat, not weather, which spoils game meat.

Finally, with the quarters glazed with blood, dried with pepper, and resting on the brushpile, place a light covering of loose twigs on the top side of the meat so that magpies, eagles, and other predators cannot peck at the flesh. Coyotes, incidentally, won't touch it for at least twenty-four hours, unless storm washes out the man scent.

Deer-sized game can be cooled on a brushpile and left unquartered if it can be handled by the lone hunter. For a large deer killed in warm weather, if the head is not to be saved for a trophy, it is best just to open up the body by cutting through the sternum at the rib cage and split the backbone so that the entire carcass can be laid flat with the hide side down.

After the carcass has been placed to cool on the brush-pile, hurry to camp for help and get it back and hang it. The meat will be set up by then, and can be moved without damage.

By-Products of the Hunt

Tanned animal hides can be used as throws for the back of a divan or as wall decorations. They can be made into vests, coats, fringed shirts, or gloves. Numerous leather-working firms which advertise in outdoor magazines will make garments from deer, elk, and moose skins.

Various uses can be found for the feet of game animals. A pair of ram or antelope feet mounted on a plaque makes a fine rack for holding a rifle on the wall. Save the forefeet of the animal by cutting them off at the knees and take them to a taxidermist.

The feet of large game animals can be made into attractive ash trays. Elephant feet make unusual ashtray stands for a trophy room; those of smaller animals are suitable for desk ash trays.

The forefeet of grizzly and brown bears can be transformed into bookends. Skin the legs from the knee joints. The feet can be left for the taxidermist. To skin the feet yourself, simply make a cut down the back of the foreleg and completely around the pad.

Sections of deer or elk antlers make fine handles for hunting knives. Several knife makers now furnish blades and tangs for the do-it-yourselfer who wants to make his own hunting knife. A thin slice of elk antler with a small hole bored in one side serves as a rustic key ring. Thread the key chain through the hole, and burn or paint your name and address in the center.

Elk teeth, which are the only pure ivory found in North America, are suitable for tie clasps. Persuade a jeweler to set a pair into a gold cap and you'll have a handsome souvenir of the hunt. Likewise, the "eyes" of elk teeth can be turned into a pair of earrings.

Ivory teeth are found only at the back of the elk's upper jaw—the teeth on the lower jaw are all calcium. Many hunters fail to remove these teeth from the skull because they don't know how or believe that special tools are required. Actually the only tools you need are your hunting knife and a couple of sticks.

First, with the point of the knife cut between the tooth and the jawbone completely around the tooth. These cuts should be made as deeply as possible, but without prying with the blade (it is apt to snap off). Just insert the tip of the blade at the outside of the tooth, then strike the butt of the knife's handle with the palm of the hand. Dig between tooth and jaw to a depth of about a half inch around each tooth.

Next, find two sticks, a heavy one to use as a hammer and a smaller one for a tool.

The tool should be about a foot long and 1½ inches in diameter. A dry spruce limb broken from a nearby tree is excellent—touch but brittle—and will snap off squarely. (A wooden tool is preferable to a pair of pliers, since the metal often scars the enamel.) The "hammer" can be a heavy piece of wood, or even a rock, weighing a pound or more.

Hold the tool firmly against the front part of the ivory tooth—that is, the edge nearest the animal's nose—and hit it sharply with the hammer. One sharp blow will dislodge the tooth without damaging it. Whittle the remaining flesh off the root area with a pocketknife, and the tooth is ready to be made into an ornament.

The brown "eye" of the tooth is the valuable part, and its depth depends on the age and condition of the elk. But to deepen the brown of the eye, and impart a deep brownish luster to the tooth, all that is necessary is to place the tooth into the canvas pocket of a pair of jeans, add a spoonful of unused coffee grounds, and keep it there for a couple of weeks. This will impart a beautiful brown polish to the ivory.

Bear Fat for Boots

The hunter who bags a bear, either black or grizzly, has the makings of a fine boot conditioner—the fat that coats the bruin during the autumn hunting season. Bear fat will not only make leather boots far softer than many boot greases, but will to some degree waterproof the boots.

Perhaps the best time to apply bear fat to boots is just after the animal has been killed and skinned. Simply rub the boots on the fat remaining on the carcass or the skin.

To keep bear fat for future use, it is necessary to render the fat and store it in a cool place. Chunks of fat can be rendered in a skillet or even a tin can at camp, and the melted oil allowed to set in a can or jar. Do not add salt as it will damage leather. At home it can be kept in cold storage, or in an outside building during winter months. It sets up as a pure white lard. I know several mountain men who use the lard from a fat, young black bear for cooking.

How Indians Made Arrowheads

Arrowheads were usually made of flint or obsidian, rocks that chip or flake easily when worked with an abrasive tool. Indian camps were often located in areas where there was an abundance of these rocks.

To make an arrowhead from a large piece of obsidian, a small piece was broken off by striking it a glancing, oblique blow with a rock. If the obsidian was hit at the center, it would split or shatter. Obsidian tends to "shear" when struck in this way, and a thin slice usually comes off the main piece. The slice may be broken further with judicious strokes of the rock. Of course, when metal became available to the Indians, they used it for breaking obsidian.

When a thin, elliptical piece of obsidian was broken off, it was chipped into an arrowhead with a tine of deer antler. The tine was squared at the point, and after a little use became rough enough to catch the edge of the obsidian. The arrowhead was folded in a piece of buckskin to prevent injuring the hand and to enable the worker to hold the piece solidly on his knee.

By working on one side of the edge, then on the opposite side, the arrowhead could be shaped and thinned as desired. Notches were chipped at the base of the head for binding it to the shaft.

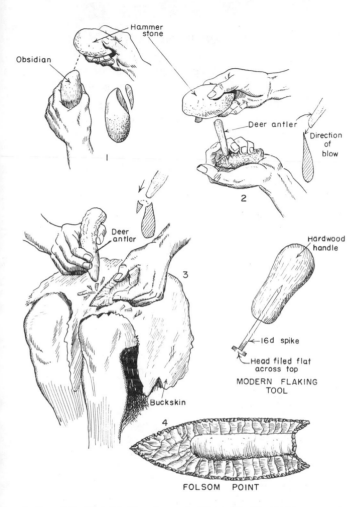

Hammer stone

Obsidian

1

Deer antler

Direction of blow

2

Deer antler

3

Hardwood handle

16d spike

Head filed flat across top

MODERN FLAKING TOOL

Buckskin

4

FOLSOM POINT

Indian chipped small piece from obsidian with stone hammer (1). With small length of deer antler, he chipped large flakes, forming the basic shape of the arrowhead (2). He completed the job with a large antler tool (the larger the antler, the finer the flake), putting a sharp edge on the arrowhead by fine flaking (3). Finished Folsom point (4) shows fine flaking along edges, large flakes on total surface. Groove to fit shaft was knocked out with blow on either side.

Arrowheads can be made today in the same way, but a better tool than a deer antler is a 16d spike embedded in a piece of hardwood. Cut off the point of the spike, leaving a 3½-inch shank, and insert it in a hole drilled in a small piece of hardwood. File the surface of the head of the spike so that it is flat. After a little use, the head will become rough enough to bite well in chipping the obsidian. Be sure to hold the head in a piece of leather so it won't slip, and be careful that the hand holding the tool doesn't slip against the sharp edge of the stone.

20

Fishing How-To

Emergency Fishing Kit

A wilderness fishing kit for emergencies must be portable enough to be carried on your person, otherwise you're apt to leave it at home. A simple kit consisting of four items will catch fish in the wilderness.

1. Dozen fly hooks.
2. Ten-yard roll of monofilament fishing line.
3. Small bobbin of silk thread.
4. Six paper clips.

The twelve hooks should be of assorted sizes, ranging from #12 to #4. They should be of the wet-fly type, and of good quality. The majority of hooks should be of average size, #6, #8, #10.

To the sophisticated angler, casting into his home stream with expensive equipment, this may not seem to be much of a fishing outfit, but I have used these items to catch fish in wilderness country.

Our remaining wilderness areas are remote areas, and the fish there are unused to anglers and generally easy to catch. Also, in most North American wilderness areas grayling will be found, and this species is particularly easy to catch. I have caught numerous grayling, up to 16 inches long, using only emergency tackle.

The monofilament can either be attached to the end of a springy branch or used as a handline. A better rod can be made by bending the paper clips into guides and lashing them to the branch with the silk thread, as explained in a later article.

If worms or other bait cannot be found, the thread is also used to tie emergency flies. Full instructions for tying flies in the wilderness are given in the next article.

Half a dozen wooden matches, paraffin dipped to be waterproof, should be included to start a fire for cooking the fish.

The entire kit will fit into a plastic envelope, which should be sealed tightly with plastic tape. If it is sewed into the pocket of your fishing jacket, you'll be sure not to leave it behind when you venture into remote areas.

Tying Emergency Flies

I once proved to a group of skeptics that it was possible to catch fish with emergency flies tied with materials found on the spot. We were on Tanada Lake, in Alaska. The first fly was made with some hair cut from my chest and a wormlike strip of blue wool from my shirttail. The second was tied from a tuft of my wife's hair and a tiny strip of silver foil from the wrapping of a roll of film. The third fly was made from a single bald-eagle feather found along the shore.

These flies were all tied without a fly vise, bobbin, pliers, head varnish, wax, or any equipment save the bare hooks. The hooks were held in the hand while the flies were tied.

The first two flies were tied in this manner: The thread was tied into the hook's eye and wound spirally down to the shank where it was half-hitched. A few hair fibers were tied on for a tail, and held by two more half-hitches. The shirttail "body" (or foil strip) was tied at the rear and

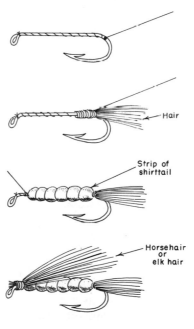

Four steps in tying emergency fly with strip of shirttail and animal hair.

Hair

Strip of shirttail

Horsehair or elk hair

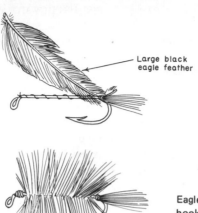

Large black
eagle feather

Eagle feather wound on hook shank to create Palmer-type fly.

wound on to the head of the hook. The thread was similarly wound on spirally to the same point where it was secured by more half-hitches. Lastly, the hairs used as a streamer were wound on at the head. Four or five half-hitches just behind the hook's eye completed the job.

The third fly was made using only a hook, thread, and the black eagle feather. Several fibers from the quill end of the feather were bound on for a tail. The tip was then tied at the shank, and wound spirally up the length of the hook, Palmer fashion, and secured at the head. A "head" was wrapped on with several turns of the thread, and several half-hitches finished the job.

With these three flies, four people, taking turns with a fly rod, caught over a dozen grayling weighing up to 1½ pounds. Every fly caught fish, and not one of the crude patterns was worn out.

Tying Flies at Camp

If you have more equipment and materials, you can of course tie better flies. Remember that fish will take flies that attract but do not resemble natural insects. This is especially true of backcountry fish, unused to contact with fishermen.

A pair of pliers, held by your partner, will serve as a fly vise. Lacking pliers, you can sharpen the point of a stick and cut a slit in the tip in which the hook's point is held.

Fly tails can be made of horsehair, squirrel hair, hemp fibers, or yarn from a sweater. Material for fly bodies includes strips of cloth or yarn, hair of a muskrat, squirrel, badger, deer, elk, moose, bear, or pet dog. Even human hair is usable. A rubber band wound spirally in several layers along the shank makes an effective fly body. Strands of burlap from a potato sack make one of the most natural-looking fly bodies imaginable. Grouse, ptarmigan, or sage-hen feathers, bunched together and wound on in the shape of an insect body, are all useful. The main thing in dressing bodies on flies is to make them somewhat elongated, elliptical, and the size of insect bodies.

Hackle is meant to simulate the insect's legs. If feathers are available, one can be wound on at the head. But when no feathers are available, the best thing to do is wind on a streamer. Streamers can be made from bundles of animal hair or from feathers from the shoulder area of large upland birds. If you can find waterfowl feathers, or even the primary feathers of magpies or crows, you have good material for streamers.

A third type of emergency fly—a nymph—can be made of skimpy materials; for example, a bunch of belly hair from a muskrat. Hold a small bunch of hairs between thumb and forefinger and bind them to the shank with spiral turns of thread. Leave a few hairs sticking out at both front and back to resemble tail and feelers.

A hardback nymph can be tied of the same material, with the addition of a small bunch of hair from a squirrel tail, elk, deer, or horse. Tie on the hairs before wrapping on the body so they protrude an inch behind the hook. After tying on the body hair double all but a few of the tail hairs over the nymph's back and tie down at the head. The few hairs sticking out in front simulate the feelers.

Painting Metal Lures

For some reason, fish will strike a lure of one color on one day but will shun it on another. I have found this to be true of cutthroat trout on the Snake River. One day they'll hit a plain brass wobbler, the next day they won't. But if I

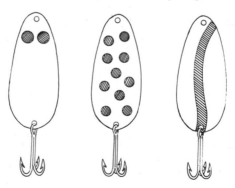

Suggested patterns for painting metal lures.

painted a pair of black eyes on the wobbler they'll hit it. Sometimes a pair of red eyes, or a red stripe, makes them hit.

To add these color variations to lures, I keep a few bottles of fingernail polish in my tackle box. The best colors are red, black, and orange. With these colors I have often changed an unproductive lure into a "taker."

Some of the designs I've found to be effective are a pair of eyes, a stippling of black dots, or a single wavering red stripe running the length of the lure. If the experiment proves unsuccessful, it's easy to scrape off the polish with a knife and try again.

Emergency Landing Net

If you damage your landing net while on an extended fishing trip, or even forget it at home, it's possible to make one from cord or old fishing line. Use the original frame if it's available; otherwise make a new one by bending a long, slender willow into a loop and tying it in place. The loop formed may not be symmetrical, but this won't detract from the utility of the net.

Next cut a number of 6-foot lengths of cord. Double each length at the center and attach it to the loop, as shown in the drawing. These double lengths should be spaced about 2 inches apart.

To weave the cords into a net, tie each of the adjacent cords of a pair, about 2 inches from the frame, with an overhand knot. After you have completed one row of knots there should be a series of half diamonds around the

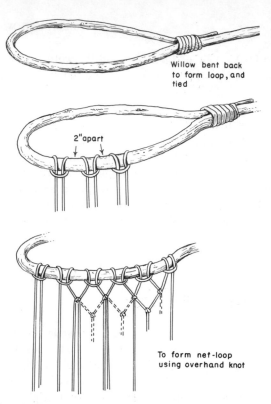

Willow bent back
to form loop, and
tied

2"apart

To form net-loop
using overhand knot

Improvising a landing net from a willow and string.

frame. To finish, continue tying the adjacent cords until you reach the ends.

As the tying progresses downward, the lengths forming the diamonds are minutely shortened, tapering the net. When the cords are used up, or when the desired length is reached, tie them together at the bottom.

When only a portion of an original net is damaged, new cords should be tied around the loop only at that section. The cords are then tied to the ends of the original net.

Tying Tapered Leaders

The advent of nylon monofilament has made it possible to tie your own tapered leaders. You can use spools of monofilament specially made for leaders, or lengths of old spinning lines. One of the most useful leaders for trout fishing tapers from an average diameter of 8-pound test down to 3-pound test. This 6-foot leader will handle large trout, and the tippet will accommodate flies down to a #12. The average trout angler can't handle much more than 7½ feet of leader, especially with big trout in fast water.

Blood knot for tying tapered leader.

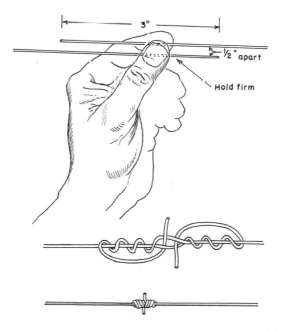

One problem in landing fish in heavy water with a long leader is that the knot joining leader and line will usually run up through the tip guide during the landing process and stick.

To tie this leader, use four tests of nylon monofilament: 8 pound, 6 pound, 4 pound, and 3 pound. In choosing this material, pay as much attention to the diameter of the material as to the listed strength. In many cases, 8-pound-test material will be the same diameter as 6-pound test. The basic idea in any tapered leader is to create an extension of the tapered line itself, down to a fine tippet which will allow the line and leader to cast the fly smoothly.

Cut a length 20 inches long of each of the four grades of monofilament. Start with the length of 8-pound test and join it to the length of 6-pound test with the blood, or barrel, knot. To tie this knot, lay the two strands of material side by side, a half-inch apart and overlapping about 3 inches. Next, with the thumb and forefinger of the left hand, grasp the two strands at the center of the overlap and hold them apart. This creates a space between the two strands which is held during the knot tying.

Wind the end of the leader at the left of the fingers three times around the strand next to it and poke it *downward* through the space temporarily held between thumb and forefinger. Then wind the end of leader to the right of the fingers three times around the other length, and poke it *upward* through the space. Finally, pull on both ends of the two lengths of leader until the knot forms and jams tight. The result will be a tiny knot with an end sticking out on opposite sides. These are clipped off just a trifle longer than flush.

With the same knot, tie the 6-pound and 4-pound lengths, and then the 3-pound tippet. After all knots are tied, pull the leader taut for a moment or so to straighten it.

Dropper Loop

A level leader is not as delicate as a tapered leader but it's adequate for fishing bait or large wet flies. Generally a 3-foot level leader is sufficient. Anything longer will be difficult to cast.

When fishing with a level leader, you may want to tie on a dropper to fish a brace of wet flies or a combination of fly and bait. Here are two simple ways to do it:

1. Lay a length of monofilament for the dropper alongside the main leader at its midpoint. About 8-pound test is right, to give the dropper the stiffness needed to keep it from winding around the leader. Grasp the dropper and

Tying a dropper on a level leader. When loop is cut at point shown, it unfolds and becomes dropper.

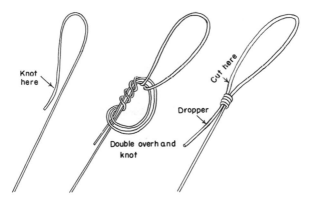

Knot here

Cut here

Dropper

Double overhand knot

the leader and tie them together with a double overhand knot. Clip off the surplus end of the dropper, leaving a single length of monofilament running parallel to the leader.

2. At a point about 12 inches from the end, double the leader back upon itself and grasp the two strands halfway up. Tie a double overhand knot at this point. Then clip the leader just below the knot, allowing the loop to unfold into a new length, with the short piece above the knot becoming the dropper.

Splicing a Fly Line

To repair a broken fly line on an extended fishing trip, or to tie on a line of smaller diameter to replace a ruined taper, you must be able to splice. A knot of any type joining the two segments is intolerable since it will not feed through the guides of the fly rod. A simple splice can be made in a few minutes with a sharp knife and a yard of silk thread.

How to splice a fly line.

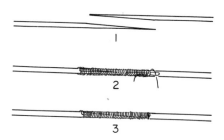

Lay each end of the two segments to be joined on a flat board. Sharpen the knife to a razor-like edge. One inch from the line's end make a diagonal cut, tapering the line from its full diameter to a point. Take care that the line does not roll while you make this cut as this will spoil the finished splice. Cut the end of the other line in the same way. When the two tapered ends are laid together, the line will retain its original diameter along the length to be spliced.

The splice is made by "whipping" the two ends with the silk thread. Begin by laying a few inches of thread along the splice; then a fraction of an inch above the taper, start to wind the line around the two ends, over the length of thread which has been laid along them. Each turn must be tightly wrapped next to its predecessor, with as much tension as the thread will withstand without breaking. Should the line break, it's best to start over.

When a half inch has been wound, the protruding thread end may be pulled under the winding so that it will not show. Continue winding until a point just beyond the cut ends is reached, as this will tend to smooth the splice. Finish the splice by folding the running end of the thread back over the part which has been wound, so that all further windings will be made upon it. When the winding is finished, carefully pull the free end of the thread, taking up all the remaining thread that has not been used. You'll find that this surplus can all be pulled up between the windings. The extra is cut off close to the winding.

If you have some fly varnish, lacquer, or even fingernail polish at camp, coat the splice with it, work it in with the fingers, coat again, and allow to dry.

When thoroughly dry, the line will cast freely through the guides of the rod. There will be a slight bump in the line, but this won't matter if the trout are biting.

Weighing a Fish with a String

Have you ever caught a big fish and wanted to weigh it on the spot? If you don't have a scale along, you can still determine the weight of your catch with only a piece of string and a stick. The stick should be about 18 inches long and uniform in diameter. Cut a small notch about 1 inch from each end. Tie a length of string at each notch. Now tie the end of one string to the fish's jaw. At the end of the other string tie some object of known weight—a boot, a pound of bacon, a can of beans. Tie a third length of string to the middle of the stick with a slip knot. You have now fashioned a crude steelyard with which it is possible to weigh the fish.

Holding the middle string in one hand, lift the stick off the ground so the fish and weight dangle freely. By sliding the string along the stick, find the fulcrum—the point where both objects balance. Mark the fulcrum on the stick and measure the distance from this point to each side string, or notch.

If you don't have a rule or tape, break off a small piece of twig about 1 inch long and use it to measure in "units." The twig need not be exactly an inch in length as long as it is used for all measuring.

The formula for calculating the weight of the fish is: $1 \times A = B \times 2$. As shown in the drawing, 1 = weight of object; 2 = weight of fish; A = distance from fulcrum

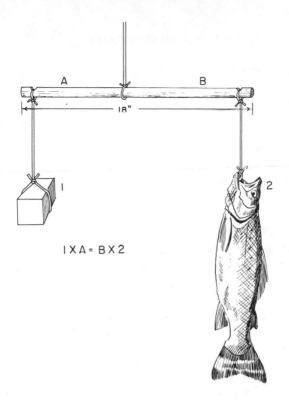

$I \times A = B \times 2$

Crude scale of stick, string, and object of known weight.

to notch on object's side; B = distance from fulcrum to notch on fish's side.

For example, suppose you are using an object that weighs 2 pounds. The distance from the fulcrum to the string supporting the object is 4½ inches, or units. The distance from the fulcrum to the string supporting the fish is 7 inches, or units. Therefore, $2 \times 4½ = 7 \times B$, or $7B = 9$. (B equals the unknown weight of the fish.) Answer: 1-2/7 pounds, or 1 pound, 4-4/7 ounces.

Measuring a Fish with Your Hand

In early times, the human hand was used as a unit of measurement. During the settlement of the West, the size of a horse was determined by how many "hands high" it was at the withers. The hand is still useful in field measuring fish, antlers, or game.

The average adult hand measures approximately 6 inches wide across the palm—from the fleshy outside at its greatest width below the little finger, to the tip of the thumb. Thus six "hands" would be equivalent to a yard.

To measure smaller distances, lay a grass stalk, leaf, or string across the hand and fold it in the middle. This gives you a 3-inch measuring stick. Fold it again and an inch and a half can be marked off.

With practice, you can measure smaller distances simply by placing the finger of the other hand into the palm. A finger in the center will show 3 inches on either side. This distance, either measured again by the finger into three parts, or just visually marked off, will serve as a gauge for small measurements.

Cleaning Fish

Game fish should be cleaned soon after being caught, otherwise the blood lying against the backbone tends to deteriorate, causing spoilage at this point first. The method of cleaning most small game fish is as follows:

If the fish has noticeable scales, remove these first by holding the fish at the tail and scraping toward the head with a knife or fish scaler. Then remove the entrails by

Two cuts for cleaning a fish. Ventral cut is shown by dotted line. Knife cuts forward to sever gill coverings from jawbone.

making two cuts. One is a straight incision running from the anal vent almost to the tip of the lower jaw. At the point where this cut terminates well up through the gill coverings, make a second crosswise cut. Just behind the V of the lower jaw tip the outer gill coverings end in a thin membrane, also V shaped, joining the gill coverings to the lower jaw. Push the knife tip through this thin membrane on one side, under the pointed tip of the gill coverings, and out the opposite side—with the edge of the knife toward the head of the fish. Then cut the remaining V-tip

627

of the gill coverings from the jawbone itself. Hold the tip of the gill coverings, which has been severed from the lower jaw, tightly between thumb and forefinger of one hand, and with the other hand grasp the fish by the lower jaw. Now separate the two sections, pulling the gills downward. In most cases, a continuous stripping motion will pull all the gills and entrails from the fish. The only part that tends to stick is that small area where the gills join the back at the fish's neck. Often it is necessary to pinch this area so the gills break free of the backbone.

With the entrails stripped away, remove the layer of blood lying against the fish's spine. Two or three strokes with the thumbnail will usually push this blood out, especially if it's rinsed with water. Then cut a small V across the anus and remove it. The fish is now ready for cooking, with the head and outer gill covering integral with the body.

For larger fish like salmon and steelhead, the procedure is the same except that a bit of cutting is necessary at the point where the top of the gills join the backbone. Usually this will not break away with a pull. Also, to remove the blood at the spine, it is necessary to sever the membrane on either side of the layer of blood, then scrape the blood away. A good tool for doing this with king salmon and large steelhead is a metal teaspoon.

Keeping Fish Cool

Freshly caught fish will deteriorate, soften, and spoil within a matter of hours unless some provision is made for keeping them cool. Cleaning fish soon after they are caught will delay this spoilage somewhat, but more should be done. The best way to prevent spoilage is to place the cleaned fish in an ice cooler. During early spring fishing, a snowbank is a natural ice box. Otherwise cleaned fish can be kept moderately cool by placing them on a layer of grass or moss in the creel. If the grass is kept slightly damp, by periodically sprinkling it with a handful of water, cooling will take place by evaporation.

An 18-inch square of burlap makes a good creel cooler. Wipe the dressed fish free of slime, fold them individually into the burlap, and put them in the creel. Sprinkle them every hour or so with a handful of water from the creek.

Besides helping to keep fish cool, burlap has another fine virtue as a creel liner. Much of the odor of dead fish comes from the slime. Burlap will collect most of the slime so that it does not permeate the willows of the creel. The burlap can be washed at home. To further avoid fish odor in a creel, give it heavy coats of varnish each season, on the inside as well as the outside.

If fish must be kept at camp for several hours, in hot weather, burlap can be used to keep fish fresh. Fold the fish separately in the burlap and tie the bundle. Hang it on the shady side of a big tree, near a stream if possible, where a breeze will strike it. Evaporation will keep the fish cool if the burlap is kept lightly moistened.

With the addition of a large tin can, you can make a better cooler. After wrapping and tying the fish in the burlap, punch a very small hole in the center of the can's bottom and thread the can, with the open end up, on the cord. Hang the bundle of fish by the cord, with the can just above. Fill the can with water. The slow seepage of water down the cord through the hole in the can will keep the burlap moistened and cool the fish. If the hole is small enough, the can of water will last for hours.

One last tip: If fish are dressed, wiped dry, wrapped in ordinary newspaper, and buried in moist ground near the water's edge, they will keep cool for hours.

Making Sinkers

Sinkers are used to get a lure down to the proper depth. They are available in great variety, and are so inexpensive that there is ordinarily no need to make your own. But in emergencies, or when commercial ones won't do a particular job, you can improvise sinkers from a variety of materials.

A tiny, irregularly shaped rock will make a temporary sinker if the leader can be tied to it without slipping. Attach it to the line about 18 inches above the bait or lure, or on a dropper, so it doesn't frighten the fish.

During my boyhood fishing days, I caught many trout by double half-hitching a simple shingle-nail onto a speckled ten-cent fishing line. A paper clip, part of the emergency fishing-kit, can be bent into a tiny roll and suspended from a dropper leader. A .22 or larger bullet, cut deeply with a knife and then squeezed around the leader, makes an adequate sinker. Similarly, BB shot from an air rifle, or pellets from an air gun, make good sinkers. Even a short length of wire will do in a pinch. Often, lacking a cutting tool as well as a sinker, I have cut a piece of wire simply by pounding it between two rocks.

Sometimes commercial sinkers are inadequate in certain situations. As an example, steelhead in Idaho's Salmon

Special sinker for fishing deep in rocky rivers.

River must be fished deep, and the bottom is practically all rocks. This means that a lot of terminal tackle is lost. An angler I know partially solved the problem by developing a sinker with a special shape. It is made from flat sheet lead, approximately 1/16 inch thick, 3/8 inch wide, and 2 inches long. The ends were tapered by cutting ½ inch off one corner. A tiny hole was bored in one end and a snap swivel attached to allow the sinker to drift along the bottom without twisting.

The sinker is attached to the end of the monofilament line, with the lure attached to a dropper 18 inches up. The sinker is allowed to bump along the river's bottom, with the baited hook above the rocks where there is less danger of snagging. The thin sinker wiggles through most of the crevices without snagging.

Similar long, but round, sinkers can easily be made by cutting off lengths of lead wire—the kind bulletmakers use for the cores of small-diameter bullets—flattening one end and punching a hole in it, and either attaching a snap swivel or threading the sinker on the dropper.

If you really like to tinker, molds are available with which you can cast your own sinkers. Or you can make molds in any shape from hardwood and pour in molten lead.

Replacing Guides

Guides on fishing rods occasionally come off and have to be replaced. If this occurs during a fishing trip, a temporary

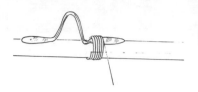

Method of winding thread
to replace a rod guide.

replacement job can be done with a yard or so of silk
thread.

To fix a guide that has become loosened, cut off all the
thread windings on both sides rather than try to wrap over
them. Then lay the guide in position and hold it in place
with the left hand.

Wind the thread around the guide and rod so the end is
beneath the turns, as shown in the drawing.

After sufficient turns have been made to bind the thread
so it won't unwrap, revolve the rod with the left hand,
holding the thread taut with the right. Continue winding
past the end of the guide's foot and onto the rod.

To secure the wrap, lay a 3-inch length of thread,
doubled, on the wrap before making the last few windings,
as in the drawing. The windings should cover this doubled
thread almost to the loop. Then pass the end of the winding
thread through the loop, and pull the two ends of the
doubled thread under the wrap, burying the winding
end. Snip off the ends and wrap the other foot of the
guide. Coat the finished wrap with fly varnish, lacquer, or

fingernail polish, if available. Otherwise, the wrap will hold until you get home to apply the varnish.

Replacing a Tip Guide

If the tip guide of a fishing rod comes off, the proper way to replace it is to scrape away all cement on the rod tip, smear the tip with ferrule cement, and replace the guide. Allow to dry before using the rod.

If ferrule cement is not available, you can secure the tip for the duration of a fishing trip by doubling a small length of silk thread over the tip of the rod end and pushing the guide back on. The added thickness of the thread will hold the tip in place.

If the guide is damaged and unuseable, a temporary guide can be made from an ordinary paper clip. Straighten the soft wire of the clip, but leave one of the original bends, forming an eye with two legs. Bend the eye slightly forward. Place the guide in position with the legs under the rod tip, and wrap it in place with silk thread in the same way as in wrapping a guide (*which see*). Coat the finished wrap with varnish, if available. A bare wrapping will last the duration of a short fishing trip, but a permanent guide

Paper clip used as substitute guide for rod tip.

should be installed as soon as possible. The soft metal of the paper clip will eventually ruin the finish of a fly line.

Lubricating Ferrules

A jointed fishing rod should be assembled by *pushing* together, not twisting, the male and female ferrules. To unjoint the rod, always pull the ferrules apart in a straight line. Do not twist them. If you can't unjoint a rod alone, get a partner to help you, each grasping the rod on either side of a ferrule. Avoid grasping the rod near a guide; you may strip it off or bend it.

In order to seat firmly, ferrules must fit tightly, but particles of grit or a bit of erosion sometimes cause them to stick. Some form of lubrication is then needed. Oil is not suitable as it will eventually thicken and worsen the condition.

The best lubricant I've found for ferrules is the natural oil occurring in human hair. To lubricate a ferrule, merely push the male element through your own hair, twisting it and working it around for a few seconds. This will impart just the right amount of lubrication for a day's use and can be repeated each time the rod is used. Of course, as you get older you may have to find another method.

Finding Natural Baits

One of the most available natural baits is the earthworm. It is found in soft soil nationwide. A good place to look for earthworms is along stream banks where the earth is moist but not wet, in farm fields, cultivated gardens, croplands, orchards, and hayfields. Ditchbanks, grassy root areas around irrigated fields, and the ground around small mountain springs also are good places to dig.

Another large white worm, the grubworm, is found in sandy, unplowed areas around cottonwood groves along stream banks. In the spring, sagebrush areas adjacent to stream banks are good places to look for white grubs.

A smaller white worm, the woodworm, is found in old conifer stumps throughout the pine belts of North America. This worm is over an inch long, has a hard, dark head, and lives on wood. You can detect the presence of woodworms by the relatively fresh, round holes appearing in old rotted stumps and logs. Chop into such wood with an ax and you'll find the holes will terminate in sawdust. The worms will be in the sawdust. The wilderness traveler often comes upon rotted logs torn apart by a wandering bear for the ants and woodworms inside. These rotten stumps and logs are a good sign of woodworms.

Ordinary black crickets are good bait. They are often found under rocks and old boards, especially around abandoned buildings. The larger Mormon cricket, which once plagued the agricultural crops of Utah and is now found in many desert areas of the West, is a good bait for large fish. These large, nasty-looking insects can be killed with a long branch stripped of leaves except for a bunch at the end.

Such a stick swatter is the best way of killing grasshoppers, which are one of the best natural baits, especially for trout. Grasshoppers of several varieties are found in sagebrush lands, dry mountain sidehills, and most abundantly in hayfields. The best grasshopper for bait is the small grayish hopper with yellow belly which develops to full maturity from midsummer to late fall. This hopper is just over an inch in length.

If the woods traveler is fortunate enough to locate an old game-kill, or a domestic animal which has died in some outlying range country, and can get to it before predators have cleaned up the remains, he is apt to get a fine bait for whitefish—maggots. These tiny larvae, which develop from the eggs of blowflies and other large flies, are a deadly bait for mountain whitefish. Thread them on a #12 hook.

Several species of flies themselves can be used as bait. The blue horsefly, which is found in most timbered areas in spring and early summer, and whose bite is so painful, is one of these. Threaded on a small hook, and drifted through a pool, it will often take fish.

Hellgrammites are a productive natural bait, especially for mountain whitefish, which will take either the dark or the pale-yellowish species. Both are found on the underside of mossy rocks in stream riffles. The easiest way to catch hellgrammites is to slant a piece of door screen in the water below a shallow riffle, then stir the rocks upstream from it. The insects will dislodge from the rocks and flow down against the screen. A piece of burlap can be used in the same way. Lacking either, simply stir up rocks and pick up the insects as they float downstream.

Small bullheads or sculpins are good bait for large fish. Look for them under large, mossy rocks in shallow riffles. A distrubed bullhead will try to escape under another rock. The best way to catch it is to spear it with an ordinary table fork as it pauses under the edge of the rock. This has now become illegal in some states, so check the regulations. If you are quick, you can catch a bullhead with your hand.

Suckers and minnows are popular baitfish. Try a worm-like strip of meat cut from the shoulder area of a large sucker. Suckers lurk in deep, slow-moving pools and can be caught on worms fished along the bottom. Minnows are the natural food of many species of fish. The easiest way to catch them is with a wire minnow trap baited with breadcrumbs. Lacking a trap, find a shallow eddy containing a school of minnows. Stay out of sight and throw a fist-sized stone into the school. You may stun one or more and be able to scoop them up.

Large trout often go for a mouse bait. Tie the mouse onto a large hook, with the point just below the belly, and allow it to drift into deep pools.

The eggs of large fish make good natural bait, though it is hard to affix them to a hook. It helps to coat the eggs with sugar first, then allow them to dry.

Freshwater clams, which occur in many streams, are good bait for large trout or steelheads. Found in beds, in the deep riffles of large streams, clams can be dug up with a pitchfork. The wilderness traveler will have to use his hands. Open them by cutting the junction of the halves, slice the flesh into strips, and impale them on a large hook.

Removing Embedded Fishhooks

There are relatively few fishhook accidents, since most people are aware of the hazard of barbed hooks. However, occasionally a fishhook will become embedded in someone's flesh.

If the hook is embedded in a finger, ear, or other area with its point nearly protruding from the opposite side,

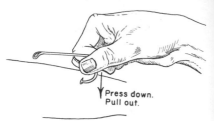

How to remove a fish-hook if point cannot be pushed through skin.

Press down.
Pull out.

the best way to remove it is to cut the shank, push the point through, and remove the hook. Remove the hook as soon as possible, as there will be a certain amount of numbness and the victim will feel less pain. Numbness may be increased by squeezing the flesh around the hook just prior to removal.

If the hook has sunk into the flesh, and it is not feasible to push the point through, the hook must be pulled out in the opposite direction from which it entered. To pull the hook straight backward would result in the barb sinking deeper into the flesh. Instead, the hook should be held, either with pliers or between thumb and forefinger, and pressed against the skin, as in the drawing. This pressure will open the entrance hole and a quick pull on the hook will usually remove it without undue pain or tearing the flesh.

If this procedure is not possible and a doctor is available, discontinue the fishing trip and seek medical aid, especially if the injury is in the eye area.

Once the hook is removed, the hole should be disinfected. Wash thoroughly with soap and water. Swab well with iodine, mercurochrome, or other disinfectant, if available. The chlorine in such products as Chlorox is a disinfectant. Dilute before applying to the wound.

How Indians Caught Fish

Before the advent of the metal fishhook, the Indians developed several productive ways to catch fish, especially larger species such as migrating salmon, fish in school, or fish in shallow water. They used the bow and arrow to shoot salmon migrating over riffles and in the small creeks during spawning runs. They snagged fish with bone hooks

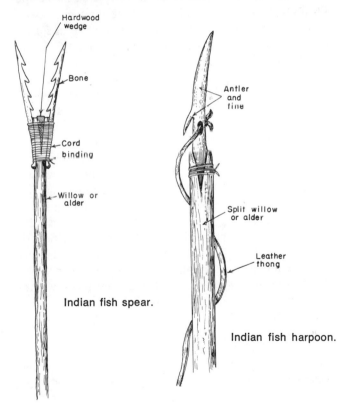

Indian fish spear.

Indian fish harpoon.

attached to cords, tossing the weighted hook into a pool containing several fish, allowing it to settle to the bottom, then jerking it upward as the fish passed over it.

Spearing fish in shallow water was productive, and several types of crude spears were used. One of the best was made of two pieces of sharpened bone, barbed on the inside, and fastened to the end of a split willow or alder. A thin, triangular piece of hardwood was placed in the split before binding it with cord, to separate the two pieces of bone. The spear was thrust or thrown at a fish in shallow water. If it hit, the barbed edges would prevent the fish from slipping off as it was retrieved.

Small harpoons were used in much the same manner on larger fish such as Chinook salmon, when they could be caught in schools in river pools, or in riffles in spawning creeks. The head of the harpoon was often made of a segment of deer antler, with the tine worked down to form a thin barb. The end of the antler was shaped and inserted into the split or hollowed end of an alder or willow pole, and bound temporarily by a thong. A small hole was then bored through the harpoon head, to which a long leather thong or strong cord was attached. The harpoon was thrust or thrown, and if the head was embedded in the fish, the handle was pulled away, and the fish hauled in by the cord. The harpoon had an advantage over the spear in that it could be thrown farther and both parts retrieved, whereas a heavy fish might carry the spear away.

Indian Fish Wheel

The Indians of Alaska and Canada developed an ingenious device for catching salmon in the muddy and silt-laden rivers of the North where the fish could not be seen or caught with lures. It was called a fish wheel.

The fish wheel was built on a log raft which had an opening in the center to allow the wheel to revolve in the water. The wheel itself contained four spokes radiating

Indian fish wheel.

from each end of a log axle. The two longer spokes held a pair of baskets woven of willows. The shorter spokes were braced by saplings across the ends. The log axle turned in round notches cut in planks which had been hewn from a log. A log box was built on the raft just behind the wheel.

The raft was placed in the river, against the bank, on a point below a bend. The current turned the wheel on its axle, like a waterwheel, and as the salmon came around the bend and past the point, the baskets scooped them up and dropped them in the log box.

Today, the Indians still use fish wheels of this sort, but the baskets are made of chicken wire instead of willows and the framework is made of lumber. Only the Indians have legal permission to use these fish wheels.

How Indians Dried Fish

Since the salmon runs were seasonal, the fish caught with the fish wheel had to be preserved to last through the year. Indians of the North dried the salmon. They cut fillets on both sides of the fish, but did not cut through the tail, leaving both fillets hinged together at this point. The fillets could then be hung on a drying rack. After the fillets were stripped from the bones, they were scored on the flesh side with lateral cuts of a knife. The fillets were hung on the drying rack with the flesh side out.

Drying racks were built of poles near the fish wheels. The racks were covered with popple branches to form a roof, shading the drying fish from the sun. Sometimes a small birch fire was built under the rack and allowed to

Birch
smudge fire

Fillets
scored

Indian fish-drying rack.

smoulder, keeping away the flies, quickening the drying process, and imparting a smoky flavor to the fish. When salt became available, the Indians used it in drying fish. Indians along the Yukon River and other salmon streams of the North still dry their catches in this way.

21

Camping How-To

Making a Safe Camp

The basic consideration in choosing a campsite is the availability of water and wood. A campsite should be *near* a supply of good water, but not so close that it presents a hazard. High shorelines and island-points are good places to make camp. So are knolls in timbered country, and open spots above creeks or springs. The camp should be so located that in case of a sudden storm or flash flood the site will not be inundated. For this reason low river banks, gulley bottoms, dry washes, and similar low areas are not good places to camp.

Similarly, if wood is used for fuel, the camp should be set up close to the supply, but not where timber is a hazard. Tents should not be set under tall, dry trees which may blow over in a high wind—the "widowmakers" of the Northwest. It isn't safe to make camp directly under tall trees which will drip rain or snow on tents and equipment. Moreover, tall trees draw lightning.

The area around any camp should be cleared of brush so sparks from the campfire won't catch. Clearing a campsite of brush also prevents tripping or stumbling, especially at night. Stumps of small saplings should be cut off close to the ground. Paths leading to the water supply, the garbage pit, and the latrine should be cleared of brush and rocks.

The tent should be pitched so that its flap faces the camp area, with its rear toward the timber. Guy ropes should be tied so that campers won't trip over them, and shielded by boxes or other objects. Low, overhanging limbs are a hazard for woodchoppers and should be cut before anyone swings an ax.

If an open fire is used, the fireplace should be sturdy so that pans of hot water or food will not upset and scald someone. It's also a good idea to keep a large pot filled with water near the fire in case flying sparks hit tarps, drying clothes, etc., and start a blaze.

The chopping block should be set back from the main working area and a firm camp rule established that the ax always be kept sunk in the block. Similarly, saws should be placed out of the way where they will not fall or be tripped over. Unsheathed knives should never be left on the ground.

Orderly storage of food boxes, camp utensils, and personal gear helps to make a safe camp. Items that are out of place, after a camp routine is established, are always a danger. Leveling the ground in the traffic area may prevent such misfortunes as folding chairs tipping over or articles skidding off uneven tables.

Finally, a few simple camp rules should be established by the one in charge: no loaded guns allowed in camp;

no fishing rods allowed in the traffic area; no alcoholic beverages allowed before evening. Abiding by a few such sensible rules often saves a camp from tragedy.

Keeping Matches Dry

Here are some ways to keep wooden matches dry in camp:

In a pint fruit jar.

In an empty Alka-Seltzer bottle.

In an empty centerfire cartridge case. Dip the heads in paraffin, and whittle a wooden plug for the case's mouth.

In a hole drilled in your rifle's buttstock. The buttplate must be removed, the hole drilled, and the plate replaced.

In a plastic wrapping sewed into the pocket of an outdoor garment. Dip the heads in melted paraffin.

In a waterproof matchcase purchased at a camping supplier.

Fire Starters

Fire starters are often necessary to get a poor quality of wood to burn. They may be found in the woods or made at home and taken along.

One of the best natural fire starters is dry pine, spruce, or fir needles. Even during rain or snow, a handful of these can be found on the lower limbs of big trees that will be dry enough to burn well. Such dry needles are reddish in color and easily recognized.

Another good fire starter found in conifer country is pitch, the resinous substance often found in old stumps. Called "pine-gum" in the West, it is yellowish in color, and in old stumps has the hard appearance of resinwood lamination. If an old stump looks gray, it's apt to be old, soggy, or rotten. If it looks yellow, it's apt to contain pitch.

A few shavings of pitch will start a fire at the touch of a match. Old-timers usually break off a few hunks every time they find a pitch stump, take them to camp, and solve the fire-making problem for the duration of the trip.

The simplest fire starters are a few birthday candles. Half of one of these little candles will be enough to start a fire with even soggy wood. A few of them in a coat pocket weigh practically nothing and won't melt and ruin the coat.

Another good fire starter can be made of newspaper rolled tightly into a half-inch roll, wound tightly with thread, dipped into melted paraffin, and cut into half-inch plugs. The bits of thread which remain act as wicks.

The tiny wax-paper cups used for jelly containers in cafes can be used as forms for making fire starters. Fill the cups loosely with coarse, dry sawdust from a softwood such as pine. Sawdust from a sawmill works fine. Poke a 1½-inch

Fire starters can be made by pouring paraffin into blind holes bored in a pine board and filled with sawdust and twine wicks.

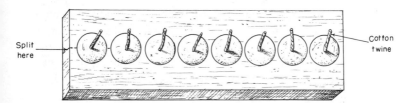

Split here

Cotton twine

length of old cotton shoelace into each cup to serve as a wick. Pour hot, melted paraffin into the sawdust until the cup is full. The wax causes the sawdust to adhere, and the mixture will burn quickly when the wick is lit.

Small pocket-sized fire starters can be made by boring a series of 5/8-inch holes nearly through a 1-inch, straight-grained pine board. Place a short length of cotton twine into each hole for a wick, and fill the holes loosely with coarse sawdust. If coarse sawdust is not available, the chips made by boring the holes can be used. Allow the twine wick to project through the center of the sawdust. Pour hot, melted paraffin into the sawdust in each hole. After the mixture has cooled and the wax has set, split the board lengthwise with an ax or knife and remove the fire starters from their forms.

Sharpening Axes and Knives

One of the best implements for sharpening an ax was the old-fashioned grindstone, turned by a treadle and cooled by a dripping can of water suspended above it. The old grindstone is largely gone, and today's best tools for sharpening an ax are a shop grinder with an emery wheel and an oilstone. The oilstone is used to put a fine edge on the blade.

When using the grinder, grind slowly so that the temper of the steel is not drawn and the edge is not ground down. Sharpen toward the cutting edge by holding the bit on the grinder so that the wheel turns toward the ax, not away from it. Contact should only be made for a few seconds at a time so as not to generate too much heat.

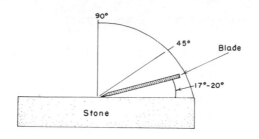

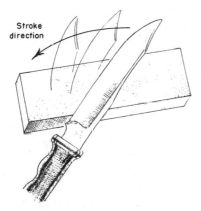

Proper way to sharpen a knife.

When finishing the edge with the oilstone, push the stone toward the edge, not away from it, at an angle of about 20 degrees. Some people move the stone in a circular fashion.

Most camp axes are used for felling trees and for splitting wood. The felling bit should be thinner than the bit used for splitting, but unless a double-bit ax is used, the ax must be a compromise. The bit of most good factory axes will be about right for splitting wood, but will be, or

649

rapidly become, too thick for felling. As an ax wears, and is sharpened only on the edge with a stone, the blade becomes thicker and should be periodically thinned down on a shop grinder.

Knives should be sharpened at home and touched up periodically as they are used at camp. They should never be thinned down on an emery wheel but with a hone or stone.

Most stones for sharpening knives are of carborundum. The larger ones usually have a rough side and a fine side. These are good stones for sharpening knives at home. For field use, a smaller stone such as the official Boy Scout stone is adequate.

The very best knife-sharpening stones are Arkansas stones quarried from natural rock. These come in various degrees of hardness, from "soft" to "hard." A hard stone and a soft one are an unbeatable combination for putting a fine edge on any knife. The stone should be lubricated with a light oil when sharpening. If none is available, water or saliva is an acceptable substitute.

The best stroke for sharpening a knife blade, and the only one to use with a fine knife, is a scything movement toward the user, with the blade held at an angle of 17 to 20 degrees, bringing the entire blade along the stone from hilt to tip. This movement, repeated several times, will bring the edge particles into line on one side of the blade. Then turn the blade over and push it away from you in a similar arc.

An implement long neglected for sharpening fine knives is the "steel" used by butchers. This rod of hard, fluted steel puts a keen edge on a knife in short order. Hold it almost vertically in front of you and stroke the blade down one side and then the other, maintaining the same angle. Steel sizes range from about 18 inches long to a 4-inch pocket model made in Germany. I recently stayed with a professional seal hunter off Alaska's Afognak Island who could skin a hair seal in three minutes flat. His knives were the best handmade products obtainable, and he would use nothing but a pair of steels for sharpening them.

Chopping Wood Safely

The average camper need not acquire the skill of the professional woodchopper. He will use an ax to fell trees and chop them up for firewood, cut brush around tents, and perhaps hack a trail for a packstring through down timber. There is an art to using an ax which can only be acquired through experience, but anyone can learn to chop safely.

The camper will probably use one of three types of axes: a single bit with a 1½-pound head and 26-inch handle; a double bit with a 2½-pound head and 28-inch handle; a single bit with a 3-pound head and 35-inch handle. The first type is adequate for most woodchopping around camp. The larger double-bit ax, owing to its longer handle and heavier head, is better if no pounding is to be done. One bit is intended for felling, the other for splitting.

The basic technique in using an ax is to "throw" the head at the target rather than falling on the handle with the body's weight. It is quite like tossing an apple which has been impaled on a stick. Hold the ax over the target and get the "feel" of the situation, as in approaching the ball in golf. Swing the head back, then forward, letting the weight of the ax head do the work.

When felling trees or cutting up long logs, chop at about a 45-degree angle to the grain of the wood. Split wood along the grain.

Before starting to chop, cut away all foliage or overhanging limbs which might interfere with the backswing. Don't chop when people are around; the ax head can slip off the helve, or the ax itself slip from the hands. Flying wood is also a hazard.

Notch small tree on either side. Cut one notch on large tree lower than other, on side you want tree to fall.

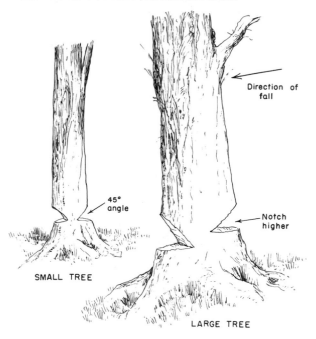

Direction of fall

45° angle

Notch higher

SMALL TREE

LARGE TREE

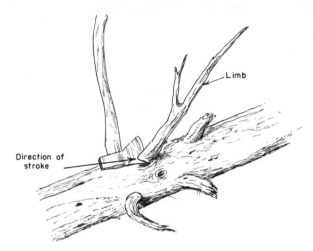

When trimming a large log, cut limbs from this side.

Cut down standing trees by making opposite notches at the base of the trunk. The bottom of the notch should be cut flat, and at right angles to the tree. The upper surface should slope so that the chips can be "pried" out at the end of each stroke by slightly tipping the bit downward.

Small trees can be cut down by chopping two opposite notches at the base, with each notch reaching approximately halfway through the tree.

With large trees, cut the second notch just above the first notch and the tree will topple in the direction of the first notch. At the first indication that the tree is about to give way, move away from the direction of the fall and from the stump as well. The tree may "jump" off the stump when it falls and strike you. Cut off limbs by striking their lower sides flush with the trunk.

653

Splitting Wood

The first thing to do before attempting to split wood is to get a large log to use as a chopping block. This block should be large enough to be stable and cut squarely across both ends. When only one end of the block is square, this end should be placed upward and the surface of the ground smoothed so that the block will stand straight. Otherwise splitting wood on it can be dangerous.

All objects around the chopping block should be removed, as they may catch the backswing. If a double-bit ax is used, the bit with the thicker edge is better for

Chopping block for splitting wood safely.

Chopping
block

QUARTER CUT   SLAB CUT

Two methods of splitting a log.

splitting. If the bit is too thin, like the edge used for felling, it tends to cut deep rather than to spread the wood.

There are two basic cuts used in splitting. One of these is "quartering." The log to be split is placed on the chopping block and first cut in half. A small log can often be split with one blow. With larger logs, one blow is often

Splitting a log with a large knot.

Split above knot —
weakest part of grain

not enough. It is better to strike the first blow at the edge of the block, weakening the wood at this point. Strike the next blow just inside the first blow, further weakening the wood. Successive blows, struck on a line across the center, will eventually split the log. Cut the halves in the same way, as shown in the drawing. Some choppers lay the halves on the block flat side down, and split them this way. This is often necessary when splitting small or knotty logs, or logs with unsquare ends. When splitting a knotty log, try to hit it above, and in line with, the knot. As this is the weakest part of the grain, the log will split easier.

Use a wedge to split tough-grained conifer logs.

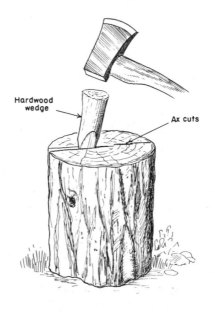

Hardwood wedge

Ax cuts

Experienced choppers often hold the ax in one hand and hold the log half with the other. The trick is to move the hand just before the ax strikes the wood.

A second method of splitting logs is to "slab" the wood, as shown in the drawing. This produces flat boards for making camp furniture or for propping up table legs, etc.

Logs that have been chopped into lengths, rather than sawed, cannot be stood on end to be split. They must be laid on the chopping block, round side up, and quartered.

It is often difficult to split the large, tough-grained logs cut from conifer trees. To make the job easier, find a piece of dry hardwood and make a splitting wedge. In most conifer country, mountain mahogany, maple, or other hardwood is available. Taper a couple of foot-long pieces which are 2 to 4 inches in diameter, making a pair of wedges. Drive the ax into the center of the log end a few times until you can insert one of the wedges in the cut. Pound the wedge into the log with the head of the ax, widening the split, and insert the second wedge. If the wedges are driven into the log at opposite sides, they should split it apart. One wedge, driven into the center of the log, will often do the job.

Sawing Wood

At large camps firewood is often cup up with a portable power saw or with some type of handsaw. The best handsaw for this work is the bowsaw. It is efficient and portable, and is available in lengths from 30 inches up to 5 feet.

The log to be sawed should be rested on a chopping block or log so that the cut is slightly off the block,

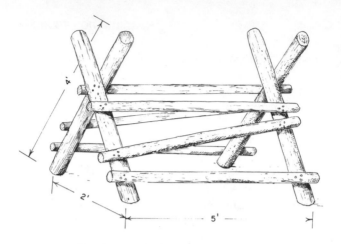

Simple sawhorse for cutting wood at camp.

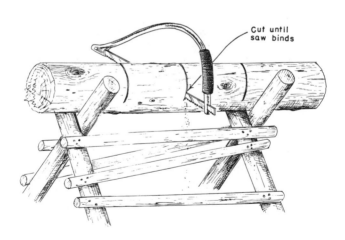

Cut until
saw binds

When log becomes sawhorse length, cut until saw binds, then lay log on the ground and chop from opposite side.

allowing the weight of the cut-off piece to open the kerf and prevent the saw from binding.

If considerable cutting is to be done, it pays to build a rough sawhorse from small poles found in the area. The drawing shows how a simple sawhorse can be knocked together with a few spikes. The logs are laid in the crosses, and cut beyond the support—again to avoid binding the saw. When the log has been shortened to sawhorse length, saw only until the blade binds in the wood. Then lay the log on the ground and complete the job by chopping with an ax on the opposite side of each cut. If green wood is cut, binding of the saw can be prevented by smearing the blade with kerosene.

Camp Cupboards

The food supply at camp is often left in packing boxes because there is no lumber available with which to build cupboards and neatly store the supplies. Camp cupboards

Cardboard boxes serve as camp cupboards.

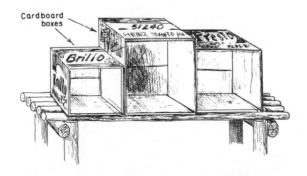

can be made, however, from the boxes in which the groceries were brought to camp. Also needed are some poles, a few spikes, and baling wire or rope.

A kitchen cupboard should be placed at a suitable working height. Build a stand about 30 inches high of four husky poles sharpened and driven into the ground, two crossbars spiked across the ends, and several slender poles laid on the crossbars. The stand can be placed inside the cook tent, or outside in mild weather. If a storm comes up, a tarp can be thrown over the cupboard.

The cupboard itself can be made of several types of boxes. The cardboard cartons in which grocery stores pack supplies are suitable. So are wooden orange or apple crates, or a few alforjas boxes. Turned on their sides, and placed in a row on the stand, the boxes can be stored with food and utensils so that an orderly cupboard is available to the camp cook. If enough boxes are brought to camp, a double-

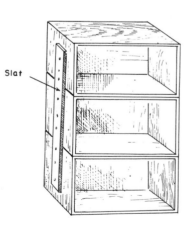

Join cardboard or wooden boxes with a slat to make a bank of cupboards.

Slat

decker cupboard can be arranged, with the second layer covering the joints of the first. Place the heavier items in the lower row of boxes and the lighter supplies on top. If the boxes are light or flimsy, they can be reinforced with a small slat as shown in the drawing.

Several types of boxes are available at large military surplus stores which can easily be converted to camp cupboards. One of these is the bomb-kit container; another is the portable officer's field desk. These boxes are of plywood with metal binding and are light and rugged. They make fine containers for hauling food in cars and boats, or on packhorses.

Camp Tables

A rustic table built of native materials is far more stable and roomy than the folding card table often taken along on auto-camping trips. The table can be made in two ways. One is simply to construct a stand similar to the one previously described for supporting a camp cupboard. If it is to be a large table, built with heavy corner posts, it is not necessary to sharpen the posts and drive them into the ground. They can be cut square at the ends and stand upright. In this case, side rails should be nailed or lashed to the posts to give the table stability. The poles used for the top should be slightly flattened on top and bottom to lie flat and provide a smooth surface. They are nailed or lashed to the crossbars.

If the corner posts are driven into the ground, seats can be built integral with the table, but a third pair of posts should be used, one on each side between the corner

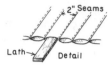

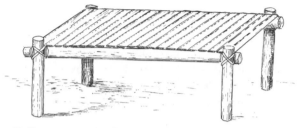

Roll-up camp table of seamed canvas and lath.

posts, for added stability. Nail or lash three poles to the ends of the corner posts at a height of 18 inches. These poles should extend 18 inches beyond the corner posts on each side and form the supports for the benches. Several slim poles of suitable length are then nailed to these supports.

A portable top for this camp table can be made from a length of 3-foot canvas of 10-ounce weight and wooden lath. The canvas should be 1 foot longer than the desired length of the table top.

Double the canvas and sew seams, beginning at the fold, across the width at 2-inch intervals. When the seams are made, cut lengths of wooden lath 1 inch shorter than the width of the canvas and insert them into the pockets formed by the seams. Then sew the open end of the canvas, locking the laths in the pockets. Finally, sew a pair of cloth tapes to one end. In storage or transit the canvas can be rolled into a tight bundle and tied with the tape. At camp it is unrolled on the framework of the table and forms a stable top.

Camp Stools

Unless you are auto-camping, chairs and stools are hard to transport. However, several types of stools can be made at camp which, although short on upholstery, are rugged and provide seats for tired campers.

The traditional camp stool has always been a short log, broad enough to make a seat, and cut square at each end. But in areas where large-diameter logs are not available, a stool can be fashioned from a slim log and a slab of wood cut as shown in the section on splitting wood. Smooth both surfaces of the slab and nail it to the log.

Simple camp stool—a slab nailed to a log.

camp stool made from a half log fitted with legs.

At a semipermanent camp where tools can be packed along, fancier stools can be made of split logs. The logs should be at least 12 inches in diameter and about 18 inches long. After splitting a log, bore a pair of holes at each end, angling inward. Cut four small saplings for legs, about 15 inches long, preferably of green hardwood, and pare down the ends to fit in the holes. If the holes have been bored at an angle, the legs will spread and you'll have a sturdy stool.

Homemade Baker Tent

To make a baker tent the following materials are needed:
1 piece of canvas 3 by 36 feet.
1 piece of canvas 6 by 6 feet.
From the 36-foot length cut three pieces, each 11 feet long. Sew them together to form a rectangle 9-by-11 feet in size. Hem the edges of the sheet along its 9-foot sides,

and fit grommets at the corners and sides if desired. This is the roof of the test.

Cut the 6-foot square of canvas diagonally, forming two equal triangles. Sew the long side, or hypotenuse, of each triangle to the long sides of the roof, with the tip of the triangle flush with the edge of the roof. These form the sides of the tent.

On the underside of the roof, a few inches above the point where the sides end, sew four large loops of hemmed canvas. These should be large enough to admit a 4-inch ridgepole, as shown in the drawing.

Sew loops for tent pegs at the four corners and midway between. (If the canvas has been fitted with grommets this is unnecessary.) Sew two loops on the lower side of the

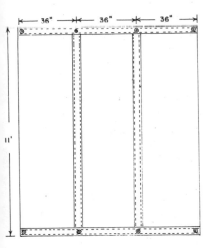

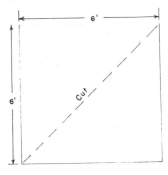

Pattern for cutting canvas for baker tent. Piece at left forms the top; piece at right, cut along diagonal, forms the sides.

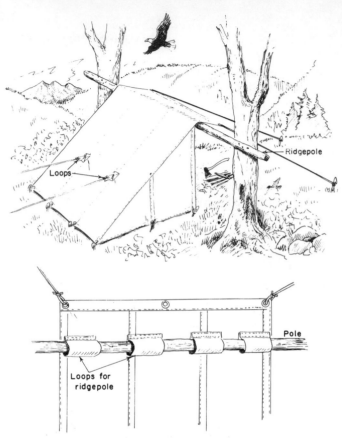

Baker tent erected between two trees. Detail shows loops sewn on underside of roof to admit the ridgepole.

roof, 2 feet from the bottom edge and 2½ feet from each side. Small guy ropes tied to these loops and pegged to the ground will prevent the roof from sagging.

The finished tent may be waterproofed with a commercial solution applied according to the directions, or with paraffin. To waterproof the tent with paraffin, shave 2 pounds of paraffin into a container and heat to melting. Next, heat a tubful of water to the boiling point. Remove the tub of water from the stove and place it outside or at a safe distance. Into a smaller container pour 2 gallons of white gasoline. Place the container of gasoline into the tub of hot water. As gasoline has a lower boiling point than water, the gasoline will boil. Pour the melted paraffin into the container of gasoline. Fold the tent loosely and immerse it in the gasoline-paraffin solution. Allow it to soak for a while and then hang it on a clothesline until the scent has gone.

Lantern Case

The glass-globed gasoline lantern provides excellent illumination in camp, but it's a fragile piece of equipment to transport safely. The simple lantern case shown here will protect a lantern from the jouncing it usually gets in transit. It was built for a Coleman single-mantle lantern. Adjust the dimensions to fit your own.

Cut the sides of the case from ¼-inch plywood. These are screwed to the corner posts, which are cut 1½ inches shorter than the sides. Allow the sides to overlap the posts ¾ inch at each end. Cut the bottom of ¾-inch plywood or pine, of a size to inset the sides, and screw it at the corners to the ends of the posts. The lid, also of ¾-inch stock, is cut to fit flush with the case edges. Cut another piece the same size as the bottom, and screw it to the underside of the lid so that it insets the case. Attach the lid to the case with strap hinges, and add a hasp and handle.

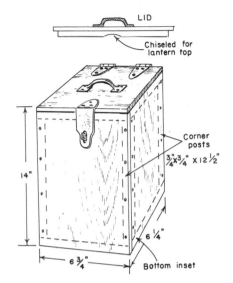

LID

Chiseled for lantern top

Corner posts

$\frac{3}{4}"x\frac{3}{4}" \times 12\frac{1}{2}"$

14"

6 $\frac{1}{4}"$

6 $\frac{3}{4}"$

Bottom inset

Case for holding camp lantern tight during travel.

If the box is the correct size, the top of the lantern should just prevent the lid from closing. Chisel a small depression in the underside of the lid to fit the lantern's top, thus holding it snugly in the case. Finish the case with a couple of coats of varnish stain, perhaps dark oak.

With the lantern well fitted, such a case can be transported in any position and absorb the usual bumps encountered on an outdoor trip.

Alforjas Boxes

Alforjas boxes were originally designed to fit inside the canvas panniers used with sawbuck packsaddles. They are also useful for packing personal belongings on camping trips in cars, boats, and airplanes. An added advantage is that these light boxes can be used with packsaddles without panniers by simply lashing them to the saddle with a sling hitch. To be most useful, alforjas boxes should be built to fit into panniers, whose dimensions are somewhat standardized. The box shown in the drawing meets these specifications, and it is easy to make.

Half-inch lumber, or 3/8-inch plywood, is used for the sides and bottom, and 1-by-10-inch lumber for the ends. The ends can be cut in a mild V-shape to conform to the side of a horse, as in the drawing, or left straight. Use flatheaded wood screws or cement-coated 6d box nails for joining the sides and bottom to the ends. Attach a 1-by-2-inch cleat to each end of the box with four screws. This cleat slants to allow the lash ropes to run from the front ring of the saddle under one cleat, across the front of the box, under the other cleat, and back to the rear saddle ring. When the lash rope is drawn tight with the completed

Alforjas box with V-shaped ends to fit horse's side.

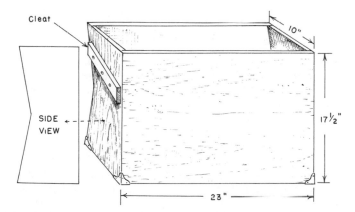

Cleat

10"

SIDE VIEW

17½"

23"

sling hitch and tied, the box will ride securely on either a Decker or a sawbuck packsaddle.

The corners of the box can be reinforced with brass corners, or with rawhide which is soaked and shaped to fit, and tacked solidly in place.

Packhorse or Car Kitchen

It is often desirable to have cooking equipment and basic food items packed and ready to go at a moment's notice for an overnight camping trip. Building a pair of camp kitchens is a good solution.

If you live in a region where packtrips are common, the kitchens should be built to fit panniers. A suitable size is 24 inches long, 18 inches high, and 10 inches thick, or wide. One of the best materials for the end pieces is 1-by-10-inch planed lumber. A good material for the bottom and both back and front is 3/8-inch plywood. If very heavy material is to be carried, ½-inch plywood is better for the bottom.

The kitchen differs from an alforjas box in that the top is closed, and the front is hinged at the bottom and anchored to the top with either a hasp latch or a window latch. The advantage of the hasp is that it may be padlocked. Two-inch strap hinges are used to attach the front panel to the bottom.

The inside of each kitchen is fitted, according to the user's needs, with plywood shelves and upright cubbyholes. Usually the lower part of the box has no partitions, leaving space for storing large items. The upper half is partitioned

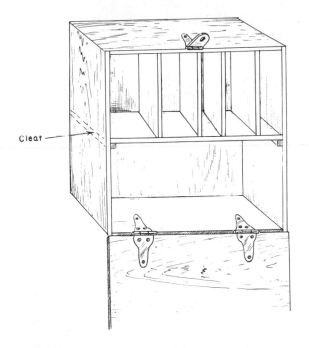

Clear

Camp kitchen should be compartmented for neat storage.

into small sections to hold plates (vertically), cups (nestled), knives and forks, condiments, etc.

At camp, the kitchens are simply lifted off the pack animal or out of the car or boat, and the front opened. Everything inside is ready for immediate use. Often when table room is at a premium, the kitchen can be set on a block and used as a table. A pair of restraining chains, one at either side, can be attached to the front to hold it in a horizontal position.

Emergency Jack

At camp it is often necessary to move large logs or rocks that are in the way. On the road, your car may get stuck in the mud so badly that the car jack can't dislodge it. In both situations, it's possible to make a jack with only a length of ½-inch rope and a couple of poles.

One pole is a 3-foot length of stout log, cut square at one end. The other is a pole 12 to 15 feet long and 3 to 5 inches in diameter. Cut a shallow notch in this pole about 3 or 4 inches from the larger end. Stand the small log upright on

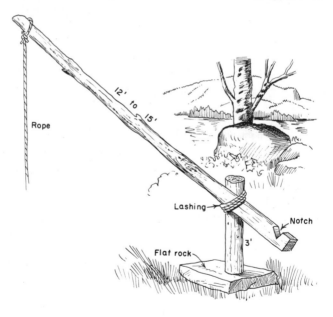

Emergency jack for moving big boulders or stuck vehicle.

its square end and lash the pole to it. Hold the pole at right angles to the upright and use a diagonal lashing, finished off with several turns of frapping. The lashing should be somewhat loose so that the pole will not bind.

The result is a long lever attached to an upright. The height at which the lever is placed can be regulated by shifting the lashing up or down the upright. In use, stand the upright log on a flat rock, a patch of hard ground, or a wood slab. Point the long end of the lever skyward, and hook the short end under the vehicle or object to be moved. Lift the object as high as possible, and block it up with logs. Move the lashing upward on the upright, and take another "bite." Repeat until the object has been lifted as high as is necessary.

You can get an even longer "bite" if a piece of rope is attached to the end of the long pole. The pole can then be angled higher, giving greater leverage.

Saw-Blade Covers

Exposed saw blades can cause nasty wounds, and ruin tents, bedrolls, and other camp gear. Saw blades should have some kind of protective cover during transit and at camp when not in use.

One of the simplest saw-blade covers is a length of burlap or a gunnysack. If the burlap is wrapped around the blade and tied with cord, only a very violent blow will cause the teeth to penetrate. Start the wrapping at one end of the blade, with a corner of the sack. A good cord for tying the material in place is butcher's cord, the kind used to tie salami ends.

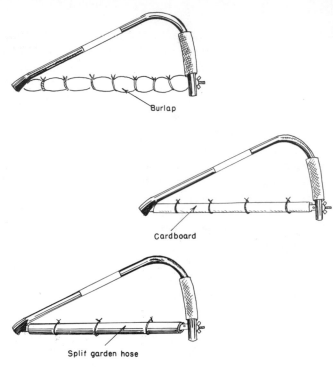

Burlap

Cardboard

Split garden hose

Three types of saw-blade covers.

A better-looking and long-lasting cover can be made from cardboard carton material. Cut a 3-inch strip the same length as the blade, and fold it lengthwise. Insert the blade and tie the cardboard in place with several pieces of cord.

For short saws, a length of rubber or plastic garden hose makes a fine blade cover. Cut the hose the same length as the blade, then split it along its full length. The split hose, slipped over the saw blade, is fastened with cord every few inches.

674

The blades of long crosscut saws can be transported safely enclosed between two lengths of ¼-inch plywood, slightly larger than the blade size and at each corner.

Extra blades for bowsaws can be safely carried in tight rolls packed in flat cardboard boxes or wrapped with several turns of burlap and tied solidly. The rolls should be tied securely with wire before they are packaged. A rolled bowsaw blade that springs loose is a hazard to everyone nearby.

Making Ax Sheaths

Ax blades should be kept covered in transit or at camp. Not many ax makers supply sheaths, but you can make your own.

A good sheath for a double-bit ax can be made from two small sheets of heavy-gauge steerhide, several copper rivets, a length of light leather strap, and a small buckle.

First, draw a pattern on heavy paper of the two sides of the sheath. These sides should be exactly the same shape and size. It is necessary to make two to achieve a precise fit around the curves of the blade. An allowance for the rivets of ¾-inch should be left at both edges and along the underside.

Trace the pattern of the two halves onto the leather and cut them out with a sharp knife. Then rivet the two pieces of leather together around the edges of the bit and along the underside, leaving a space for the handle. Space the rivets 1 inch apart. The top of the sheath is left open. Copper rivets-and-burrs are the most lasting fasteners for

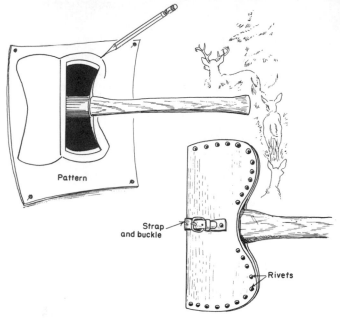

Sheath for double-bit ax.

joining the leather sides. The two-element rivets available at 5-and-10 stores are nearly as suitable.

After riveting the two sides, rivet a small buckle to one side of the sheath. On the opposite side, rivet a short length of strap with punched holes. This strap is buckled across the top of the sheath and holds the ax solidly in place.

A sheath for a single-bit ax can be made from a long piece of leather, or two smaller pieces if a single piece is not available.

If one piece of leather is used, draw a pattern on heavy paper as shown in the drawing. Allow ¾ inch at the edge for riveting. The flap is optional. If two pieces of leather

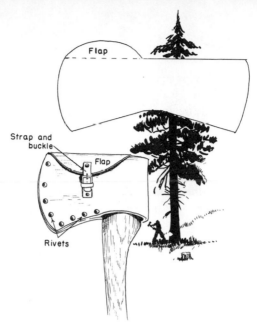

Sheath for single-bit ax.

are used, cut two patterns, leaving enough leather at the back to be able to rivet the sheath over the butt of the blade.

If the sheath is made of two pieces, rivet on a strap and buckle similar to the one on the sheath for a double-bit ax. If a flap has been cut on one side, fold it over the face of the ax and rivet a short strap to it. Then rivet a buckle to the side.

Knife Sheaths

The short sheaths that are sold with many knives are not entirely safe for strenuous activities such as horseback riding and climbing. The knife often slips from the sheath and is lost or stabs the wearer during a bad fall. It is easy and inexpensive to make a rugged sheath that will fit most types of knives.

For an average-size knife, a foldover sheath of heavy, stiff steerhide is durable and safe. It should be long enough to cover the entire blade and most of the handle. Only enough of the handle should protrude so that the fingers can catch the butt and pull the knife from the sheath.

Draw a paper pattern to fit the knife, leaving sufficient room at both edges for riveting or lacing, and transfer it to the leather. Cut the leather and soak it in warm water until it's soft. With a blunt tool, such as the end of a folded pocketknife, form-fit the softened leather to the knife. This is done by inserting the knife into the folded leather, and carefully molding the leather to its shape. The important areas to work down are the hilt and along the grip itself. If the leather is somewhat soft, the approximate shape of the knife can be imparted to the sheath.

Next, carefully remove the knife without disturbing the flexible, shaped sheath and allow the leather to dry. When dry, the sheath may be riveted or laced along the edge to a point just above the hilt. Care should be taken that there is enough room in the sheath to admit the hilt but that it will fit tightly.

Small, hammer-on rivets may be used, but they will enlarge the size of the finished sheath. It is better to lace the open side of the sheath with a length of ¼-inch buckskin, or similar soft leather such as the lace known as tooling calf.

Before lacing, holes must be punched in the edges of the open face of the sheath. These should be approximately

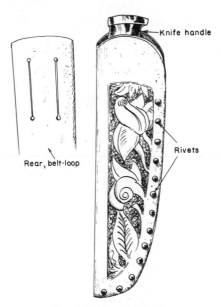

Knife handle

Rivets

Rear, belt-loop

Sheath for hunting knife.

3/32-inch holes, spaced ¼ inch apart, and staggered along opposite sides.

An overhand lacing is simplest for the beginner. Experienced leather workers may use one of several types of edge stitching. To begin the overhand stitch, lay a couple of inches of the lace between the halves of the sheath at the bottom end. The first stitches will be around and over this length of lace, binding it down firmly and out of sight. Continue lacing the edges to the finishing point at the approximate middle of the grip. It is easiest to complete the lacing without regard for tying in the end. Then with an awl or nail loosen the last half-dozen stitches, poke the end of the lace under these stitches and between the edges of the sheath. Starting with the last tight stitch, tighten the

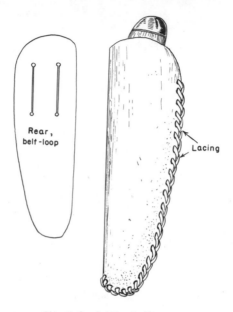

Rear,
belt-loop

Lacing

Sheath for folding knife.

loosened laces again. At the last stitch, a loop will occur. Pull the loop under the final stitches, as with whipping a rope end, and cut it flush. This conceals both ends of the lace and prevents it from unlacing.

A belt loop may be riveted on the rear side of the sheath. However, to prevent the knife from slipping out of the sheath it is better to cut the belt loop in the sheath itself. To cut the belt loop, make two rows of tiny holes 1½ inches apart, with ¾ inch between the rows. Then slit the leather between the holes. The loop should be cut so its lower end is just above the hilt. When the belt is inserted, the inside of the leather loop will bear against the grip of the knife and hold it tightly.

Folding sheath knives, shaped like large pocketknives, are becoming increasingly popular. They are safe to carry since their blades are folded, but they are too large for the average pocket. The easiest way to carry them is in a sheath.

Such a sheath is made by folding a piece of leather to fit the knife, then lacing it around the edges, nearly to the top. The sheath should be long enough to cover all but an inch of the knife, which can be grasped with the thumb and forefinger. The edges are laced as above. The belt loop is similarly punched and cut in the rear side, near the top.

Emergency Needle

A rugged needle for patching canvas, sewing soft leather, and other tasks can be improvised from the metal key used for opening many types of food cans. Simply straighten the key with a pair of pliers, and pound it straight with a hammer. Then sharpen the tip with a small file. Lacking a file, use a small sharpening stone. Tarps, tents, bedroll covers and other camp gear can be repaired with such a needle, using cord, fishing line, or leather laces.

Emergency needle made from slotted can key.

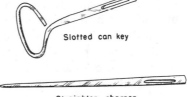

Slotted can key

Straighten , sharpen

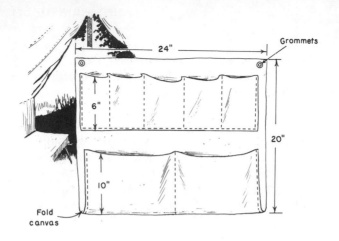

Canvas tent bag keeps personal articles in order.

Tent Bags

When camping in a tent on an extended trip, it is difficult to keep personal articles in order. A tent bag for keeping shaving kit, toothbrush, extra socks, and other items handy can be made of a piece of canvas. A good size for such a bag is 20 by 24 inches. To make a bag of that size you'll need a piece of canvas 24 by 30 inches, and another strip about 6 by 24 inches.

First hem the edges of the larger piece of canvas. Then fold the 30-inch side to form a 10-inch pocket at the bottom. Stitch the edges and sew a seam up the middle, dividing the pocket into two compartments. Sew the smaller strip of canvas 3 inches from the top, stitching it along the bottom and at both ends. Then sew vertical seams at intervals, separating the pocket into five or six compartments. Finally, set grommets into the top edge 2 inches from each corner. The bag can be hung from nails driven into one of the poles that support the sides of a wall tent.

Bough Bed

The air mattress and the folding camp cot have made outdoor sleeping a comfortable experience. There are times, however, when an air mattress springs a leak, or when backpacking in the wilderness it's necessary to improvise a mattress from conifer boughs.

Cut several armfuls of green boughs from small spruce or other conifer trees. The boughs should be about 18 inches long and thick with foliage. Begin by making a pillow approximately 3 feet wide and from 8 to 10 inches

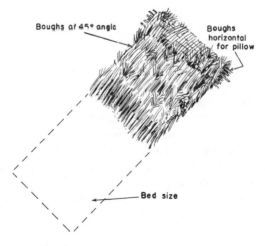

Boughs at 45° angle

Boughs horizontal for pillow

Bed size

How to lay boughs for a camp bed.

thick. Starting in the middle, lay individual boughs so that the butts point outwards.

Then lay more boughs on the pillow with their butt ends touching the ground. These are placed at an angle of 45 degrees, leaning toward the pillow. Lay each succeeding row of boughs at the same angle, pressed tightly against the previous row, so that the tips stand a foot off the ground and form a thick mat. Continue laying rows of boughs until the bed area is completely covered. For the bed to have a comfortable spring to it, sufficient boughs should be used. If there are not sufficient boughs in an area, it is best to make the shoulder area thick and skimp on the foot. Or place a small log on each side of the bed to prevent the boughs from spreading under your weight.

Leaf Bed

During the fall season, when leaves are shed, a wilderness camper can gather dry leaves and use them for insulation and softness under his outdoor bed.

Leaves, unlike thatched boughs, will not remain in place during the night but will slip from under the sleeper. To prevent this, make a bed frame of four logs, as shown in the drawing. The side logs can be placed 30 inches apart. The cross logs are cut to bed width, then spiked inside the side logs at proper length. It helps to make notches on the outside of each side log, then drive the spikes through these into the ends of the cross logs.

If the logs for the frame are about 6 inches thick, or even larger, they will prevent the leaves from scattering. Level

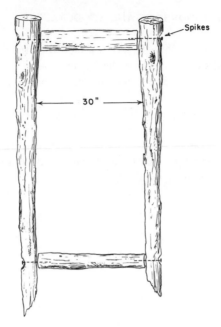

30"

Spikes

Wooden frame for a leaf bed.

the ground inside the frame, pile the leaves inside and smooth them down. The blankets or sleeping bag are placed on top.

Grass-and-Pole Bed

If the ground where you want to make your bed is wet, you can make a mattress of grass and poles. First make a bed frame as described for a leaf bed. On top of the frame, place small, dry poles fairly close together, and lash or nail them to the end logs. Small jackpine, lodgepole pine, or spruce poles are suitable. Then invert the entire framework so that the poles attached to the frame become the bed's bottom. Place the framework so that the head is slightly uphill. Sometimes it will be necessary to smooth the ground and pile dirt higher at one end.

Finally, spread grass or leaves inside the framework, and lay the bag or blankets on top. The poles will protect the sleeper from moisture in the ground, and keep the leaves from scattering. This type of framework and mattress also can be used on snow or sheer rocks.

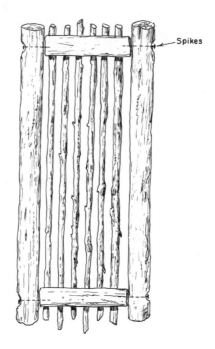

Spikes

Wooden frame for a grass-pole bed.

Bales of straw or alfalfa hay used similarly will make good outdoor mattresses. Horseback hunters often divide a bale of hay for mattresses, and then feed it to the stock on the last day of the hunt. A camper who is near farmland can arrange to get ample mattress material from a stubblefield or haystack.

Dead-Man Tent Stakes

Tents are normally staked down with commercial tent stakes, or wooden stakes cut from saplings and sharpened on the spot. However, when a tent must be set up on sandy

Log anchors tent rope securely in sand.

ground, or snow, or on a gravel bar, stakes won't hold. In such places the best method of staking a tent is to use a "dead man" at each corner.

A dead-man tent stake is merely a stick of wood, a long rock, or even a long chunk of ice tied to the tent's guy rope and buried in the ground. For an average-sized tent, a dead man 18 to 24 inches long will be ample, even in sand.

Dig a hole where each dead man is to be placed. The depth of the hole depends on the softness of the footing. In pure drift sand, a hole 2 feet deep will be ample. Tie a length of wire, rope, or strong cord to the center of the object to be used as an anchor. This should be long enough to extend above the ground after the dead man is buried. Bury the dead man in the hole and tamp the earth over it. Then tie the rope to the loops of the tent.

I have watched Eskimos stake fox traps in snow with this method. They set the trap, then ran the wire from the trap's stake chain into a hole in the snow.

With the small oil stove they melted snow in a pot and poured it slowly over the length of wire in the hole. It only took moments in that 30-below-zero temperature for the water to freeze solidly into a bar of ice along the hole's bottom. They carefully tramped snow on top, immobilizing the trap. When timber is not available, a winter camper can use the same procedure to pitch his tent on snow.

Trenching a Tent

It's a good idea to trench your tent, even though it doesn't look as if it will rain. Especially in mountainous country, sudden showers often occur during the night and an inundated tent takes a bit of the fun out of camping.

If the ground on which you have chosen to pitch your tent slopes slightly, pitch the tent with its rear uphill. You should sleep with your head toward the rear of the tent.

With a shovel, ax blade, or sharpened board, dig a small trench around the tent. The trench should be about six inches from the back and side walls and extend beyond the front. Keeping the trench close to the tent will prevent anyone stumbling over it. Pile the dirt from the trench along its outer edge, forming a little dike. This small dike of dirt, spread evenly around the tent's back and sides, will divert water flowing downhill. Water coming off the canvas will run into the trench and around the outside of the tent. Bevel the ground between the tent walls and the trench to keep water from running under the tent.

How to Dispose of Garbage

Bury all tin cans, food remains, and other garbage which will eventually disintegrate and become part of the soil. When burying garbage, dig the pit far enough from camp to avoid flies or odor, and deep enough so that when it's covered with dirt, bears and other animals will not be able to unearth the garbage and scatter the remains.

Garbage that will burn should be sorted out and piled in an open area where there will be no danger of setting a forest fire. If part of the refuse is wet and won't burn, it is permissible to pour a little gasoline from a lantern onto the pile and start the fire by tossing a match onto it from a distance. When the fire is blazing well, stir it with a stick until everything is burned. Take care that the fire does not become too large and cause an accident.

Garbage that won't burn or disintegrate in the ground, such as glass bottles, should be taken home or disposed of in barrels provided in many camping areas. In some of the remaining wilderness areas, campers are now required to do this. In the Bob Marshall Wilderness Area in Montana, for example, campers are required to pack out all glass bottles and tin cans—anything that won't burn.

Coffee can nailed to tree keeps toilet paper dry.

Camp Toilet-Paper Holder

A 2-pound coffee can, nailed through the bottom into a tree next to the latrine, will keep toilet paper dry at camp. The can should slant slightly downward to prevent rain or snow from dripping off the trees and into the can. Owing to the length of the can, it is hard to drive the nail with a hammer. The best way is first to punch a hole in the bottom from the outside. Then, while holding the can in position, insert the nail into the hole and drive it into the tree by holding the end of a short limb against the head and hitting the protruding end with a rock.

Simple Camp Utensils

Making extra dishes around a camp is easy. A plate can be made by slabbing off an inch-thick board from a length of pine log and shaving down the top surface with an ax. Hold the head of the ax in one hand and push it like a block plane over the face of the board, shaving it until it becomes smooth. It is not necessary to remove the bark on the edges.

To make a knife, use a 6-inch length of any small, dry hardwood limb, shave a 3-inch "blade" with a pocketknife, and round off and bevel the edge. The knife will cut butter and spread it, cut boiled meat and similar food, and even steak if it is tender.

Similarly, a usable fork can be made of an inch-thick slat of straight-grained pine, spruce, or Port Orford cedar. Cut the slat to about 8-inch length, and flatten 2 inches at one end to nearly 1/8 inch thickness. Next cut a V in the end

Method of shaving a slab to make a dish.

1½ inches deep and hollow out the tines. Smooth the edges and surfaces of the tines and shape the handle. It is best to make the tines first; if they break it is easier to begin again before working on the handle.

If there is a 20-inch length of galvanized wire in camp, as well as a small file, a fine fork can be made for heavy work such as turning meat or pick roasting corn from the coals. Bend the wire at the middle to form a U. Then twist the two ends together into the shape of a fork. Sharpen the tines with a file or stone so they will spear

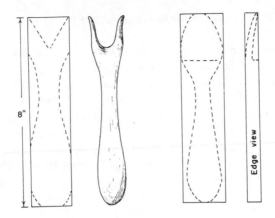

Fork and spoon whittled from slabs of wood.

Simple cooking fork made from
a length of galvanized wire.

large pieces of food. Be sure to clean the fork after meals, otherwise the metal may contaminate food.

Wooden spoons for cooking and eating can be carved from a slab of wood 1 inch wide and ½-inch thick. This slab may be cut from any straight-grained wood, but a pine split is best. About 1½ inches from the end, carve a spoon blade by first making a notch on the top side, then tapering the bottom side from a point 1½ inches back to the tip. Shape the flat blade to form an oval and carve the handle to the rough form of a spoon. If you have the time and inclination, you can use soft wood and hollow out the blade.

Camp cups are easy to make from new tin cans. Cut the can through the center, leaving an inch uncut at the seam.

Edges folded and hammered

To make a camp cup, cut tin can along dotted line, fold and hammer edges.

Then make two vertical cuts so that a strip of metal about 1 inch wide is left, extending from the can's center to the top. Hammer a fold in the raw edge of the cup and pound it smooth. Do the same with the edge of the strip. Then bend the strip into the shape of a handle.

Small frying pans can be made in the same way from gallon-sized fruit cans. Coffee- and teapots can be made from any tin can of suitable size by adding a wire bail. Punch two holes on opposite sides at the top of the can and twist the ends of the wire through these holes. The length of the wire should be about twice the can's diameter to form a loose loop. A good wire for this purpose, and one of the handiest items around any camp, is 1/16-inch copper wire. It is strong but easily bent with the fingers.

Camp Tongs

A pair of tongs is handy around an outdoor camp for moving coals, logs, hot pans, and other tasks. A pair can be made in a couple of minutes from a green stick. The stick should be cut twice as long as the desired length of the finished tongs. Cut a notch at the center about two-thirds through the stick. The sides of the notch should form a

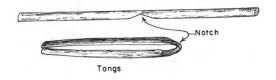

Notch

Tongs

Wood tongs serve many useful purposes around camp.

wide angle so the stick will fold. Flatten the inner side of each end to aid in gripping objects.

Doodle Hook

Another useful wooden tool around an open cooking fire is a doodle hook. Made from a green, forked stick, it is a handy tool for lifting the heavy lid of a hot Dutch oven, a pot of boiling coffee, or a pail of hot water from the fire. If the end is sharpened, it can be stuck in the ground near the fire and always be ready for use.

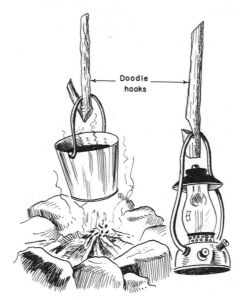

Doodle hooks

Two types of doodle hooks.

In areas where green wood is unavailable, another form of doodle hook can be made from a length of dry wood about 18 inches long. About 2 inches from one end cut a deep notch. The upper edge of this notch should be long and sloping, the lower edge short and steep. Hook the notched stick under the handle of a pot or lantern and use it as a lifter.

Walloper

If you dislike cleaning greasy pots and pans with your hands, make a walloper. All you need is a dishrag or pot scourer, a 10-inch stick, and a nail.

The stick should be approximately ¾-inch in diameter, peeled and smoothed. Simply nail the dishrag to the larger end of the stick, first folding it so the nail head won't pull through. To prevent the mesh of a metal scourer from slipping off the head of the nail, cut a washer of leather, or whittle one from a small piece of wood.

Camp Toaster

One of the best camp toasters is simply a length of forked alder or willow. If the fork is cut to a 3-inch spread, the tines will hold a slice of bread firmly. A 2-foot handle prevents burning the hands. Simply impale a slice of bread on the tines and toast it over coals.

Another toaster, for holding several slices of bread, can be made from a larger forked alder or willow. The fork should extend a foot or more from the main branch at

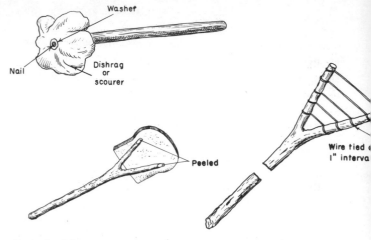

Forked stick toasts single slides of bread. Larger forked stick with wire grid toasts several pieces.

about a 45-degree angle. Tie pieces of wire across the fork, at 1-inch intervals, forming a grid. This grid will hold several slices of bread for toasting over coals.

Grub List

Because of individual requirements and preferences, there are as many grub lists as there are campers. No single list could possibly fit everyone. One husky camper may want meat three times a day; another may want fruit. The way to make up a grub list that will satisfy everyone and provide balanced meals is to use the principle of multiples.

First figure the number of meals anticipated during the trip. Say there will be three fellows going, and the camping trip is for four days. This means there will be twelve breakfasts, lunches, and suppers. Incidentals will be left until later.

The next step is to begin with a basic menu for one of the day's meals—say, breakfast. A good outdoor breakfast consists of orange juice, bacon and eggs, hotcakes, coffee, and perhaps a small dish of fruit. This basic breakfast is then broken down into one-person servings. This is most important, since the total amounts depend on the reasonable accuracy of this estimate.

A 6-ounce serving of juice is reasonable. Three strips of sliced bacon, or about 3 ounces, is average. Two eggs per person. One good recipe for hotcakes calls for 1 egg with enough milk to make 1 cup mixture, into which is stirred 1 cup of prepared pancake mix. This will make 6 large pancakes, approximately 5 inches in diameter. So for the individual's hotcakes, there will be ½ egg, ½ cup of milk (or ¼ cup of canned milk diluted with ¼ cup water), and ½ cup of hotcake flour. Butter and syrup, jelly, or jam are normally used on hotcakes. One ounce of butter is ample, and 3 ounces of syrup will do. One ounce of granulated coffee will make what a normal person wants for breakfast, as will ½ ounce of sugar, and 1 ounce of canned milk. Let's assume that the fat from frying the bacon will cook the hotcakes, and that 1 pound of salt and a can of pepper will last the entire trip. Also, figure 6 ounces of canned fruit to a serving.

Multiply all individual servings by 12 and the result would be the following breakfast list:

Orange juice—72 ounces, or about 4½ pints
Eggs—2½ dozen
Hotcake flour (prepared)—6 cups or about 3 pounds
Butter—12 ounces, or 1 pound with a bit extra for frying

Syrup—36 ounces, or a bit over two pints
Coffee—12 ounces, or for practical purposes, 1 pound
Sugar—6 ounces, or around ½ pound
Canned milk—30 ounces, or 2 large cans and 1 small can
Canned fruit—72 ounces, or about 4½ pints

This is a reasonable estimate of what three people would eat for breakfast for four days. Next comes the remodeling of the list to suit individual tastes and requirements.

For instance, the menu might be altered to have ham instead of bacon for two breakfasts, so an estimated amount of ham is included and a proportionate amount of bacon is left out. If one person eats only one egg for breakfast, the egg total is revised accordingly. Perhaps only two people eat canned fruit after their hotcakes, so only two-thirds of the fruit total is included. One person may like tea for breakfast instead of coffee. If he uses 2 tea bags each time, then he'll need 8 tea bags, and the coffee total may be cut down one-third. If jam or marmalade is used on hotcakes half of the time, then the syrup total may be cut, and the jam estimate added. In many instances, in good fishing or hunting country, there is a possibility that fresh fish or liver and onions may be used for breakfast, instead of bacon, eggs, and hotcakes. This may be anticipated, but should never be depended on. Finally, in estimating a grub list, include those items that make camp eating so much fun—such as a cookie or two after the morning coffee.

The other meals are planned in the same way. When the total amounts are figured for twelve breakfasts, lunches, and dinners, *all* should be increased as much as 25 percent to have ample food in case of emergency.

Using a Space Blanket

One of the finest items recently developed for campers is the space blanket, a sheet of fiberglass enclosed in two layers of material and used principally as an insulator. Many blankets are silver on one side and red or blaze-orange on the other. The blanket is lightweight and can be folded into a pocket-sized package.

A space blanket is waterproof to the extent that prolonged dampness will not penetrate it. It can be used as a ground cloth for sleeping, or as a cover for duffel or a packboard load during a sudden rain, or as a seat while trail watching on damp ground.

But it is as a wrap that the space blanket is most useful. Draped around the shoulders Indian fashion, so that it creates a kind of "tent," the blanket will keep you warm in the chilliest weather. The Indians understood the principle of insulation and used a blanket in this way when they wanted to keep warm. Their body heat warmed the space inside the draped blanket and insulated them from the cold. Any blanket will keep a camper warm, but the advantage of the space blanket is that it's light and made of the best insulating materials.

The red or blaze-orange side of the blanket is designed to serve as a safety wrap on a deer stand. The average olive-green camp blanket camouflages a hunter too well, and he's apt to be mistaken for a deer. Wearing a blaze-orange space blanket is a good precaution.

The blanket is also useful as a signal flag in an emergency. Tied high in a tree or on a long pole, and waving in the breeze, it can be seen from an airplane and from over a half-mile away on the ground.

Transplanting Trees and Shrubs

Have you ever come upon a fine specimen of small spruce, pine or fir in the mountains and visualized it growing on your home lawn? Here's how to transplant it:

Choose a small tree or bush for transplanting, one that has a symmetrical shape. It makes no sense to transplant a ragged tree. It will not improve through the years.

The tree must be removed without disturbing the roots or exposing the taproots to air for too long. The best way to accomplish this is to transplant the tree without removing the dirt from the roots. Spring is the best time to do this, before summer growth begins and the sap begins to flow freely.

Dig a small, circular trench around the tree, gradually going deeper until you've dug under the roots. With small trees no higher than 2 feet a block of earth 15 inches in diameter will be adequate.

It will be difficult to remove the tree without the soil breaking away from the root system unless some kind of container is used. I have found that the best container is a half-bushel peach basket. When the tree is sufficiently loosened in the ground, lift it out with the shovel and, steadying it with one hand, place it in the basket. Shovel fine dirt into any spaces between the root dirt and the basket and tamp it down with the handle of the shovel. This is important, as it seals off air from the exposed root ends. Then slowly pour a bucket of water around the base of the tree. This helps to settle the earth and further seals the roots from air.

When the tree has been firmly implanted in the basket, carefully move it to the site where it will be transplanted.

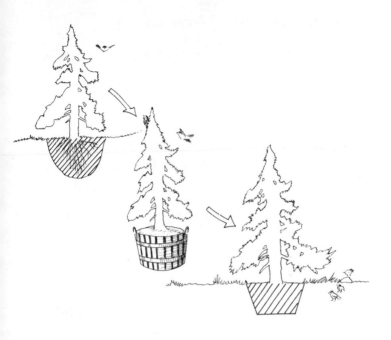

Three steps in transplanting small tree.

It is wise to decide in advance where you want to transplant the tree, to avoid having to rectify a mistake by digging up the tree a second time.

Having chosen the exact spot for the tree, dig a hole the size of the basket. Then lower the basket into the hole by the handles. Tamp dirt around the outside of the basket and slowly pour another bucket of water over the buried roots. After the water has settled, sift a little dirt over the top, sealing off the air.

With proper care, a transplanted tree will "take" in the earth. As the roots begin to grow again, the wooden basket will decay and the new roots will grow through it. In a few years the basket will be completely decayed and the tree firmly rooted in the ground.

How to Bank a Campfire

When sleeping near the heat of an open fire in cold weather, you must bank the fire to last through the night. This means it must be arranged so as to protect the coals from an undue amount of oxygen.

Build the fire an hour or so before retiring and allow it to burn down to a bed of coals. Shovel a ring of dirt around the fire about the height of the coals. Then sprinkle the dead ashes which are left at the edges of the fire over the top of the coals, covering them completely with a thin layer. Banked in this manner, a fire will burn and emit warmth for several hours. The dirt and ashes will admit just enough oxygen to keep the fire burning without completely smothering it. To replenish the fire, scrape the top away and place a few bits of dry wood onto the remaining hot coals. Fan the coals with a hat, or blow on them. They should blaze up and ignite the wood.

How Indians Carried Fire

The Indians had no matches to start a fire with a flick of the wrist, so they often carried their fire with them from one campsite to the next. They used the hollow horn of a buffalo or wild sheep as a container. After cleaning the inside of the horn, they filled it with fine ashes from the fire, added coals on top of the ashes, and more ashes around and on top of the coals. The ashes insulated the horn so it wouldn't get hot, and kept air from the coals so they wouldn't burn up. Keeping the horn in an upright position, the Indians were able to carry their fire great distances. When they reached their new campsite, they prepared a bed of dry tinder, poured the hot coals on top, and fanned the smouldering wood into a blaze.

Plastic Water Carrier

In semiarid regions the water supply may be some distance from a suitable campsite, and water must be carried a considerable distance. If you are backpacking and have only small utensils, this can become a real problem.

A square sheet of plastic neoprene, often used to cover packboard loads, makes an excellent water carrier. Tie the opposite corners of the sheet with a square knot. Then push the sheet into the water until it fills. Grasp the two knots and lift. The sheet forms into a bag and may be carried half full of water.

A 4-foot-square sheet of heavy neoprene will make a bag capable of carrying at least 2 gallons. I have carried water in such a bag for over a half-mile out of a rocky canyon without much loss. The bag may be hung from a suitable tree limb in the shade and used as a permanent water container.

If the water situation ever becomes critical, and it is necessary to catch rainwater, a large sheet of neoprene is useful. Such a sheet is often used as a tent floor or lean-to shelter. Lay the sheet on the ground in an area where its center will be a bit lower than its edges. If necessary,

How to use a plastic sheet to carry water.

the edges can be propped up with rocks or dirt. Rain will gravitate toward the sheet's center, where it can be dipped up.

Using Clorox Bottles

A handy item to have around camp is an empty plastic Clorox bottle in half-gallon size. It can be used as a water jug, and if you are in doubt about the purity of the water supply, it will disinfect the water at the same time. Chlorine, which this product contains, is often used in tablet form to disinfect culinary water, and the commercial product will work just as well as the tablets.

The ratio is eight drops of Clorox per gallon of clear water, and twelve drops to the gallon if the water is turbid. If a half-gallon bottle of Clorox is emptied at home and held upside down for about ten seconds, there will be just about the required four drops remaining on the bottle's inside. If the empty bottle is taken to camp and filled with water, the water will be disinfected.

Because of its plastic construction and inset handle, the bottle stores well among other types of dishes and cooking utensils without danger of breakage. Such a bottle is especially useful for carrying fresh water in a boat.

Cut Clorox bottle along dotted line to make boat bailer.

This bottle also makes one of the best boat bailers imaginable. To make the bailer, leave the cap on the bottle and cut the lower end in the form of a sugar scoop, as shown in the drawing. Grasp the bailer by the handle and scoop the water out of the boat. The plastic material will bend a trifle and can be forced into corners where a metal can won't fit.

Camp Coat Hangers

The sportsman who leaves the city wearing a business suit, and travels by plane, boat, or automobile to a fishing or hunting camp, rarely finds a place to hang his dress wear when he arrives. His suit usually ends up in a pile under his cot.

A simple coat hanger can easily be made from a curved, dry limb around 18 inches long. Remove the bark, and scrape off the fuzz which is common to dry wood,

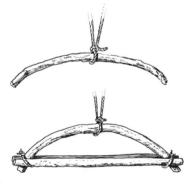

Simple coathanger (top) holds pants with addition of two sticks tied at each end.

otherwise it will shed particles on the garment. Cut a small notch in the center of the hanger's underside and suspend it from a loop of cord. With the coat on the hanger, the ends of the cord can be tied around the tent's ridgepole or looped over a nail.

A pants bar can be added by tying a straight branch to the ends of the hanger. Two bars will keep the press in the pants better than one.

Hauling Ice Water in a Car

When traveling in desert regions it is necessary to take along a sufficient supply of water, and if you want to preserve fish or game birds on the return trip you'll need ice as well. With the new plastic collapsible containers, it's possible to have both. These containers come in 1-gallon and 5-gallon sizes. For one-day trips a couple of gallon-size containers will suffice, but for trips of several days in very hot weather you'll need the 5-gallon size.

Before leaving home, fill the containers nearly to the top, and put them in the freezer. On the trip, when water is needed it is poured from the containers of ice, which will be slowly melting. If you have an insulated cooler to keep food supplies, the containers can be kept in the cooler and the packages of food piled around them.

The ice will keep for a remarkably long time. On a one-week fishing trip in Baja California, six of us took along 85 gallons of frozen water in these collapsible containers. We had enough drinking water for the week, and had enough ice left to preserve several coolers full of tuotuava and corvina steaks and butter clams.

Indian Tipis and Wigwams

The Indians built many different types of dwellings—pit houses, log houses, pueblos, tipis, and square wigwams, to name a few. Of them all, the tipi seems to have taken the strongest hold on our imagination, for when we think of Indians, we generally think of them living in tipis.

The tipi was used by many different tribes, especially by the nomadic hunters of the Great Plains and central Canada. As every schoolboy knows, it was a conical-shaped framework of poles covered with animal skins or bark. The Plains Indians used buffalo hides to cover their tipis; the Canadian Indians the skins of caribou. When a tribe moved from one hunting ground to another, they often dragged the poles of their tipis behind their horses and used them again.

The tipi was constructed by tying three slender poles near the ends, standing them upright to form a tripod, and then leaning other poles against the top with their ends fitted in the crotch. The base of each pole was planted firmly in the ground. Space for an entrance was left at the front of the structure. If birch bark was to be used as a covering, large sheets were cut by girdling a tree in two places and cutting away the bark in one piece. These sheets were flattened and sewed around the framework.

The Indians understood the principle of the draft and chimney, and left an opening in the top of the tipi. The low entranceway provided draft for the fire, which was built in a stone pit in the center of the dirt floor, and the smoke escaped through the opening in the top. The Indians eventually discovered that smoke flaps at the top greatly improved the draft; these were added by extending the

Indian tipi.

covering material to form V-shaped flaps on each side of the opening. If more draft was needed, the bottom edges of tipi covering were raised.

In regions where there were no trees to make tipis, but where willows were available, certain tribes made square wigwams. The framework of these wigwams consisted of

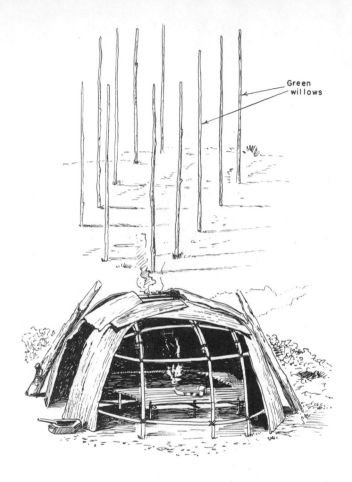

Green willows

Square wigwam.

numerous long willows, sharpened at the ends and implanted in the ground on the four sides of the wigwam's perimeter. If the willows were long enough, they were bent over to form a canopy and their tips buried in the ground.

Wigwams were made of shorter willows by bending them in from each side and fastening them where they overlapped. This framework was covered with bark, skins, or blankets. The fireplace was located in the center of the wigwam, and the smoke escaped through an opening in the top. A low entranceway provided the draft.

A wilderness traveler can easily make such a square wigwam in willow country and cover it with neoprene plastic sheets, tarps, or canvas. A simplified "covered-wagon" wigwam can be built more easily by using willows on only two sides and fastening them at the top.

Indian Steam Bath

Before the first white men came to North America, the Indians had discovered the many mineral springs throughout the land and bathed in them regularly to cure their ailments. The same springs were used for generations, and today many spas stand at the sites of these early Indian health resorts. In Idaho, Lava Hot Springs and the Mud Baths along the Salmon River attract many visitors. Years ago I visited a hot spring in British Columbia, along the Liard River, which Canadian Indians had once used. I hiked to the spring along an old, worn Indian trail.

When they were unable to visit a mineral spring, the Indians often built their own steam baths for curing aches and pains. These baths were small, square wigwams with a rock firepit in the center. The bather sat on a block of wood, with his head above the framework if he wished. The fire in the pit was kept burning until the rocks were

Rock fire-pit
at center of floor

Indian steam bath.

hot. The bather then got inside, poured water over the rocks, producing steam, and closed the entranceway.

Campers with time on their hands can easily make an Indian steam bath in willow country, using canvas tarps or neoprene sheets for covering the wigwam.

How Indians Made Rabbit-Skin Blankets

A singular talent of the North American Indian was his ability to use almost everything in his environment to supply his simple needs. In the Far North, for example, the Indians used the skins of the abundant snowshoe rabbits to make warm blankets. In winter the pelage of this rabbit (actually a hare) turns white—a camouflage coat in

714

the snowy landscape. At this time the skin is at its prime and does not shed its hair.

The rabbit skins to be used for a blanket were stretched and dried, and cut into long strips. The strips were cut in

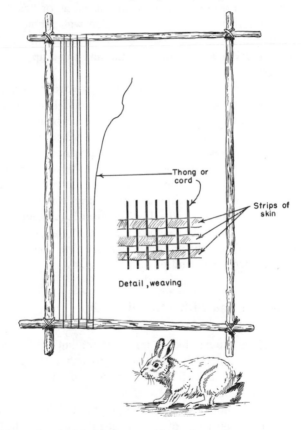

Wood frame laced with thong or cord formed warp for weaving blanket of strips of rabbit skins.

two ways. With a flat skin—that is, one that was split along the belly line—the rough edges were cut off and the circular skin cut in a spiral, starting from the edge and working toward the center, until the entire skin was cut into a single strip. If the skin was removed in one piece, or "cased," so that it formed a tube, the strip also was cut in a spiral, starting at the tail and working toward the head. The latter method saved a little of the skin, and the strip tended to curl less.

The frame on which the blanket was woven was simply a rectangle of poles lashed at the corners. This frame was wound with a long thong cut from the hide of a deer, moose, or caribou, forming a warp on which to weave the blanket. The rabbit skins were then woven through the thongs of the warp, the end of one skin being sewed to another as the work progressed. When the entire warp was filled, the thongs were cut from the frames and tied together to prevent the blanket from unraveling. These rabbit-skin blankets were so warm that the Indians continued making them even after woolen blankets were available from The Hudson's Bay Company.

Driving a Nail with a Handkerchief

This may sound like a magic trick, but it's actually a simple method of driving a nail into a tree if you lack a hammer or a rock. It's always handy to have a few nails in trees around camp for hanging gear.

Fold a handkerchief until it is about 2 inches square. Place it in the palm of your hand, holding it so it won't unfold. Grip the nail between the second and third fingers,

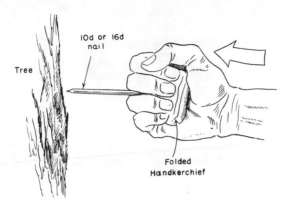

Handkerchief folded in palm cushions hand.

with the head held tightly against the handkerchief. Now stand about a foot in front of the tree, draw back your arm, and punch the nail into the tree much as a boxer throws a body punch. A strong blow will drive a 10d or 16d nail at least an inch into the wood. Don't try it with shorter nails; you're liable to bruise your knuckles against the bark.

22

Cooking How-To

Balanced Meals

There are outdoor chefs who can prepare meals that rival the creations of a hotel chef working in a modern kitchen with the latest appliances. I have been nourished in the outdoors by such delicacies as barbecued trout, T-bone steaks, baked potatoes with sour cream, blueberry pancakes made from wild berries picked on the spot, braised ptarmigan, baked salmon, and cakes, pies, and pastries of every description.

The average outdoorsman need not be able to cook such elaborate dishes, but he should know what constitutes a balanced meal and should master the basic techniques of outdoor cooking so he can prepare edible and enjoyable meals over a campfire or portable stove.

A balanced outdoor meal should contain proteins, carbohydrates, fats, and vitamins. The outdoorsman with limited cooking experience will find it easier to remember these components in terms of actual foods—meat, potatoes or macaroni, vegetables, bread and butter, fruit. Obviously the same menu can't be repeated at every meal because people demand variety. Eggs will furnish the protein at breakfast, if meat isn't served. Hotcakes will replace bread and butter. Juices, instead of fruit, will provide vitamins. Rice may be substituted for potatoes or macaroni. A good stew may contain everything except dessert.

With the many prepared foods available to campers today, anyone who likes the outdoors can learn to cook well enough to get by for the duration of a trip. All he needs to know is how to make acceptable coffee or tea, cook such staples as bacon and eggs, read printed recipes, and use a can opener. It helps if he understands what each of the basic cooking processes does to food, and can cook simple foods with a minimum of utensils. After that, to become a fine outdoor cook he only has to buy a good outdoor cookbook and follow directions. The real secret is practice.

Cooking Fires

The advent of such fuels as propane, butane, and gasoline for portable stoves, and the current popularity of camping vehicles, has greatly reduced the need for the wood cooking fire. Nevertheless, there are many times when the outdoorsman must use wood for cooking, particularly in wilderness areas. Outdoorsmen have cooked their food over hardwood, softwood, willows, brush, sagebrush, and even buffalo chips.

Most outdoor cooking fires are used before they are ready. The cook builds a fire, and when it is burning well he begins to cook. Generally speaking, this is wrong. The fire should be allowed to burn for a considerable time until a bed of hot coals is formed. Coals provide a more uniform heat and will not blacken utensils as badly as will flame.

When wood fuel is used in a camp stove, it isn't necessary to let the fire burn down to coals. The metal of the stove, and the confinement it gives the fuel, induce a regular heat while the fire is burning. But in an outside fire, blazing wood, especially in a strong breeze, produces an erratic heat which alternately cooks and cools. A bed of hot coals produces an even heat which the cook can regulate simply by shifting the cooking utensils.

To stabilize the cooking heat further, it is best to use heavy utensils. A heavy griddle, Dutch oven, or skillet won't heat up as quickly as a thin steel skillet but it will hold heat long after it has been removed from the fire. This helps to maintain an even cooking heat with no danger of flash burning the food.

A further way of controlling the heat from an outside cooking fire is to use some kind of grid over the fire. This may be an old refrigerator or oven shelf supported by rocks placed on either side of the fire, a homemade steel grid with legs, a small sheet of metal, or merely two rows of rocks flanking the fire, set close enough together to support a pot. One of the best grids available in conifer country is a pair of green logs of similar diameter placed on opposite sides of the fire. When the coals are ready, they are raked with a stick into the opening between the logs. The pots and pans are placed on top of the logs. Logs 3 feet long and from 6 to 8 inches in diameter are fine for this purpose.

Frying Foods

To fry foods means to boil them in oil. The amount, or depth, of the oil is important. Foods may be fried in shallow oil, as when cooking bacon or steaks. Or foods may be deep-fried—plunged into deep boiling oil and completely covered. Such foods as shrimp, doughnuts, and French-fried potatoes are often deep-fried.

Frying is a poor form of cooking compared with other methods. Frying coats pieces of food with a layer of fat which is digested late in the digestive process, largely through the action of bile. Despite this fact, frying is much used in outdoor cooking because it is easy, quick, and tasty for foods such as fish and steak. The newer shortenings and frying oils are better than the old standby lard, since food does not absorb them as much and they drain better after cooking. Also, people engaged in vigorous outdoor activity have hearty appetites and good digestive systems. Fried foods rarely cause them discomfort.

However, the amateur outdoor cook should still try to keep fried foods to a minimum, alternating with other forms of cooking. For example, if fried ham has been served for breakfast, roast or boiled meat for supper would be better for health.

Boiling and Stewing

Another form of cooking is boiling. Such camp foods as vegetables and less desirable or tougher cuts of meat often are boiled in water to which salt has been added. Butter, flavoring, and condiments may be added after the food is cooked. A tough cock sage grouse, or the leg cuts of an elk or moose, can't be tenderized by frying. But boiling them for several hours will render them edible. Often a piece of tough meat is boiled for a time, then fried to make it more palatable.

Care should be used in boiling tough meat of any kind. If the cooking water is brought to and kept at a rolling boil, it often tends to toughen already tough meat. Instead of boiling, it is far better just to simmer the meat and water.

This leads us to another form of cooking—stewing. Stewing is a good cooking method for the outdoorsman, especially if he isn't in a hurry. A stew can be set on the coals, a little dry wood added now and again, and gradually cooked over a period of several hours. Stewing preserves the juices of meat and vegetables which are lost in other forms of cooking.

There are two things to remember when making any kind of meat-vegetable stew:

First, the ingredients should be placed in the pot to cook in the order of their toughness, or the length of time it takes to cook them. For example, tough meat should be started first, and raw carrots added before such items as diced potatoes or cooked string beans. Such flavoring as catsup, or a can of tomato sauce, would be added last.

Second, the stew should not be allowed to reach a full boil but be kept at a bubbling simmer. Simmering, in addition to tenderizing the meat, retains the flavor of the stew. A final virtue of stewing is that a good stew gets better as it goes along. What is left over from a big supper is just as good when heated up and served at breakfast.

Elevation affects cooking time for both boiling and stewing, since water boils when the vapor pressure equals the atmospheric pressure. Thus at sea level the boiling point is higher than it is at high altitudes, as anyone who has boiled eggs above timberline in the Rockies has discovered.

Baking

Baking is a cooking process which employs hot, dry air as the heating medium rather than hot fat or water. The outdoorsman normally uses one of a few basic utensils for baking: the oven of a sheet-metal camp stove, a reflector oven, or a Dutch oven. A substitute for a Dutch oven can be made by inverting one heavy cast-iron or cast-aluminum skillet over another of the same size. If a good fit is obtained, the air inside the oven will be heated evenly.

At some large camps that are used annually, and at some western ranches, outdoor ovens are built of brick, cinder blocks, or native stone. These have grates inside and are equipped with steel doors—somewhat on the order of the outdoor adobe ovens that Indians in the Southwest have used for decades. These large ovens are ideal for baking large quantities of bread and cakes, and an understanding of their construction and use will help the camper who must use a smaller oven for baking.

Besides bread and pastries, apples, potatoes, fish, ham, and squash can be baked. These foods are often smeared with a thin layer of melted butter or shortening before placing them in the oven. This thin layer of fat or butter not only keeps the food from scorching on the side that touches metal, but it also imparts a better flavor to the crust.

For the average camper, the primary thing to remember in baking is to produce an even heat around the food and to maintain the heat long enough to bake the food without scorching it. This takes experience.

The stove oven and the Dutch oven maintain an even heat throughout. A reflector oven, which is openfaced, depends on an even flow of heat from the hot coals in front of it. To produce the maximum degree of reflected heat the top and bottom faces of the oven must be set at about a 45-degree angle to the coals.

Roasting

Roasting is a form of cooking in which food is subjected to heat from an open fire. As with baking, hot air is the heating element, and is radiated over the surface of the food. The food often rests on a metal roaster or pan and is covered so that moisture and juices will not be lost. The juices are condensed by contact with the upper part of the container and drip back on the food, a kind of self-basting which prevents scorching or burning.

The American Indians used to roast food in many simple ways. Birds, fish, or pieces of meat were placed on the end of a forked stick and held before an open fire. Again, entire birds were often wrapped in heavy mud and placed in hot coals to cook. Then the caked mud was removed, exposing the cooked, moist meat. Ears of corn were similarly roasted in mud.

The Indians of the Southwest used the roasting process as a military expedient. In the rimrock country of Arizona, I have repeatedly come upon huge pits full of blackened embers. When an Indian tribe was being pursued by white soldiers, they often sent their squaws ahead to dig these pits, line them with coals, and roast the trimmed, gourdlike bodies of agave and century plants. When the retreating braves came upon the pits, cooked food was awaiting them. The soldiers, having to extend themselves with packed gear, often could not catch up with the braves, who traveled light and found their food along the way.

Today, Boy Scouts often roast food in such simple ways when learning survival techniques. But practically speaking, the camp cook generally will roast meat on top of the camp stove, inside a camp oven, or in a Dutch oven on the hot coals of a campfire.

Broiling and Barbecuing

Other methods of cooking outdoors are broiling and barbecuing. Broiling means to cook over an intense heat, usually a flame, and normally is used for meats. In the home electric or gas oven, the heat usually comes from above; at camp the heat usually comes from below.

Broiling is a good way to cook meat at camp. Portable charcoal broilers can often be taken along. If meat is seared on both sides, then cooked a bit more slowly until done, the charcoal imparts a delicious flavor.

Barbecuing, of course, is a specialty at western ranches where outdoor pits are often built. An entire animal, such as a sheep or a small pig, or perhaps a large piece of beef, may be barbecued in one of these pits. This entails building a fire hours in advance to create enormous quantities of hot coals. The food is wrapped in wet burlap, canvas, or large green leaves and placed in the pit on the hot coals. The entire pit is then lightly covered so that moisture will not escape.

A covered barbecue "pit" may be built above ground from two halves of a steel drum or steel culvert. The lower half, set on legs and equipped with a grid, contains the charcoal. The upper half is hinged to the lower half so that it can be closed on the coals and food. I recently had the pleasure of eating some prime beef which had been barbecued in such a "pit" at the famed Y-O Ranch in Texas. A huge piece of beef was barbecued for five hours, then served with the trimmings and a special barbecue sauce.

Tempering a Griddle, Skillet, or Dutch Oven

Three of the most useful camp cooking utensils are a large griddle, a skillet, and a Dutch oven, all of cast iron. Most camp foods can be cooked in one of these three utensils. Generally the griddle is used for cooking bacon, eggs, and hotcakes, the skillet for frying a variety of foods, and the Dutch oven for baking or roasting.

Before using any of the three utensils for cooking, old-timers would "burn them in," or "temper" them. To temper a new griddle, either of cast iron or cast aluminum, place it on a stove and heat it for about an hour. Then cover the entire cooking surface with some form of fat. The best thing to use is the rind from which bacon slices have been cut. If a large piece of rind is not available, a small amount of cooking oil may be used.

With the griddle hot, and the surface covered lightly with oil, use a spatula to smooth down the cooking surface. This

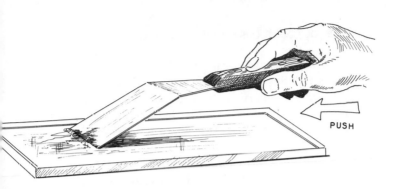

Tempering a griddle with a spatula.

surface may appear to be entirely smooth, but it will have tiny particles of metal which will cause food to stick unless they are worked down. Invert the spatula, as shown in the drawing, and push the blade repeatedly across the entire cooking surface of the griddle. Apply a fair amount of pressure, and be sure to scrape the corners as well as the center.

During the scraping, the oil or grease will become slightly blackened from minute particles of metal and dust from the factory surfacing. Wipe the griddle surface clean two or three times during the tempering, and apply more oil or grease.

After an hour of such scraping a new griddle will be ready for cooking hotcakes. When finished, wipe the griddle with a paper towel or dry cloth, but *do not* wash it with water. After future uses do not wash the griddle but coat it lightly with bacon rind or cooking oil and dry it with a cloth or paper towel. Food particles that stick to the surface are burned off by heating the griddle and then drying it while a light film of cooking oil remains on the surface. The light film of fat or oil will work into the pores of the metal and food will not stick to it. It will also prevent rusting. And the hot oil cleans just as well as soap and water.

A Dutch oven may be tempered in much the same way. It is heated, lightly oiled, and heated again until the cooking oil or fat smokes. Then it is wiped with a dry paper towel or dish cloth. The walloper described previously is a good tool for doing this without burning the hands. The underside of the lid is tempered in this way, as well as the bottom part of the oven. An occasional light coating of oil or bacon fat applied to the entire surface will keep it from rusting.

Two types of Dutch ovens. Older model, right, has concave lid for holding hot coals.

Rim holds hot coals

This should be done especially before traveling or when storing the oven for long periods of time.

The best Dutch oven for baking bread is not the modern one with its rounded, convex lid, but one of the older models with a rimmed, concave lid and three legs. The legs keep the oven level on a bed of coals, and also raise it slightly above the coals if desired. The rimmed lid is nearly airtight and designed to hold hot coals in its concavity. These produce an even heat inside the oven, even when it is removed from the coals. Many campers take along a few charcoal pellets and use them for this purpose.

Baking Bread and Biscuits

Loaf bread is baked in a Dutch oven in the same way it is baked in a home oven. The loaves are formed, allowed to rise, then coated with melted butter and placed in the hot oven. It takes practice to get the heat just right, but if the oven is set on a firm bed of hot coals, just at the side of the fire, and its lid filled with hot coals, bread will bake in approximately one hour without burning.

Fresh biscuits are always welcome in a camp. If a stove is not available, biscuits can be easily made in a Dutch oven. They are mixed, formed, and baked just as in the home oven.

Biscuit mixes, with all ingredients already in the flour, are available at any grocery store. One of the best, especially for the lazy camp cook, is a product called Krustease which mixes with water and forms a stiff batter. The beauty of this product is that it will also make hotcakes, dumplings, and waffles.

Doughnuts

A special treat around a camp on a rainy day is a batch of doughnuts. Here is a fine recipe which calls for fresh (not sour) milk, so diluted canned milk can be used. The recipe will make forty-eight doughnuts.

1 cup sugar
3 teaspoons baking powder
2 tablespoonfuls melted shortening
2 eggs, slightly beaten
1 cup fresh milk, or ½ cup canned milk mixed with ½ cup water
½ teaspoonful vanilla flavoring
1 teaspoonful salt
½ teaspoonful cinnamon
½ teaspoonful nutmeg
1/8 teaspoonful ginger
4¾ cups flour
½ teaspoonful lemon flavoring

Mix and blend the eggs and sugar. Sift the flour and mix with the salt, spices, and baking powder. Then add milk, shortening, and flavoring to the flour mixture and mix into a dough. Chill the dough. Roll the chilled dough on a floured board into a sheet about ¼ inch thick.

Cut the sheet of dough into doughnut shapes with an empty tin-can top—about 2¾ inches in diameter—which has been floured. Break the center of each doughnut with the fingers into a rough hole. Immerse the doughnuts in approximately 3 to 4 pounds of boiling lard or cooking oil, turning when done on the bottom side, and cook until done. Allow the doughnuts to drain on a paper towel and sprinkle with sugar. Save the hot fat for other uses.

Southern Fried Pies

A fine camp recipe for a cold, snowy day is a batch of southern fried pies. A regular pie-crust dough may be used, or the same one used for doughnuts. The filling is made from packaged raisins.

Plump two cups of raisins by putting them in 1½ cups of cold water, add 1 tablespoonful of butter, and boil for one to two minutes. Next, stir 1 cup of sugar with 3 tablespoonfuls of flour and a few grains of salt. Add enough water to the sugar-flour mix so that it can be stirred. Stir this mixture into the raisins and allow to boil for two to three minutes, stirring constantly. Remove from the heat and allow to cool slightly.

Cut the dough into circles about 5 inches in diameter. Pour the raisin filling onto one-half of each circle, fold over the other half, and pinch it around the edges. Use enough filling to make each pie about ½ inch thick.

Fry the small pies in a hot Dutch oven, using enough cooking oil or fat to prevent them from sticking. Cook with the oven's lid on until the tops are brown. The same raisin mix can be used with a standard pie-crust mixture to bake regular pies on a tin plate in a Dutch oven.

Biscuits in a Flour Sack

My maternal grandfather hated to wash dishes. When my grandmother was sick, and he had to do the cooking, he taught us boys that a used dish became a dirty dish that had to be washed. To avoid this chore, he always mixed his biscuits in the top of a 50-pound sack of white flour.

After meticulously washing his hands, Grandpa would soberly tell us, "Always leave a little clean dirt on your hands, to mix off into the bread. It improves the flavor."

That is how I learned to mix biscuits in the top of a flour sack. The same procedure can be used at camp when a mixing pan is not available.

First, mix ½ cup of canned milk with ½ cup of cold water. Add 2 tablespoons of melted bacon fat and mix well. Smooth down the top part of the flour in a sack and make a small depression in the center. If the sack is only partly full, roll down the sides until the level of the flour is about 2 inches from the top of the sack. Into this depression, sprinkle ½ teaspoonful of salt and 2 level teaspoonfuls of baking powder. Then pour a little milk-water mixture into the depression. Mix in the flour, either with a spoon or by folding small amounts of flour over the liquid and mixing it together. Add more of the milk and water, mixing it with the flour. Keep the mixture stiff, not liquid. With care, all the liquid can be mixed with flour until a stiff dough remains. Knead the dough into a ball, and pinch off small portions which will become biscuit-sized when baked.

Bullburgers

One of the best ways to use lesser cuts of elk, deer, moose, or caribou meat is to make them into bullburgers. This allows you to use all parts of the animal without waste. You'll need a small food chopper, with a medium-coarse blade, for grinding the meat. The burgers will be better if the meat is ground twice.

Bullburgers may be made at camp, or at home from meat that has been frozen. Before grinding meat into burgers, allow it to cool thoroughly for several days. Tough, old bull animals should age from ten to fourteen days to break down the fibers of the meat.

When making burgers at camp, select cuts to be chopped on the basis of how fast they age. Rib and brisket cuts age quicker than the loins, hams, and shoulders. If the burgers are to be used immediately, it is all right to include areas of fat. However, if the meat patties are to be frozen, it is best to cut out most of the fat and substitute fat pork. Deer fat especially tends to become rancid with age when frozen. If you send your game to a processing plant, tell them to double-grind the meat and add 25 percent fat pork.

The simplest recipe for wild-game bullburger is to mix the ground meat with sliced or diced onions, shape it into flat patties nearly half-inch thick, and fry in a heavy skillet, on a heavy griddle, or in a Dutch oven. Serve on heated, buttered buns or toast, or as part of a regular meal, with a few slices of dill pickle and catsup.

Bullburger can be used in a variety of combinations. The meat can be formed into small, round patties (1½ inches diameter). Prefry the patties and add them to nearly cooked macaroni. Another fine recipe, suitable for camp or home, requires large green peppers, one per person. Hollow out the peppers and slice them in half, lengthwise. Boil in enough water to cover for 20 minutes. While the peppers are boiling, fry small burgers, about the size of the pepper halves, mixed with diced or sliced onions. Salt and pepper the burgers before frying. When both peppers and patties are done, mix a tablespoonful of flour into the fat remaining from frying the burgers, and stir until it browns. Add the water in which the peppers were boiled, stirring constantly, and thicken into a sauce. Place a slice of bread or toast on each plate, add the sauce and a half pepper, open side up. Put a patty inside each pepper half, add sauce, and serve.

To combine bullburgers and chile, follow this recipe. Break half a pound of burger into small pieces with a fork, and fry in a skillet. When browned, salt lightly, then add a 16-ounce can of prepared chili con carne and mix with the meat. Heat to near boiling. Add water as it cooks to give the desired consistency. If thin, eat in a bowl with crackers or bread. If thick, spread over toast or buns.

For a hot lunch that is quickly prepared and nourishing, try Mexican burgers. Ingredients needed are:

½ cup chopped onion
1/3 cup chopped peppers
½ pound bullburger
6-ounce can of tomato paste
½ cup water
1¼ teaspoonfuls salt,
   pinch of pepper, or to taste
1-2 teaspoonfuls chili powder
1 small can of pork and beans

Break the bullburger into small pieces with a fork and saute in a skillet, with the chopped peppers and onion, until brown. Stir the tomato paste into the half cup of water and add to the meat. Add salt, pepper, and chili. Finally, add pork and beans, stir well, and heat until piping hot. Serve over buttered toast with fresh salad or fruit.

How to Cook Tongue

One of the best cuts of meat from a big-game animal, the tongue, is often left behind in the woods. The tongue of elk and moose is especially good, and of considerable size. It is easily removed, after the animal's head has been detached, by cutting up from the throat area and freeing the tongue from its base.

To prepare tongue, wash it and then boil it for two or three hours in salted water (1 tablespoonful salt to the gallon). After boiling, peel off the skin with a sharp knife. The meat can be thinly sliced and used for sandwiches. Deer tongue is prepared in the same way.

Cooking Sheep Ribs on an Open Fire

The meat of wild sheep is among the most delicious of all game meat. Of the various cuts, none surpasses the ribs, especially when cooked over an open fire. I watched a Tahltan Indian hunter cook sheep ribs in this way, his only utensil a length of green spruce.

He built a roaring fire and allowed it to burn down to coals which gave off a regular heat. Meanwhile he prepared the large slab of ribs by paring down the loin area so that it equaled the thickness of the rib area and would cook evenly. He found a length of green spruce and sharpened both ends, shoved one end into the ground, about a foot from the edge of the fire and slanted slightly toward it.

He impaled the ribs on the stake at the center, a bit toward the top, with the outside toward the fire. Almost at once, the meat began to bubble as the fat melted. As the meat cooked, the fat basted it and kept it from burning. The Indian regulated the heat by moving the coals of the fire. When they died down, he put on a little dry kindling. He turned the ribs when they were done on one side.

After an hour or so, the meat was ready. He pulled the stake from the ground, sliced off a rib for each of us, and salted them. We ate the ribs with our hands, like corn on the cob. I've seldom eaten better meat.

Later the Indian told me that when a hunter of his tribe had to travel long distances in wilderness country, he carried only a rifle, a small rucksack, and some salt. When he killed an animal, he used the ribs first, cooking them the way he had shown me. He put the remains in the rucksack, and ate some for lunch the next day. The following day he would dry, smoke, and cut the rest of the meat into long slices. Packing as much meat as possible in his small rucksack, the hunter would continue his journey, and when the meat was nearly gone, he would kill another animal. The Indian told me that he'd once crossed most of British Columbia with only a rifle, a rucksack, and some salt.

Moose Nose

Among the Indians of the North the cooked nose of a moose has long been considered a delicacy, for the long bulbous section, from the end of the septum to the tip, contains considerable meat. The entire nose was chopped or sawed off, coated with mud, and placed in a bed of hot coals. After several hours it would be completely cooked. When the caked mud was removed, most of the hair would come off and the rest could be scraped away. The meat was separated from the bone, salted, and eaten. Moose nose may still be prepared this way in a hunting camp.

A more sophisticated way of cooking moose nose is to boil it. The entire nose section, including the lower part of the upper jawbone, may be used, or only the bulbous nose area. First parboil the nose in a large kettle for forty-five minutes. Then remove it and place in a container of cold water to cool.

When the nose has cooled, pick off the hair. Immerse the nose in sufficient fresh, cold water to cover it. Add a couple of onions, a clove of garlic, and a tablespoonful of salt. Allow to simmer until tender, and then leave overnight in the same liquid. In the morning, the white meat of the bulbous section may be thinly sliced and used for sandwiches or snacks. If desired, elk tongue and moose nose may be pickled in vinegar.

Eskimo Steak

In the winter of 1959, while I was hunting in the Arctic, an Eskimo hunter named Ookeelah (which means Run Fast) showed me how to prepare Eskimo steak.

Inside his tiny igloo he thawed out some pieces of fresh caribou meat which he'd brought from his little village of Point Hope, Alaska. The meat was from the animal's brisket area and contained fat marbling. When it was thawed, Ookeelah cut it into ¾-inch cubes. He boiled these tiny cubes of raw meat in a pot on the puny gas stove he used to heat tea water when traveling. He used chunks of ice from a nearby lake for water. He added a couple of pinches of salt to the boiling water.

When the meat had boiled for nearly a half-hour, Ookeelah set the pot on the table. Then he heated some seal oil he'd rendered from the blubber of a hair seal and poured it into a tin cup.

We ate the meat by impaling a cube on a fork and dipping it into the warm seal oil. He called this "Eskimo steak" and told me soberly that his people had to eat it or else they would get sick. Living in that harsh land, and lacking green vegetables and other sources of vitamins, the Eskimos had discovered that the oil of the seal compensated for their vitamin deficiency. They ate only the brisket and ribs of the inland caribou they occasionally shot—the meat containing fat. In his broken English, Ookeelah assured me that the hams of the caribou were "—for dogs and good white-man food."

Potatoes and Onions in Foil

Easily prepared at camp with a minimum of utensils, this combination of potatoes and onions cooked in butter is often called German-fried spuds.

To prepare, peel the potatoes and slice thinly. Mix with peeled, sliced onions. A good ratio, if you like onions, is 1 onion to 3 potatoes. Add salt, pepper, and butter—about 1 tablespoonful of butter to each pint of potatoes and onions, mixed well.

Shape the mixture into a small rectangular loaf and wrap in foil. Cover lightly with hot coals. A quart-sized loaf should cook between twenty and thirty minutes.

If a small charcoal grill is available, the potatoes may be cooked on it. Wrap in two layers of foil to prevent the package from breaking open during handling. The layers should be folded on opposite sides. Turn once, when half cooked. It is often possible to tell when the potatoes are done by smelling the steam escaping from the folds.

Bullburgers, wieners, or pork chops go well with German-fried spuds.

Corn in Mud or Foil

To roast ears of sweet corn in an open fire, leave on the husks, smear them with thick mud, and bury them in a bed of hot coals. The mud cakes, holding in the moisture and flavor much as in pressure-cooking, and prevents burning. After approximately twenty minutes, remove the ears from the coals and strip off the caked mud and husks. Eat on the cob with butter and salt.

Roasting ears may also be wrapped in foil and cooked in hot coals. Again, the husks should be left on. Cooking time will be about twenty minutes, depending on the thickness of the husks and the size of the ears.

If roasting ears of corn are picked from a garden or purchased from farmers along the road, do not peel away the outer husks as is often done in supermarkets. With the green husks intact, the ears can be roasted in hot coals without first covering them with mud or foil. The trick is to gather all the husk ends together over the tip of the ear

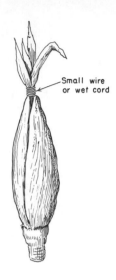

Tie husk ends before roasting corn in hot coals.

and tie them with a short length of thin wire or a wet cord. The wet cord will burn through during the cooking, but it will hold the husk ends over the end of the cob long enough to prevent burning. Tying the husks keeps the steam in while the corn is roasting. Ears of sweet corn cooked in this way don't have the swampy taste imparted by certain types of mud. And corn roasted in any manner retains its garden flavor better than corn boiled in water.

Making Jerky

The American Indians, through necessity, made a great contribution to the process of preserving fresh meat. Their problem was three-fold. First, fresh meat was a main part of their diet, and game animals were normally killed at considerable distances from their villages. Second, it was hard during summer season to use up an entire animal before spoilage set in. Third, on their travels they needed a food which was light but sustaining, and could be carried.

The Indians solved all three problems by cutting meat into long strips and drying it in the sun. Smoke, and salt when available, were used in the curing process to some extent.

Indians of the North country still jerk much of their fresh meat. Within the past decade I have been in the Alaska bush and seen Indian hunters kill a moose. They would camp for several days while they cut the meat into long strips, hang it from drying racks made of willow and alder, and cure it in the sun, keeping a slow birch fire going beneath it. While traveling down the Yukon River, between Dawson and Eagle, Alaska, I photographed the long drying racks where literally hundreds of king salmon, taken from the fish-wheels of the river, had been hung in strips and were being smoke-dried. Again, at a hunting camp at Beaver Creek, Alaska, the part-Indian female cook made moose jerky from the trophy bull I had shot, and it was delicious.

Many hunters like to make venison or antelope meat into jerky. Not only does it add variety to the camp menu, but is a palatable and sustaining meat for lunches and snacks.

There are dozens of recipes for making jerky, but they all require drying the fresh meat before spoilage can occur. How thick and wide the strips of meat are cut is determined to some extent by the season. If it is sunny when the drying process begins, the strips are cut larger than they would be in wet weather.

Here is a basic recipe for deer or antelope jerky. It is very simple, and a good one for the beginner:

Cut the meat, preferably ham or shoulder, into long strips 1-inch wide and ¼-inch thick. Cut with the grain. Pare off all fat, as it will turn rancid in jerky.

Next, lay the strips on a breadboard or other flat board, and sprinkle them generously on both sides with black pepper. Use approximately twice as much as for steak or chops. Rub the pepper well into the meat with the hands. When this is done, thread a length of white cotton cord through the end of each piece of meat, using a large darning needle. The cord is for hanging the strip.

Fill a 5-gallon can with water and bring to a boil. Blanch the strips of meat in the boiling water by immersing each piece for ten seconds, removing it, and immersing it for another ten seconds.

Lightly brush each piece with prepared liquid smoke. Then hang the strips to dry. In an arid climate, they may be hung on a line in a cool, dry room where it will take from eight to ten days to dry. The strips also may be hung from a pole outside in the sunshine, protected from flies by a cheesecloth "tent," and high enough so dogs can't get at them. It should take three or four days for the meat to dry. Store the dried meat in cloth bags, preferably hung off the ground, or in cold storage.

Other recipes differ largely in the mixture of spices and how they are applied to the meat and the size of the strips.

The curing salt may be applied directly to strips, instead of blanching them in boiling salt water. Curing salt can be obtained from a processing plant. Rub the salt thoroughly into the strips and leave them in a cool place overnight before hanging them to dry. You can make your own curing salt from 1 pound of salt, 6 ounces of Prague powder, 2½ ounces of sugar, and 1 ounce of white pepper, all mixed thoroughly. For those who like jerky very hot, 1 ounce of cayenne pepper may be added. This mixture is sufficient for 40 to 50 pounds of fresh meat.

If damp weather is a problem, or if your patience is limited, the drying process may be speeded up by putting the thin strips into pans so they do not touch and slowly drying them in a warm, but not hot, oven. The oven temperature should be between 100 and 150 degrees, and the strips should be turned occasionally. Drying also may be speeded by putting the strips in a meat smoker which has a low heat output.

For the person who wants to make jerky at home, and can use an electric oven, here is a fine recipe:

Cut strips of lean meat (deer, antelope, elk, or beef) 1/8 inch thick and lay them in a dripping pan or small dish pan. Sprinkle the first layer with a good brand of seasoning salt, as you would salt a steak. Put one drop of liquid smoke onto each strip and brush it evenly with a pastry brush. Pepper the strips with seasoning pepper, and sprinkle them again with a light coating of granulated sugar. If you like garlic, sprinkle the strips lightly with garlic salt. Line the pan with a second layer and add the seasoning. Continue adding layers of strips, seasoning each layer until the pan is nearly full or the meat runs out. Let the pan of meat set from five to seven hours. For tough meat, overnight is not too long.

Get as many oven shelves as possible—one for each bracket is desirable. Take each shelf out of the oven, cover it with the prepared strips, and replace it. Set the temperature for 100 degrees, and heat the strips from six to seven hours. Strips cut thicker than 1/8 inch may take longer. When the strips are dried brittle, the jerky will be done. It may then be stored indefinitely in cloth, paper, or plastic bags, in the home freezer or refrigerator.

Venison Chili

Exceptionally fine venison chili can be made at camp, if preparation is made in advance and a few necessary items brought along. The ingredients needed are as follows:

2 pounds ground or diced venison
1/3 cup diced onions
1/4 teaspoonful minced garlic
2 teaspoonfuls ground cumin
3 tablespoonfuls flour
1 teaspoonful salt
1/4 teaspoonful pepper
2-1/2 cups tomato juice
2 tablespoonfuls chili powder

The venison may be diced by cutting it into ¼-inch cubes with a sharp knife on a flat board, or it may be run through a small food grinder.

Saute cubed or ground meat, with the onions and garlic, in a Dutch oven, for about fifteen minutes, stirring occasionally. Add cumin, chili powder, flour, salt, pepper, and stir. Then add the tomato juice. Cover and cook for another fifteen minutes, uncover and cook for fifteen minutes more.

Serve hot over preheated chili beans. This recipe serves eight people.

If deer meat is not available, elk, moose, or caribou may be substituted. Venison is best, however, owing to its finer texture.

This same recipe may be used at home to prepare chili in bulk for freezing. After preparing the chili mixture, allow it to cool thoroughly and put it in pint-sized plastic refrigerator bags. Tie the bags shut and put in the freezer. Chili made in this way should be used within a six-month period.

Beans and Ham Hocks

One of the best camp meals, especially in cold weather, is a mixture of dry beans and ham hocks. The following recipe serves three people.

Wash 1½ pints of dry, white beans, place in a large pot, and cover with 2 inches of water. Place on the fire and allow to simmer, adding water as required so the beans do not cook dry.

Cut ham hock which still contains some meat into small chunks and add to the beans after they have simmered for three hours. Add salt, pepper, and a dash of catsup. Simmer for another hour and serve with buttered bread and fresh fruit.

Camp Coffee or Tea

Most outdoorsmen drink a lot of coffee, and can make a good cup with the home percolator or drip coffeepot. Some don't do so well over a campfire.

Camp coffee is best when made in an enameled coffeepot. However, it can be made in an aluminum pot, a kettle, or even in a Dutch oven. Some of the best camp coffee ever made has been brewed in a 2-pound coffee can rigged with a wire bail.

Use regular-grind coffee, one heaping teaspoonful to each cup of water. Those who like their coffee strong add an extra spoonful "for the pot." Fill the pot with the required number of cups of cold water and set on the coals to heat. As the water heats, add the equivalent number of spoonfuls of coffee.

The coffee grounds will stay on the water's surface as the water heats, and will "grow" as the water reaches the boiling point. The coffee must be watched carefully at this stage or else it will boil over. If you're using a coffee can, lay a green alder across the top. It will dampen the rolling boil as the water reaches the top.

When the water boils, allow the grounds to settle and mix with the boiling water for approximately thirty seconds, then take the pot off the coals to let the coffee settle, or brew. Set the pot just far enough away from the heat so that it will remain hot but not simmer. In five minutes, the coffee will be ready to pour. If it hasn't completely settled, add a dash of cold water.

Many outdoorsmen of the Far North prefer tea instead of coffee. They say it keeps them warmer on the trail. Tea can be made at camp in an enameled teapot, an aluminum pot, or a metal tea pail used by many Canadian woodsmen. The pot used for making tea should not be used for making coffee.

Do not boil tea. Heat the water to the boiling point, add the tea leaves, and remove the pot from the fire to steep.

An average mixture is one level teaspoonful of tea leaves for each cup of water. The steeping time depends on individual taste, but after about three minutes tea will become bitter. If an earthenware pot is available, first put in the tea and then add boiling water for a couple of minutes.

Tea bags are very handy for making camp tea, but the quality of the tea in bags is generally poorer than that sold in bulk. Many campers like black tea, others prefer green. Canadians and Alaskans have developed a taste for the wild Hudson Bay tea, often called Labrador tea or mountain tea. This grows wild on small bushes having rosette-shaped leaves. These green, waxy leaves will give off a delicate odor similar to eucalyptus. This is one way of identifying the plant. It is found in the northern tier of the states near the Canadian border, in Canada, and in much of Alaska. Fur traders used it to supplement their supply of regular tea, and some later came to use it exclusively.

To make Hudson Bay tea for two people, pick about a dozen leaves and boil them in water for three minutes. (It takes time for the hard leaves to give up their flavor.) Then remove the leaves from the water and bring it to a boil. Combine the Hudson Bay tea with a little black tea and you'll have a delicious, warming drink.

Hudson Bay tea leaves may be picked and dried, and taken along for future use. The best way to dry the leaves is to place them in a brown paper bag near the camp stove. A quart dries in a few hours and weighs very little.

Making Hotcake Syrup

Occasionally at camp the syrup runs out before the hotcakes. Rather than disappoint hungry campers, make your own syrup of sugar and water. Just pour a cupful of granulated white sugar into a heavy skillet and place the skillet over the fire. Stir the sugar until it is an even brown. Add a cup of boiling water and stir vigorously until the sugar is dissolved. Do not allow the sugar to burn or turn black. The result is a tasty syrup that blends well with hotcakes. If a little maple flavoring is available, a half teaspoonful will improve the taste of the syrup.

Tin Can Chowder

A tasty chowder can be made at camp from surplus fish. A large tin can, or several small ones, serves as a cooking pot, though a Dutch oven is best. The ingredients needed are:

2 cups shredded fish
1 cup diced potatoes
1 small diced onion
½ cup diced celery stalks
4 slices thin bacon diced, or salt pork if available
½ cup canned milk
Salt and pepper

If fish from a fish-fry are left over, these may be used. Otherwise, fresh fish should be boiled for seven minutes in a clean cloth. The flesh can then be picked from the bones.

Brown the bacon in the can or oven, then add the onion and cook over low heat until partly done. Add potatoes, celery, and two cups of water (this may be the water used for boiling the fish). Salt to taste. Allow to simmer until the vegetables are tender, then add the fish and milk. Pepper to taste, heat to near boiling, and serve.

Steamed Clams

Outdoorsmen who travel along ocean beaches often find clam beds that yield a couple of bushels. If you've dug soft shell clams, you can steam them at camp with only a large bucket and a piece of large-mesh screen.

Cut a circle from the screen having a diameter just 8 inches larger than the diameter of the bucket at a point

Pattern for cutting steaming basket, top, and finished basket, which is placed in bucket rim down.

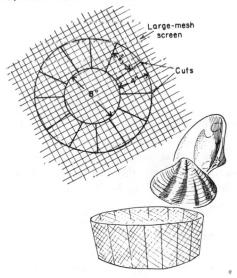

4 inches from the bottom. Then cut the circular screen in spokelike segments, as shown in the drawing. Bend in the segments to form a small basket. Place this basket, rim down, into the bucket. The flat part of the screen will now be 4 inches from the bottom of the bucket.

Fill the bucket with about 2 inches of water and set on the fire or stove to boil. Place the washed clams inside, on the screen, and put on the lid. The water is kept at a rolling boil, but does not touch the clams; the steam from the water cooks them. The clams will open in several minutes. They are done, ready to eat off the shell. Serve with buttered garlic bread.

Fillet of Tuotuava

When the tuotuava, or white sea bass, are running in southern waters fishermen usually fillet their catch and bring it home on ice in a cooler. The fish often weigh over a hundred pounds, and filleting is the best way to handle them.

Campers can enjoy a superb fish meal on the beach if they prepare for it in advance.

The big fish are skinned and filleted. The fillets to take home may be cut larger; those to be cooked on the beach are cut about 3 inches long by ½-inch wide and just under ½-inch thick.

Prepare a batter of cornflake crumbs, fresh egg, canned milk, a product called Dixie Fry, and the product Bisquick. The proportions of this batter are entirely flexible. The best way is to mix one beaten egg with a full cup of canned milk, then add equal parts of the other three ingredients until a thick batter is formed.

Dip the fillets into this batter, then deep-fry them in cooking oil. A large Dutch oven is excellent for this purpose. Fill it with about 2 inches of oil. The screen device suggested for steaming clams is adaptable to frying fillets. Use it as a basket for lowering the fillets into the oil. Cooking time is approximately fifteen minutes, or until the fillets are golden brown.

Serve with fresh homemade bread, hot if possible, and spread with garlic butter. Lacking homemade bread, serve stone-ground bread, cut into slices 1½ inches thick, heated in a reflector oven or a Dutch oven, and generously spread with melted butter.

Cooking Fish Without Utensils

The go-light backpacker often needs to cook fish without utensils. Here's how to do it:

One way to cook fish fillets without utensils is to salt them, impale them on a green stick and toast them over the fire until they are cooked on both sides, taking care that they don't crumble and drop off the stick when they are nearly done. It is always best, of course, to let an open fire die down to a bed of coals before using it for cooking.

Another way to cook the fillets is to place a flat rock in the bottom of the fire pit when building the fire. After the fire has burned down to a bed of coals, scrape them away, exposing the red-hot rock. Flatten a tin can by cutting out both ends with a pocketknife and lay it on the rock. A fillet can then be cooked on the flat tin. Lacking a tin can,

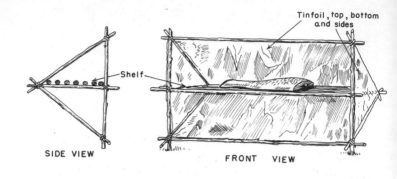

SIDE VIEW   FRONT VIEW

Tinfoil, top, bottom and sides

Shelf

Reflector oven for baking fish.

cover the rock with tinfoil or cook the fillet right on the rock itself.

Indians used to cook fish on a spit over an open fire. They would thrust a green stick completely through the fish, from mouth to tail, and suspend it over the fire on two forked sticks. As the fish cooked, it was rotated until done.

To bake fish, you can make a reflector oven with a few green sticks, some tinfoil, and a few nails or wire. First make the sides of the oven by nailing or wiring three short willows in the form of a triangle. Fasten crosspieces to these sides to form the oven, as shown in the drawing. A shelf of green sticks supports the fish. Cover all inside surfaces, except the shelf, with tinfoil. Set the oven in front of a bed of hot coals, with the fish on the shelf. The reflected heat bakes the fish.

Small fish may be salted and baked whole. Larger fish should be cut into fillets, with the skin left on, and baked with the skin side next to the shelf. The skin prevents the fish from crumbling and falling through the gaps in the shelf.

Baked Lake Trout

Here is a recipe for trout that are too large to cook in a skillet. First stuff the trout with a dressing like that used for turkey. Lay it on its side in a baking pan and spoon a row of dressing around the fish. Then place strips of smoked bacon across the fish. Cover the pan and bake in a medium oven until nearly done. At this point, pour a can of condensed tomato soup over the fish and bake until the soup thickens into a paste. To serve, cut the fish crosswise into ample portions and add dressing.

Crumbed Trout

One of the finest ways to cook medium-size trout is to skin them, dip them into a batter of bread or cracker crumbs mixed with buttermilk, then fry them to a golden brown in hot butter.

Fish in Foil

This is a simple way to cook pan-sized fish, especially trout, and preserve the flavor and moisture of the fish.

Clean the fish, then salt and pepper lightly, and coat with butter inside and out. For a 12-inch trout, use about 1 tablespoonful of butter. Wrap each fish individually in a layer of aluminum foil, folding the edges of the foil tightly, otherwise as the butter melts it will escape.

Allow the cooking fire to die down to a bed of hot coals, and rake them over the foil-covered fish. Allow to cook without disturbance. Cooking time depends on the size of the fish and the quality of the coals. For a pine-wood fire, and a 12-inch trout, the cooking time is just twenty minutes. To serve, simply open the foil and use it as a plate on which to eat the fish.

Pan-sized fish may be wrapped in foil and cooked on a grill over charcoal. Turn once, after approximately three-fourths of the cooking time has elapsed. Part of the butter will be lost from leakage, but this won't affect the taste of the fish.

Smoking Fish

In wilderness country where the fish are cooperative, often more are caught than can be eaten at camp. Rather than waste extra fish, you may want to preserve them and take them home. Smoking them is the answer.

We once found a smokehouse in British Columbia which Indians had built and abandoned, and used it for smoking our catch. Slender aspen poles had been formed into a small wigwam about 4 feet high and covered with sheets of green bark from the larger trees, leaving a tiny aperture at the top. A small pit for the fire had been dug just inside the bark covering. The draft was regulated by moving the sheets of bark. The fish were placed on a small platform of green alders near the top. The only flaw in this smokehouse was that, unless you were careful, the bark covering would catch fire and burn up the entire outfit.

A better smokehouse can be made by using a canvas tarp for a covering. Build the platform about 3 feet high by driving four green alder poles into the ground and wiring or nailing crossbars at the tops and a few inches down. Lay green alder sticks across these crossbars to form platforms. Build the fire just inside the front of this framework, preferably in a shallow pit that extends outside the house, into which the fuel can be fed.

With the fire started, and the fish on the alder shelves, wrap the canvas around the framework, leaving only a small opening at the top. This allows enough upward draft to keep the smoke coming up through the house so the fire will not die out.

With two lengths of stovepipe and a cardboard carton about 2 feet square, you can build another type of smokehouse that is even better. Find a cutbank about 4 feet high, and from the shoreline of a lake or stream. At the edge of the cutbank build a small framework of willows or alders similar to the one just described. The carton should fit over the top of the framework. Cut a small door 4 inches square in the bottom of the carton for a draft. Leave one side of the door uncut so it can be bent open and shut.

Next build a small cairn of rocks, sod, or dirt on the shoreline, two stovepipe lengths from the smokehouse. Lay the stovepipe between an opening in the top rear of the cairn and the interior of the smokehouse. Cover the pipe with dirt or support it with rocks to keep it in place.

Build a small fire in the cairn and add green alder or aspen wood to make it smoke. Regulate the smoke by placing a piece of tinfoil, a tin plate, or a sheet of metal cut from a large tin can on top of the fire. The smoke travels up to the smokehouse and smokes the fish without danger of burning them by a sudden blaze of fire.

For smoking fish at home, make the smokehouse out of a 50-gallon oil drum. Cut out both ends. At a point about 6 inches from the end that will be the top, run three small iron rods through the barrel through holes cold-chiseled in the sides. Onto these lay a small wire grate (the shelf from an electric oven). Place a few green willows across the top of the barrel, and on top of these lay one of the cut-out ends. This will keep most of the smoke inside the drum, but allow enough draft for the smoke to rise through the barrel. Place the fish on the wire grate.

Smokehouse made from oil drum.

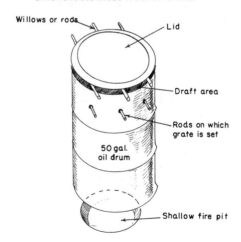

Dig a shallow pit just inside the rim of the barrel, and build a small fire, adding green wood to make it smoke.

Prepare fish for smoking by soaking them overnight in a strong solution of salt water. This drains the blood and seasons the fish. Small fish, such as 1-pound trout, should be smoked about seven hours. When the fish are deep brown and wrinkled they are done.

The best wood for smoking fish is apple wood. Often an angler near some rancher's orchard can arrange to save the prunings from spring orchard work, take them home, and use them for smoking up a batch of spring-caught trout. In the hills, the best wood is green aspen splits. Both apple and aspen impart a fine flavor to smoked fish.

Finally, here's a more sophisticated smokehouse you can build in your backyard from an old refrigerator. The shelves for holding the fish already exist.

Obtain a small one-burner hotplate. Take out enough of the seal around the refrigerator door to admit an electric cord, and put the hotplate inside the refrigerator on the bottom. Place a shallow metal pie-tin filled with hardwood sawdust on the hotplate. Shut the refrigerator door and turn on the hotplate. The fish will be smoked. If there isn't enough draft, remove more of the door seal. The hardwood sawdust must burn without flaming. Regulate the amount of air entering the refrigerator, or shift the tin on the hotplate, to produce the right amount of smoke. Only stainless steel refrigerator shelves should be used. The old-time cadmium-plated shelves might, under certain conditions, taint the fish.

This lazy man's smoker can preserve fish in half the time it takes an outside smokehouse, for all the smoke is condensed and used. Hardwood sawdust can be obtained from furniture manufacturers.

One-Dish Meals

The modern camper, motor-home, and trailer all allow more latitude for the outdoor cook. One can haul more fresh fruit, vegetables, and even meat to the jumping-off spot than before. Too, these added items to the meals can be easier taken in to camp for the first day than before, or used prior to leaving the camper's convenience. Here are two good one-dish meals which are easy to fix:

Skillet Stew (Serves 2)

Saute ½ chopped onion in 1 tbl. butter, margarine, or cooking oil until slightly browned. Add 2 tbl. chopped green peppers, and 2 medium, quartered tomatoes (several cherry tomatoes could be used). Cook with skillet covered for two minutes.

Add 1 zucchini (sliced about ¼-inch thick), 1 Polish sausage, 1 frankfurter (both sliced about ½ inch thick). Salt to taste (just a sprinkle pleases most people).

Cover skillet and steam for 3 to 4 minutes, until zucchini is slightly cooked but still crisp, and the sausages heated through. Add 1 or 2 tbl. of water before steaming, if more moisture is needed.

Serve over cooked noodles.

Sauted Grouse

Salt and pepper 2 pieces of grouse, ptarmigan, pheasant, or domestic chicken breast which has been boned. Dredge with flour. Put 1 tsp. cooking oil and 1 small chopped onion in skillet. Add chicken and brown.

Add ½ tsp. tarragon, 4 sliced mushrooms, a squeeze of fresh lemon, and ¾ cup of water or broth.

Simmer about 30 minutes. Add ½ sliced cucumber. Steam 2 minutes. Serve over hot cooked rice (preferably the 1-minute kind.

Solar Cooking

Recently there has been considerable interest in the possibilities of solar cooking, due largely to the national trend towards conservation of energy. Wood has always been the standard cooking fuel for outdoor cooking as well as fuel for the campfire—both so vital to the outdoor experience. Most of the real "outdoor" areas, especially in Canada and Alaska, are wooded or brush-covered, providing fuel that need not be transported. Also, the wood normally used for fires has been small stuff—dry branches, small saplings and poles, and blow-down—found on the spot or nearby, and much of which otherwise would be wasted. The supply of heavy logs and commercial timber used in the lumber industry, or the overall national supply of wood, has not been affected by this use of wood for camping fuel.

Despite the availability of wood, there are situations and areas where solar cooking would be handy. These include large areas which contain small amounts of fiber fuel, vast regions of hot arid country with long periods of intense sunlight, and seasons when outdoor fires are not desired or are prohibited because of fire hazard.

The basic problem for solar cooking is three-fold—finding periods of continuous, intense sunlight; concentrating the rays of this sunlight in some manner onto a small cooking surface; and making this fit into a "stove" or utensil small enough to be handily transported.

Numerous experiments have been tried to accomplish this, including the use of a battery of convex lenses, solar heating cells, and reflectors such as mirrors. So far, solar cooking for the outdoorsman is largely in the experimental stage.

As an example, the Cooperative Extension Service of a large southwestern university, in cooperation with the U. S. Department of Agriculture, has developed a simple experimental solar cooker built of materials no more elaborate than cardboard boxes, aluminum foil, an unpainted coat hanger, glue, and tape. The frame into which this cooker is set is nothing more than an average-sized cardboard box with the top and front cut out, and a small hole in each side, near the top and front, through which the spindle goes.

The cooker element is somewhat on the order of a reflector cooker, but in the shape of a partial cylinder, or the smaller "half" of a length of round log, split just off-center, and hollowed out. The nearly semicircular ends of the cooker are made of heavy cardboard, and the rounded part of the partial cylinder is similarly made of a rectangular piece of cardboard, fastened around the curved portions of the ends with tape. The length of the partly cylindrical element is just shorter than the width of the frame, so it will fit inside.

The inside, concave surface of the resulting element is lined with aluminum foil, as are the insides of the ends. Each end is marked at a point called the focal point of the reflecting surface, or concave side. This focal length is exactly one-half the length of the radius, were the cylinder extended to full round. The spindle, made from the straightened unpainted coat hanger, when inserted longitudinally through the focal points, will be where the reflected rays of the sun, from the curved aluminum, will converge. In intense sunlight, by rotating the element to catch the rays, the cooker will cook hot dogs.

To use the cooker, the spindle is poked through an end-hole in the frame, then through one end of the element lengthwise, through the frankfurter, through the opposite end of the element and frame, and is then rotated to focus the rays. All holes for the spindle should be friction-tight.

When experimenting with, or using solar cooking, one vital fact should be remembered. Solar cooking is often slow-cooking, and sufficient temperature, over enough time, should be maintained to kill all harmful bacteria. According to the U. S. Department of Agriculture, bacteria in foods are killed at temperatures of 165 degrees F., maintained for 2 hours or more.

Camp Oven

Also available is a recently developed portable camp oven which can be used for similar outdoor cooking needs. This small oven measures just over 15 inches in each dimension, is completely insulated, has an oven section, and an integral heating compartment. The heat is provided, inside the oven, by canned heat or Sterno cans, and it has a handle for carrying. One model is called the "Campoven," and it will bake most any kind of food.

23

Photography How-To

Night Pictures

Most modern cameras are equipped to take flash pictures, and that is the simplest way to take outdoor pictures at night. Modern flashbulbs and flashcubes are not only inexpensive but very small for the amount of light they emit.

However, on backpacking or wilderness trips where every ounce counts, and flash equipment is excluded for reasons of portability, night pictures can be taken using only firelight. The fire should be allowed to burn down to a bed of coals to permit the subjects to stand close to it. When ready for the picture, toss a small armful of dry brush or twigs onto the coals so that the fire flares up. When the fire blazes up to the height of the subjects' knees, and their faces are illuminated, snap the picture. For black-and-white film with an ASA rating of 125, try an exposure of one second with the diaphragm set at f4.5, at a distance of 12 feet.

If you can seize the moment when dusk is falling, and the fading light of day can augment the firelight, an interesting photo can can be taken. The light of the fire should be slightly stronger than the daylight. Test the light by squinting the eyes; the difference will then be readily apparent.

How to Make "Etchings"

Have you ever seen an attractive black-and-white picture in a magazine and wished to preserve it? If the picture has been printed on paper having a clay base, it can easily be transferred from the page to a piece of plywood. The result will resemble an old etching and will be an appropriate decoration for a wall in your home or vacation cabin.

In order to accomplish this transfer, obtain a product known as polymer medium from an art-supply store. This is sold under a variety of trade names. You'll also need a small brush.

To determine whether the magazine is printed on a paper with a clay base, wet a finger and run it over a page. If some of the coating comes off and has a chalky feel, the base is clay. Most coated paper used in "slick" magazines today has a clay base.

Cut the picture from the magazine and trim the margins. Then cut a piece of ¼-inch plywood to a size larger than the picture, leaving a suitable margin on all sides. Smooth the face and edges of the plywood with fine sandpaper. Dip the brush in water, and paint the face of the plywood with the polymer medium. Immediately place the picture face down on the plywood, being careful to put it exactly in position the first time as it is almost impossible to remove it once it contacts the polymer medium. (It's a good idea to rule corner marks for placement on the plywood.) With the picture in place, smooth it down with the back of a plastic comb, removing all air bubbles. Smooth from the center of the picture to the edges.

Allow the picture to dry for fifteen minutes. Then immerse the plywood board in a pan of warm water for a minute or two, until the paper is loosened and can be carefully peeled off. Allow the board to dry completely.

The picture will now be reproduced on the plywood, but in reverse. Just enough of the grain of the wood will show through to give the appearance of an old etching. Of course, copyright laws forbid anyone to use pictures in magazines for commercial purposes, so your "etchings" should be only for your own enjoyment.

Rustic Picture Frames

An outstanding photo deserves to be enlarged, and will be further enhanced by an attractive, rustic frame. If you are at all handy with tools, it is satisfying to make your own frames for your favorite outdoor photos.

The best wood for making rustic frames is pine, spruce, or fir. Select a straight, dry sapling or branch about 2 inches in diameter with just a trace of green in it. If the wood is slightly green, the bark will remain on the frame longer. The pole need only be long enough to cut two sides of the frame, since it will be split in half and both halves used. When determining the length, be sure to figure the outside dimensions of the frame, to allow for the mitered corners.

The first step is to remove the rough bark from the pole with a sharp pocketknife. Shave it off in strips, leaving the

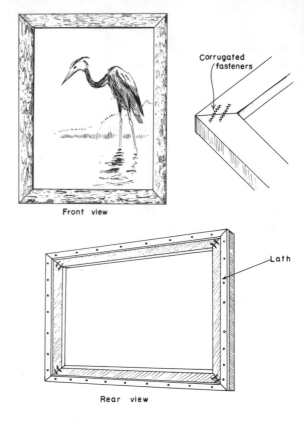

Corrugated fasteners

Front view

Lath

Rear view

Chipped conifer frame enhances outdoor pictures.

cambian layer underneath. Do not scrape down to the white wood. If the bark tends to stick in some areas, leave it intact.

Next, with the pocketknife chip the surface of the wood to produce a mottled effect. Cut the chips about ½-inch wide and up to an inch long. It just takes a flick of the wrist to cut each chip The chips should be cut in some sort of pattern, such as a spiral, yet should not look too regular.

After creating an attractive pattern on the surface, split the pole in half, lengthwise, with a power saw or a handsaw. Sand the raw edges smooth. Cut the four sides of the frame, mitering the corners at a 45-degree angle. These corners must be cut accurately; for the best results use a miter box and backsaw.

The easiest way to join the corners of the frame is to use glue and corrugated metal fasteners. Coat both surfaces of the miter joint with glue, then lay the frame face down and drive two fasteners into the center of the joint.

If you have a router or table saw, you can mortise a recess in the back of the frame into which the picture and glass will fit. Otherwise, glue and nail thin lath, ½-inch narrower than the frame, to the back of the frame, and create a recess to insert the picture and glass.

Finally, apply several coats of clear varnish to the frame. Some varnish turns yellowish with age, and if a darker tone is desired, this type should be used.

Rustic Plaques

Beautiful rustic plaques for mounting trophy heads, fish, mottos, or souvenirs can be made from a thick log. Select a log that is slightly green and do not remove the bark. To make a round plaque, saw a straight slice about 1 inch thick from the end of the log. To make an eliptical plaque, saw the slice on a diagonal. Allow the slices to dry in the shade to prevent splitting and shedding of the bark. When dry, plane and sandpaper the face and apply a few coats of varnish or lacquer.

Camera Harness

Most cameras are hard to carry. Either they swing clumsily from a strap around the neck, or they pull on the pants in a case at the belt. To make the chore easier, I designed a harness for carrying a small camera close to the chest, without dangling, where it is always ready for taking a quick picture.

Harness holds camera snugly against chest; elastic band permits raising it quickly to the eye.

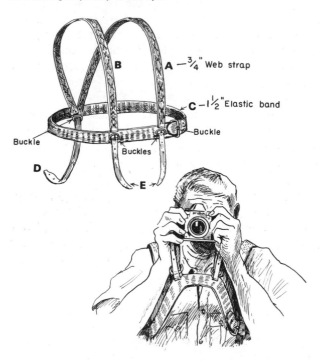

As the drawing shows, two ¾-inch web shoulder straps (A and B) are sewn to a 1½-inch elastic band (C) which buckles around the torso. At the rear of band C is sewn a ½-inch leather strap (D) with a buckle. Two other ½-inch straps (E), with buckles, are sewn to the front of the harness just below the shoulder straps. These thread through the rings on the camera and buckle it tightly against the chest. The rear strap (D) loops under the belt and is buckled.

The harness keeps the camera held securely in place, ready for instant use. When you want to take a picture, the elastic body band will stretch and allow the camera to be raised to the eye.

Combination Filter-Sunshade

If all outdoor photos could be made while shooting with the sun at one's back, there would be no need to use a sunshade. However, it is often necessary to shoot into the sun, and if sunlight strikes the lens directly, or bounces off the camera into the lens, the film can be ruined. This can be prevented by shading the lens.

Standard sunshades are usually funnel-shaped and have a metal ring which fits over the lens mount. The average sunshade for a lens of 4-inch focal length is about 3 inches —a little too bulky to carry in a shirt pocket. Years ago, I made a filter sunshade which fits easily into a shirt pocket, and have used it consistently with a particular camera.

To make such a sunshade, get a yellow filter mounted in a metal ring that fits on your camera's lens mount. You'll also need a length of cardboard mailing tube. The inside diameter of the tube should be slightly smaller than the di-

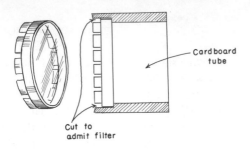

Cardboard tube

Cut to admit filter

Small filter-sunshade, made from cardboard tube, guards lens from sun's rays.

ameter of the filter ring. Cut a 1¼-inch length of tube and smooth both ends. Thin the rear end of the tube with a pocketknife so the filter ring will fit about ½-inch into the tube. Cement the filter ring in the tube at this point. When the cement has dried, paint the entire surface of the tube with flat black paint. Give the edges two coats for added protection, then wrap the tube with a couple of layers of black friction tape. The filter ring will slip on the lens mount and hold the sunshade in place.

When carrying the filter-sunshade in the shirt pocket, the glass often collects moisture and must be dried before use. To prevent this, keep the gadget in a small plastic bag. Then, when you have to take a quick picture, the filter will be dry.

Portable Background for Flower Photos

When photographing wild flowers in the woods, it is often difficult to eliminate distracting background material. You can tramp on obstructing foliage, and open wide the diaphram of the lens to blur the background, but a better method is to create an entirely new background.

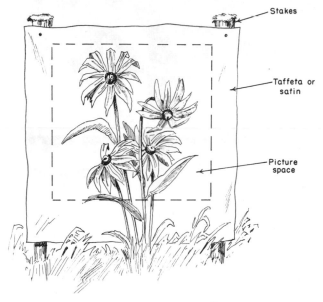

Stakes

Taffeta or satin

Picture space

Squares of taffeta or satin in a variety of colors can be used as background for photographing wild flowers.

A few pieces of taffeta or satin, about a yard square, rolled on a cardboard tube and carried in your car, will provide you with a handy backdrop for photographing wild flowers. I have found the most useful colors to be red, blue, black, and silver. To support the backdrop, drive two sharpened stakes into the ground about a yard apart behind the flowers. Fasten the cloth to the stakes with thumbtacks.

24

Horses and Horse Gear

Choosing a Suitable Horse

On most western packtrips the outfitter normally assigns each rider a horse on the basis of his experience, age, and size. A youngster usually gets a small, gentle horse; a heavy person a large, stout horse; an experienced rider a spirited horse. Occasionally, you will be given the chance to choose your own mount from those in the corral, and you should know a few things about horses to make an intelligent choice.

There is no foolproof way to choose a good horse just by looking it over. Horse buyers and professional horsemen are often fooled, giving rise to the numerous droll stories about horse swapping. Nevertheless, it is possible to observe a group of horses and eliminate the undesirables.

One basis for selecting a horse is the way it moves about the corral with other horses. If an animal constantly bites and kicks the others viciously, it is not apt to be even-tempered on the trail.

Another feature to look for is the stride of an animal. The stride should be clean; the feet should come forward in a straight line, not swing out to each side. The head should be held high, the ears and eyes should look alert. The legs should be clean and slim. Riding horses are unlike work-horses in that they don't have a lot of shaggy hair around the fetlocks.

The size of a horse is important when it is being chosen for riding on mountain trails. A slim, racy-looking animal may be fine for flat-country riding, but for mountain use a horse should have a broad chest, a strong back, and a chunky build. Reject a horse with a deeply swayed back and a pot belly.

If you are not an experienced rider, you'll want a horse that is well broken to the saddle. It's possible to single out a well-broken horse by the numerous small white patches, about the size of a thumbnail, just behind the withers and behind the shoulders in the middle of the rib cage. These marks are made by a saddle which is too tight and puts undue pressure on the horse at these points. If the horse's mane is worn just ahead of the shoulders, it may mean that it has been wearing a collar and has been used as a work-horse—that is, it is "double broken."

To gauge a horse's disposition, approach the animal and try to pet it. (Always approach a horse from the front or side, never from the rear.) If the horse lowers its ears, rolls its eyes showing the whites, and snorts, it may be too wild for anyone but an experienced rider. If the horse sidles gently away from your grasp, it is probably friendly but doesn't want to be saddled and ridden at the moment; but if it submits to a few pats on the neck and some soft words, it may be gentle enough to ride.

Once you've made your choice, and the horse has been saddled and bridled, you can put it through a final test to determine whether or not to take it on the trail. If the horse responds well to neck reining and to knee pressure, it's a good sign that it has been well trained. A horse that responds sluggishly may be slow on the trail and will have to be continually urged along the way.

How to Catch a Horse in the Open

The standard way to catch horses grazing in a meadow is first to drive them into a corral, then catch each animal by approaching it slowly and placing a halter on its head. One horse is often corraled at night and in the morning used as a wrangling horse for rounding up the others.

In areas where there is no corral, horses can be driven into a small grove of trees and confined while one or two are caught. The remaining animals often collect around those already tied. A makeshift corral of lariats tied to trees will keep horses confined while they are caught and saddled. When catching grazing horses, one should move slowly and talk gently. Yelling at a horse is the surest way to make it bolt.

A nosebag filled with a quart of grain is a good lure to use in catching a horse. Hard-working horses on a ranch are normally fed twice a day, and they quickly learn to associate the sight of a nosebag with food. Dangling a nosebag before a reluctant horse, and shaking the bag so it can hear the grain, is a good way to coax it into a halter. Soft words help, too. Once the horse can be induced to put its nose in the bag, it is an easy matter to grasp its hackamore or halter. If it's not wearing either, grasp the mane and gently drop a rope around its neck. The horse will generally remain still long enough to allow you to knot the rope into a loop or put on a hackamore or halter.

Nosebag filled with a quart of grain is a good lure.

Halters and Bridles

The basic difference between a halter and a hackamore is that the former is made of heavy strap leather with buckles and rings, and the latter is made of rope.

In placing a halter on a horse's head, hold the head loop in the right hand and hold the noseband open with the left. Bring the head loop up the horse's face and over the ears in one gentle movement, encircling the nose with the noseband. Free the ears from the headband and allow them to point forward in their normal position. Many horses, especially those that have been misused, dislike having their ears touched, so adjust the ears quickly and gently. Finally, bring the lower strap, or throat latch, under the throat and fasten it at the left side of the face. The horse can then be led away to be saddled, fed, or tied.

In tying a horse to a hitching rack or corral, the knot should be at about the same height as the nose, with 3 or 4 feet of slack between. A good knot is a slip knot around the pole, finished off with a half-hitch to prevent the horse from rubbing or pulling the knot undone.

The horse is controlled by a head harness called the bridle. Bridles vary in design, but they all work on the same principle. They are made of strap leather, braided leather, or rawhide. A leather band runs from the mouth area over the head and behind the ears. The two ends of the band are attached to the bit. In most models another band encircles the nose, and in some another narrow band, the throat latch, fastens under the throat.

The bit is the part of the bridle which is used to control the animal. The mouthpiece of the bit varies according to how "hardmouthed" a horse is. A snaffle bit has a

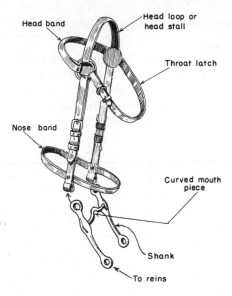

Typical horse bridle and standard bit.

mouthpiece which is either a straight metal bar, or a bar joined at the center by two connecting loops. This type of bit is normally used for draft horses or racers. The standard bit, which is generally used when hunting on horseback or trail riding, has a mouthpiece with a mild bend at the center and long shanks. The lower ends of the shanks have loops for admitting the reins. When the reins are pulled, the curved mouthpiece presses against the roof of the horse's mouth. This pressure, and the pressure of the chin strap, causes the animal to slow or stop.

Well-trained horses are often ridden with a bridle without a mouthpiece. The horse is controlled by a snug-fitting noseband and chin strap. When the reins are tightened, the prying action of the long bit shanks restrains the horse. This bit is called a hackamore bit.

Many outfitters and guides prefer to bridle a horse over the halter or hackamore, since the animal then can be tied more securely when the rider dismounts to stalk game. The beginner should keep his horse tied by the halter rope while putting on the bridle. A horse tends to back when being bridled, and if it is not tied it may get away.

To bridle a horse, grasp the headband in the right hand, the bit in the web of the left hand, and in one easy motion lift the headband over the horse's nose so that its right side crosses the face. As the bridle is pushed upward on the face, the mouthpiece will contact the mouth. A horse accustomed to the bridle will open its mouth when the metal touches its teeth. Otherwise, place the thumb of the left hand into the mouth, behind the teeth, and press until the horse opens its mouth. Try to bridle a horse on the first try; if you fail, the horse resists even more in subsequent tries. Once the bit is in the mouth, place the headband over the ears and fasten the throat latch, if any, snugly but not tightly. During cold weather, it is advisable to warm the mouthpiece before putting it in the horse's mouth by holding it in the palm of the hand for a few minutes.

Saddling a Horse

The stock saddle is the type most commonly used for hunting and trail riding, especially in the West. This saddle has a wide pommel, a relatively low cantle, heavy skirts, and a sturdy horn. It may have one or two cinches. Such saddles weigh anywhere from 20 to 40 pounds; 30 pounds is a good weight for the average rider.

Two dimensions are important, the "swell" and the "seat." The swell, or the front width, should be 13 or 14 inches. The length of the seat may be from 13 inches, for a woman, to 16 inches, for a heavy man. A 15-inch seat is standard and will fit the average man of medium build.

The best stirrups for everyday use have flat, leather-covered bottoms. Stirrup length has to be adjusted for the individual rider, and ought to be approximately the length of his arm.

To saddle a horse, place two blankets, or one blanket and a pad, on its back so they are even on both sides. The

Stock saddle is used in the West for hunting and trail riding.

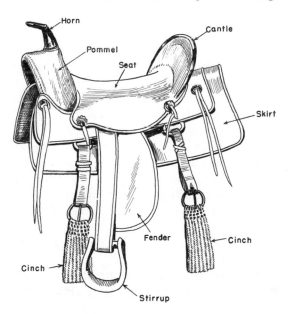

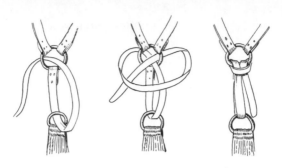

Latigo knot for fastening cinch to ring.

front part of the blankets should extend about 2 inches beyond the saddle skirts when the saddle is in place. If a blanket and a pad are used, the blanket goes on first. For hard riding, two blankets are necessary to protect the horse's back.

With the blankets in place, grasp the pommel and swing the saddle onto the horse, freeing the cinch or saddle strings if they catch under the saddle. Holding the horn, gently wiggle the saddle in place so that it settles snugly onto the blanket. Lift the stirrup and hook it over the horn to expose the cinch ring.

Grasp the cinch under the horse's belly, pull it up to the saddle ring, and fasten it to the ring with the latigo strap. The knot used is shown in the drawing. Some cinches are rigged with a tackberry—a metal hook that is wrapped in the latigo and hooks to the cinch ring. With a tackberry, a cinch can be tightened quicker since it is unnecessary to tie the latigo knot; the latigo is simply tightened and the knot secured.

Most horses, knowing the constriction of a tight cinch, will hold their breath while being cinched. When they exhale, the cinch will be loosened. To offset this, the cinch should be retightened before mounting.

Staking a Horse

During summer and fall, when horses are allowed to graze at night on grass in the area, it is necessary to stake them to the ground. The stake should be about 3 feet long and 3 or 4 inches in diameter, sharpened at one end, and driven into the ground about 18 inches. A ½-inch rope from 20 to 40 feet long is used to anchor the animal to the stake. Small trees or brush within the area should be cut so they

Bowline allows loops to revolve around stake as horse grazes.

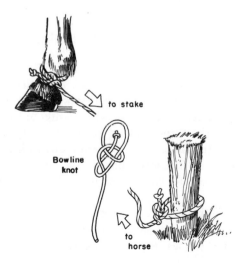

to stake

Bowline knot

to horse

won't catch the rope as the horse feeds in a circle. Otherwise the animal may hurt itself or break loose.

It is best to tie the rope to the horse's foot rather than to its head. A horse will exert less pressure on the rope with its foot, and it is less likely to get tangled in the rope and injured. The left foot is preferred since a horse is accustomed to being handled from the left side. The best knot to use is a bowline, tied loose enough so it doesn't rub. The bowline is also used to tie the rope to the stake, as it allows the knot to revolve as the animal feeds.

A staked horse should be checked periodically, to be sure the rope hasn't tangled and to shift the stake when the animal has overgrazed its limited range.

Tethering a Horse

Sometimes a horse is tethered instead of staked—that is, it is tied by its head to a movable anchor such as a large log. This permits the horse to drag the log and prevents injury should it tangle the rope or fall. Also, the horse can feed over a wider area than if it were staked.

Horses to be tethered usually wear a halter or hackamore which has a short rope spliced to it. The tethering rope is knotted to the halter (or hackamore) rope with a bowline tied in each with the loops linked. The bowline is one of the easiest knots to untie after it has been subjected to strain.

An Alaskan Indian once showed me how to tether a horse on open plains where only low bushes grow. He found several little bushes growing closely together, bushes

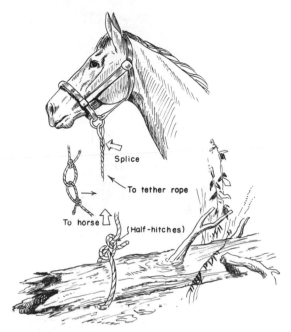

Splice

To tether rope

To horse (Half-hitches)

Tethering a horse to a movable log.

whose branches were only ½ inch in diameter. Had he tied his horse to one of them, the animal could easily have escaped. But the Indian grabbed two handfuls of bush, brought the tops together and tied them with an overhand knot. The green, flexible branches bent without breaking. He then wrapped the horse's reins tightly three turns around the knot, doubled the reins back and tied three half-hitches around them. The horse was firmly tethered and could have been left for several hours if necessary.

Tethering a horse to low bushes.

Hobbling a Horse

In many remote areas, horse permits are issued to out-fitters which allow them to graze their stock at certain prescribed spots. Most riding horses and pack stock are hobbled at night when put out to feed. If mules are used, a bell mare is hobbled among them. Mules tend to stay close to a bell mare. The outfitter may keep one horse tied at camp to help him find the hobbled stock in the morning.

There are many types of horse hobbles. One of the most dependable consists of two leather straps, equipped with heavy buckles, which are joined by a short chain with a swivel at the center. The straps buckle around the horse's front legs just above the fetlocks. Light hobbles, often used when a rider leaves his horse to stalk game, are made of a single strip of braided rawhide with a slit or loop at one end and a knot at the other. The leather strip is doubled and looped around one of the horse's front legs; the two ends are then twisted three or four turns and joined around the other leg.

Two types of horse hobbles: buckled straps joined by a chain and swivel; light rawhide hobble often used by hunters when staking game.

The early Mormons invented a novel type of hobble to protect their stock from being stolen by roving bands of Indians. It consisted of rings and fastenings which had to be manipulated correctly, like a puzzle, to undo it. Before the braves could figure out how to solve the puzzle, the horse's owner would often be upon them.

Horses soon become used to hobbles, and instead of trying to take separate strides will accept the constriction and simply jump away with long bounds. Still, even an experienced hobbled horse cannot go as far in a night as can an unhobbled horse, and wranglers usually are able to locate the animal in the morning.

Feeding and Watering a Horse

If a horse is confined in a corral it usually is fed cured grain and hay three times a day. When it is to be ridden for a full day, it is fed in the morning and in the evening. An average-sized horse needs about 15 pounds, or quarter of a bale of hay, at each feeding. Alfalfa, grass, and timothy, singly or in mixture, are typical hay feeds. In addition, heavily worked horses are usually given about 2 quarts of cured grain, normally oats with a little beardless barley added. However, if a horse is fresh from the pasture and is unused to cured grain, it should be given only 1 quart or a bit more at each feeding.

When a few horses are being fed in a corral, they usually are given their hay in a manger and left untied. But if there are many horses, or if the horses are strangers to each other, it is safer to tie them at the manger by their halters or hackamores, giving them enough leeway to reach the bottom of the manger.

Grain usually is fed to horses in individual nosebags after they have eaten their hay. All the horses should be fed grain at the same time, otherwise fights are apt to occur. Grain can be measured by cupping both hands and using them as a scoop; four handfuls make about 2 quarts.

Normally, horses require an hour or more to eat their ration of hay, about fifteen minutes to eat their nosebag of grain. Enough time should be allowed before setting out on a trip for them to eat their fill. On returning to the corral, they are fed in the same order—first hay and then grain.

Bridles should always be removed before feeding horses hay or grain. A horse can "crop" a small amount of grass along the trail while wearing a bridle, but it can't eat much dry hay with one on. If a horse is fed while tied to a tree or post, rather than at a manger, it should be checked every twenty minutes or so to see that it can reach all the hay. A feeding horse tends to nose to the bottom of a hay pile, scattering the hay beyond its reach, and the scattered hay must be swept back.

Horses in a corral should be watered after they are fed. Usually they are led by their halter ropes to a nearby stream. A horse can drink with a bridle on, but should not be compelled to except when on the trail.

When a horse is being ridden, it should never be allowed to drink its fill when overheated and sweating. It should be allowed only a few swallows, or none at all, until it cools off. Otherwise it is apt to founder.

How to Curry a Horse

A horse should be curried occasionally to remove loose hairs and dirt and to improve its appearance. Currying also seems to improve a horse's disposition; the cleaning and grooming leave it soothed and tractable.

A steel-toothed comb and a stiff-bristled brush are used for currying. Hold the comb in the right hand, the brush in the left, and begin on the left side of the head. Brush the animal's cheeks but don't comb them unless they are unusually dirty. If combing is necessary, use a light stroke; this is a sensitive area with short hair. Always brush with the grain of the hair. Comb the forelock and mane and gently brush the forelock over the forehead and the mane toward the side it naturally lies. Then continue combing and brushing the horse's left side, working downward and back on the neck and downward over the body and legs. Exert enough pressure with the comb to remove loose hairs and dirt, but not enough to hurt the animal. Less pressure should be exerted on the brush; it is used to wipe off the loose material scraped up with the comb and to smooth the hair into a glossy coat.

Comb the tail in the same way as the mane, and then curry the right side. Give special care to the area where the saddle rides; any dirt left in this area will cause sores from the pressure of the saddle and rider.

How to Mount a Horse and Ride

When ready to mount, approach the horse from the left side, grasp the reins in the left hand, and with the same hand grasp the horse's mane just ahead of the saddle, or grasp the saddle horn. The reins should be fairly snug between the bit and the left hand. Turn the stirrup outward with the right hand, and raise the left leg and insert the toe well into the stirrup. With the right hand, grasp either the horn or the cantle of the saddle and with a slight spring, using both arms to pull yourself up, swing the right leg over the horse's back and seat yourself in the saddle.

A cowboy would never turn his horse in order to mount from the uphill side, but a beginner who has to mount in uneven terrain should not hesitate to do so. It's a lot easier. Only if the outfitter or owner gives you the nod should you try to mount a horse from the right side. Most horses won't permit it, but if a horse has been used frequently in the mountains, it may be accustomed to being mounted from the right side, which is often the uphill side.

The first thing to do after mounting is to straighten the saddle, which usually is pulled off center by the pressure of mounting. To do this, grasp the horn and, standing on the right stirrup, jerk the saddle to the right.

Next, it's a good idea to check the length of the stirrups to be sure they fit properly. Even an expert horseman is unable to ride properly with stirrups of improper length. If the stirrups are too long, your rump will bump the saddle with each stride the horse takes; if too short, you will soon develop cramps behind the knees. Stirrups are the right length if you can stand in the saddle, with your full weight on the stirrups, and have 1 to 2 inches of space between the saddle and your crotch.

After adjusting the stirrups, settle into the saddle and "find your seat." This is difficult to explain, but it is a matter of finding the position that is comfortable both for you and the horse. Sit straight in the saddle, not far enough back to ride on the cantle nor far enough forward to press against the pommel. Do not twist to either side, as this will injure a horse's back. The soles of the boots should contact the bottom of the stirrups with a firm pressure, the heels pointing downward, and the legs should firmly grip the horse's sides.

A horse is controlled largely by the bridle reins. The reins are not used to *pull* the horse's head to one side or the other. Riding horses are trained to respond to neck-reining. To neck-rein a horse, hold the reins together in the left hand, slightly above the saddle horn, without any slack. To turn the horse to the right, move the hand holding the reins laterally to the right so the left rein lies snugly on the horse's neck. Exerting pressure on the left rein will cause the animal to turn its head to the right. At the same time, lean toward the right and press the left knee against the horse's side. These combined movements will cause a trained horse to turn to the right. To turn a horse to the left, follow the same procedure on the other side.

To start a horse from a standing position, make an exaggerated kissing sound by pursing the lips and sucking in the breath, simultaneously pressing the knees against the horse's sides. With less spirited horses, a slight kick or two with the heels is sometimes necessary.

To stop a horse, pull gently on the reins and say, "Whoa, boy!" Never pull harshly on the reins or jerk them. With a proper bit, a horse can be stopped by gentle, but firm, pressure.

It is often said that, from the outset, you should show the horse you are the boss—and it's a good maxim to follow. But it doesn't mean that you should mistreat a horse in order to dominate it. A horse should be handled with firmness and kindness. If it disobeys your wishes, correct it with a gentle voice, the proper use of the reins, and perhaps a kick or two in the ribs to accent the instructions. A horse should never be beaten, yanked by the bit, or yelled at constantly.

In mountainous country, a horse should be allowed to rest frequently. If the terrain is exceptionally steep, this may be necessary every 20 yards or so. An animal should not be permitted to climb until it lathers unduly or is exhausted. When climbing on horseback, lean forward in the saddle, and when riding downhill lean back. If the descent is steep, it's a good idea to dismount and lead the horse.

When riding across blowdown country, don't force a horse to jump over large logs. And in boggy or swampy areas, if a horse hesitates and resists crossing, trust its instinct and don't force it. Likewise, when riding along a mountain trail with numerous switchbacks, it's best to slow the horse and give it its head; the animal can normally cross bad spots on its own. The safest way of negotiating any rough terrain is to dismount and lead the horse; the difference in weight makes it easier for it to maneuver.

On crossing a stream, a horse usually wants to stop and drink, and should be allowed to. When you stop for lunch, let the horse crop grass, making sure it is safely tethered, and loosen the cinch to allow it to feed more easily.

If the ride has been long and arduous, and the animal is obviously tired, get off and walk the last mile or so into camp. Once at camp, the horse should be immediately unsaddled, fed, and watered—and left with a few kind words and a pat on the neck. This is a good horse's reward for working hard, and it expects it and deserves it.

A word about carrying extra gear on a saddle horse. If a rifle is carried in a scabbard, try to balance the weight and keep the saddle straight by carrying something on the opposite side. A compensating pressure on the stirrup on the opposite side is often sufficient to balance the saddle. Small items should be carried in a pair of small saddlebags tied behind the cantle. No more than 8 pounds should be packed in saddlebags, and the two bags should be equal in weight so they balance.

How Indians Rode

Before the Spaniards came, there were no horses in the New World. Indians in the Southwest and on the Great Plains hunted on foot and used dogs to pull their belongings. The Spaniards tried to keep horses from the Indians, but in 1680 the Pueblo Indians of New Mexico revolted and stole large herds. Thereafter, horses spread across the West and changed the Indians' way of life.

Though lacking the white man's riding gear, the Indian was nevertheless a superb horseman. His saddle was usually a skin or blanket tossed over his pony's back, or lashed under the animal's belly with a length of rawhide. His bridle and reins were a length of rawhide or braided thongs tied into the horse's mouth. One method was to tie both ends of the rawhide around the horse's lower jaw and loop the rest around its neck. Another was to tie one end of rawhide around the jaw and use a single rein. The animals were trained to neck-rein.

Indian "bridle" was often a length of a rawhide tied to the horse's lower jaw and used as a single rein.

To mount his pony, the Indian grasped its mane with both hands and pulled himself upward, balancing himself on his chest across the horse's withers. From this position, he swung his leg across the horse's back and sat upright. Or he might simply grasp a lock of mane with both hands, standing at the horse's shoulder and facing its rear, and swing himself into the saddle in one graceful motion.

How to Choose Riding Boots

The best boots for riding a horse are cowboy boots. These boots are designed especially for riding, and they are not only comfortable but have several safety features. The pointed toe slips quickly and easily into and out of the stirrup; the plain stitching of the toe sheds rain or snow; and the high arch and heel prevent the foot from slipping through the stirrup and the rider being dragged by the horse. If a boot does stick in the stirrup, it will pull off the rider's foot, leaving him free. With unpredictable horses, and in field emergencies, such features are often lifesavers.

Despite all this, the average outdoorsman has no business riding with cowboy boots unless he is accustomed to them. When using a horse for big-game hunting or camping, the majority of time is spent walking or climbing. Unless one is used to wearing cowboy boots, walking for any amount of time will cripple the feet, throw the normal posture out of line, and cause aches and undue weariness.

The best riding boot for the average outdoorsman is the one he uses for his regular outdoor activities. If one is hunting big game, the riding boot to use is the one normally worn for stalking. If one is camping, the best boot for riding is the strong, rugged shoe or boot meant for general camping.

The best all-round boot for dry-weather hunting, camping, hiking, or other summer activity is a lightweight leather boot with 6- to 8-inch uppers, "cord" soles, and leather laces. This all-purpose boot is the best choice for riding. If possible, the toes should be smooth on top, without stitching. This will help shed rain or wet snow that otherwise would collect in the seams and sink into the boot.

For very wet weather, experienced horsemen simply put a pair of rubber arctics over their cowboy boots—the high-heeled, pointed-toe type which are especially designed for this purpose. The average outdoorsman, however, is better off in wet weather with rubber-bottomed pacs. These do not fit exceptionally well into stirrups, but since they will be used more for walking than for riding, they are the best compromise. While riding in rain or wet snow, water continuously drips on the shoes, draining down the lower legs and onto the boots. Good rubber-bottomed pacs will keep the feet dry. In cold weather, a pair of sheepskin innersoles should be used in conjunction with the pacs, to keep the feet warm while riding.

The one safety precaution to observe when riding with rubber pacs is always to keep the balls of the feet on the stirrups. In this position, the feet can easily be pulled free.

How to Shoe a Horse

Shoeing a horse correctly requires farrier's tools: a hoof knife, rasp, shoeing hammer, and pinchers. It also requires experience—and considerable strength if the horse is unwilling. Shoeing a horse string is such specialized work that many outfitters hire a professional horseshoer to do the chore for them. A good job of horseshoeing will last approximately a month on stock which is daily traversing rocky mountain country. Often the shoes will last a full hunting season, but if a shoe does pull off, and you are without professional help, it is useful to know how to replace it. This can be done with nothing more than a horse rasp, horseshoe nails, and a claw hammer. An average riding horse takes a #2 shoe and #5 and #6 horseshoe nails.

Tie the horse with a short rope to a tree or hitching rack on level ground. Place the tools near the foot to be shod, so that, once started, you can do the job as rapidly as possible. A horse dislikes having its foot held up for a long time.

To shoe a horse's front foot, stand at the animal's shoulder and grasp the hairs of the foot at the pastern joint. Pull the front foot upward, and say, "Raise up." A horse previously shod will usually raise its foot at this command. If not, pulling up on the hairs will cause the horse to raise its foot.

When the foot is raised, place it between your knees, facing the horse's rear, and hold it there firmly. Using the rasp, clean the frog of the hoof of any gravel or rocks, and then smooth down the entire bottom surface. If the animal has been previously shod and has just slipped a shoe, the surface of the hoof need only be smoothed down for about 1/8 to 1/4 inch. Next, smooth the edges by rubbing them with the rasp at right angles.

Now place the shoe on the flat surface of the hoof to see whether it fits. If the shoe is a bit too wide, it must be heated (even in a campfire) and then held at the center with a pair of tongs or pliers, and the ends pounded slightly together. If too narrow, the heated shoe must be spread a trifle by pounding it over a pointed rock that fits between the points of the shoe.

Once the shoe has been fitted, hold it in place and nail it to the hoof with four nails on each side. This is the vital part of the operation. A horseshoe nail is not symmetrical; the head bends slightly to one side and the point of the nail is beveled. In placing the nail into the slot of the shoe, the head of the nail *must* be tipped towards the inside of the hoof and the beveled point must head towards the outside of the hoof.

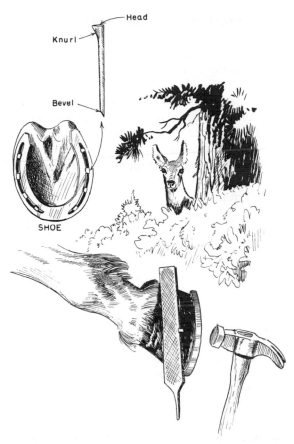

Head

Knurl

Bevel

SHOE

Horseshoe nails are driven through slot and into hoof at a slight angle so they will protrude from the side. Points are then twisted off with claw hammer, clinched and filed smooth.

In driving the nail, the beveled point will then go approximately ¾ inch into the hoof, gently curving so that it will protrude slightly from the side. If driven the opposite way into the hoof, the nail would slant in the other direction and penetrate deeply into the central part, or "quick," of the hoof.

As each nail is driven, twist off its point with the claws of the hammer. To do this, grasp the nail between the claws and twist clockwise. The nail will break at the junction with the hoof. Twisting off the point is necessary, for if a horse lowers its leg while the nail protrudes, it may sink into your leg. This is why professional horseshoers wear a leather apron.

When all eight nails are driven, and twisted off, the hoof may be lowered temporarily so the horse can rest. While it rests, smooth the part of the hoof just below each protruding nail. The hoof will be broken at these points and must be smoothed so the nails can be clinched. Use a corner of the rasp to do this.

Again lift the hoof, hold it between your legs, and place the edge of the rasp at the point where each nail protrudes from the hoof. Tap the head with the hammer. If the rasp is held flat against the hoof, the broken ends of the nails will be bent outwards. After each end has been tapped against the rasp, finish the clinching with the hammer, tapping the ends against the hoof and giving each a light stroke with the rasp.

The average person should not attempt to shoe the hind feet until he has had considerable experience in shoeing the front feet. It's harder for a horse to stand with its hind foot lifted, and many horses will kick anyone trying to fit a shoe on the hind foot. It is more important to be able to replace a front shoe than a rear one, since a horse can travel without a rear shoe more easily than it can without a front shoe.

Tying a String of Horses

When several packhorses are taken on a trip, they are often tied together to prevent them from feeding along the trail or running off. But it is necessary to fasten them together so that if one horse stumbles and falls over a bluff, it won't pull the entire string with it. Western outfitters generally use a length of rope spliced into a circle, one end of which goes over the tree of the packsaddle of the first horse and is connected with baling twine to the halter or

Special knot used for tailing horses on smooth terrain.

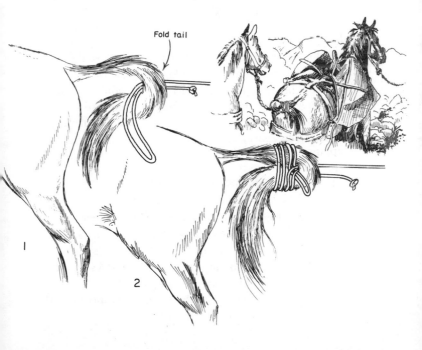

hackamore rope of the horse behind it. Another spliced loop ties in the next horse in the string, and so on down the line. The sisal twine is strong enough to hold the horses on the trail, but will break if one falls.

If a wrangler has to bring in several unsaddled horses over smooth terrain, he often uses a different method—called "tailing" the stock. The tail of the first animal in the string is folded into a loop, just below the fleshy part, and is attached to the halter or hackamore rope of the horse behind it with a special knot, as shown in the drawing. The other horses are joined in the same way, one behind the other.

But even tailing can be hazardous. In Wyoming, two hunters decided to bring in a fresh bearskin on a horse unused to the smell of bear. After several unsuccessful attempts to load the hide, they had to blindfold the horse and tail it up short to a gentle horse named Brownie. When they removed the blindfold, the loaded horse went berserk. As one of the hunters described it, "He reared and bucked like fresh out of a buckin' chute. He jerked so hard Brownie was lifted clean off his hind feet—his rear end never did come down for thirty minutes!"

How to Make a Rope Hackamore

If a standard hackamore is not available, a horse is often led by a rope tied around its neck. This isn't always satisfactory, for an animal so tied is hard to handle and tends to pull back or graze unduly. There are two ways, however, to make a hackamore out of a rope tied by a bowline around a horse's neck. As shown in the drawings, the

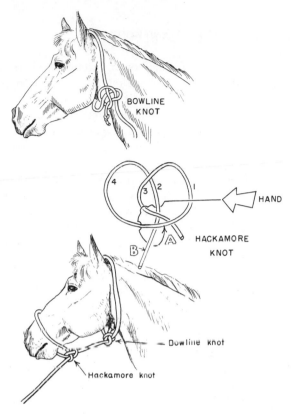

BOWLINE KNOT

HAND

HACKAMORE KNOT

Bowline knot

Hackamore knot

Hackmore knot forms a nose loop which helps in controlling a horse.

hackamore knot forms a nose loop which aids in controlling a horse.

The simplest way to tie a hackamore knot is to grasp the rope near the bowline and double it into a loop about 20 inches long. Tie two overhand knots in the loop, and snug the finished knot close to the bowline. This loop forms the noseband. Then undo the bowline around the horse's neck, slip the loop over its nose, and retie the bowline to fit.

The second hackamore knot is a little more complicated, but it's a favorite of veteran horsemen and worth knowing. To learn to tie this knot, get a few feet of rope and practice without a horse. Hold the rope with both hands palm upward, one end extending about 18 inches from the right hand. Now, gripping the rope with the fingers, turn the palms down. You'll find that you've formed two loops. Lay the loops on a table so they form a figure like the one in the drawing. The strands in the drawing are numbered 1, 2, 3, and 4. Following the path of the arrow, reach over strand number 1, under 2, over 3, under 4, and around the running end, B, and grasp the rope at point A. Holding both ends in the left hand, pull with the right hand—and you've tied the hackamore knot.

Once you've mastered forming the loops and reaching through to tie the knot, try tying the hackamore on a horse. Use the animal's neck to support the loops, and once the nose loop has been formed, retie the bowline to take up any slack.

How to Throw a Sling Hitch

A sling hitch generally is used to lash cargoes wrapped in tarps on a Decker packsaddle. With this hitch, cargoes of uneven weight or size can be perfectly balanced and don't have to be packed in panniers.

To tie the hitch, knot the end of the sling rope to the front ring of the saddle, and thread the other end through the rear ring, as in Figure 1. Loosen the cross loop

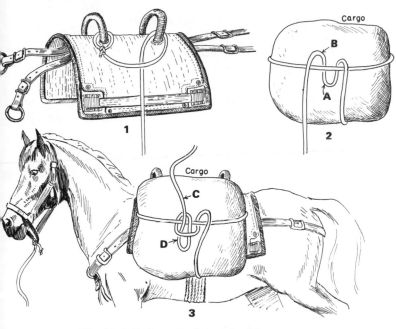

Sling hitch tied on a Decker packsaddle.

sufficiently so the cargo will fit inside it. Lift the cargo high on the side of the saddle, and holding it there with one arm, put the cross loop around it. Then grasp the vertical rope, pull it under the cargo, and draw it tight. Bring the rope up the side of the cargo, over the cross rope, and push a small loop (A in Figure 2) under the strand. Pull down on A, tightening the hitch. Grasping the rope at B in Figure 2, pull it through loop A. The resulting knot is shown untightened, for clarity, in Figure 3. To complete the hitch, grasp the rope at C and tie two half hitches around loop D.

The other cargo is lashed to the right side of the horse in the same way, but the sling rope is knotted to the rear ring. When both cargoes have been loaded and hitched, they are further secured by running the remaining rope of one hitch across the top of the saddle, pushing it through loop D and bringing it back over the saddle again.

Loads of uneven weight are balanced as they are hitched. The heavier one should be held high on the saddle and tied there with the cross rope, the lighter one allowed to ride farther down, over the curve of the horse's body. This balances the uneven weight.

How to Throw a Barrel Hitch

The barrel hitch is often used with a Decker or a sawbuck packsaddle for packing elongated cargoes such as the hind quarters of elk or package of tents and poles. The drawings show how it is tied on a sawbuck saddle.

First, tie the end of the lash rope securely to the front sawbuck, as shown in Figure 1. Form a loop below the front sawbuck, bring the running end back over the front sawbuck and over and behind the rear sawbuck, forming a second loop. The end of the rope should now be hanging from the rear sawbuck.

Insert the cargo in the loops (Figure 2). Tighten the front loop so that the cargo is in the correct position, and take up the slack toward the rear loop. Tighten the rear loop, bring the running end under the cargo and up to rope A, and tie it with two half-hitches.

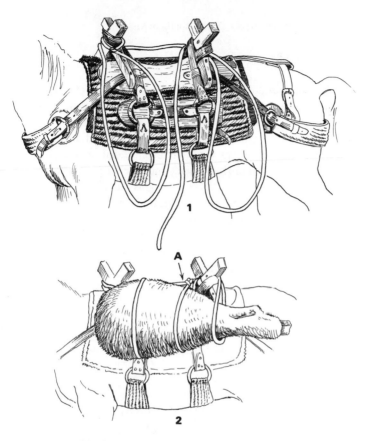

Barrel hitch tied on a sawbuck packsaddle.

Lash the second cargo to the other side of the pack animal in the same manner. Elk quarter should be covered with tarps, but they may be packed as shown if none is available.

How to Throw a Diamond Hitch

The diamond hitch is the best-known hitch for lashing down a load on a packhorse or mule. It is normally used after the cargoes have been lashed on with another type of hitch or the panniers have been loaded, and a top pack, covered with a canvas tarp, has been added. The diamond hitch is used with both sawbuck and Decker packsaddles.

A lash rope about 25 feet long is needed to throw a diamond hitch. One end is knotted (called the running end); the other end is tied to a cinch.

Stand at the horse's left shoulder and lay the running end of the rope along the top of the load so it extends to the horse's tail. Wrap the cinch end of the rope around the horse and load, and catch the rope in the cinch hook (Figure 1). Allow the loose rope to fall to the ground at the horse's shoulder.

Bring the loose rope over the strand that runs along the length of the horse and tuck a small loop under the strand that encircles the horse and pack (Figure 2). Reach under this loop, over the encircling strand, and grasp point A. Pull the rope through the loop, forming a second loop (Figure 3). Grasp the rope at point B (Figure 3), tighten the hitch, and pull this rope across to point C (Figure 4) and under the pack. Now grasp the rope at poind D (Figure 4) and bring it under the top pack at point E. Tie the end of the rope, as shown in Figure 5, with a looped half-hitch. When seen from the top, the center of the hitch will form a diamond.

The beauty of the diamond hitch is that no segment of the rope is tied but is free to distribute the tension of the hitch over the entire rope. In effect, this prevents any section of the hitch from loosening.

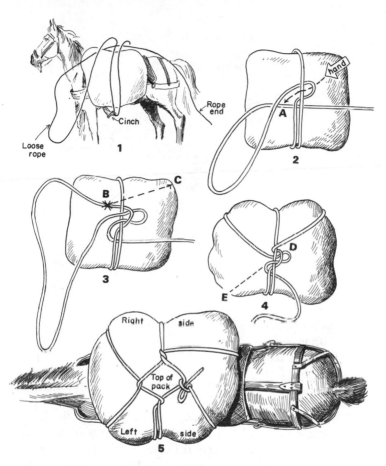

Labels in figure: Rope end, Cinch, Loose rope, 1, hand, A, 2, B, C, 3, D, E, 4, Right side, Top of pack, Left side, 5

Diamond hitch.

How to Throw a McNeel Hitch

The McNeel hitch often is used instead of the diamond hitch to lash down cargoes or panniers after they have been secured to the packsaddle with a sling hitch.

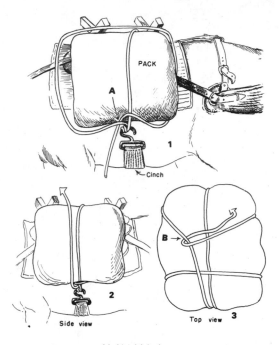

McNeel hitch.

To throw the hitch, stand at the left side of the horse and toss the cinch end of the lash rope across the animal's back, over the load. Grasp the cinch as it comes under the horse and hook the lash rope on the left side of the animal, under the load at the belly line. Two turns with the rope are made in the cinch hook, as shown in Figure 1.

Maintaining tension on the rope at the cinch hook, form a large half-hitch in the running end, large enough to completely encircle the cargo (Figure 1). The end of the rope should come *under* the half-hitch just above the cinch hook (A).

Tighten the half-hitch around the left-side cargo by pulling the running end, as shown in Figure 2, and bring the rope to the top of the load.

At this point, bring the running end across the saddle to the forward end of the right-side cargo, down the front end, under, and up the rear end. The lash should look like Figure 3, which is a top view. Run the end under the lash at point B. Tighten the rope and tie at B with a looped half-hitch, completing the job.

How to Throw a Gilligan Hitch

Professional outfitters and packers display a fierce pride toward their work. No professional packer will admit that any horse or mule is too tough for him to handle. Once in the hills with his packstring, a packer will never give up on an unruly animal. A packer friend, on one occasion where a mule lay down, told me quietly, "I'll load that mule or kill him." He loaded the mule. A packer is also proud of the appearance of his loaded packstring. He simply will not be caught in the company of another packer with his cargoes looking sloppy. After a long pack on a tough mountain trail, he will stop his string within a quarter-mile of base camp and repack his cargoes so that his outfit will look shipshape when he arrives.

In the Selway country years ago, there was a packer named Gilligan, who reputedly came into camp one day with his packs in a mess. Tarps were dragging, half off the mules; cargoes were tipped to one side; and blankets had slipped halfway out behind the saddles. Being very tired, Gilligan hadn't made that final stop to reshape his load.

And so to this day a sloppy job of packing is known as a Gilligan hitch.

Therefore, the way to throw a Gilligan hitch is simply to take a length of rope, some duffel, and a pack animal, and begin tying things on without rhyme or reason.

How to Make Shotgun Chaps

A pair of chaps is indispensable to anyone who rides a great deal in heavily wooded terrain where branches and brush tear cloth pants to shreds. The best type for dry-weather riding is a pair of shotgun chaps, which take their name from the slimness of the legs. These chaps may be obtained at a riding outfitter, but if you have a tanned deerskin or elk skin you may want to make your own, largely for the fun of doing it and for the pleasure of wearing clothing of your own making.

You'll need a pattern from which to cut the chaps from the skin. If you already own a pair of store-bought chaps, you can of course use them as a model for cutting a paper pattern. Otherwise, an old pair of work pants will serve as a pattern. Put them on and have someone mark them for cutting as shown in the drawing.

The first mark begins at the top of the outside seam, at the belt line, and angles across one buttock, under the crotch, and up one side of the fly to the front belt line. The other leg is marked in the same way. Another mark runs down the outside of each leg, beginning 1 inch from the first mark at the top of the outside seam, and goes straight down the leg to the cuff, ending 2 inches behind the seam. The marks that end at the top of the fly are then

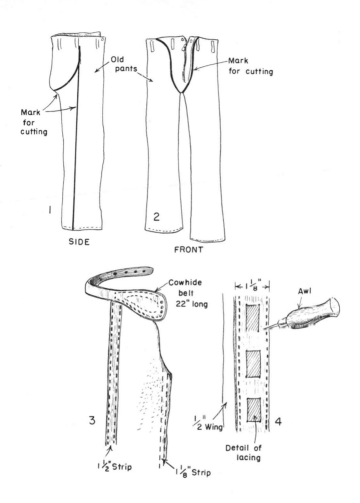

Mark pattern for chaps (Figures 1 and 2) on pair of old pants.
Figure 3 shows position of strips and belt, with detail of
lacing in Figure 4.

rounded off to form the characteristic "belt" of the chaps. This mark should begin 3 inches below the belt line and curve across the front to a point 3 inches from the original mark.

After the pants have been marked correctly, cut out the pattern with a pair of scissors. This pattern is not necessarily the true pattern, since the pants from which it was cut may have been a little too large or too small. The standard sizes for the legs of shotgun chaps are as follows: for slim builds—22 inches wide at the top of the thigh; for medium builds—23 inches; for heavy builds—24 inches. The legs taper to 20 inches at the bottom.

Lay the pattern on the skin and adjust the measurement to suit your particular physique. This adjustment, if necessary, is made on the inside of the legs. Then add 1½ inches for the seam. When the measurements are correct, mark the leather and cut out the legs with a sharp knife.

The next step is to make the belt for the chaps. This should be cut from medium-heavy cowhide. It consists of two pieces. Each piece conforms to the curved top of the legs. It should taper from 3 inches at the front to 1½ inches around the side and back. One piece is fitted with a buckle at the small end, the other terminates in a pointed strap with holes. Each belt half should be about 22 inches long, allowing for riveting the buckle and for wearing the chaps over the pants.

Sew the belt halves to the legs, or give the material to a shoemaker and let him do it on a machine.

It is now necessary to reinforce the edges of the legs, and this too is a good job for a shoemaker. Cut two strips of leather the same length as the legs, one 1-1/8 inches wide, the other 1-1/2 inches wide. Sew the 1-1/8 inch strip to

Finished chaps laced in front with buckskin.

the front-outside edge, leaving a small wing of the leg material as shown. Sew the 1-1/2 inch strip on the inside of the rear edge of the leg material, flush with the edge (that part coming from the rear and which will be underneath). As shown in the drawing, the strips are sewn with two seams.

The edges of each leg can now be laced together to form the "barrels" of the shotgun. To do this, cut a lace of ½-inch leather somewhat longer than the legs. Using an awl, punch a series of holes through the outside strip and the leg, as shown in the drawing, and cut the leather between each set to make a slit. Now turn this strip down on the inside strip and use the first set of holes as a template to punch the second set, thereby making sure all the holes line up. When holes have been punched in both legs, lace the edges of each leg together, and rivet the ends of each lace to keep it from pulling out. While you're riveting, it's a good idea to rivet the belt at the point where it leaves the leg. This will prevent the stitches from tearing.

The legs of the chaps must now be fastened at the front of the belt. This is done by punching a matched set of holes in the front ends of the belt and lacing them together with a length of ¼-inch buckskin. Lacing is used here instead of rivets or a buckle so that if a rider is thrown, and his belt catches on the saddle horn, it will break apart.

25

Miscellaneous How-To

Walking Stick from a Hoe

Ice often forms in low spots on a trail, and when covered with fresh snow these pose a hazard for the hiker. With a sharp-tipped walking stick made from an old garden hoe, you can punch into such spots and prevent a bad spill. In summer such a walking stick is useful for crossing streams.

Cut off the hoe where the shank joins the blade, using a hacksaw, torch, or grinder. Heat the shank in a forge, or even in an open fire, until it is hot. (With an open fire, be careful not to burn the handle where the shank enters the ferrule.) Straighten the heated shank by hammering it on an anvil, the flat side of an ax, or a large rock. Then sharpen the end with a grinder or file. Cut the handle to a comfortable length for your height.

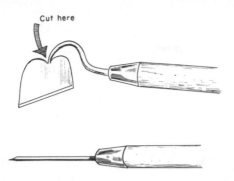

Sharp-pointed walking stick, made from a hoe, prevents spills when hiking on icy ground or when crossing streams.

The handle of an old hoe is often brittle and may split, so coat it lightly with linseed oil. In time, your hand will rub the oil into the wood, and the handle won't sliver or crack unduly.

Walking Stick from a Sapling

A sharp-tipped walking stick can be quickly improvised in camp if you have a 16d spike, a length of small-gauge wire, and a short nail or flathead screw. Cut off the head of the spike by notching it on opposite sides with a file, then breaking it off with the claws of a hammer. Sharpen the spike slightly at this end. Find a dry sapling about 1 inch in diameter and 5 feet long, trim off the branches, and whip the larger end with the wire for about 1 inch. Finish the whipping by winding the wire around the small nail or screw, which should be imbedded in the wood at the proper

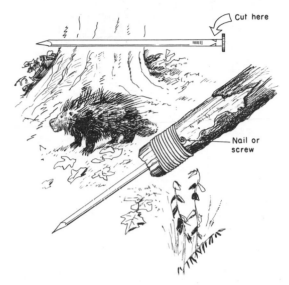

Walking stick improvised from a spike and sapling.

place, and then set flush. Finally, drive the spike into the end of the staff. The whipping will prevent the wood from splitting.

Loseproof Pocketnife Case

If you have a habit of losing your pocketknife in the outdoors when you most need it, here's a simple case you can make from a strip of thin leather that will fit in your pocket and secure the knife to your belt.

For an average-sized pocketknife you'll need a strip of leather about 20 inches long and 1½ inches wide. Cut it according to the pattern shown in the drawing. Fold the 1½-

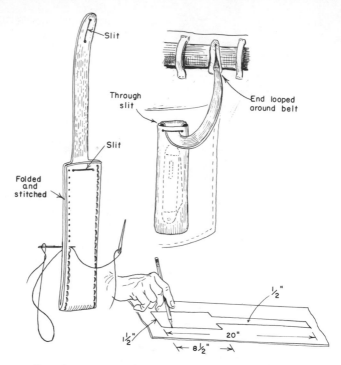

Strap keeps pocketknife case closed and secured to belt.

inch width back on itself and sew together the three edges. Then turn the case thus formed inside-out.

Cut a ½-inch slit in the case 3/8 inch from the top (see drawing). Cut another slit 1 inch long and ½ inch from the end of the narrow strip. That's all there is to making the case.

Insert the knife, pass the end of the strip through the slit in the case, and pull it tight, sealing in the knife. Slip the end of the strip through your belt, pass the case through the slit in the end, and drop it in your pocket. You'll never lose your pocketknife again.

Survival Knife

This is a handy tool to take along on outdoor trips. Made from a power hacksaw blade, it will cut or saw the toughest materials, yet it's small enough to tie to the frame of a packboard for use in an emergency.

Get a 16-inch blade and cut it in half on the edge of an emery wheel. Cut it at an angle, with the teeth on the long side. Then grind the blade to the shape of a skinning knife, rounding off the diagonal end, and leaving a few inches for a handle. Grind slowly, cooling the blade often, so as not to draw the temper of the steel. When the blade has been ground to the proper shape, sharpen the smooth edge on the wheel, and then hone it on a stone to a fine finish. Finally, wrap the handle with a few turns of electrician's

Survival knife from hacksaw blade.

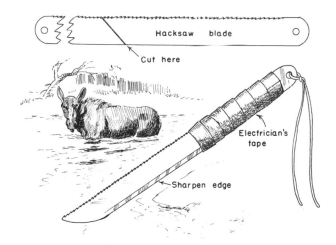

tape, leaving the hole in the end exposed. Then tie a length of buskskin thong in the hole with which to tie the knife to a packboard or other safe place.

A standard hacksaw blade can be turned into a smaller knife in the same way. This one will be about 3 inches overall, but it will do many small cutting jobs.

How to Make Knifes

Hunters with an unmounted deer, elk, or moose rack can use the antlers for making handsome knife handles. A variety of blades are available that can be transformed into rugged knives by anyone who can work with tools.

Start with a kitchen paring knife, or a larger utility knife with a 5-inch blade. The knife should be of top-quality steel, as it is foolish to expend time and energy on making a handle if the blade is inferior. A paring knife makes a good fish knife, a utility knife a good hunting knife. For the handle, select a length of tine from a deer antler. The wide end, where it joins the main beam, serves as a hilt, tapering to a narrow butt.

With a backsaw, saw the tine in half lengthwise. Mark the position of the holes in the blade, and carefully drill the handle from the outside. Attach the antler halves to the blade with long copper rivets, filing off the heads of the rivets and tapping them in place with a ball-pein hammer. Smooth and polish the ends of the rivets so they are nearly flush with the handle.

A more challenging job is to make your own blade from an old file. A 6-inch flat bastard file is suitable. Grind it slowly on an emery wheel into the shape of a knife blade,

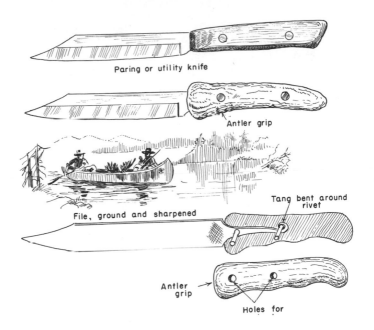

Paring or utility knife

Antler grip

Tang bent around rivet

File, ground and sharpened

Antler grip

Holes for

Paring or utility knife fitted with antler grip (top). Knife made from file (bottom) is secured in grip by bending tank around rivet.

being sure not to draw the temper of the steel. When the blade has been shaped and nearly sharpened, bore a hole through the large part of the tang.

To attach the antler handle, it's necessary to chisel a small mortise on the inside surface of each half. This mortise should be cut to the shape of the tang, and only as deep as half its thickness. Outline the tang with a pencil on the antler surface to get the correct shape.

When the mortise has been cut, hold the tang in the mortise, mark the position of the hole, and drill through both halves of the handle. Then drill a second hole in each half about 1 inch from the butt.

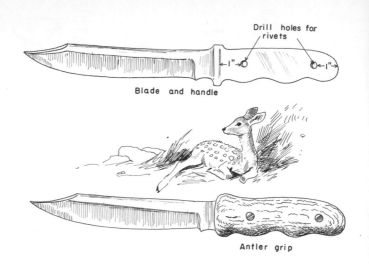

Drill holes for rivets

←1"→

Blade and handle

Antler grip

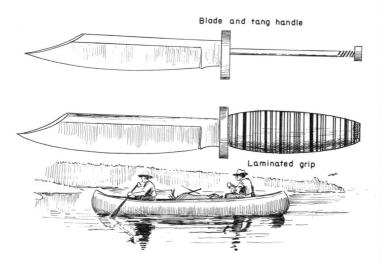

Blade and tang handle

Laminated grip

Knives without grips are available for the do-it-yourselfer.

822

Fit the antler halves on the tang and rivet them in place. If the mortise has been cut accurately, the two rivets will hold the handle firmly on the tang. However, if the fit is not exact, or if the blade is long, the tang can be secured firmly to the handle by bending its tip into a small loop, boring another hole in the handle aligned with this loop, and installing another rivet. The blade can then be honed to a fine edge.

A few companies, such as the Indian Ridge Traders of Ferndale, Michigan, sell knife blades without handles, especially for the do-it-yourselfer. The blades come with tangs or with round rods. Those with rods can be fitted with laminated handles of leather, aluminum, hard rubber, or antler.

How to Make Rustic Furniture

Chipped conifers, which were described in the article on making picture frames, will make attractive rustic furniture for summer homes. The basic tools needed are a saw and a power drill or hand brace with extension bits up to 1¼ inches in diameter.

The table shown in the drawing is a good piece for the beginner to build. The legs are about 4 inches in diameter and 30 inches long, the rails 2 inches in diameter, their length determined by the table's size. Remove the bark and chip the legs and rails, but do not varnish them, before assembling the table.

Two sets of rails join the legs together and brace the table. The top rail is set 2 inches from the top of the legs, the second rail 6 inches. The rails can be made of saplings 2 inches in diameter.

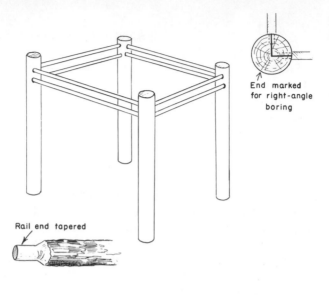

End marked
for right-angle
boring

Rail end tapered

Angle
iron

Chipped
wood
edging

Leg and rail assembly for building rustic table. Top is attached with angle irons.

When cutting the rails to size, allow 4 inches at each end for inserting them in holes in the legs. Taper each rail end with a pocketknife or drawknife to a diameter of 1¼ inches. The rail ends should taper sharply from the original diameter; the last 2 inches should be uniform in diameter. Tapering will remove the chipped bark, but the white wood will look attractive on the finished piece.

Bore 1¼-inch holes 2 inches deep in the top of the legs to receive the rails. As an aid in boring the holes at a true right angle, it helps to scribe a right angle, with a square, on the top of each leg. Align the bit with these marks as you drill and the holes will be true.

Assemble the rails and legs with glue.

The top can be made of ¾-inch plywood. It should extend beyond the legs 4 inches on each side. Finish the edges

Rustic bed is built with same leg and rail assembly.

Large
lower rail

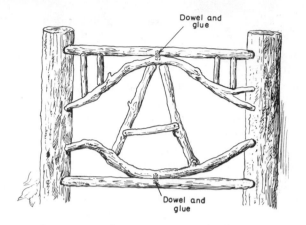

Decorative headboard displays owner's initial.

Elliptical log slab can be turned into a handsome coffee table.

by gluing on half-round branches chipped to match the legs and rails.

At this stage, sand the top, and the legs and rails where necessary, and finish with a couple of coats of varnish.

Attach the top with 4-inch angle irons. Use lag screws to attach the angle irons to the legs, flatheaded wood screws to attach the irons to the top.

A rustic bed can be made of chipped conifers using the same leg-and-rail method. Use two short posts for the footboard and two longer posts for the headboard, with two rails along the sides and ends. Cross rails support the box spring and mattress. The footboard may be braced with a crossbar between the posts. The headboard is braced with a crossbar near the top.

A more elaborate headboard can be created by using curved branches, either to form a symmetrical design or your own initials.

If you can obtain an extra-large log, and can persuade a sawmill to saw off an eliptical slab about 3 inches thick, you can turn it into an attractive coffee table. The slab should be dried indoors before working on it. When it has cured without splitting or shedding its bark, sand one side smooth. Bore four holes in the underside of the slab, angling outwards, and fit four short legs of chipped-wood saplings. Glue the legs in place and shape the ends to stand flat on the floor.

Antler Door Handles and Drawer Pulls

Deer antlers make attractive door handles and drawer pulls for summer homes and other places where a rustic decor is appropriate. Generally the smaller tines on an antler are the right size for handles and pulls, and they should be slightly curved. When cutting the tine for a door handle, include part of the main beam at the joint. This is rounded off and forms the top of the handle. The ends must be ground flat so they butt evenly against the surface on which the handle or pull is mounted. Drill a hole through each end of the tine, and attach it to the wood with Phillips-head screws.

Door handle made from deer antler.

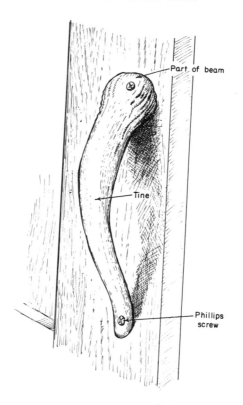

Index